Catt

"The best one-volume history of the legendary era of the cowboy and cattle empires in thirty years. *Cattle Kingdom* redefines our understanding of the era beyond the traditional boundaries of the West . . . Knowlton's flowing prose style is enjoyable to read . . . Knowlton has added a superb volume to the agricultural, cultural, economic, and environmental historiography of cattle ranching and cowboy history in the American West."
— Stuart Rosebrook, *True West*

"Mr. Knowlton writes well about all the fun stuff: trail drives, rambunctious cow towns, gunfights, and range wars. What makes it a 'hidden history' is the way it enlists all of these tropes in support of an intriguing thesis: that the romance of the Old West arose upon the swelling surface of a giant economic bubble . . . *Cattle Kingdom* is *The Great Plains* by way of *The Big Short* . . . His book coasts along just fine on the strength of his curiosity and storytelling ease. And his empathy."
— Stephen Harrigan, *Wall Street Journal*

"*Cattle Kingdom* is the smartly told account of rampant capitalism making its home — however destructive and decidedly unromantic — on the range. Related this way, the story . . . offers ample conflict and drama delivered with a fresh and winning perspective."
— *Dallas Morning News*

"Lively . . . [the] analysis does not bog down the storytelling. Knowlton deftly balances close-ups and bird's-eye views. We learn countless details . . . More important, we learn why the story played out as it did."
— *New York Times Book Review*

Cattle Kingdom

THE HIDDEN HISTORY
of the
COWBOY WEST

Christopher Knowlton

MARINER

HarperCollins*Publishers*
Boston   New York

First Mariner Books edition 2018
Copyright © 2017 by Christopher Knowlton

Mariner
An Imprint of HarperCollins Publishers, registered
in the United States of America and/or other jurisdictions.

www.marinerbooks.com

Library of Congress Cataloging-in-Publication Data is available.
ISBN 978-0-544-36996-2 (hardcover)
ISBN 978-1-328-47025-6 (paperback)

Map by Mapping Specialists, Ltd.

Book design by Kelly Dubeau Smydra

Printed in the United States of America
24 25 26 27 28 LBC 11 10 9 8 7

Illustration credits appear on pages 425 and 426.

For Pippa

To be a cowboy was adventure;
to be a ranchman was to be king.

— Walter Prescott Webb,
The Great Plains

Contents

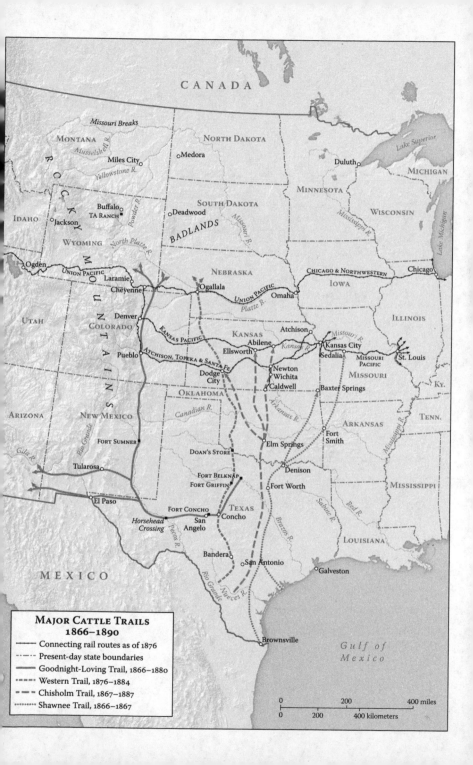

CANADA

Missouri Breaks

MONTANA

Miles City

Musselshell R.

Yellowstone R.

Buffalo
TA RANCH

Powder R.

NORTH DAKOTA

Medora

Duluth

Lake Superior

MICHIGAN

IDAHO

Jackson

WYOMING

North Platte R.

SOUTH DAKOTA

Deadwood

BADLANDS

Missouri R.

MINNESOTA

WISCONSIN

Lake Michigan

Mississippi R.

Ogden

UTAH

UNION PACIFIC

Laramie

Cheyenne

ROCKY MOUNTAINS

Denver

COLORADO

Pueblo

KANSAS PACIFIC

ATCHISON, TOPEKA & SANTA FE

Ogallala

NEBRASKA

UNION PACIFIC

Platte R.

Omaha

IOWA

CHICAGO & NORTHWESTERN

Chicago

ILLINOIS

Atchison

KANSAS

Abilene

Ellsworth

Kansas R.

Kansas City

Sedalia

Missouri R.

St. Louis

MISSOURI PACIFIC

KY.

Dodge
City

Newton

Wichita

Caldwell

Baxter Springs

MISSOURI

ARIZONA

NEW MEXICO

Rio Grande

FORT SUMNER

Tularosa

Gila R.

El Paso

OKLAHOMA

Canadian R.

DOAN'S STORE

FORT BELKNAP

FORT GRIFFIN

FORT CONCHO

San
Angelo

Concho

Arkansas R.

Elm Springs

Fort
Smith

ARKANSAS

TENN.

Denison

Fort Worth

MISSISSIPPI

Mississippi R.

Horsehead
Crossing

Pecos R.

TEXAS

Bandera

San Antonio

Brazos R.

Sabine R.

Red R.

LOUISIANA

MEXICO

Rio Grande

Nueces R.

Galveston

Brownsville

*Gulf of
Mexico*

MAJOR CATTLE TRAILS
1866–1890

———— Connecting rail routes as of 1876

–·–·– Present-day state boundaries

———— Goodnight-Loving Trail, 1866–1880

▪▪▪▪▪ Western Trail, 1876–1884

▪ ▪ ▪ Chisholm Trail, 1867–1887

·········· Shawnee Trail, 1866–1867

0   200   400 miles

0   200   400 kilometers

Introduction

Throughout the summer and fall of 1886 a series of puzzling natural occurrences unfolded on the open range of the American West. In the Dakotas, Montana, and Wyoming, the sky turned so hazy at times that a pale halo formed around the sun. Exceptionally dry and hot weather sparked prairie brushfires that burned out of control. Elsewhere, hatches of grasshoppers, known as Rocky Mountain locusts, grew into deafening swarms and ate the little grass that was available.

John Clay, the Scottish-born manager of the Cattle Ranch & Land Company, rode out to inspect the Wyoming rangeland, taking the old pony express route through Lost Soldier and Crooks Gap: "There was scarce a spear of grass by the wayside. We rode many miles over the range. Cattle were thin and green grass was an unknown quantity except in some bog hole, or where a stream had overflowed in the spring. It was a painful sort of trip. There you were helpless. There was no market for young cattle, your aged steers were not fat, and your cows and calves were miserably poor." He could not shake a sickening sense of foreboding.

Lincoln Lang, a rancher in the Badlands, noticed that beavers were furiously at work on the walls of their lodges and piling up unusual quantities of saplings for winter food. Others observed that the winter coats of the elk and the moose grew in thick and heavy. Birds, especially the cedar waxwings and the Canada geese, flocked and migrated south a full six weeks earlier than normal.

Over in Montana, the veteran trail driver E. C. "Teddy Blue" Abbott noticed snowy owls perched on fence posts and paused on his horse to examine them from a distance. In his sixteen years on the open range, he could not recall ever having seen one before.

Teddy Blue's boss, the cattle baron and former gold miner Granville Stuart, noticed the owls too. One local Native American tribal leader wagged his finger at Stuart and warned him that the birds were the ghostly harbingers of a harsh winter to come.

The cattlemen were already grumpy. Beef prices had been in sharp decline for several years now, which had prompted many of the cattle operations to take fewer steers to market. That meant there were more cattle on the already overstocked open range. The problem was compounded when a presidential order, signed by Grover Cleveland in July of the prior year, forced the cattle herds off the giant Cheyenne and Arapaho Indian Reservation in the Indian Territories, part of what today is Oklahoma. The cattlemen drove many of those herds, comprising some 210,000 head of cattle, onto the northern ranges and then moved them from valley to valley, like the pieces on a giant checkerboard, in an effort to find the little remaining grass and water available in areas still free of the suddenly ubiquitous barbed wire.

Many of the veteran cattlemen had grown rich during the boom — the greatest agricultural expansion the country had ever seen. But there were worries that they had overexpanded and overleveraged themselves to keep abreast of the rapidly evolving industry. By some accounts, total investment in the cattle industry now exceeded the capitalization of the entire American banking system. By other accounts, Cheyenne, Wyoming, the epicenter of the boom, had the highest median per capita income in the world. Many of the country's richest families and individuals—Marshall Field, the Rockefellers, the Vanderbilts, the Flaglers, the Whitneys, the Seligmans, and the Ameses—were now cattle investors.

The open range was crowded with speculators and new money and giant cattle conglomerates. At the Cheyenne Club, the posh watering hole of the cattle barons, there were whispers about lax management, overcounting of cattle herds, even the questionable solvency of some of the larger outfits. One of the most prominent members, a former president of the club named Hubert Teschemacher, had actually resolved that fall to liquidate his ranch at a loss, to the consternation of his Boston and New York investors. Another club member, Moreton Frewen, a Sussex squire who founded the first joint-stock cattle company registered in England, arrived in town after a year away and wrote to his wife how quiet Cheyenne seemed. It was as though its boomtown businesses, anticipating some calamity, had come to a momentary standstill.

Twenty-eight-year-old Theodore Roosevelt, who had just completed his third year as a cattle entrepreneur in the Dakota Territory, displayed a shrewd understanding of the situation when he wrote that fall, in an article for *The Century Magazine*, "In our country, which is even now getting crowded, it is merely a question of time as to when a winter will come that will understock the ranges by the summary process of killing off about half of all the cattle throughout the North-west."

His assessment would prove accurate.

A week before he left the Dakotas to return to New York via the Northern Pacific Railroad, Roosevelt said goodbye to his two best hired men, Bill Sewall and Sewall's nephew Wilmot Dow, who had managed the Elkhorn Ranch for him. The two men had decided to return east with their wives to their native Maine. Sewall had argued from the outset that the Badlands were unsuitable rangeland for cattle. Roosevelt had contradicted him and now would pay the price.

A short time later Roosevelt's Badlands neighbor, the Frenchman known as the Marquis de Morès, departed for Paris, as he did every fall, leaving behind his towering slaughterhouse and immense beef-packing plant, by far the largest plant west of Chicago, a monument that matched his own ambition and ego. Although he wouldn't admit it to a local reporter, who had heard rumors and questioned him at the train station, his empire was teetering on the brink of insolvency.

The first snowstorm arrived in November, followed in December by a gale-force blizzard that would last for three days. Granville Stuart was caught on a stagecoach between Musselshell and Flat Willow when the second storm hit. The visibility was so poor that he and the other passengers took turns walking in front of the team of horses with a lantern to guide them.

In January a brief thaw arrived, accompanied by a warm wind known as a chinook, but the thaw served only to melt the snow enough to create a thick crust when the cold returned, which it did, with conviction, a few days later. The next storm lasted for ten full days. The temperature dropped to an excruciating twenty-two below zero Fahrenheit and kept falling, to twenty-eight below, to thirty below, and finally, on January 15, to forty-six below zero. Over in the Dakotas the temperature reached sixty degrees below zero in places and remained there. The snow was so fine that it stung the face. Whipped by the wind, it pushed through crevices and under doorsills and left little piles as fine as the sand of an hourglass.

The cattle tried to drift before the storm, but the icy crust on the snow scraped the flesh from their knees and hocks. Those that sought refuge in the gullies and coulees were soon buried in snowdrifts, where often they suffocated to death. When another group of cattle arrived to seek shelter, soon they would add a second layer of carcasses. Others were trapped against barbed-wire fences where, immobile, they froze in the wind. The calf-bearing cows died first, followed by the old bulls, and finally the heifers and the steers. When the worst of the cold arrived, even the fattest steers died on their feet, literally frozen in their tracks.

That winter on the northern ranges would be the coldest on record.

Most of the ranches had trimmed their staff for the winter months, leaving few cowboys available to try to move the cattle to safety. Teddy Blue described the situation: "Think of riding all day in a blinding snowstorm, the temperature fifty and sixty below zero, and no dinner. You'd get one bunch of cattle up a hill and another one would be coming down behind you, and it was all so slow, plunging after them through the deep snow that way; you'd have to fight every step of the road . . . It was the same all over Wyoming, Montana, and Colorado, western Nebraska, and western Kansas."

Cattle wandered onto the frozen rivers, where they fell into air holes. They walked out onto the ice, and the ones behind pushed the ones in front into the icy water. Teddy Blue estimated that six thousand of Granville Stuart's cattle were lost this way. "The ice kind of sloped down to the holes. I remember when we was trying to push them back into the hills, there was one poor cow that had slipped through, and she had her head up and was just holding on by her head. We couldn't get her out — our horses weren't shod for ice — and so we shot her."

The weakened cattle soon made the gray wolves fat and bold. When Lincoln Lang came across a wolf pack eyeing a starving steer from a safe distance, he took revenge by mercy-killing the steer and lacing its carcass with an entire bottle's worth of strychnine. The next morning he found fifteen large wolves dead in the snow — in his opinion, a record kill from a single piece of bait.

Another barrage of storms, less severe but more frequent, blew through in February, and the surviving cattle were by now in desperate shape. Dying herds wandered into the towns, looking for food and shelter. Cattle smashed their heads through the glass windows of ranch houses or tried to push through the doors; in their frantic hunger they ate the tarpaper off the sides of farm buildings. From indoors the ranchers listened to the desperate lowing of cows, and the knowledge that they could do nothing to save them wrenched their hearts. More than a few would hear that lowing in their dreams for months to come.

The deadly winter proceeded, almost biblical in its ferocity and duration, as though it had every intention of humbling and shaming anyone who had participated in the great cattle boom.

When the thaw finally arrived in April, the stench of death replaced the snow. The corpses of cattle crowded the coulees and the arroyos and blanketed countless fields. Carcasses were found hanging from trees — trees that the cattle had scaled from snowbanks in an effort to eat the branches. The dead bodies clogged the drainages and the spring creeks and damned sections of the rivers. Said Lincoln Lang, "One had only to stand by the river bank for a few minutes and watch the grim procession ceaselessly going down, to realize in full depth the tragedy that had been enacted within the past few months." Cowboys quickly coined a name for the debacle: the Big Die-Up.

Teddy Roosevelt returned to the Badlands to inspect the damage and reportedly rode on horseback for three days without seeing a single living steer.

The animal loss, as well as the financial loss, at first seemed incalculable. As Granville Stuart observed, "This was the death knell to the range cattle business on anything like the scale it had been run on before . . . A business that had been fascinating to me suddenly became distasteful. I wanted no more of it. I never wanted to own again an animal that I could not feed and shelter."

Roosevelt, who had lost over two-thirds of his herd, wrote to his friend Henry Cabot Lodge, "The losses are crippling. For the first time I have been utterly unable to enjoy a visit to my ranch. I shall be glad to get home." To his sister Anna he wrote, "I am bluer than indigo about the cattle; it is even worse than I feared; I wish I was sure I would lose no more than half the money I invested out here. I am planning how to get out of it."

One of the greatest speculative bubbles of the Gilded Age was over. Yet its full impact on American identity, on industrial development, on the conservation movement, even on American foreign policy, was still to be felt. Perhaps no boom-bust cycle has had as lasting an impact on American society as the rise and fall of the cattle kingdom, and yet, oddly, this epic saga is largely forgotten today.

Here, then, is the story of the open-range cattle era, the tale of how ranching emerged as an industry across a land once dismissed as the Great American Desert, and how cattle displaced bison, herd by herd, until "cattle fever" grew into an investment stampede.

Why, the reader might ask, do we need a new history of an obscure cattle boom at this point in American history? The fact that it has been over forty years since this story was last properly told is perhaps reason enough. The other reasons are fourfold. In the wake of recent oil, real estate, and dot-com bubbles, every American has been reminded of how often our free-enterprise system subjects us to the shocks of boom-bust cycles. One goal here is to shine light on the psychology and greed that drive an investment mania, and on the financial and human catastrophes that result from the bursting of a commodity bubble. There are lessons to be learned. Second, for this writer, a former financial journalist and investment manager retired to Wyoming and prospecting for literary ideas, the story stood out as an apposite morality tale about the price paid by those who ignore economic and ecological realities in their single-minded pursuit of the American Dream. Third, hindsight and a deeper understanding of the natural world today allow us a wider frame of reference for studying an environmental disaster such as the Big Die-Up. Finally, the era provided an opportunity to tell a remarkable tale: the story of the cowboy and his rise to mythic stature.

This book traces the arduous trail drives of the longhorns from the mesquite and thorn scrub of southern Texas to the pop-up cattle towns of Kansas. It then follows the beef through the gates of the gory slaughterhouses of the Union Stock Yards in Chicago to the celebrated New York City dining palaces of the Delmonico brothers, who first popularized the American steak. It will show what life was really like for a cowboy, along the dusty trail and in the saloons, and how the myth that grew up around him was remarkably at odds with the realities of his daily existence. That myth, while inaccurate, proved remarkably durable, especially after its definitive embellishment by the author Owen Wister. It gave birth to an enduring genre of entertainment and has influenced our national politics in surprising ways.

One destination will be Cheyenne, Wyoming, the greatest of the cattle towns of the north, and its boomtown shops and grand homes. A visit to the private clubrooms of the exclusive Cheyenne Club will reveal the cattle barons at work and at play, and show how their high times ended with the questionable use of vigilante justice.

At a more personal level, this book depicts how opportunities and challenges arose for young men, rich and poor, recent graduates of Harvard College or farm boys like Teddy Blue Abbott, who were daring enough to enter the cattle profession. The book will track the careers of three aristocratic twenty-five-year-olds, in thrall to cattle fever, who sought their fortune in the trade: the Englishman Moreton Frewen, the Frenchman the Marquis de Morès, and the New Yorker Theodore Roosevelt. Thanks in part to the experience of Roosevelt during his years as a ranchman in the Dakota Territory, this era gave birth to the American conservation movement.

At times the narrative takes a step back from these proceedings to examine the larger forces that shaped and spurred the industrialization of agriculture. It looks at how global trade and flows of capital drove events every bit as much as the trail drivers themselves, luring investment by Scottish and English moneymen seeking better returns on their capital. The cattle industry's connections to other nations and markets pushed the boundaries of the nation's commerce toward the emerging global marketplace. And thanks to the multicultural nature of the cattle trade — its diverse group of cowboys and cattlemen and its competition with an equally diverse population of immigrant settlers — the industry not only helped heal the regional divides created by the Civil War but also laid the foundations for the multicultural nation that is the United States today. Far more than the Gold Rush, the cattle era gave birth to a romantic notion of entrepreneurialism: the pursuit of individual freedom and economic opportunity that today sends young college graduates to Silicon Valley.

In fact, entrepreneurs in refrigeration and meatpacking, men like Gustavus Swift and Philip Danforth Armour, set the stage for the American Century with groundbreaking managerial insights that grew their enterprises into the country's first fully integrated industrial combines. Thanks to the cattle kingdom and its rapid-fire efforts to codify the raising, slaughtering, and transporting of cattle, the country took a giant step closer to becoming a predominantly industrial society.

Also fitting for a period of American history so rife with innovation, great strides were made in cattle-industry medicine and technology, breakthroughs that built fortunes and saved lives. None was more significant than the creation of barbed wire, which literally reshaped the landscape and set the stage for the era's eventual destruction — at great personal cost to so many of its key players.

Today, thanks in no small part to the impact of the cattle kingdom, we are called upon to negotiate compromises between conflicting economic ambitions and use of our public lands. We are compelled to balance free-market exploitation of our natural resources with sound stewardship of the environment. That all began in the late 1860s on the open range.

Although the cattle kingdom did not formally conclude with the Big Die-Up itself, it badly staggered the industry. The true end of the era is better signposted, according to most historians, by the most famous of the range wars that followed: the murderous and controversial crossroads known as the Johnson County War. For it is here that the cowboy and the cattleman, representing dwindling labor and capital, respectively, finally collide in a violent finale fit for a Hollywood western.

Only three of the men featured in this narrative survived on the open range until the era's close. They are the cowboy Teddy Blue Abbott, the urbane Harvard man Hubert Teschemacher, and the savvy Scotsman John Clay. They might not be as well remembered as other characters, but the personal stories of this trio round out the variety of experiences faced by young men in this treacherous business.

When the number of dead animals was finally tallied in the late spring of 1887, the losses incurred in the Big Die-Up totaled nearly a million head of cattle, 50 to 80 percent of the various herds across the northernmost ranges — the greatest loss of animal life in pastoral history. For animal carnage, only one event could possibly compete. It occurred just twenty years earlier, across the same landscape, at the outset of the great cattle era: the extermination of the American buffalo, or as it is more accurately called, the bison.

PART ONE

Birth of a Boom

1

The Demise of the Bison

On January 13, 1872, twenty-two-year-old Grand Duke Alexis Romanov, the fourth son of the Russian czar, arrived in North Platte, Nebraska, by private railcar, accompanied by an entourage of courtiers in gold-brocaded Russian uniforms. The grand duke was there for a buffalo hunt.

Two companies of American infantry in wagons, two companies of cavalry on horseback, the cavalry's regimental band, and an assortment of cooks and couriers had been assembled to meet the duke at the train station. His American hosts included luminaries such as the distinguished Civil War veteran Major General Philip Sheridan, at that time the commander of the U.S. Army Department of the Missouri, the renowned Indian fighter Lieutenant Colonel George A. Custer, and William F. "Buffalo Bill" Cody, who later became famous for his traveling Wild West Show.

The entertainment in the wilderness included a lavish feast among the tents erected at Red Willow Creek, and a meet-and-greet encounter with local tribal chiefs, including Chief Spotted Tail of the Brulé Sioux, who had been coaxed into joining the expedition, along with four hundred Sioux warriors, in return for a payment of twenty-five wagonloads of flour, sugar, coffee, and tobacco. The Americans may well have hoped that Spotted Tail would appear in his elaborate war robe, which was adorned with over a hundred human scalps taken in battle, but instead he wore a white man's two-piece gray worsted suit, a rather old one, with a blanket thrown over his shoulders. For entertainment a group of Spotted Tail's warriors performed their traditional war dance.

The first morning's hunt found the group galloping over a hillock and down onto a large herd of grazing bison. According to Cody's embellished account, the duke proved to be a poor shot. He fired his pistol erratically at the largely docile bison from horseback and missed them at a short distance. It wasn't until Cody handed the duke his own Springfield Model 1863 rifle, nicknamed "Lucrezia Borgia," that the Russian noble managed to fell his first animal, an event that immediately produced much waving of flags and hats and a champagne toast. The duke leapt off his horse and used his saber to slice off the bison's tail as a trophy.

The next day the duke managed to kill two more bison. In total, during his five-day hunting trip he would slay eight, including a pair that he allegedly shot from the window of his private railcar somewhere outside Denver. He returned to Russia with their tails, mounted heads, and tanned hides as keepsakes.

Nothing like the so-called Great Royal Buffalo Hunt would ever again occur on American soil. Just three years later such a hunt would be impossible: the bison would be gone.

For the first ninety or so years of their new republic, most U.S. citizens viewed the open areas of the America West as a barren wasteland of no intrinsic or economic value. It was seen as a geographical hinterland, the Great American Desert, fit habitat only for the "savage" tribes of Plains Indians, despite the fact that it covered several hundred million acres. This vast area comprised the Great Plains, the High Plains, the semi-arid prairies, and the foothills of the Rocky Mountains, and it stretched from the Missouri River abutting the present border of Iowa westward to the Rocky Mountains, and from the Red River along the present Texas-Oklahoma border northward to Canada. This dismissive view of the wide-open expanses of the American West persisted because of a poor understanding of the land's ecological diversity and ignorance of the fact that the area provided forage for herds of buffalo that numbered in the tens of millions.

The Native Americans who occupied these territories, some two dozen tribes of varying sizes, took a far more enlightened view of the region — and lived in a more ecologically minded and spiritual harmony with it. For many of these tribes, their culture and livelihood depended on proximity to the bison, whose animal parts they used to clothe, house, arm, and feed their people. And the Native Americans' dependency on the bison may well have involved more than a somewhat passive harvesting of resources that nature provided. It is likely that for perhaps two thousand years the Plains Indians proactively farmed the buffalo on the Great Plains, treating the area as one massive pasture under their jurisdiction. They may well have used fire to remove what once was forest, to encourage the growth of grass for bison forage — a thesis, if true, that debunks the popular myth of the American West as an unspoiled, pristine wilderness at the time of European settlement.

Those who saw the great bison herds never forgot the experience. The largest herds appeared to blanket vast valleys in their black fur, in numbers rivaling anything seen on the African savannas. In 1839 Thomas Farnham, riding along the Santa Fe Trail, reported that it took him three days to pass through a single buffalo herd, covering a distance of forty-five miles. At one point he could see bison for fifteen miles in every direction, suggesting a herd that encompassed 1,350 square miles. In 1859 Luke Voorhees claimed to have traveled for two hundred miles through a single herd somewhere along the border of Colorado and Nebraska. And a dozen years later, Colonel R. I. Dodge passed through a herd along the Arkansas River that was twenty-five miles wide and fifty miles long.

The artist George Catlin, paddling a canoe on the Missouri River in the Dakotas, came around a bend and encountered one such immense herd as it forded the river. The swimming, snorting animals had effectively dammed the water. Catlin and his terrified companions managed to pull their canoes ashore just seconds before being engulfed by the herd. They waited for hours as the bison crossed, watching them shuffle down from the green hills on one side, swim across in a solid mass of heads and horns, and then gallop up the bluffs on the far side. During this time the bison managed to obliterate a fifteen-foot-high riverbank, carving their own road up and out of the river.

The white man's perception of the plains and prairie lands finally began to change with the rapid economic developments of the decades just prior to the Civil War: the collapse of the fur trade, the discovery of gold, the arrival of the railroad, and the westward flow of immigrants along the Oregon, Santa Fe, and Mormon trails. By the early 1860s former fur hunters and California-bound settlers, trailing the odd cow along with their oxen, had helped to introduce the first small herds of cattle to the western forts and outposts. Grocers and merchants, seeking to feed the arriving miners and railroad workers, introduced other small herds. The earliest cattlemen of the West, figures such as John Wesley Iliff, a former grocer who assembled a herd outside Denver in 1861 to service the railroad crews, began to believe that domesticated cattle might be able to withstand the long winters and the aridity of the climate. If this surmise was correct, big money could be made in cattle ranching on the open range.

Iliff's contracts with the railroads and the army forts eventually proved so lucrative that he was able to buy more than a hundred miles of land along the South Platte River in Colorado. Over time, his rangelands became so vast that he could ride for a week in one direction without sleeping anywhere but in his own ranch houses. He would be the first to earn the sobriquet "cattle king."

However, if the cattle were to come, the competing buffalo would have to go, although the cattlemen rarely described the tradeoff so explicitly. At first, given the seemingly infinite number of bison, such an outcome seemed wholly unlikely. But in a stunningly short period of time, less than twenty years, the bison were forced to the edge of extinction, with no more than 325 surviving south of Canada. Meanwhile, some 5.5 million cattle, initially almost all Texas Longhorns, arrived to take their place. The two great bovine herds displaced each other, just as surely as the automobile would replace the horse-drawn carriage. Cattle, the thinking went, functioned better than the wild bison as a machine for converting grass into hide and meat, and ultimately into profits.

Although the sperm whale, the sea otter, and the doomed passenger pigeon faced similar threats from profit-hungry hunters and businessmen, nothing could match in numbers, poundage, and sheer waste the slaughter of the bison, or the speed with which this animal approached extinction. Great human effort produced horrific carnage. From the air, the change must have looked like binary environmental sleight of hand: bison out, cattle in.

This great bovine switch would mark, as the historian Richard White has written, "the transformation of the plains, deserts, and mountains from a biological republic to a biological monarchy where humans reigned, where uselessness among lesser living things was a crime punishable by death, and where enterprise was the reigning value." This domination of the American West and its various animal species became possible with the arrival of the railroad.

As the new tracks of the Union Pacific Railroad slowly inched their way across the midriff of the continent, they divided the bison population into two primary herds, one southern and the other northern. The southern herd of some five million animals would disappear in a matter of four years, from 1872 through 1875. The slightly smaller northern herd would survive longer, but facing similar assaults, it vanished by 1883. Spurs of new railroad lines sped this development: they offered commercial and recreational hunters easy access to the bison.

Railroad management encouraged this type of recreational hunting, hoping to eliminate the herds that often blocked their lines and occasionally derailed a locomotive. A carnival-like atmosphere arose when a train encountered a bison herd. Passengers were directed to shoot at the beasts from the train windows. Animals that were shot were left behind to die, their carcasses rotting along the tracks. The telegraph companies too were eager to see the bison go because the animals took turns scratching themselves against the telegraph poles. Bison could rub a pole out of the ground in a matter of hours, disrupting a vital lifeline of communication.

Commercial buffalo hunters initially operated alone or in pairs as they harvested hides to make buffalo robes and blankets. The work was so filthy and the profession considered so lowly that the early cattlemen ostracized the skinners, calling them "stinkers" because their clothes often reeked of bison blood and feces. According to Teddy Blue, "The buffalo hunters didn't wash, and looked like animals. They dressed in strong, heavy, warm clothes and never changed them. You would see three or four of them walk up to a bar, reach down inside their clothes, and see who could catch the first louse for the drinks. They were lousy and proud of it."

What began as a cottage business soon matured into a full-fledged industry. Tanned skins could be fashioned into men's overcoats, finished off with a flannel lining. Another favored product was the lap robe. It was useful for covering the knees during a ride in a sleigh or carriage, and also indoors, at a time when central heating did not exist. The best hide for lap robes was the winter pelt of the female bison, which had fur less coarse than that of the bison bull. Before long, hunters were culling females from the herds.

A discovery made at a Philadelphia tannery further sealed the bison's fate. Strips of bison hide sewn together made excellent belts for driving stationary steam engines and other industrial machinery. Almost overnight, a year-round demand for bison skins emerged. To meet the demand, syndicates of hunters were formed, armed with the latest breech-loading (rear-loading) rifles.

What followed was an orgy of slaughter.

As anyone who has encountered a bison in the wild will testify, the animal is remarkably docile and not easily provoked. Hunting bison was the big-game equivalent of shooting fish in a barrel. The historian Francis Parkman, in *The California and Oregon Trail,* described the two most common methods of hunting bison. In the first, the "still hunt" method, the hunter approached the herd quietly, on foot. "The buffalo are strange animals; sometimes they are so stupid and infatuated that a man may walk up to them in full sight on the open prairie, and even shoot several of their number before the rest will think it necessary to retreat." He might have added that this form of hunting was devoid of sport; it was butchery.

In the second and far more exhilarating technique, known as "running," hunters on horseback, riding at full gallop, charged the bison herd and singled out fleeing animals to shoot at close range. But there were problems with this method: the very real danger that the wounded bison would turn and gore the horse or its rider, and the difficulty of reloading a pistol or a rifle while bouncing along on horseback. Many hunters carried three or four bullets in their mouth for convenience, which presented its own set of risks.

But the gravest danger in running buffalo was poor terrain. A recreational hunter named Alexander Ross witnessed a horrific pile-up when his hunting group galloped across a stretch of rocky flats pockmarked with badger holes. Twenty-three horses and their riders went down at once. One horse, gored by a bison bull, died instantly. Two more broke their legs. One rider fractured his collarbone, while another mistakenly discharged his gun and shot off three of his own fingers. A third was struck in the knee by a musket ball. Despite this fiasco, the hunting party returned to camp that afternoon with 1,375 bison tongues — the only cut of meat they salvaged from the dead animals.

One hunter, Orlando A. Brown, was said to have killed 5,855 bison in a two-month period in 1876, amounting to roughly 97 bison a day. "Buffalo Bill" Cody took credit for shooting 20,000 in his ten-year career as a buffalo hunter.

In each hunting syndicate there was a division of labor. One hunter focused on the shooting. His goal was to shoot the bison broadside through the lungs from a safe distance and avoid using too much ammunition; a pelt riddled with bullet holes was virtually worthless. The shooter always began by targeting the leader of the herd, usually the eldest female, as her injury would invariably cause confusion among the rest of the herd. Those nearest to her would gather around her, only to become the next targets. Once shot, each animal collapsed to its knees or onto its side and bled to death through its nose and mouth. Another female would eventually assume leadership and try to move the herd away, only to be shot in turn. A good shooter, armed with a sixteen-pound Sharps rifle and a hundred rounds on his cartridge belt, could shoot as many as two bison a minute. He was forced to pause or switch rifles only when the rifle barrel grew too hot.

The next workers to move in on the bison were the skinners, each armed with at least a pair of knives — a skinning knife and a ripping knife. They would flay each carcass, a process that might take ten to fifteen minutes per animal. Done properly, the first incision went from the throat down the length of the belly; with bulls, care was taken to cut around the sinew of the scrotum. The next incisions were made around the skin of the head, including the ears, leaving behind the rest of the head; cuts followed along the back side of the hind legs and the front side of the forelegs. Then it was time to cut the hide away. This process started at the knees and required sharp blades and a lot of steady pulling. If a horse was available, it could be hitched to the hide to help strip it from the carcass. A good skinner could strip thirty to forty hides in a day, each weighing about a hundred pounds.

Also present as part of the syndicate were gun cleaners, cartridge reloaders, cooks, blacksmiths, wranglers, and teamsters to drive the wagons. Others stretched out and staked the pelts on flat ground to dry, first with the gory side up and later the fur side. A large operation might soon cover a couple of acres with staked hides. When both sides were ready, the skins were piled into tall stacks that had to be unstacked and spread out in the sun daily until the hides were cured. During this process the hides lost about half their weight, which made them cheaper to ship. The hides were then delivered by wagon to the nearest railhead, where warehouses were built to house them — by the tens of thousands — until they could be shipped east to tanneries in Chicago, Kansas City, and Europe.

A single pelt might sell for twenty-five cents on the hunting grounds and three dollars in Kansas City. An overcoat made from bison pelts sold for as much as fifty dollars. As one twenty-two-year-old bison hunter, Frank H. Mayer, observed, "When I went into business, I sat down and figured that I was indeed one of Fortune's children. Just think! There were 20 million bison, each worth at least $3 — $60 million. I could kill 100 a day ... that would be $6,000 a month — or three times what was paid to the President of the United States and a hundred times what a man with a good job could be expected to earn." By the late 1870s, five thousand hunters and skinners were at work in the industry.

Extravagant waste was the order of the day. By some estimates, only one in four hides proved good enough in quality to make it to retail. Hunters rarely salvaged bison meat, and when they did, they usually took only the tongue and the hump. So many skinned carcasses were left behind, rotting on the plains, that a few years later a cottage industry of "bone-pickers" grew up to collect bleached bison bones. These were carved into trinkets or converted into bone char, a product used to filter water, remove color during the refining of sugar, or process crude oil into petroleum jelly.

The last great contributor to the bison's destruction was the unwritten policy of the frontier military to deprive the Plains Indians of their most critical foodstuff — bison beef — thus ensuring their eventual dependence on the U.S. government for food rations. Historians still debate over how conscious and deliberate a plan this was, but there is no question that the military gave out free ammunition to hunters, encouraged its own forces to engage in recreational hunting of bison, and led a number of lavish hunting expeditions for the politically favored — the Great Royal Buffalo Hunt was the most famous.

As Teddy Blue observed, "All this slaughter was a put-up job on the part of the government, to control the Indians by getting rid of their food supply. And in a way it couldn't be helped. But just the same it was a low-down dirty way of doing the business, and the cowpunchers as a rule had some sympathy with the Indians."

The Native Americans understood full well what was happening and why. Satanta, chief of the Kiowa, said, "These soldiers cut down my timber; they kill my buffalo; and when I see that my heart feels like bursting . . . Has the white man become a child that he should recklessly kill and not eat? When the red men slay game, they do so that they may live and not starve." Ten Bears of the Yamparika band of the Comanche echoed the sentiment: "So why do you ask us to leave the rivers, and the sun, and the wind, and live in houses? Do not ask us to give up the buffalo for the sheep. The young men have heard talk of this, and it has made them sad and angry. Do not speak of it more."

General Philip Sheridan, who oversaw the military operations of the Trans-Missouri West during this period, is particularly culpable. It was Sheridan who laid waste to the Shenandoah Valley during the Civil War, in an effort to starve the Confederacy into submission. He used similar tactics against the Native Americans. Indeed, Sheridan is widely credited with the remark "the only good Indian is a dead Indian," a comment that he denied making. Also he reportedly urged the Texas legislature around this time to "let them kill, skin, and sell until the buffalo is exterminated, as it is the only way to bring a lasting peace and allow civilization to advance."

Such malfeasance extended to Washington, D.C., and the White House. When a federal bill designed to protect the dwindling herds passed Congress in 1874, President Ulysses S. Grant used a pocket veto to squelch its passage.

William T. Hornaday, director of the New York Zoological Park and a critic of the government's negligence concerning the bison, argued in his 1889 book, *The Extermination of the American Bison*, that the bison population may already have been in decline when politicians, businessmen, and recreational hunters set out to destroy it. Human settlements expanding along various western rivers had deprived the bison of some of its best habitat. And these animals faced increased competition for food from new entrants into the ecosystem, in particular the herds of wild mustangs, which, like the first cattle, had been introduced to the continent by the Spanish conquistadors. It is also possible that the great herds, so awe-inspiring to early observers, were actually an "outbreak population" — an explosion in numbers caused by sharply reduced predation by Native Americans; their own numbers had been decimated by smallpox, typhus, measles, influenza, and other diseases introduced by Europeans. Thus the bison population may have reached levels that were unsustainable and set to trigger a precipitous decline. The wholesale slaughter only accelerated it.

Hornaday blamed the near extinction of the bison on five causes: human greed, inexcusable government neglect, the hunters' preference for hides of the female bison over that of the bulls, "the phenomenal stupidity of the animals themselves and their indifference to man," and, perhaps most fatal, the arrival of breech-loading rifles together with other advances in firearms, such as fixed ammunition. Contagious cattle diseases also may have played a role.

With no existing environmental organizations and few influential advocates defending the animals, other than perhaps Hornaday himself, the killing spree continued until the spring of 1884. When the hunting syndicates went out that year, as usual, to shoot the bison, there were none to be found.

Just a few years later Hornaday would write, "Not even a bone or a buffalo-chip remains above ground throughout the West to mark the presence of the buffalo . . . The like has probably never occurred before in any country, and most assuredly never will again." Outraged at the loss, he had no patience for those who said the extermination of the bison could not have been stopped: "Such an accusation of weakness and imbecility on the part of the General Government is an insult to our strength and resources. The protection of game is now and always has been simply a question of money."

By 1902 only two dozen bison survived in Yellowstone National Park, protected from hunters by the penalties imposed by the Lacey

Act of 1894. From this surviving herd, with the aid of the National Park Service, the animals began a slow recovery. William Hornaday did his part by cofounding, in 1905, the American Bison Society, the first conservation organization to reintroduce animals into the wild. Today bison numbers vary from 2,500 to 4,000 in Yellowstone, and another 30,000 or so roam public and private lands outside the park, but the bison is unlikely to recover its role as a keystone species on the open prairie.

The disappearance of the bison marked the first great environmental disaster in the history of the United States. The second, this time featuring cattle, was soon in the making.

With the open range emptied of bison and the so-called Indian problem greatly reduced by the removal of tribes onto reservations, only one more catalyst was needed to launch the cattle bonanza: economic incentive. It arrived at the conclusion of the Civil War with the complete devastation of the Confederate economy. Chief among the impoverished states—the one with perhaps the worst economic prospects during postwar Reconstruction—was Texas. And it was here in the desperate southern ranch lands in the spring of 1866 that the era of the Cattle Kingdom was born.

2

Cattle for Cash

An Iowan named George C. Duffield is the only drover of the cattle era known to have kept a diary of his trail drive. His entries give a woeful account of the hardships of moving a thousand head of longhorns north from Texas to Iowa in 1866.

It has been raining for three days . . . Hard rain and wind and lots of trouble . . . Ran my horse into a ditch & got my knee badly sprained . . . Still dark & gloomy. River up. Everything looks blue to me . . . Big thunderstorm last night. Stampede, lost 100 beeves . . . found 50. All [the men] tired. Everything discouraging . . . Swam the river with a rope & then hauled the wagon over. Lost most of our kitchen furniture such as camp kettles, coffee pots, cups, plates, canteens . . . It does nothing but rain . . . the cattle all left us [in the night] & in the morning not one beef to be seen. Hunt beeves all day . . . All the hands discouraged . . . Nothing to eat . . . Everything gloomy. Four of our best hands left us . . . Rain poured down for two hours.

This was just the beginning of George Duffield's travails. A year earlier, at the conclusion of the Civil War in the spring of 1865, large sections of cities like Atlanta and Charleston had been reduced to burnt rubble. The slave-based plantation system had unraveled, adding to the massive unemployment throughout the South. There was no formal government, no police force, no courts or postal service, and Confederate currency was worthless, as were all other Confederate government securities. Everyone's savings, unless they happened to be in gold, had been lost forever.

Few parts of the South faced prospects as bleak as those of the state of Texas, much of which was still largely uncultivated and only sparsely settled: the largest city, Galveston, had fewer than ten thousand people. Texas cattle outfits tended to be small and run by hardy Scots-Irish men who were willing to defend their property from Comanche raids. Most grew corn and cotton as well as raising stock; cotton was the state's largest crop. When the young men went off to war, most of the cotton plantations and cattle ranches were largely abandoned.

But after the war the Texans discovered they did have one commodity in great abundance: wild longhorn cattle.

Traditionally, the cattle had been valued for their leather hides and tallow — the fat used to make soap, candles, and lubricants. Before the Civil War, their lean meat was not the preferred choice of the northern beef market, but Texans ate it, and it was inexpensive. Good for home use, but not a great business opportunity.

In the wake of the war, this changed. In northern cities like New York, where the economy was booming thanks to wartime spending, the standard of living was rising rapidly, and as it rose, tastes were evolving. Pork, long the staple protein of the average diet, had fallen out of favor, replaced with a taste for beef. As a result, beef prices in the Northeast were soaring: a steer worth four dollars in Texas could sell for forty to fifty dollars in New York. And in Texas, the population of wild longhorns had exploded because they had been left largely on their own during the war. The supply of these animals appeared unlimited.

It didn't take long for the desperate cattlemen of Texas to spot the opportunity and set about exploiting it. All they needed to do was trail the free cattle from the impoverished grazing grounds of southern Texas to the markets of the North and pocket the profits. A second underserved market existed as well: the forts, Indian reservations, and mining towns of the newly opened American West.

Cattle had been trailed from Texas to Missouri as early as 1842 and to California as early as 1854. Even in 1864, during the Civil War, the poet Walt Whitman recalled seeing the cattle herds sweep through Washington, D.C.: "The mounted men, always excellent riders and on good horses, dash after the recusant, and wheel and turn — A dozen mounted drovers, their great, slouch'd, broad-brim'd hats, very picturesque — another dozen on foot — everybody cover'd with dust — long goads in their hands — An immense drove of perhaps 2000 cattle — the shouting, hooting, movement, &c."

Although the maps depicting these routes suggest an orderly branch network of roads, on the ground the paths taken were often circuitous, as the drovers needed to provide water and grass for the cattle along the way. This meant following rivers and creeks and tracing the routes of old Indian and buffalo trails. The earliest endpoints were the railheads of the Union Pacific and the Missouri Pacific railroads, which were gradually extending their tentacles of track westward, now that the Civil War was over and capital was available for their expansion.

But nothing about this trail-driving scheme turned out to be quite as easy as it looked on paper.

The first challenge: a cattle drive required horses, but the freely roaming mustangs needed to be roped, corralled, and broken by a skilled broncobuster. It typically took five to six days to properly break a wild mustang. And to trail cattle north, a journey that could take three to six months, drovers needed four or five horses per cowboy.

The second challenge: the behavior and temperament of the wild Texas Longhorn itself. It was a hybrid — a cross between a brand of southern cattle and the wild black cattle first introduced to the

New World by the Spanish. The resulting animal had long, somewhat spindly legs; a narrow torso, with thin loins and rump; and a longish narrow head, featuring horns, similar in shape to the spaghetti handlebars of a bicycle, that sometimes hooked forward and sometimes out to the side. The largest spread of horns on record belonged to a bull named Champion, born around 1890 on a Mexican ranch near the Rio Grande; his horns stretched more than nine feet from point to point.

It was a challenge for cowboys to round up these wild cattle. Texas Longhorns hid in the brush during the day and did most of their foraging at night. Only briefly in the summer, when the tormenting mosquitoes were out in force, did they spend the daylight hours in open areas, where they hoped to find a breeze. Most of the time the cowboys were compelled to ride into the thorny brush to flush the cattle out. But a cow with a young calf was prepared to gore a horse to defend her offspring, and the longhorn bull was notoriously ornery: "sullen, morose, solitary, and pugnacious," as one cattleman put it. "The longer he lived, the meaner he became."

"Ask any old-time range man of the south country to name the quickest animal he has ever known," wrote J. Frank Dobie in his book *The Longhorns*. "He won't say a cutting horse, a polo pony, a wild cat, a striking rattlesnake. He doesn't know the duck hawk. He will say a Longhorn bull. Some other bulls are quick; many breeds fight, even the Polled Angus. But none of them can bawl, bellow, mutter and rage like the bulls of Spanish breed and none can move with such swiftness."

The Texas cattlemen rounded up longhorn herds, cut out and castrated young bulls to make the neutered and more docile steers that were the source of most of the best marbled beef, and branded the calves with branding irons to document ownership. Cows (females) and heifers (young cows that had not yet had calves) were saved for breeding, but all of the animals roamed free. These methods were developed by the Mexican vaqueros, whose ancestors had once wrangled herds for the Spanish missions throughout present-day California, Texas, and Mexico.

As luck would have it, the longhorn had adapted admirably to its drought-prone environment in ways that made it well suited for trail driving. A hardy animal immune to most cattle-borne diseases, it could travel two days without water, and it showed remarkable endurance. The longhorn steers soon grew accustomed to being trailed, each animal understanding its place in the hierarchy of the herd and assuming the same position in line each day, often pairing up with the same partner. The stronger, fitter steers were the natural leaders and took their place at the point of the herd; the weaker animals brought up the rear. If a steer developed a sore foot, he would drop back and limp along until his injury healed and then resume his place farther up in the herd.

Once a herd was assembled, the profit-seeking Texan faced his most grueling challenge: the trail drive itself. Since railroads throughout the South had been badly damaged during the Civil War and had never ventured far into Texas, he faced only two realistic choices, and neither was attractive. He could trail his herd to the Kansas and Missouri railheads, where the cattle could be shipped east, but on such a trail drive the Texan was likely to face hostility or even armed resistance put up by local farmers; they feared that their crops would be trampled by the herds or that their own livestock would contract a deadly disease from these cattle from farther south. The other option: the ambitious Texan could head farther west and try to reach a mining town or one of the forts overseeing the territories — always good markets for beef — but then he faced the risk of Indian attacks.

It required a minimum of eight men to drive a thousand head of cattle. The trail boss usually rode a few miles ahead, scouting out water holes and good places to graze the herd. The cook followed on the mess, or chuck, wagon. This modified covered wagon, or prairie schooner, was drawn by four horses and loaded with canned and powdered food, a three-legged Dutch oven, cooking utensils, and a barrel of drinking water. The cook was usually accompanied by the herd of horses, known as the remuda, along with the lowly wrangler responsible for their care and oversight.

Two cowboys were positioned at the point of the herd and two along each swing, or flank. The two most junior cowboys brought up the rear and were known as drag riders. Their job was to keep the slow and lame cattle moving along. They were constantly subjected to dust and spatterings of the herd's manure; they took the full brunt of its noxious odors.

The men dressed simply. Most wore wide sombrero-like hats, to keep the sun and rain off, and a collarless shirt, often with a vest over it, with pockets to hold tobacco, matches, and good-luck charms. They wore thick gloves to protect their hands against chafing caused by the lariat. A bandana could serve many purposes: worn around the neck, it offered protection from sunburn or served as a dust mask; tied around the ears, it could provide warmth on a chilly morning. Initially, according to Teddy Blue, the cowboys "had no tents, no tarps, and damn few slickers."

Their meals consisted chiefly of pinto beans, sorghum molasses, and lots of beef, accompanied by cornmeal or sourdough biscuits and gravy, all of it washed down with black coffee. This menu could vary when cowboys caught their own wild fish or game, such as trout, elk, deer, pronghorn, or wild turkey. Wild onions were considered a particular delicacy. A staple of the diet was "son-of-a-bitch stew," concocted from leftover cattle parts such as the heart, testicles, and tongue.

On a good day, a trail drive could cover fourteen or fifteen miles, usually with a break at midday for lunch.

The greatest threat facing the drovers was a stampede. It didn't take much to spook the jumpy longhorns: lightning, the appearance of a wolf, the snap of a towel. Teddy Blue, one of the most experienced trail drivers of the era — he participated in his first trail drive when he was only ten years old — describes in his memoirs a particularly harrowing stampede on a blustery, squalling night in the fall of 1888: "About ten minutes to two one night, just before time to come off guard, my partner and I met, the way you do, circling in opposite directions around the bed ground. I asked him what time it was and he popped a match — them parlor matches had just come out then. I thought he'd have the sense enough to pull off from the herd a little ways but he didn't. It was a stormy night. The cattle were up and milling, and at the flash of the match they were off."

Teddy Blue had experienced a number of stampedes and knew precisely how to respond. He spurred his horse after the herd. The trick was not to get in front of the cattle but still get close enough so that you could begin to turn them. Eventually the nose of the herd could be directed into the tail, resulting in a vortex that forced the cattle to mill in confusion, stopping the stampede.

But a stampede in the dark is especially dangerous. The first nighttime stampede Teddy Blue had witnessed occurred in 1876 on the Blue River in Colorado when he was just fifteen. It resulted in the death of a cowpuncher and his horse. Teddy Blue never forgot the sight of the bodies, discovered the next morning: "The horse's ribs was scraped bare of hide, and all the rest of horse and man was mashed into the ground as flat as a pancake. The only thing you could recognize was the handle of his six-shooter."

Teddy Blue knew that his horse could see in the dark better than he could, but still the animal faced numerous hazards, including the burrow holes made by prairie dogs, coyotes, and badgers.

On this night, the herd finally came to a halt of its own accord. But then, just as Teddy Blue was catching his breath, something new spooked the cattle; bellowing, clattering their horns, pounding their hooves into the turf, they were off again, stampeding over the dry sagebrush prairie, with Teddy Blue in pursuit.

He had barely succeeded in turning the herd when his horse, a mustang named Pete, tripped on an embankment that rose up suddenly before them. The horse stumbled, throwing horse and man to the ground. The pommel of the saddle gouged Teddy Blue in the chest, snapping three of his ribs; he lay pinned by one leg under his horse, the wind knocked out of him. At ground level the thumping of the cattle's hooves was deafening. A moment later the swing of the turning herd descended upon Teddy Blue. He stuck out his hand to protect himself. Immediately a hoof slammed into it.

As he lay there, trapped, three ribs broken, hand gashed, he felt convinced that it was his turn to be trampled into a pancake on the open range. But the side, or swing, of the stampeding herd somehow passed by without further harming him or his horse. The next morning Teddy Blue rode into camp and tried to resume his duties, despite the extreme pain from his injuries. At noon he rode up to a ranch house along the trail to ask for a glass of water. Before it could be brought to him, he fainted and fell off his horse.

Crossing rivers required special techniques. The cowboys riding at the front would try to lead the herd into the water, while the others kept the cattle moving. Once the herd started across — and sometimes the cattle would balk at reflected light or ripples on the water — it was imperative to avoid gaps in the herd, lest a lagging group break back for the shore. But nor could you hurry the longhorns and risk getting them excited because then they would panic and mill. And a mill in a river was difficult to break and potentially costly. The cows in the center of the vortex would be forced under and drowned. There were reports of as many as eight hundred cattle drowning in a single mill that could not be broken up.

At night, the cowboys each spent another two hours on horseback, in alternating shifts, circling the herd. A full night's sleep was rarely more than five or six hours. As Teddy Blue said, "When you add it all up, I believe the worst hardship we had on the trail was the loss of sleep. There was never enough sleep." Exhaustion and tension were the norm, as Iowan George Duffield discovered.

Gloomy times as ever I saw . . . This day has been spent in crossing the West Trinity [River] . . . I swam it 5 times. Upset our wagon in the river & lost many of our cooking utensils again . . . Lost my knife today . . . Cold morning. Wind blowing & hands all shivering . . . There was one of our party drowned today (Mr. Carr) & several narrow escapes & I among the number . . . Men all tired and want to leave. I am in Indian country and am annoyed by them. Believe they scare the cattle to get paid to collect them . . . Many men in trouble. Horses all gave out & men refused to do anything . . . Hard rain & a windstorm. Beeves ran & I had to be on horseback all night. Awful night. Wet all night . . . Almost starved not having had a bite to eat for 60 hours . . . Oh! What a night — thunder, lightning & rain . . . Am almost dead for [lack of] sleep . . . I am not homesick but heartsick . . . Beautiful clear night & this morning I went on guard so cold that my teeth chattered . . . Cooked dinner under a tree on the A K. River bank with two ladies . . . 15 Indians came to help us herd & tried to take some beeves. I would not let them. Had a big muss. One drew his knife & I my revolver. Made them leave but fear they have gone for others. They are Seminoles.

The cattle drives of 1866 met with decidedly mixed success.

That year the trailblazing duo Charles Goodnight and Oliver Loving drove two thousand head of cattle from near San Antonio over almost seven hundred miles to Fort Sumner in New Mexico. They were accompanied by eighteen men, including one former slave and a cross-eyed cowboy named Nath Branner who joked that he could keep one eye on the longhorn and watch out for rattlesnakes with the other. Before departing, thirty-year-old Goodnight had retrofitted a covered wagon to create the first chuck wagon; it soon became a fixture on the trail.

Fort Sumner, little more than a loose assemblage of adobe and Spanish mission-style buildings, was responsible for the oversight of the million-acre Bosque Redondo Indian Reservation, home to eight thousand Navajo forced to move there from their traditional lands in eastern Arizona two years before. But the area was ill suited to farming, and the corn crop had been devoured by cutworm caterpillars; thanks to poor planning by the government, an urgent need for food supplies arose.

The journey proved arduous: along one stretch in the Pecos Valley, the herd traveled through eighty miles of barren scrubland and heat haze without water, which killed some three hundred steers. When the longhorns finally reached the banks of the wide, reddish Pecos River, the desperately thirsty cattle stampeded into the deep water to drink, clamoring, snorting, bellowing, and roiling the river. Despite the cattlemen's attempts to untangle them, a hundred drowned. Other cattle died from drinking poisonous alkali water in nearby streams.

When they reached Fort Sumner, Goodnight and Loving were paid eight cents a pound for the steers. Goodnight slung the saddle-bag containing their twelve thousand dollars in gold over the back of a mule and returned to Texas. Loving trailed the remaining cows and calves farther north into Colorado, the most obvious market being Denver, a large gold-mining town of thirty-five hundred people with a grid of dirt streets, a slew of red-brick buildings, and a disproportionate number of gambling dens, saloons, and prostitution "cribs." There he had no trouble selling the rest of the herd.

Goodnight and Loving had just made the first financial killing in the cattle trade. And the cattle they sold in New Mexico gave birth to the cattle industry in that state.

Goodnight, who never learned to read or write, would boot-strap his share of the money into a cattle baron's massive fortune over the course of his career and own over a million acres of Texas ranch land. Loving's luck ran out on the next trip. Riding on horse-back to Fort Sumner ahead of the herd, with a one-armed cowboy named Bill Wilson, Loving was attacked by a party of armed Comanche, perhaps the fiercest of the Plains tribes. He and Wilson galloped down to the Pecos River, leapt off their horses, jumped into the water, and took refuge in the six-foot-high brakes of Spanish cane that grew along the far shore. But the Indians were close behind. They quickly captured the cattlemen's horses and then sent a group of men to wade the river. The Comanche on the far bank called out in Spanish for the cattlemen to surrender, then fired random shots into the cane. One bullet passed through Loving's wrist and his holster, then into his side. He tossed his pistol to Wilson, who managed to hold off an Indian charge. The two spent a tense afternoon and evening in a standoff with their attackers. Loving, in great pain and convinced that he was going to die from his wounds, finally persuaded Wilson to make his escape. Wilson removed his cowboy boots and trousers so that he could kick to stay afloat while treading water with his one arm. Then, remaining as motionless as possible, he floated downstream past a Comanche watchman on horseback.

In order to get back to Goodnight and the herd, Wilson, with nothing to eat and clad only in his underwear, was forced to walk barefoot for three days over terrain littered with prickly pear cacti. He used a tepee pole as a walking stick and as a defense against wolves at night. He was so covered with red dust when he finally reached the trail drive that his friends mistook him at first for a limping, one-armed Comanche.

By then Loving, still alive, had made *his* desperate escape, also by floating downstream in the dark. He found his way to a road, where he flagged down a group of Mexicans traveling with a wagon. He offered them $150 to carry him to Fort Sumner. He arrived there, exhausted but relieved, only to encounter a young, inexperienced physician who at first refused to amputate his gangrenous arm. By the time the surgery was performed, the gangrene had spread. Loving died two weeks later from septicemia.

Other cattlemen trailed their herds up what they thought was the safer route, along the Shawnee Trail to Sedalia, Missouri, the trailhead for both the Missouri Pacific and the Missouri-Kansas-Texas railroad lines. A few attempted to cross the Ozarks, where they soon lost their bearings in the woods. Worse, it proved nearly impossible to herd cattle through the trees — or to feed them. Furthermore, Missouri, bordering the unsettled territories of the West, had become a popular hideout for miscreants and outlaws. It didn't take long for groups of these men to devise a way to steal from the Texans. They would stampede the herds at night, making sure the cattle were widely dispersed, before cutting out a group and hiding it. The next day they would offer to help the cattlemen round up the scattered animals — returning the hidden cattle if the pay was good enough, keeping them if it wasn't.

Other Texas cattlemen encountered the open hostility of farmers in Kansas. They rightly suspected that the Texas Longhorns carried the disease known as Texas fever (also called Spanish fever).

Although the hardy longhorns were apparently immune to this disease, as they were to most typical afflictions of cattle, no one disputed that they carried and transmitted it, although exactly how remained a mystery. The disease usually proved fatal to northern cattle, destroying red blood cells and causing high fever, anemia, internal hemorrhaging, and usually death. Wayne Gard, author of *The Chisholm Trail,* provides a grim description of a sick herd: "The stricken cattle began to arch their backs and droop their heads and ears. Their eyes became glassy and staring. They began to stagger from weakness in their hind legs. Their temperatures rose and their appetites faded. The pulse became quick and weak, and the animals panted for air." Eventually, as the disease progressed, the animal would slump into a coma-like lethargy or become delirious, tossing its head about so violently that its horns cracked.

To struggling homesteading farmers who depended on their cows for both dairy products and drafting, Texas fever was a terrifying threat. Although quarantines prohibiting the passage of Texas cattle through the region were already in place in parts of Missouri and Kansas, they were not being enforced. Meanwhile, the desperate Texans, whose livelihood depended on their herds, were unlikely to be deterred from selling their cattle because of some loosely imposed quarantine. Conflict was inevitable.

Nineteen-year-old Jim Daugherty, with five other cowboys, drove five hundred head of cattle north in 1866 from an area near present-day Dallas, through Oklahoma, to Kansas, where a group of so-called Jayhawkers — native-born Kansans who had supported the Union during the Civil War — stopped them not far from Baxter Springs. Daugherty and one of his cowboys, John Dobbins, were leading the herd when the group, clad in hunting attire and coonskin hats, approached them. Dobbins attempted to draw his gun; the Jayhawkers shot him dead in the saddle. This caused the cattle to stampede. Daugherty raised his hands and surrendered, while the rest of his crew chased after the herd. The Jayhawkers tied Daugherty to a tree, reportedly whipped him with hickory withes, and then debated among themselves whether to hang him. Eventually, concluding that he knew nothing about Texas fever, they released him. He lost 150 head of cattle, most of them in the stampede, but he managed to sell the remainder of the herd in nearby Fort Scott, Kansas, for a nice profit despite the attrition.

Another cowboy who found his path blocked in Baxter Springs was Nelson Story, a twenty-five-year-old Ohioan. With profits he had made from a placer-claim gold strike in Alder Gulch, Montana, he had bought a thousand Texas Longhorns at ten dollars per head to trail north. He made a quick decision to divert his herd westward, around the Kansas settlements and up to Virginia City, Montana, where he knew thousands of miners were working around Alder Gulch. They would buy the cattle for ten times what Story had paid for them. The route took the cowboys up the Platte Valley to Fort Laramie, and from there they hopscotched north from fort to fort — Reno, Fetterman, Phil Kearney, through the Powder River Basin, and northwest into the Territory of Montana. This route took the herd through Sioux territory, where bands of Indians were launching regular attacks on the military forts. Story was warned that the trip would be very dangerous, but he chose to proceed anyway, arming his twenty-seven men with the latest breech-loading Remington rifles. At one point a band of Indians swept down a hillside, wounded two of his cowboys with arrows, then galloped off with a portion of the herd. Story and a handful of his cowboys went after the war party, tracked them into the Badlands, counterattacked, and reclaimed their cattle. "Did they yield the steers willingly?" one of Story's men was asked years later. "Well you might say so" was the laconic reply. "We surprised them in their camp and they weren't in shape to protest much against our taking back the cattle." From that point on, the rapid-fire Remington gave the cowboys an advantage; this weapon scared the Indians into keeping a safe distance. Nevertheless, Story took few chances, trailing the cattle at night. His party had just one fatality — a cowboy sent out ahead to hunt for game late in the trip. He was captured and scalped, his body nailed to the ground with arrows. Story was the first man to trail a herd into Montana, but it would be another four years before others, less well equipped, considered it safe to trail cattle through the Powder River Basin.

Yet the Plains Indians would play a surprisingly small part in the cattle boom that followed. Relatively little warring, other than a few skirmishes, like these early ones, took place between cowboys and Indians. By the end of the Civil War, with their numbers drastically reduced by internecine wars, disease, and starvation, most tribes had already been relegated to reservations. The Native Americans would become a consumer market for the aspiring cattle ranchers rather than hostile competitors for prairie territory. Even the once-powerful Comanche, who occupied lands on the Texas Panhandle and in western Oklahoma, lower Kansas, and portions of New Mexico, and had fought hard against the encroachment of ranchers and settlers, would surrender by 1875, their numbers decimated. Soldiers at the various U.S. military forts continued to find reasons to suppress insurrections by bands from surviving tribes, including Custer's fatal miscalculation near the Little Bighorn River in 1876, but by 1879, when the beef bonanza took full flight, Indian attacks posed no real threat to cowboys or cattlemen on the open range.

The largest and probably the longest trail drive took place in the spring of 1869, when some two hundred former Confederate soldiers and their families, seeking a better life, trailed fifteen hundred cattle and twelve hundred horses from the Brazos River in lower Texas to California. At night they frequently combined the herd's four divisions into one vast grouping.

At the peak of the cattle boom some forty thousand cowboys worked on the open range, a majority of them white southerners, many of them former Confederate cavalrymen. The rest were a mix of European immigrants, predominantly Germans and Scandinavians or their American-born sons, as well as Mexicans, former slaves who had fled the plantation system of the South, and Native Americans — they often possessed excellent riding skills.

The job — outdoor work with physical challenge — held an unmistakable appeal for young men. Meals were included, as was genuine camaraderie: the cowboys were paid to collaborate. Liquor, gambling, and in some cases cussing were strictly forbidden, but the job didn't require an education or a place to live. You didn't even need a horse: the trail boss would provide one. About all you needed was a saddle, a bedroll, and a poncho.

And who could complain about the surroundings? Most of the Confederate cowboys had never seen the open rangeland of the West. Nothing quite prepared them for the beauty and scale of the landscape — buttes and coulees and massive mountain ranges and azure skies, all on a gargantuan scale. How different it was from the flat, grassy prairies of west Texas!

They marveled at bald eagles in their snow-white headdresses, perched on the limbs of cottonwood trees. Riding across the prairie flats on a warm day, they could smell the hayfield fragrance of sagebrush and watch herds of pronghorn bounce away in unison. In the emerald-green alpine meadows bloomed wildflowers in incomprehensible profusion: primrose, harebell, phlox, larkspur, balsamroot, wild rose, paintbrush, and the hundreds of white and yellow varietals that appeared with the first snowmelt of spring and grew in gaudy abundance well into the summer. The last to appear, fireweed, grew chest-high at the end of July, blanketing the hillsides with rosy-purple blossoms and culminating the annual flower show like the finale of a fireworks display.

In autumn the cowboys heard for the first time the melancholic bugling of a bull elk at dusk. They admired the stands of quaking aspens in their shimmering golden fall foliage. All felt the visceral excitement that Lewis and Clark had experienced when they first traversed that incomparable landscape. Here was a world that stirred the soul and gave a cowboy the sense of being wildly alive while making clear his humble status in the cosmos.

Indeed, a firsthand encounter with the wide-open beauty of the American West was enough to change a man's character. "There was a freedom, a romance, a sort of mystic halo hanging over those green, grassy, swelling divides that was impregnated, grafted into your system," wrote the cattleman John Clay in his memoirs. Clay himself had arrived from Scotland in 1874. He described himself as a young man "with an eye to the main chance" and would go on to manage, among other ranches, the Swan Land & Cattle Company, a historic Wyoming cattle ranch that survived for seventy years.

Life on the open range would routinely turn callow young cowboys, like Clay, into savvy cattlemen. It would take one willful, rich, squeaky-voiced dilettante from New York City named Theodore Roosevelt and endow him with the maturity and gravitas needed to succeed in national politics. "I have always said I would not have become President had it not been for my experience in North Dakota," he would later write. "It was here the romance of my life began."

Perhaps adding to the thrill of it, the job of a cowboy entailed an astonishing number of ways to get hurt or killed. You could fall from your horse, you could be kicked in the head while roping a steer, you could be gored by a horn, you could drown while crossing a river, you could be caught in quicksand, you could be struck by lightning, you could be scalped by an Indian, you could be shot by a rustler, or you could be involved in a barroom brawl. And this list overlooks the less than fatal but uncomfortable perils of the job, such as the torment of mosquitoes and horseflies and many untreatable maladies, such as sunstroke in the summer and sun blindness in the winter, infections, sprains, food poisoning, and piles. And medical help was hard to come by; as one observer wrote, "Doctors were scarcer than Latin scholars on the range."

George Duffield could have used one:

My back is blistered badly from exposure while in the river & I with two others are suffering very much. I was attacked by a beef in the river & had a very narrow escape from being hurt by diving [under water] . . . I have a sick headache bad . . . Had a great time gathering black berries . . . Last night was another of those nights that try a man. It thundered & lightened all night & rained one hard rain . . . Beeves ran. Wind blew. Was on my horse the whole night . . . We turned south and west. The day was warm & the flies worse than I ever saw them. Our animals

were almost ungovernable . . . Lost my coat and went back for
it . . . Osages visit our camp. They are great Beggars . . . We all
right but 2 men are down with boils & one with ague . . . Could
not reach wood nor water & had to stay on the prairie without
water or fire. The country continues rough & rocky. It is almost
impassible in places. Found a human skeleton on the prairie today . . . Cattle stampeded & ran by two farms & the people there
were very angry. We were visited by many men and threatened
with the Law but think we are all right now . . . I was sick last
night had a chill & the colic this morning — feel very badly yet.
Everything parching under the scorching sun . . . A very sick
man in camp has had two severe fits. I got struck by a horse
(in the face) & have a very sore eye and am still troubled with
colic . . . I was very sick & slept none. I had severe shakes.

Ultimately, it took Duffield six months to move his longhorns
north to Iowa. Only half his cattle survived the journey.

Grueling efforts like these yielded one important early discovery: the cattle seemed able to withstand a northern winter on the
open range without supplemental feed. Some attrition had to be
expected — the odd animal that got caught in a snowdrift or failed
to find forage — but most could survive the cold months if they
were parked in a sheltered valley. The drought-resistant blue grama
grass, the buffalograss, and the tussock and bunch grasses that had
once fed the buffalo herds could now sustain the Texas cattle. And
that concept opened up new economic possibilities. Also, the acreage in open-range territories and states seemed infinite, and the
government was willing to lease it or sell it for a pittance. Or you
could simply take possession of whatever tracts you wanted, claim
the land and water rights by "prior appropriation," and pay nothing.

So despite the heavy losses and setbacks incurred during those
earliest trail drives in the aftermath of the Civil War, the Texans
persisted in pushing their herds northward. They had few mon-
eymaking alternatives. In the spring of 1867, some 35,000 head of
cattle headed up the trails; the next year, 75,000; the year after that,

350,000; and in 1871, some 600,000. The great migration of Texas Longhorns, the largest forced migration of animals in human history, had begun in earnest. In all, some ten million cattle would be driven north out of Texas, accompanied by half a million horses and some 50,000 cowboys. Recalled Teddy Blue, "From that time on the big drives were made every year, and the cowboy was born."

3

Birth of the Cattle Town

Teddy Blue Abbott saw every aspect of the open-range cattle era, from its earliest days to its violent end. He was, in many respects, the quintessential cowboy. Although small, weighing only 135 pounds, he was adept at roping and wrestling calves, and this made him especially valuable during the twice-yearly roundups.

Teddy Blue caught cowboy fever early in his youth. In 1870, when he was ten years old, he helped his father drive a small herd of cattle from Texas to Nebraska. His parents, both British, had immigrated to Lincoln, Nebraska, after his father went broke farming in Norfolk, England, where Teddy Blue was born. Despite pouring more than sixty thousand dollars ($1.4 million in today's money) of an inheritance into various farming and cattle activities, Teddy Blue's father, sullen, lonely, and tyrannical, would eventually fail in the New World too, and lose every penny he invested in farming.

The Abbott farm adjoined a parcel of property where the neighboring town had built an insane asylum. One of Teddy Blue's most vivid childhood memories involved going out one frigid winter morning with his brother Harry to feed the milk cows. Teddy Blue watched as Harry dug his pitchfork into the haystack and struck something solid. They swept aside the hay sprigs to reveal the frozen body of an inmate—a woman clad only in a nightgown. Her dead eyes, wide open, stared glassily up at them. She had fled the asylum the night before and sought shelter in the haystack; she froze to death in the bitter cold. Recalled Teddy Blue, "I took one look and lit out for home so fast I never even stopped to get on my horse." One of thirteen children, Teddy Blue knew from an early age that the last thing he wanted was to be a farmer like his father. When his oldest and favorite brother died of an illness at age nineteen, the experience cost Teddy Blue his faith in God—in his words, it "made an infidel of me." He spent much of his childhood on horseback, idolizing cowboys and skipping school. Chafing at his father's stern parenting, he ran away at fourteen to join a group of drovers near Fort Kearney on the Platte River, only to return out of concern for his mother. But by age eighteen, he had left home for good. Although he had little true understanding of the rigors that he was committing himself to, he was convinced they would be preferable to farming.

After their disappointing experiences with trailing cattle north in 1866, the Texas trail drivers knew better than to head back to Sedalia, Missouri, or Baxter Springs, Kansas. Fortunately, the railroads were by now reaching farther into the Great Plains, adding as many as two to five miles of track each day. The cattlemen realized they could avoid conflict with the Jayhawkers by targeting railheads much farther west. But this solution did not happen by accident. In one of the more inspired ideas of the time, an enterprising twenty-nine-year-old Illinois cattle merchant named Joseph G. McCoy dreamed up the idea of constructing a formal railroad depot specifically for the sale of cattle. In partnership with his two brothers, he would build what amounted to a small town to receive the cattle herds, a place where, as he wrote in his memoirs, "the Southern drover and the Northern buyer would meet upon an equal footing, and both be undisturbed by mobs or swindling thieves." It was, according to the historian Paul Wellman, "one of the great single ideas of this nation's history." What sounds like a simple enough concept could not be implemented without great resourcefulness and ingenuity — human talents that came to characterize the launching of the cattle era.

In the spring of 1867, McCoy made the rounds of various railroad companies to pitch his idea, seeking their cooperation. His first stop was the headquarters of the Kansas Pacific Railway, where he made a presentation before the company's president and executive committee. After listening patiently, the president, described by McCoy as a "pert, lively, courteous little gentleman, but evidently not a practical railroad man, and one that knew absolutely nothing about freighting live stock," smiled at him skeptically and announced that he had no faith in the idea and "would not risk a dollar in the enterprise." He did add, however, that if by some miracle McCoy pulled off the operation, Kansas Pacific would pay to build a switch and sidings that would give McCoy a place to load his cattle.

McCoy's next stop was the Missouri Pacific Railroad. Ushered into an elegant wood-paneled office, he met alone with the company's president, a large, formidable man dressed in a hand-tailored suit who sat smoking a cigar and examining a stack of business papers. McCoy timidly stated his business, suddenly self-conscious of what he described as his "rough, stogy, unblocked boots, a slouch hat, seedy coat, soiled shirt and unmentionable [underwear] that had seen better days twelve months previous." The railroad magnate bit down on the cigar and looked up at McCoy. He listened, "striking the attitude of indescribable greatness, when stooping to notice an infinitesimal object." When McCoy had finished his pitch, the company president proclaimed in a booming voice, "It occurs to me that you haven't any cattle to ship, and never did have any, and I, sir, have no evidence that you ever will have any, and I think you are talking about rates of freight for speculative purposes, therefore, you get out of this office, and let me not be troubled with any more of your style!"

But McCoy refused to give up. Less than twelve hours later, a freight agent for the much smaller Hannibal & St. Joseph Railroad embraced McCoy's idea and agreed to ship the cattle to Chicago via Quincy, Missouri, at the acceptable rate of forty dollars per stock car. McCoy later stated that this single decision by a small railroad company had dramatic implications: it helped lay the foundation for Chicago's primacy as the cattle hub of the West and ultimately the headquarters of the meatpacking industry, while simultaneously depriving St. Louis of a much larger role in the cattle trade.

The spot that McCoy picked for his depot, a Kansas hamlet and stage station named Abilene, consisted of little more than a dozen dirt-floored log huts; he once described it as "a very small, dead place." The local saloonkeeper, Josiah Jones, owned the only profitable business in town: selling prairie dogs as pets to tourists. But the location met all of McCoy's criteria. It stood far enough from major settlements to allow cattle to be trailed in without interference from Jayhawkers, and it lay in a mile-wide depression in the plains known as Smoky Hill Valley, which was amply watered and rich in long grass. A nearby military station, Fort Riley, served as a potential market for the beef and provided security from Indians.

Pooling money from his family, McCoy bought 250 acres on the town's northeast edge and began construction of his depot in June 1867, ordering hardwood from Lenape and pine boards from Hannibal. Within two months he had erected a sturdy cattle yard that could hold up to three thousand head. He also built an office and a barn, bought and installed a pair of ten-ton Fairbanks scales that could weigh twenty cattle at a time, and began constructing a soon-to-be-famous three-story hotel, which he named Drovers Cottage. Eventually costing fifteen thousand dollars to build, the completed hotel could boast plastered walls and green venetian blinds; it featured both a saloon and a billiard parlor. It could sleep 80 and feed 240. The accompanying barn could accommodate up to a hundred horses and fifty carriages.

With the work still under construction, McCoy paid a visit to the

governor of Kansas, Samuel J. Crawford, and outlined his ambitious
plans. Crawford, eager to attract business to the state, endorsed the
plan in spite of a Kansas statute requiring that Texas cattle be kept
sixty miles west of Abilene to protect the settlers from the scourge
of Texas fever. "I regard the opening of that cattle trail into and
across western Kansas of as much value to the state as is the Missouri River," the governor told a local paper. Next, McCoy printed
up handbills to be distributed in towns throughout Texas and the
Southwest, announcing the opening of the cattle town. Then he
sent three representatives on horseback in various directions to
alert any Texas cattlemen already on the trail with their herds to the
presence of the new depot. Finally, he used his contacts in Illinois
to alert the Springfield and Chicago cattle buyers that shipments
would soon be headed to Kansas.

It was an expensive and daring gamble. Days of nail biting and
waiting ensued.

Finally, a number of herds, including one destined for California,
were intercepted and persuaded to steer their cattle up to Abilene.
In all, some thirty-five thousand cattle arrived in Abilene during
that summer and fall, and twenty thousand of them were shipped
out by the railroad. The Kansas Pacific, incredulous at what McCoy
had accomplished, kept its promise by building a one-hundred-car
siding area where cattle could be loaded into stock cars. Before long,
McCoy's cattle pens at what he named the Great Western Stock
Yards could load twenty railroad cars in an hour. The following
year the number of cattle shipped out of Abilene by rail doubled.
A thousand stock cars full of cattle, eighteen steers per car, were
shipped east in June alone. The number doubled again the following year.

McCoy recalled in his memoirs, with evident satisfaction, the
day that the agent from the Missouri Pacific Railroad arrived in
Abilene, suddenly solicitous of McCoy's booming business. McCoy
told the agent that not only did he have no cattle for his railroad,
but he also suspected that he never would, and please say as much

to the company's president. "The agent seemed to relish the force of such language, and departed forthwith to deliver the message."

Joseph G. McCoy had just created the first cattle town. Much like the iconic American cowboy, the cattle town, almost as soon it emerged, became a myth-spinner. After all, it was here that the cowboy and "civilization" rubbed shoulders. It was here that the new saloons threw open their bat-wing doors to gamblers and "soiled dove" prostitutes. And it was here on the dirt streets just beyond the boardwalks that shootouts would take place — amid neighing horses, rattling wagons, and lowing cattle.

The emerging cattle towns created a kind of stage set for exotic western activities, which eastern writers imaginatively described for their readers. Almost immediately, journalists with a nose for a good story began arriving from eastern newspapers to record what was happening in towns like Abilene. Writers penning the new "dime novel" (the American equivalent of the British penny dreadful) appeared too, looking for lurid subject matter to grab the attention of their emerging readership. Serious writers like Mark Twain and Stephen Crane came through as well, eager to participate in this curious new chapter in the conquest of the West and to generate firsthand material for their journals and short stories.

Perhaps the most unlikely of these literary aspirants was a high-strung young opera writer from Philadelphia, who traveled west for his health after suffering a nervous breakdown. He began to take copious notes on the passing scene, not yet sure what to write or how to write it, but mesmerized by everything that he saw and heard. His name was Owen Wister.

Several cattle trails leading to different cattle towns were soon established. The one running from Red River Station in Texas to the cattle yards of Abilene would be named after a man of Scottish-Cherokee heritage, Jesse Chisholm, who only a few years earlier had used a portion of the route to profitably trade with the Plains Indians. The Western Trail reached up to notorious Dodge City, and the

Goodnight-Loving Trail stretched up to Cheyenne. The Shawnee Trail, the only great cattle trail that predated the Civil War, led to Kansas City and St. Louis.

The effect on the hamlet of Abilene was nothing short of astonishing. In a whirlwind of construction, log huts and tents gave way to wood-frame and then brick buildings. A grid of streets soon formed. By 1870 the town had three thousand citizens and boasted four hotels, ten boarding houses, five dry goods and clothing stores, nine or ten saloons, and a handful of other establishments. Just a year later the Novelty Theatre opened, with an actor-manager in charge. By then a red-light district had emerged on the outskirts of Abilene, which, by some estimates, featured thirty brothels for servicing the hundreds of cowboys regularly passing through the town. In 1871, the year McCoy became mayor, he moved these houses to the edge of town, creating an area that came to be known as McCoy's Addition or, more colorfully, the Devil's Half-Acre.

McCoy's success was such that other Kansas cow towns sprang up in quick succession, among them Ellsworth, Newton, Wichita, Caldwell, Hays, Dodge City, and Hunnewell. Montana had its Miles City; Wyoming, its Cheyenne and Medicine Bow; on the Panhandle arose Tascosa; in Nebraska, Roswell, Ogallala, and Lincoln. These towns were built along spurs of the railroads that reached farther west and south, shortening the trail drives for the cattlemen.

In his celebrated 1902 cowboy novel, *The Virginian: A Horseman of the Plains,* Owen Wister would capture the shared features of these brand-new cattle towns:

Medicine Bow was my first and I took its dimensions, twenty-nine buildings in all, — one coal chute, one water tank, the station, one store, two eating-houses, one billiard hall, two tool-houses, one feed stable, and twelve others that for one reason and another I shall not name. Yet this wretched husk of squalor spent thought upon appearances; many houses in it wore a false front to seem as if they were two stories high. There they stood rearing their pitiful masquerade amid a fringe of old tin cans, while at their very doors began a world of crystal light, a land without end, a space across which Noah and Adam might come straight from Genesis.

In their early days, lacking the rudiments of a local government or any semblance of municipal services, least of all electricity or running water, these towns were nothing fancy. The streets remained unpaved and, by all reports, were littered with tin cans and broken bottles. The British travel writer Isabella Lucy Bird was not much impressed with Cheyenne, Wyoming, during her visit in 1873: "It is an ill-arranged set of farm houses and shanties; and rubbish heaps, and offal of deer and antelopes, produce the foulest smells I have smelt for a long time. Some of the houses are painted a blinding white; others are just unpainted; there is not a bush, or a garden, or a green thing; it just straggles out promiscuously on the boundless brown plains . . . It is utterly slovenly-looking and unornamental, abounds in slouching bar-room looking characters, and looks a place of low, mean lives." It was a far cry from a comely English village, with its thatched cottages and green cricket pitch.

And yet to a cowboy, arriving after having spent two or three months sleeping on the ground outdoors during a journey of more than a thousand miles from the cattle lands of southern Texas, the sight of a cow town on the horizon was most welcome. Like sailors on shore leave after a long passage at sea, the trail drivers longed for rest and relaxation and for whatever entertainment and diversions the newly erected village might offer.

Once the herd was corralled at the stockyard or pastured on the outskirts of town — or perhaps purchased by a speculator, or handed off to a cattle baron eager to expand his western herds on the open range, or sold to a slaughterhouse or a feeder from Illinois who intended to fatten up the steers for a year before slaughter — the cowboy would be paid for his labors. The pay usually came in the form of five- or twenty-dollar gold pieces. His salary: $25 to $40 a month, but double that if the cowboy owned and used his own horses. Still, the pay was not impressive. A foreman, by contrast, might earn $125 per month.

With money jangling in his pocket, the cowboy then rode into a newborn town built largely as a playground with him in mind, designed to deftly and swiftly separate him from those hard-earned wages. Given his age, his limited education, and his pent-up appetite for alcohol, pleasure, and recreation, that is precisely what would happen.

4

Cattle-Town High Jinks

A cowboy's highest priority upon arriving in a cattle town was to get clean. To do that he would check into a boarding house or a ramshackle hotel or perhaps just a bunkhouse, where accommodations consisted of a dormitory with cots. Here he could shave, and shower or bathe, often encountering rows of bathtubs and sinks where communal toothbrushes hung on strings, alongside communal towels, hairbrushes, mirrors, and combs. In his book *Roughing It,* Mark Twain described one such comb as apparently handed down ever since the age of Samson and Esau, gathering hair and "certain impurities."

Scrubbed, clean-shaven, and refreshed, the trail driver then joined the hundreds of other cowboys wandering the dirt streets and the new wood boardwalks of the busy town. While the shops were open, he might go in search of personal supplies, such as thread and tobacco. He might decide to get a haircut (thirty-five cents) before visiting a photography studio — the latest fad — to get his black-and-white portrait taken. Teddy Blue remembered following exactly this order of events: "I bought some new clothes and got my picture taken . . . I had a new white Stetson hat that I paid ten dollars for, and new pants that cost twelve dollars, and a good shirt and fancy boots. Lord, I was proud of those clothes! When my sister saw me, she said: 'Take your pants out of your boots and put your coat on. You look like an outlaw.' I told her to go to hell. And I never did like her after that."

Another cowboy arriving in Abilene in 1868 from the Chisholm Trail, footsore after walking all the way from the Kansas border with a herd (a party of Osage Indians had stolen the cowboys' horses), was a young man named Joe Horner, who would later play a starring, even notorious, role in the open-range era, under a different name — Frank M. Canton. But at eighteen years of age in 1868, his feet badly blistered, he was just glad to arrive in Abilene. He used his pay to buy himself a .44-caliber Winchester rifle and a pair of ponies.

The next stop for all cowboys was the local saloon.

This establishment dominated the main street of every cattle town. Usually the building was deep and narrow, with a false front; its bar ran the length of one long wall. Most bars were 50 to 60 feet in length, although some, like the one in Denver's Albany Saloon, reached 110 feet. They were constructed of polished oak, mahogany, or walnut, often imported from Chicago or Europe. The top-of-the-line bars were made of polished Circassian walnut and sold by Brunswick-Balke-Collender, a company today better known for manufacturing high-end billiard and pool tables. Behind the bar, on the back-bar mantle — also known as the altar — a long mirror allowed you to see behind you as you stood and drank. In a high-end saloon, like the Alamo in Abilene, the Varieties in Dodge City, the Gold Room in Cheyenne, or Doc Thayer's Gold Rooms in Newton, you were likely to find brass cuspidors, also known as spittoons or gaboons — one for every four or five men standing at the bar, since many chewed tobacco. At the far end of the room you might find gaming tables, billiard tables, and perhaps just enough open space for a dance floor and a fiddle band.

These western saloons, sporting their distinctive swinging bat-wing doors, had evolved from roadhouses, which marked the various station stops along the stagecoach lines, and from the tent saloons that trailed the teams who constructed the railroads. From the outset, these earlier establishments were well known for serving rotgut liquors, often a toxic mix of whiskey, tobacco, molasses, and red peppers known as Forty Rod, Tangle Leg, Tarantula Juice, Coffin Varnish, Taos Lightning, or Bust Head. A shot of this concoction had the potency to make, by one consumer's account, "a hummingbird spit in a rattlesnake's eye." Such rotgut sold for ten dollars a gallon but, perhaps mercifully, was often watered down when sold by the shot. "Some of that frontier scamper juice would draw a blood blister on a rawhide boot," according to Ramon F. Adams, a Texas historian and apparent authority on the subject. "It made you wonder how they kept such stuff corked. Three drinks would grow horns on a muley cow," he added.

Happily, just as the saloons began to replace the roadhouses, dramatic advances were made in the Northeast in both the bottling and marketing of alcohol. E. G. Booz, for example, introduced his Old Cabin Whiskey in a bottle shaped like a log cabin. Other whiskies — rye was particularly popular at the time — arrived in bottles with blob tops and corks or fancy glass stoppers. Popular mixed drinks included Cactus Wine, made from tequila and peyote tea, and Mule Skinner, a mix of whiskey and blackberry liquor. Ale and stout, once available only from a barrel, could now be found bottled in pottery jugs and were served warm until well into the 1880s. If you wanted a soft drink, you could order ginger ale or a drink called High Mucky Muck, the taste of which has been lost to posterity.

The rapidly expanding selection soon included drugstore tonics, such as Dr. B. J. Kendall's Blackberry Balsam, Hostetter's Bitters, and Dr. Simmons' Liver Regulator, known as "the cowboy's friend." According to the book *Saloons of the West*, "Allegedly, medicinal and sometimes mildly alcoholic, these shrub-root-based concoctions were widely advertised as blood purifiers, aphrodisiacs, as being good for common skin disorders, irregularity and other bowel ailments, kidney, bladder, and liver cures, as a help for poor appe-

tites, 'male weaknesses,' and for a host of other quasi-medical calamities limited only by the imagination of the bartender and the
gullibility of his customer."

A shot of whiskey generally cost fifty cents, and a glass of beer
ran twenty-five cents, or "two bits." A bottle of champagne might
sell for twelve dollars.

The most popular game at the gambling tables across the West
was faro, a card game much like poker in which each player opposed the dealer, who dealt from a single deck of cards. Ordinarily,
the player enjoyed decent odds against the house, but the dealing
box, or "shoe," was easily, and often, rigged. Poker was played with
a twenty-card deck comprising the face cards and the ten card of
each suit; the game featured no draw — all twenty cards were dealt
at the start of each hand. If you opted for billiards, then balkline or
three-cushion were the games of choice. Pocket billiards had fallen
out of favor, and straight pool would not be invented until 1910. In
the bigger saloons, monte, dice games, keno, and darts could also
be found. Gambling in its various forms was popular, but not all
cowboys fell prey to the professional gamblers or the card sharks
and pool sharks. Recalled Teddy Blue, "I couldn't see giving it to
them tinhorns. You knew they were going to take it away from you.
And besides, I never had time to gamble; I couldn't sit still long
enough; I always had to be up, talking, singing, drinking at the bar.
I was so happy and full of life, I used to feel, when I got a little whiskey inside me, that I could jump twenty feet in the air."

For Teddy Blue, the women were a cattle town's greatest attraction. In a saloon at the peak of the cattle era, a cowboy was likely to
encounter three varieties of "ladies." At the top of the pecking order
were the hurdy-gurdy girls, the professional dancing girls; they were
usually poor but respectable farm girls from the Hesse region of
Germany who traveled around the western states and Canada, accompanied by a chaperone. They were available for dances but were
definitely not to be solicited for sex. Next were the ordinary dancing girls, found in both saloons and dancehalls, and cowboys could
pay them for the privilege of a dance (twenty-five cents a twirl); as

a rule, these girls were not in the sex trade. Finally, and most prevalent, were the saloon girls, who were almost always prostitutes.

If the cowboy was interested in sex, he faced a variety of choices because there were prostitutes at every price point. The best dressed and most expensive were the parlor-house girls found in the brothels, which were usually run by madams who themselves were former prostitutes. Saloon girls fell somewhere in the middle in terms of affordability, and the least expensive and by all accounts the least attractive — by cowboy standards anyway — were the "crib girls" who occupied dilapidated one-room shacks on the outskirts of town. They were often older prostitutes or those afflicted with alcoholism or drug addiction (usually to laudanum, a mixture of opium and alcohol), or women of ethnicities deemed less sexually desirable, such as Native Americans and Chinese immigrants. An encounter with a prostitute might cost a cowboy anywhere from one to five dollars, depending on the class of prostitute.

Most of the prostitutes were shipped in for the summer season from St. Louis, Omaha, Chicago, and St. Paul. Others moved from town to town, following the trail herds north and finding work in saloons wherever they could. As Teddy Blue recalled,

Some of those girls in Miles City were famous, like Cowboy Annie and Connie, the Cowboy Queen. Connie had a $250 dress embroidered with all the different brands — they said there wasn't an outfit from the Yellowstone down to the Platte, and over in the Dakotas too, that couldn't find its brand on that dress . . . We all had our favorites after we got acquainted. We'd go into town and marry a girl for a week, take her to breakfast and dinner and supper, to be with her all the time . . . I suppose those things would shock a lot of respectable people. But we wasn't respectable and we didn't pretend to be, which was the only way we was different from some others . . . If I'd have been a woman done what I done, I'd have ended up in a sporting house.

Teddy Blue insisted that most of the cowboys treated the women well: "better than some men treat their wives." He mentioned examples of cowboys who abused prostitutes and how their peers ostracized these men. Though this may have been the case, it is also fair to say that Teddy Blue's examination of the plight of these women went only so far. Many "soiled doves," whose average age was about twenty-three, were "fallen" women, abandoned by boyfriends or families, or widowed and left destitute, with no other means of earning a living. Others, as remains the case today, were products of dysfunctional families or had suffered abuse as children.

Their work entailed many perils. Subject to the whims and potential violence of the men, they faced the constant threat of disease — and not only sexually transmitted diseases such as syphilis, popularly known as "the calamity" in light of the poor prospects for a cure, or gonorrhea, which was equally prevalent. Tuberculosis, potentially a death sentence, was another risk. Others included pregnancy, almost invariably culminating in a dangerous abortion. Rubber condoms had become widely available in the late 1850s but were still relatively expensive, as were early versions of the diaphragm. Despite these options, many prostitutes struggled to get by as best they could by using the rhythm and "withdrawal" methods. By some estimates, 20 percent became pregnant at some point in their career.

Prostitutes had little or no chance for social advancement. Few cowboys would seriously consider marrying one, and likely could not afford to anyway. Escape from prostitution was almost out of the question. Those few who did manage to marry often ended up with saloon owners or men who pimped them. The rest ended their careers in the cribs and saw their lifespan shortened by poverty, despair, and often alcoholism or drug addiction. As Michael Rutter put it in his history of prostitution in the West, "This line of work never had a good retirement plan."

By the time Abilene began its third summer, two to three hundred prostitutes were working there. And each of the cattle towns that sprang up along the westward-expanding railroad had a red-light district of its own. Ellsworth had its Nauchville, Wichita its Delano district, Tascosa its Cuntville. The cowboys weren't solely responsible for all this vice or the easy money and loose morals that so quickly tainted the reputation of the cattle towns. Similar shenanigans had prevailed in the mining camps and towns. Commerce, of course, fueled it all. After all, in these towns the economic machinery of the nascent western cattle industry first kicked into gear. As Walter Prescott Webb explained it in *The Great Plains,* "If Abilene excelled all later cow towns in wickedness, it also excelled them in service — the service of bartering the beef of the South for the money of the North." In each town the better hotels and saloons were crowded with not only cattle buyers, commission men willing to lend against the value of the cattle, various middlemen, and speculators, but also the railroad agents who stood by to negotiate the freight rates for hauling cattle by stock car. Also, visiting ranchers and hunters, railroad workers, tourists, journalists, professional gamblers, and various local people were all eager for a night on the town. And inevitably, the towns grew especially rowdy at night.

Initially the cattle towns lacked courts, police, and jails. The rowdy cowboys, of course, liked it that way. When Abilene's first group of selectmen posted a sign that strictly forbade cowboys from bringing guns into town, the cowboys responded by riddling the sign with bullet holes. When the first jail was erected, they promptly tore it down. When it was eventually rebuilt, the cowboys sprung from it the first prisoner, a black cook from a recently arrived trail drive who had been arrested for drunkenly trying to shoot out the cattle town's new streetlights.

High jinks were to be expected when dealing with large gatherings of men in their late teens and early twenties. Teddy Blue recalled galloping his horse, Billy, into the parlor of the infamous Mag Burns's parlor house in Miles City, on a dare. When the madam slammed the door behind him and threatened to call the sheriff, he somehow managed to exit with the horse through a window and ride off before the sheriff could catch him. Realizing that something needed to be done about the general disorderliness, Abilene's town trustees settled on hiring two Texas marshals, who arrived by train, took a quick look at the situation, and jumped on the next train back to Texas. The town finally found and hired as its first marshal a former New York City police officer named Tom "Bear River" Smith, who had worked as a construction supervisor for the Union Pacific Railroad and had experience as a boxer. On two occasions, to the astonishment of a saloon full of rowdy cowboys, he used his fists to subdue and disarm a threatening gunman. Sadly, just over a year later, he lost his life while trying to arrest a pair of ranchers at their spread a few miles outside Abilene. When Smith tried to charge the men with committing a local murder, guns were drawn, shots fired, and Smith's deputy fled the scene, leaving behind Smith, who was wounded. One of the ranchers grabbed an ax off a stump and all but beheaded the lawman.

The next man to accept the job as Abilene's marshal was none other than James Butler "Wild Bill" Hickok, described as "a tall, graceful, pantherish man, almost as vain about his looks as a woman, a great gambler, and possessed of great courage." Hickok was an able ambidextrous shooter who wore his holstered pistols, .36-caliber Navy Colts, hung from a military belt, with their butts facing forward. This made it easier for him to wear the guns while sitting at gambling tables, where he spent most of his leisure hours. But to draw, he needed to twist his wrists inward to grab the pistol handles, a technique known as a cavalry draw. In total, he would kill eight men in gunfights.

Before taking the job in Abilene, Hickok had worked as a constable in Monticello Township, Kansas, and then as an outfitter and wagon master for the Union army during the Civil War. The Abilene town fathers paid him a handsome salary of $125 a month and an additional fifty cents for every stray dog he shot or impounded. Before long he had headquartered himself at the Alamo Saloon, where he could further supplement his income by gambling. According to legend, he took special care to play cards only at tables where he could keep his back to the wall, a practice later adopted by the character Shane, in the book and movie by that name. By all accounts, Hickok was an effective lawman — at least until he quarreled with Phil Coe, an owner of the rival Bull's Head Saloon. The origins of the quarrel remain disputed: they may have involved a dancehall girl named Jessie Hazel or Hickok's alleged complicity in a gambling kickback scheme. Hickok had also annoyed Coe by insisting that Coe paint over the Bull's Head Saloon's profane sign, which depicted a bull in a state of full sexual arousal. The outcome was a shootout on Texas Street on the night of October 5, 1871.

Phil Coe had been drinking with friends. Then, walking out onto the street, he fired recklessly at a stray dog, attracting the marshal's attention. The two men suddenly found themselves face-to-face, apparently little more than eight feet apart. Everyone else on the street scrambled for cover. It was a mismatch. Both men drew simultaneously, but Coe shot wide. Hickok, both guns firing, shot Coe in the stomach, a "paunch wound" that would prove fatal, as virtually all gutshots did; Coe expired after three days of pain and suffering. No sooner had Coe collapsed than a second figure came running out of an alley. In the dim light, Hickok thought it was another adversary, so he turned and fired again. The man he accidentally killed was Mike Williams, a former bartender who now worked as a security guard for the Novelty Theatre. Williams was a close friend of Hickok. For the remainder of that autumn, Hickok carried a sawed-off shotgun when he patrolled the streets of Abilene.

The worst cattle-town shootout took place in Newton, Kansas, in 1871, an event that came to be known as the General Massacre. Here, in Perry Tuttle's dancehall, a Texan named Hugh Anderson opened fire on the local marshal, Mike McCluskie, slaying him in retribution for the shooting death a week before of a fellow Texan. But McCluskie had an acolyte named Jim Riley, a tubercular young man with a hacking cough who slavishly followed McCluskie around town. On witnessing his mentor's death, Riley bolted the door to the dancehall and began shooting wildly at Anderson and his gang. When the carnage ended, four more men were dead or dying, and another four, including a couple of bystanders, were badly wounded. Riley managed to escape and was never found. The massacre earned Newton the sobriquet Bloody Newton.

Dodge City, the longest-lived of the cattle towns, boasted a distinguished cast of lawmen and gunmen, and both frequented its saloons. Among them were the brothers James, Ed, and Bat Masterson. Also present were Mysterious Dave Mather, who later served as a marshal in a variety of western towns and saw his share of gunfights; Bill Tilghman, who would go on to be city marshal of Perry, Oklahoma, sheriff of Lincoln County, and chief of police in Oklahoma City; and finally, Wyatt Earp, survivor of the shootout at the OK Corral in Tombstone. It hardly seems a coincidence that all of these gunmen were buffalo hunters early in their careers.

Often the victims of the Dodge City gun battles were wrapped in a blanket and buried at Boot Hill, a cemetery on the hill overlooking the town, so named because the dead were usually buried with their boots on.

For ten years Dodge City claimed the title of cowboy capital of the world. It endured longer than other cattle towns in part because the land around it was considered unsuitable for settlers, or so-called nesters. The centerpiece of the town was Dodge House, which opened in 1873, boasting fifty rooms. In room 24, the consumptive gunman and dentist "Doc" Holliday located his dental practice. Downstairs, the hotel featured decent food and imported wines. A tongue-in-cheek sign in the lobby read, SHEETS WILL BE CHANGED . . . ONCE IN SIX MONTHS — OFTENER IF NECESSARY . . . BEDS WITH OR WITHOUT BUGS.

Here in Dodge City, the "Beautiful, Bibulous Babylon of the Frontier," the term "red-light district" was first coined. The name derived from the blood-red glass panels in the doors of the Red Light House brothel. Appropriately, the town boasted one of the most renowned and beautiful prostitutes of the American West, a woman with the stage name Dora Hand, a former showgirl reportedly estranged from her prominent Boston family. According to the historian Paul Wellman, "By all accounts, she was a beautiful creature, with a face and voice which gave men strange nostalgic dreams of better days and finer surroundings." She would die young, however, from a gunshot fired at random into the wood cabin where she was sleeping.

While fabled shootouts, like the one in Newton, did occur in cattle towns, the press often exaggerated the violence. Much of this had to do with a sense of rivalry and economic competitiveness between the towns. The editor of a local newspaper, hoping to drum up business for his town, took every opportunity to question the safety or desirability of neighboring towns a few miles down the tracks. For example, the *Ellsworth Reporter* reprinted a letter to the *Topeka Commonwealth* from "A Cattle Man" which disparaged the grazing ground around Wichita for its alarming number of flies and mosquitoes and touted the area around Ellsworth. The *Wichita Eagle* retaliated by citing Ellsworth's short grass and lack of water. Similarly, Dodge City and Caldwell regularly mocked each other: "Caldwell is way behind the times as a cattle town," wrote one Dodge City editor. "They didn't have any bull fight on the 4th [of July]."

Most of the best gunmen understood that it wasn't speed that mattered in a shootout, but rather accuracy. If you drew smoothly, and calmly took aim before firing, you were far more likely to inflict damage than if you reeled and drew your revolver from the holster as fast as you could. Furthermore, if you stood sideways, as done in European duels, instead of face-to-face with your opponent, you made yourself a far smaller target. Hickok had earned his reputation as gunman in what may have been the first classic walk-and-draw gunfight. In July 1865 in Springfield, Missouri, he fell out with a former friend, Davis Tutt, over losses in a poker game, losses that included Hickok's prized Waltham pocket watch. At six in the evening the two men approached each other from opposite ends of the town's public square. When they were about fifty paces apart and still on the move, they drew and fired. Tutt missed. Hickok's lucky shot struck Tutt in the heart, killing him instantly. Hickok's exploits as a gunman made him the first western hero of the newly popular dime novels.

But it was no accident that Wild Bill Hickok chose to carry a sawed-off shotgun to defend himself after his shootout with Phil Coe in Abilene. A shotgun was a much better weapon than a revolver in a gunfight, and it easily surpassed the six-shooter as an aid to law enforcement. The historian Lewis Atherton cited the case of perhaps the most successful law-enforcement officer of the cattle era, Nathaniel K. Boswell, a former drugstore owner who served as a sheriff in the Territory of Wyoming for a decade beginning in 1869, while doubling as deputy U.S. marshal at Laramie. Boswell later became a long-serving chief detective for the Wyoming Stock Growers Association. His weapon of choice was a Parker or Remington double-barrel shotgun, not a six-shooter. (The pump shotgun was not introduced by Winchester until 1893.) Boswell never engaged in reckless shootouts, choosing instead to conceal himself before apprehending culprits. Consequently, he never failed to make an arrest and never let an arrested man escape. Furthermore, he never received so much as a scratch during his many years of service, earning a deserved reputation for both bravery and resourcefulness. So much for the image of the lawman as a daring gunslinger! This myth, largely invented by the press, later became a staple of the western, both on television and in the movies. Most cattlemen who lived long enough to watch these programs considered them "highly unrealistic in their use of gun play."

In fact, most cowboys did not carry weapons at all. If they did own an expensive six-shooter, it was likely the Colt Single-Action Army, introduced in 1873 and known as "the Peacemaker." Its price — a hundred dollars per pair — would have been a huge amount of money for a cowboy. The cowboy who did own a revolver usually kept it in his bedroll because a loaded six-shooter worn around the waist was both cumbersome and heavy when riding or walking. And most cowboys knew that wearing a six-shooter in a cattle town was an invitation to gunplay; most preferred to avoid altercations. Cowboys tended to settle a dispute with a fistfight. A revolver was best used to kill snakes, put wounded animals out of their misery, or signal for help. As Leon Clare Metz wrote in *The Encyclopedia of Lawmen, Outlaws, and Gunfighters,* "The image of the ordinary Western cowboy as a fast and accurate gun-fighter has practically no validity."

A more useful weapon for hunting game was a single-barrel rifle, ideally one made by Henry or Winchester, whose rifles had replaced the heavy Sharps rifles used by the buffalo hunters. By the 1870s, Winchester was making rapid improvements in its handsome weapons. The Model 1866 "Yellow Boy" and the Model 1873 rifles came in a variety of calibers and were especially popular on the open range. The magazine held fifteen cartridges, all of which could be fired in fifteen seconds. A gunman adept at loading the gun could get off sixty shots in a minute.

Some cowboys simply disliked guns. Surprisingly few ever saw actual gun violence in the towns that they visited. Indeed, cowboys were highly motivated to stay out of trouble. If caught committing a crime, they faced the most rudimentary and arbitrary forms of criminal justice. The local justice of the peace or the police-court judge handled all minor cases, and these men were, as likely as not, also the local saloonkeepers. District judges, who handled federal and state crimes, from robberies and holdups to rapes and murder, served the larger territories. But these judges had to travel vast distances to dispense justice, and they struggled to convene juries; an offender had no guarantee of a timely trial, let alone a fair one.

Mark Twain described one such jury as composed of "two desperadoes, two low beerhouse politicians, three barkeepers, two ranchmen who could not read, and three dull, stupid, human donkeys! It actually came out afterward that one of these latter thought that incest and arson were the same thing. The verdict rendered by this jury was, Not Guilty. What else could one expect?" Twain had a point: few of the district judges were experienced or competent; many could barely read, let alone write. Their jurisdiction might encompass twenty or thirty counties and entail a crushing caseload. Dockets were simply overloaded, and proper courthouses were scarce or nonexistent. Worse, the laws themselves often lacked specificity.

One legendary dispenser of arbitrary justice was Roy Bean, owner of a saloon in the west Texas town of Langtry. Bean's saloon was named the Jersey Lillie in honor of the great English beauty and actress Lillie Langtry, a figure of particular fascination across the West, thanks to her notoriety as a mistress of Queen Victoria's son Bertie, the Prince of Wales and the future Edward VII. Bean, who referred to himself as "the Law west of the Pecos," was famously lax in his interpretation of the statutes. He fined felons whatever money they carried on their person and then kept it. He released horse thieves if they returned the stolen horses. He once fined a dead man forty dollars for carrying a concealed weapon, then used the money to pay for the dead man's coffin, headstone, and grave-digger, while he kept the dead man's pistol to use as his gavel. When a lawyer used the term "habeas corpus" in a trial, Bean threatened to hang him for using profanity in the courtroom. His most out-rageous ruling involved an Irishman accused of killing a Chinese worker. Friends of the Irishman threatened to destroy Bean's saloon if he ruled the death a murder. Bean, after flipping hastily through *The Texas Statutes*, announced, "Gentlemen, I find the law very ex-plicit on murdering your fellow man, but there's nothing in here about killing a Chinaman. Case dismissed." He charged five dollars for officiating at weddings and ten dollars for divorces, and always concluded a wedding ceremony by admonishing the bride and groom with the well-known words that concluded the death sen-tence: "And may God have mercy on your soul!"

Life might be cheap in a cattle town, and the law only erratically enforced, but the towns were hardly deadly if you went about your business and took care to avoid trouble. In fact, no one was killed in Abilene in 1869 or 1870. Ironically, no one died in a cattle-town gun-fight until the arrival of the sheriffs and marshals, who were hired to prevent such murderous acts. Even in Dodge City's worst year, 1878, only five men died in gunfights. The historian Robert Dykstra counted only forty-five homicides in all of the Kansas cattle towns during the cattle era, an annual average of 1.5 homicides. Thirty-nine were from shotguns, and only six from handguns. Of the forty-five victims who suffered bullet wounds, less than a third returned fire. Many, apparently, were unarmed. Few of the dead were cowboys. (By comparison, in New York City some four hundred murders occurred each year in the late 1860s, making the homicide rate roughly equivalent to that of the cattle towns. The same is true of arrests: in 1865 some 68,800 arrests were made in New York City, with its population of some 850,000.)

The eastern readers of dime novels would have been shocked to discover how little gunfighting actually went on in the cattle towns. The published accounts consistently exaggerated the swagger of the cowboys and the number of shootouts. Edward L. Wheeler's Deadwood Dick series contributed heavily to this myth, although the town in his dime novels was always more of a gold-mining settlement than a cattle town — and mining settlements were indeed far more violent. "Deadwood is just as lively and hilarious a place during the interval between sunset and sunrise as during the day," he wrote. "Saloons, dance-houses, and gambling dens keep open all night, and stores do not close until a late hour. At one, two and three o'clock in the morning the streets present as lively an appearance as at any period earlier in the evening. Fighting, shooting, stabbing and hideous swearing are features of the night; singing, drinking, dancing and gambling another." The dime-novel authors understood that little money was to be made by depicting these towns as they actually were during the summer months, which is to say, similar to a college town on a Saturday night, or perhaps a Florida beach resort during spring break. Rowdiness and carousing were the norm, and yes, the prostitution and gambling and drinking were real, but death by gunfire was infrequent.

Disease was a far greater scourge — the threat most likely to cut short a cowboy's life. The problem was exacerbated because cattle towns were located at a great distance from proper medical facilities.

Teddy Blue told the harrowing story of volunteering to keep company with a young ranch hand from his outfit who was dying of tuberculosis. Together they holed up in a hotel room in the cattle town of Miles City. "He kept having hemorrhages, blood all over everything, and I took newspapers and spread them on the bed-clothes and on the floor. He didn't want me to leave him for a min-ute. We were just two boys in a strange land." The ordeal lasted a week; Teddy Blue remembered it as the worst of his life. At the end, the boy asked Teddy Blue to lie down beside him and let him rest his head on his shoulder. "In a few minutes he mumbled something about Ethel, his sister I think, and then he was gone." Exhausted and distraught, Teddy Blue went down to the hotel bar for a drink. There he encountered a captain he knew from Fort Keogh, dressed in his civilian clothes. The captain, on hearing what had happened, took pity on Teddy Blue and, in a gesture of respect for what he had done, removed his hat and overcoat and handed them to Teddy Blue and told him to go for a walk to get some fresh air. "So I went out, but I went to a honky-tonk the first damn thing—trying to get [the death] off my mind."

Tuberculosis, or consumption, was prevalent in the West in part because eastern doctors prescribed moving to the West as a pos-sible cure. But the climate did little good for most of these patients, and the disease may have been more contagious at higher altitudes. Doc Holliday, for example, was a "lunger" sent west, and he died of TB at the age of thirty-six. It wasn't until 1882 that the German microbiologist Robert Koch attributed the cause of the disease to a species of bacillus—but even then a cure in the form of antibiot-ics was still decades away. Penicillin would not be discovered until 1928.

Tuberculosis was not the only threat. Another scary disease, ty-phoid, killed some 30 percent of those who contracted it—it could be spread through unsanitary water or milk. Typhus, or spotted fe-ver, transmitted by bedbugs, lice, and fleas, killed some 20 percent of its sufferers.

But the most deadly killer among the terrifying diseases of the Old West was smallpox. Airborne and easily transmitted by coughs or sneezes, the virus was a quick death sentence for as many as half who contracted it. Those who did survive often bore alarming facial scars from the blisters. When a cowboy named Johnnie Blair died of smallpox in Tombstone in 1882, his contagious body lay rotting because no one dared touch it. Finally a fellow cowboy lassoed him around the ankles and dragged him out of the building to his gravesite.

Many a cattle town became the victim of its own success, attracting, by virtue of its apparent wealth and economic opportunity, settlers and homesteaders looking for somewhere to farm and build a new life. These folk tended to be responsible, hardworking citizens, often from New England or the Middle Atlantic states, who quickly found themselves at odds with the cowboys, gamblers, "soiled doves," and general riffraff. The newly appointed town fathers would float various initiatives meant to control the pandemonium, banning firearms and imposing stiff fines for gambling and prostitution. These efforts often drove the more disreputable establishments out of business, but they sometimes chased away the cattlemen and their profitable trade as well.

Other towns, like Newton, never had a chance to develop a local population of settlers. When the railroad and the cowboys moved farther down the railroad line, the remaining businesses quickly went broke and the towns disappeared almost overnight. When Abilene lost its cattle trade, the iconic Drovers Cottage was disassembled and moved to Ellsworth, where it enjoyed a second act.

Each cattle town, like any new business, was vulnerable to competition. Another town could, and often did, spring up, farther down the tracks and closer to Texas, to compete with it. Consequently, Abilene's heyday lasted only four years. Newton thrived for just one. Dodge City, the largest and the last of these towns, looked for a time as though it might survive much longer. Ultimately, as we shall see, forces other than competition caused its downfall.

But whatever their future, in the 1860s and '70s the cattle towns, for all their famous rowdiness and lawlessness, were already serving a number of useful purposes. They were kick-starting — or perhaps "spurring" is the right word — the financial engine of the great cattle boom, which quickly gathered momentum. Consistent money — even small fortunes, if all went well on the drive — could now be made by trailing cattle. Thanks to the cattle-town stockyards and the dealers, meatpackers, and middlemen who gathered there, ranches began to proliferate on the open range. These establishments became steady buyers and sellers of Texas cattle, and in turn could be easily bought and sold.

Of no less importance, these towns were helping to unite the North and the South in mutually profitable commerce, an important step toward healing the ruptures caused by the Civil War. As McCoy wrote in 1874, "The feeling today existing in the breasts of all men from both sections [of the country] are far different and better than they were six years ago." The towns became quintessentially American melting pots of culture and peoples. Ethnically diverse men — a mix of Americans, Canadians, Mexicans, Germans, Swedes, Frenchmen, Englishmen, Irishmen, and Scots — were elbowing up to the saloon bars together. According to the historian Lewis Atherton, the eight hundred inhabitants of Abilene in 1870 represented a remarkable twenty-seven different states and thirteen foreign countries.

The much-mythologized cowboy was, from the start, different from other characters of American folklore, such as Johnny Appleseed or Paul Bunyan. He was far more of an everyman, a blank slate onto which every young boy could project his own image. The cowboy provided a fascinating, enviable alternative to a cramped, indoor urban lifestyle or the dull, repetitive tasks of a farmer or factory worker. As Lewis Atherton has written, "The fears thus engendered by a rapidly burgeoning industrial and urban age encouraged people to idealize the life of the American cowboy." But Joseph G. McCoy understood that economics, not the romance of the West, lay at the core of business in a cattle town. Yet despite all his effort and ingenuity, McCoy never made the kind of fortune that he had hoped to in Abilene. The Kansas Pacific Railroad, soon known as the Union Pacific, reneged on its promise to pay McCoy five dollars for every stock car of cattle shipped — an agreement that he some-how neglected to get in writing. McCoy soon moved his capital-intensive operation to Ellsworth, where he built another stockyard, but there, as well, progress and the cattle trade moved on too rapidly for him to score big. He would later try his hand at selling refriger-ated railcars and barbed-wire fencing — he even counted cattle for the U.S. Census Bureau. In 1874 he published a memoir, *Historic Sketches of the Cattle Trade* — one of the best and earliest descrip-tions of the emerging industry. He also worked for the Cherokee Nation as a land-tax collector, and in 1890 he ran unsuccessfully as a candidate for U.S. Congress.

Abilene, Kansas, endures to this day, with a population of sixty-eight hundred. Its most celebrated native son is the World War II five-star general and U.S. president Dwight D. Eisenhower. Grow-ing up there, he was fascinated by stories of the lawman Wild Bill Hickok. After high school, Eisenhower worked as a night super-visor at a creamery on the site where Drovers Cottage had once stood.

5

Lighting the Fuse

O n the afternoon of Thursday, April 10, 1877, a calm and clear day, the steamship *Algeria*, an iron-screw steamer of 3,379 tonnage, pulled into New York Harbor carrying forty saloon passengers and eighty steerage passengers. The trip from Liverpool, with a brief stop in Queensland, Ireland, to pick up mail, had taken the normal ten days, slowed only modestly by a steady headwind and a gale that shredded one of the steamer's topsails. Enjoying his first transatlantic passage was James Macdonald, the award-winning agricultural correspondent for the newspaper *The Scotsman*. Macdonald was on assignment to report on the emerging American beef bonanza, which suddenly threatened to upend the British stock-growing industry.

As the *Algeria* entered the mouth of the Hudson and headed toward the steamship piers on Manhattan's West Side, the ship passed another steamer headed in the opposite direction. The passing ship rode unusually low in the water. One of Macdonald's fellow passengers shouted out so that the others could hear, "Guess that's a

Gunion steamer laden with American beef. Why, she's almost out of sight!"

As Macdonald confirmed the following the morning, the Gunion Line's steamer did indeed carry a large cargo of refrigerated dressed meat, or as the British preferred to call it, "dead meat." A thousand pounds of refrigerated American beef were now arriving weekly in both Liverpool and Glasgow. To everyone's amazement, the beef tasted every bit as good as the average fresh beef in Britain, and the quality was predicted to improve quickly as the Americans rushed to better their breeding stock. Prices of British beef were forecast to drop by 15 to 25 percent in the face of this unexpected competition, creating consternation throughout the British stock-growing establishment. If the reports were true, American dead meat would, as Macdonald wrote, "cut away the most important item of profit that can be had from farming in the Old World at present." The results could be "ruinous." Understandably, the subject of dead meat was big news. Recently, the House of Lords had taken up the matter. Macdonald was assigned to make sense of these new developments for *The Scotsman*'s readership in London and Edinburgh. He aimed to dispel the hype and correct or verify the "glowing reports" of a booming U.S. cattle trade. "These notes shall be nothing if not impartial," he promised.

The beef trade between Britain and the United States was not new. Pickled beef had been traded for over fifty years but was essentially a niche business — primarily because so many diners found the consistency of pickled meat unpalatable. But the severe rinderpest epidemic that struck Britain in May 1865 transformed the trade. By September 1867, the disease had wiped out some 500,000 head of cattle, including half the dairy cows of Cheshire County, a center of the dairy trade. It took an act of Parliament to finally halt the epidemic. In February 1866, the Cattle Diseases Prevention Act made the slaughter of infected herds compulsory. The Americans seized the opportunity of the resulting beef shortage and began to ship live cattle to Great Britain in the holds of steamships. Unfortunately, this method of transport proved unreliable. A report in the

Manchester Guardian of October 23, 1894, shows what could, and did, go wrong:

> According to news just received from New York, the Liverpool steamer "Europe" had a most trying experience on her last trip from New York to London. The "Europe" had a miscellaneous cargo when she sailed from New York for London, and 584 head of cattle and 599 sheep. On the 8th of October she encountered a north-west gale in the evening, during which the rudder chain parted and the vessel's head could not be kept on to the sea. In consequence the steamer got into the trough. Sea after sea came over, until the cattle pens on the main and spar decks were flooded. This washed away the bedding of the animals, who could not then keep a footing on the slippery decks. The cattle were flung to the deck time after time. The crew got oil-bags and put them over the side to prevent the sea breaking over the ship, but between one and two o-clock in the morning of the 9th the pens on the port side, forward of the bridge, gave way, and the cattle which had been tied there were thrown out on to the slippery decks and made frantic efforts to get on to their feet. This they did for such a long time that they for the most part became too weak to continue the struggle and died. The ship rolled very much, and occasionally the bullocks were hurled into the sheep pens, and struggled often until they were killed. The decks presented a shocking scene, being strewn over with dead or dying cattle. The crew in the meantime were doing all they could to repair the rudder chain and make the vessel steer. This was accomplished later in the day, and then the work of clearing up the decks was commenced. This was a very arduous task, and it was said that the men had to throw overboard no less than 223 dead cattle and 188 sheep, whilst others had to be killed.

Even when American cattle did survive the Atlantic crossing, the threat remained that they carried their own contagious diseases, such as pleuropneumonia. As a precaution, Parliament passed the Contagious Diseases (Animals) Act in 1869; it didn't preclude the shipping of live American cattle but did require that the animals be slaughtered within ten days of arrival.

It would be simpler to ship beef already slaughtered and dressed. The problem was how to keep the dressed beef cool enough to avoid spoilage. In New York an entrepreneur named John I. Bate set about designing a system to keep the dead meat at a steady thirty-eight degrees Fahrenheit. His prototype involved fans and ice. The airtight hold of a steamship could be loaded with blocks of ice, and hand-cranked fans could blow air over them. Thus cooled, the air could chill the racks of meat hanging nearby.

The first two shipments cooled by this system arrived in London in perfect condition in 1875. Bate promptly sold the system to the New York meat wholesaler Timothy C. Eastman, who expanded the business. Eastman soon persuaded the steamship companies to use steam energy to operate the fans. Then he shrewdly marketed the meat by delivering a free load to Queen Victoria at Buckingham Palace. Over the next four years more refrigeration methods were developed, among them the Cravens process, which moved cool air over the beef by means of a system of pipes. Soon seven companies were shipping refrigerated beef to Britain on all eight of the transatlantic steamship lines. But Eastman still dominated the trade, which remained immensely profitable. It cost Eastman only twenty-six dollars to purchase, slaughter, dress, and ship a steer whose meat he could sell in Liverpool for ninety dollars.

The speed of global transport had recently leapt forward, thanks to the completion of two huge construction projects. First, the driving in of the gold railroad spike on Promontory Summit, Utah, in May 1869 put the finishing touch on the transcontinental railroad. The railroad allowed for smooth, rapid transport of goods back and forth across the American continent. Then, just six months later, on November 17, the Suez Canal opened after ten years of digging. The canal enabled steamships to move goods from India into the

Mediterranean without having to travel around the Cape of Good Hope, providing similar savings in time and expense.

As Macdonald saw it, part of his mission was to make sense of so much rapid change in transport, agriculture, and finance. He began his investigation in the New World by visiting the beef-packing plant and the enormous refrigerated warehouses that Eastman had constructed in Jersey City. "The Yankees are rough butchers and truly the sight in the slaughter-house was not inviting," he wrote to his readership, with droll understatement.

Over the next four months Macdonald would talk to anyone who knew anything about the emerging American cattle trade — ranchers, farmers, beef packers, and regulators. He traveled 11,420 miles by train — averaging 22 miles per hour, at a cost of 3½ cents a mile, visiting most of the states in the West and the Midwest. He concluded that the new competition from American beef producers was not likely to be as injurious as feared. Yes, a new competitor had emerged, "not death-bearing but formidable, and gradually becoming more so." But the British beef establishment still had time to respond. His recommendation was to concede the low end of the beef market to the Americans and instead focus on the high end, using the best feed and animal-husbandry practices to produce the finest possible British beef. "Keep few, keep good, keep well," he urged.

But it was Macdonald's report filed from Texas that caught the attention of his readership. His trip by rail from Washington, D.C., to central Texas had taken thirty-six hours. At one point he shared a crowded passenger car loaded with forty immigrants, mostly young and middle-aged men headed for California, Texas, Colorado, Kansas, and Missouri. They were looking, they told him, for better opportunities than they had found on the farms or in the factories of the East. A basic rule of thumb in the cattle business stipulated that every one hundred Americans required eighty head of cattle to satisfy the market. Only a few of the states were, by this definition, self-sufficient because "the tide of emigration has overcome the bestial ranks." And this was, he reminded his readers, an enormous country. The state of Texas, for example, was five times the size of England.

Once he had begun to explore the state, Macdonald reported, he had discovered that the Texas cattle business was highly profitable. Then Macdonald delivered his humdinger: "A gentleman who had been engaged in the stock trade for many years in the south of Texas assured me that, though he has seen a few reckless Americans go to the wall at cattle-raising, he had never known a Scotchman or an Irishman to fail; 'they all make money.' The same gentleman gave it as his opinion that at the present day, capital invested in cattle-raising in Texas was paying more than 25 per cent per annum."

Twenty-five percent per annum! This kind of market intelligence, offered by such a reputable reporter, had to be taken seriously. And the Scottish business establishment in Edinburgh did just that. As the Scotsman John Clay observed, "The financial officers of that conservative old city had found a new mine to exploit. The drawing rooms buzzed with the stories of this last of bonanzas; staid old gentlemen who scarcely knew the difference betwixt a steer and a heifer discussed it over their port and nuts."

The Scots well understood what we today call "first-mover advantage." Historically, they had punched above their weight — that is to say, above the English — by being more willing to take risks and to do so earlier when an opportunity arose. They had also shown a knack for financial innovation, creating, just a few years before, the first "terminable debentures," or short-term bonds, designed with a duration of only a few years. Before this innovation, all available bonds fell into the category of highly conservative long-term securities, like our thirty-year mortgage. This innovation alone drew £25 million of English capital into Scottish financial institutions by the 1880s, worth £2.2 billion in today's money.

The challenge for the Scots was how best to invest this capital. American mining and railroads and land mortgages had proven profitable, but they were unpredictable and thus speculative. Now along came the western cattle trade — an industry that the Scots knew something about. Scotland and Ireland had long been the grazing grounds for the herds of Great Britain. Scots had trailed the local longhaired Highland cattle to market for hundreds of years.

Rumors of the phenomenal success of the Ulster Scot cattleman John Adair, who had been early into the game, lent further credence to what Macdonald was reporting. Adair owned a forty-thousand-acre estate in Ireland, where he was now building his own castle and ruthlessly evicting tenants to create private hunting grounds. He had moved to New York as a young man and made his first fortune by lending cheap British money to capital-starved American real estate companies, pocketing the spread in what today would be known as a "carry trade." In 1874 he had moved the business to Denver, recognizing the West as the next great economic bonanza. Before long, on a guided buffalo hunt, he met Charles Goodnight, the creator of the Goodnight-Loving Trail, the first man to trail his cattle into New Mexico and the onetime partner of Oliver Loving. Goodnight and Adair went into business. Adair put up the capital, some $50,000, in return for two-thirds of the profits; Goodnight assumed the role of manager. The JA Ranch on the Texas Panhandle eventually owned 100,000 head of cattle. Reportedly Adair had sunk $365,000 into a business now worth $3 million; in addition, he had already paid himself dividends of $70,000. Wasn't this irrefutable proof of first-mover advantage?

Up in Dundee, Scotland, a slightly different financial dynamic was at work.

Dundee, where marmalade had been invented in 1797, had for a time been the center of the Scottish linen trade. But the Crimean War of the 1850s curtailed the amount of flax that could be imported from the Baltic states, and without flax the Scots could not make linen. The Dundee merchants shifted gears to focus on the manufacture of jute. Much like hemp, jute is a coarse vegetable fiber that can be spun into a durable thread, which in turn can be used to produce rope as well as burlap and other rough cloths. The Dundee merchants began to import raw jute from the Indian subcontinent, from the area later known as West Bengal, in Bangladesh. The linen looms in Dundee were retrofitted to produce jute cloths such as burlap, but the coarse fiber was difficult to weave. Whale oil brought in by the Dundee whaling fleet provided a clever solution to the problem: the oil, mixed with water and sprayed on the fibers, made the jute easier to work with.

The jute merchants showed impeccable market timing: the outbreak of the American Civil War in 1860 created a historic boom for jute products. Both sides of the conflict needed burlap sandbags, canvas tents, wagon covers, and ropes — all made from jute in Dundee. By the end of the war, 130 jute mills operated in Dundee, and their owners, mostly local families, had become jute barons. Fat with profits but concerned about overinvesting in the jute business, which already had begun to move offshore, these mill owners began to look for other places to grow their money. The best that they could hope to earn on their savings was around 4 percent annually, the prevailing interest rate in Great Britain. In the United States, as John Adair understood, you could lend out your money and get paid as much as 16 percent in annual interest. But a 25 percent return sounded even better. In Dundee, western cattle companies quickly became the investment vehicle of choice — and the first of these, the Prairie Cattle Company, lived up to everyone's expectations.

Both cities in Scotland had developed a coterie of shrewd, patient investment managers who were good at recognizing opportunities and appraising risk. Many had agreed to pool their capital, and to do that it was essential that they know and trust one another. By no accident, they all belonged to the same social and sporting clubs, attended the same church (Scottish Presbyterian), and supported the same educational causes.

One of their most successful members was Robert Fleming, the son of a Dundee shopkeeper. In 1873 Fleming had founded the first overseas Scottish investment trust, known as the Scottish American Investment Trust, to invest in distressed American railroad bonds. By helping to reorganize these railroads, he had consistently delivered 40 percent annual returns for his general partners. He would go on to even greater acclaim in the City of London as the founder of the merchant bank Robert Fleming & Company. It was Fleming, more than anyone else, who taught his fellow Scotsmen to think like venture capitalists and to invest abroad.

Following Fleming's advice proved much easier than it would have been just a few years earlier. In 1855 Parliament had passed the Limited Liability Act. For the first time, investors were no longer on the hook for the liabilities, or debts, of an enterprise if it should fail — or sink, in the case of a ship. The investor might lose whatever money he had put up to buy his shares, but that was all. This simple act of limiting liability had instant implications for both investment and trade. The vast wealth and savings of the British aristocracy, as well as that of the emerging merchant class, began to pour into the shares of new limited liability companies, which offered better returns with controlled risk. A later act, in 1862, allowed any seven individuals to form a so-called joint-stock company by means of a memorandum of association, with the choice of limited or unlimited liability.

The Scots would take the lead in the creation of joint-stock companies. Many would be assembled specifically to buy up existing western ranches or start western cattle companies from scratch. They would beat the English to the opportunity. The English, however, were not far behind.

The English too had taken note of Macdonald's postings from America. Intrigued by what they read, they formed the Royal Commission on Agriculture and sent two members of Parliament — Clare Read and Albert Pell — on reconnaissance to the American West in the fall of 1879 to explore opportunities for British investment. To escort them, the two commissioners hired a savvy twenty-eight-year-old cattle expert named John Clay, who had immigrated to Ontario with his family only five years before. Ever since, he had been actively engaged in shipping fine breeds of cattle to America to improve his family's stock.

For the next fifty years John Clay would be witness and party to every major event in the western cattle business. He would help the

Scots set up their first cattle companies and become the hands-on manager of a pair of the most storied western ranches. He would serve as president of the Wyoming Stock Growers Association, the most powerful political organization in the cattle kingdom. He would eat and drink with the most famous cattle barons at the prestigious Cheyenne Club, and, as the capstone to his career, would launch his own successful cattle commission company in Chicago, walking the floor of the Exchange Building at the Union Stock Yards, where herds were bought and sold. His memoir, *My Life on the Range,* published privately in 1924 and full of lively portraits of his contemporaries, endures as one of best-written records of the cattle era.

After a couple of months spent touring the West in the company of young John Clay, Read and Pell submitted their report. The conclusion? "The acknowledged profits upon capital invested in cattle are 25 to 33 per cent; even the latter figure is probably below the mark." So it was true: 25 percent returns on capital were the norm! As the historian Edward Everett Dale observed in *Cow Country,* "It was said that the announcement of an important gold discovery could hardly have created greater excitement throughout the Island Kingdom than did this report of Read and Pell."

The news arrived at a time when the British aristocracy and landed gentry faced an urgent need to find new, more profitable investments. This privileged group, comprising fewer than a thousand families, owned most of the property holdings of the British Isles and the accumulated wealth of the vast British Empire. In many cases these estates had been first assembled, or greatly expanded, on the lands of the monasteries dissolved and confiscated by Henry VIII during the English Reformation. Land had been a profitable and predictable investment for over a century, and many of these families had taken on large debts in order to enlarge their holdings or simply because the cost of borrowing was so low. But a new merchant class was now challenging the financial preeminence and political power of these grandees, thanks to fortunes made in banking, trade, and textiles and other manufacturing enterprises.

The most significant challenge arrived with Parliament's repeal of the Corn Laws in February 1849 (in British usage, "corn" may denote different kinds of grain, including wheat).

The idea behind the abolition of the laws, which had kept the price of wheat high, had been to lower the cost of bread for workers by removing the tariffs on imported wheat and thereby enable the manufacturers to lower their workers' wages, thus improving manufacturing profitability—or so the theory went. After the repeal, the price of wheat indeed fell, as expected, but so precipitously that Britain's wheat crops were no longer competitive with the wheat imported from India and Argentina. This situation became aggravated when the currencies of these two foreign countries began a spiral of devaluation. By the middle of the century, the problem was compounded when American wheat grown in the Midwest, along with Ukrainian wheat, began arriving by steamship. What had once been the most productive and profitable farmland in the world —fields of winter wheat and barley in the Cotswolds, for example —was suddenly unprofitable. The now uncompetitive British tenant farmers were unable to pay rent to their landlords, resulting in enormous financial strains on England's great landed estates, many of which were leveraged. Rental incomes at many estates dropped by a half to two-thirds between 1872 and 1890. The value of the land was halved.

The fictional BBC series *Downton Abbey* realistically depicts one such aristocratic family's struggle to stay afloat. An actual example can be seen at Chastleton House, an English National Trust property in Oxfordshire, built by a wealthy wool merchant between 1607 and 1612. The rent rolls, which are on display, show the family's tenant farmers falling deeply in arrears on their payments in the mid-nineteenth century, a trend that led inexorably to the family's financial ruin.

The British grandees and gentry saw only three choices open to them. The families could pursue a strategy of retrenchment, selling off land, downsizing, and curtailing their incomparable standard of living. Or they could arrange for the oldest son, the heir to the estate, to marry into an extremely rich American family and thereby replenish the fortune. Or they could look for fatter returns from their other investments, to offset their estate's agricultural losses and the rapidly diminishing value of their land. In other words: cut costs, merge, or diversify. Ideally, they could pursue all three, which many attempted to do.

Compounding the problem, Britain faced a glut of rich sons who had little or nothing to do to occupy themselves. The system of primogeniture, by which only the eldest son inherited the family's estate, had succeeded in holding together many great estates for generations, but it left the younger sons in a state of career limbo. Many had been educated at top universities in classical subjects and trained to be gentlemen — for whom the idea of work in a trade was anathema. A career in Parliament required an independent income, and, following the three Reform Acts, was no longer so easily arranged. Other careers in the military, the civil service, or medicine required specialized training. Similarly, jobs in the clergy, once an honorable career path for such young men, had fallen out of favor. An article titled "What Shall I Do with My Son?" was published in the literary monthly *The Nineteenth Century* in April 1883 and widely circulated. It spelled out the problem: too many young men of leisure were engaged in the feckless pursuits of fox hunting, shooting, horseracing, gambling, partying, and enjoying London club life. In short, there were too many Bertie Woosters. As one observer remarked, "They had too much time to dress up, too few problems to tackle." Some of these young men were being sent out to various parts of the empire as so-called remittance men. Settled abroad, they lived off family allowances, although this strategy did not come close to solving the problem.

But perhaps operating a cattle ranch in the American West could serve as new and more gainful employment for these hapless young men.

The Field, an upscale magazine launched in 1853 and still found today in the reading room of nearly every club in London, was one of the last British periodicals to weigh in on the beef bonanza. Its lengthy article on the cattle trade reflected this preoccupation with the future of the sons of the upper class. The author, William A. Baillie-Grohman, an Austrian-born big-game hunter writing under the pseudonym "Stalker," addressed himself directly to this audience of young dilettantes: "It is a rough life; indeed, coming straight from his English club existence, it will at first, perhaps, repel him. But the roughness has its good sides, a short experience generally sufficing to weed out the effeminate and unmanly." Baillie-Grohman went on to reassure the aspiring young British cattleman that he would not be alone in the New World — he would find plenty of his fellow countrymen happily employed there: "You see the heir-apparent to an old English earldom mowing, assisted by the two sons of a viscount; you can watch the brother of an earl feeding the thrashing machine . . . There, in not a few instances, you will find the survival of what has gained England her grand repute — sterling manliness and uncompromising honesty."

"Stalker" concluded by cautioning those venturing forth to be sure to make allowances for the idiosyncratic American notions of democracy. "That marked feature of America, social equality, which, while it has often a way of expressing itself in a very extravagant and disagreeable fashion, is undoubtedly a main factor in the unusually rapid growth of the Great West, and must never be forgotten by the English settler."

Macdonald's articles and Read and Pell's parliamentary report were far from alone in pointing out the profits to be made in the western cattle business. In the United States, the individuals who did the most to promote the emerging cattle bonanza were the small-town newspaper editors in the cattle towns themselves. For example, the *Cheyenne Daily Sun* wrote in its issue of January 14, 1879, "It is time for Wyoming to wake up! She is the only exclusively pastoral region in the United States, and her plains and valleys offer better inducements to capital and settlements than any other State or Territory now known to mankind." Nathan Addison Baker, editor of the *Cheyenne Daily Leader,* wrote sixty-three articles extolling the riches to be derived from the cattle trade and Wyoming's superlative environment, a cattleman's paradise.

But the newspapers had plenty of company. Ramon F. Adams, who compiled a bibliography of all the books and pamphlets written on the cattle era, stated, "Every Western state and territory, and often each county in a territory, issued a pamphlet emphasizing the many attractions of the district for the land-seeker, most often stressing its advantages for cattle raising." And every western railroad did the same, commissioning its press agents and others to write laudatory books and brochures on the seemingly boundless opportunities the West had to offer. Dr. Hiram Latham was probably the first, in 1871, in his *Trans-Missouri Stock Raising*, which first appeared as a series of articles in the *Omaha Herald*. By no accident, the land that he touted as the best for cattle grazing was situated along the route of his employer, the Union Pacific Railroad. Unfortunately, Latham's own efforts at cattle ranching led to his bankruptcy only two years later. He left the country to manage a narrow-gauge railroad in Japan.

Other writers joined the promotional bandwagon, keeping up a steady drumbeat of hype. General James Brisbin, hoping to build a career as a broker between western cattlemen and eastern investors, authored *The Beef Bonanza; or, How to Get Rich on the Plains*, published by J. B. Lippincott in 1881. Showing what the historian Gene M. Gressley called "a complete lack of restraint in describing the fortunes to be made in the cattle industry," Brisbin wrote of "immense profits" that could only grow in the future and of weather that was the healthiest on earth. He cited dozens of examples of cattlemen who had made their fortunes. "The West! The Mighty West!" he boomed in his preface, and then went on to insist that no matter where the immigrants settled, they would be better off than they had been in the East. Fabulous profits and unlimited financial success awaited. "I can not imagine why people remain in the overcrowded East," he opined. As for the cattle trade: "the beef business can not be overdone" — there would always be a ready market for the meat.

In 1884 the Scotsman J. S. Tait issued a small brochure titled *The Cattle-Fields of the Far West.* By his estimate, the annual profits for a ranch ranged from 33⅓ percent to 66½ percent. All of these profits were, of course, tax free — at the federal, state, and local levels. (Before 1913, income tax was levied only during wartime. Upon ratification of the Sixteenth Amendment to the Constitution in 1913, Congress gained authority to impose an income tax, eventually resulting in the system of taxation familiar to us today.) Even prestigious publications like *Harper's New Monthly Magazine* got drawn into the excitement. In a long article published in November 1879, A. A. Hayes Jr. breathlessly extolled the virtues of the business: "It will be plain to any one who will examine carefully into the matter that under ordinary and favorable circumstances profits will mount up each year in an increasing ratio, and he can readily make figures for himself."

Again and again writers spelled out the virtues of the business. Articles featured tables depicting how little money was required to venture into the business. These reports showed how a herd of cattle would grow exponentially through breeding. They estimated that a herd would double in size within seven years, with enough steers sold along the way to cover the expense of running the ranch and perhaps even to pay back the initial investment.

What were these initial investments?

Brisbin figured that you needed only $25,000 to get started, a sum that you could borrow. He recommended buying a herd of 1,750 cattle comprising a mix of, say, 300 yearlings and two-year-olds, 600 cows, and 600 steers of varying ages; the remaining 250 calves would likely be thrown in for free. Your expenses in the first year would run you a little over $5,000, including the cost per year of two cowboys and a foreman and their board ($2,160), nine horses ($675) and their grain for a year ($385.50), a wagon with two mules and harness ($525), a ranch house ($200), and farm implements such as a mower, horse rake, and plow ($200 for all three). Then throw in an extra $1,000 for incidental expenses. These costs would grow modestly as the ranch expanded, requiring more staff. The sale of 300 beeves (horned cattle) and old cows at the end of the first year should net $8,200, cover all your expenses, and allow you to reinvest the difference in your stock, a process that would then repeat every year. At the end of six years, even if you had borrowed that initial $25,000 and paid interest that had compounded at, say, 7 percent to $10,061, you could now pay back both the borrowed principal and interest and you would be left with a highly profitable ranch valued at $51,278. In ten years the profits would be much larger; in fact, each year's profits henceforth would exceed the entire initial $25,000 investment. Brisbin insisted that his numbers were conservative; he allowed for the fact that 3 percent of the cattle would be lost annually to straying, predators, or bad weather and that just 84 percent of the cows would bear calves.

In *Harper's New Monthly Magazine*, Hayes, writing for a more affluent audience, calculated that you might need to spend $50,000 for a ranch of 10,000 acres in Colorado, and another $72,000 for a herd of 4,000 good cows costing $18 each. To these you would add and breed eighty Hereford bulls bought at $50 apiece, bringing your total investment to $126,000, for a decent-size spread, noting that you would own your own land. By his estimates, such a ranch would throw off combined profits of $114,651 over the next three years. The land would likely appreciate at 10 percent each year, the rate at which land prices had been rising in Colorado. The business would have assets of $283,800 at the end of that period, already doubling the initial investment, at least on paper. Hayes admitted that these calculations did not allow for the possibility of disease. He recommended insuring against the threat. A decline in cattle prices seemed highly unlikely, given the unmet demand for beef in the United States and Europe, specifically in Great Britain.

All such estimates overlooked the fact that, for various reasons, as few as one in four of the cattle might ever leave the ranch. That meant the actual cost per head might be four times higher than calculations based on the simplified formula that many promoters used, which spread those underestimated costs over the entire herd.

The Colorado Live Stock Record summarized the growing fever of optimism: "Cattle is one of those investments men cannot pay too much for, since, if left alone, they will multiply, replenish and grow out of a bad bargain." Similarly, David W. Sherwood, a Colorado cattleman, wrote in to the upscale weekly sporting journal *Spirit of the Times* to inform its readers that cattle ranching offered the best, most infallible investment proposition of the day: "I do not hesitate to say that this is the grandest opportunity for investment that can be offered. There are no uncertain risks attached to the business to eat up profits, as the losses are almost nothing and the profits many times those afforded by other investments."

The last of the great promotional tracts, Walter von Richthofen's *Cattle Raising on the Plains of North America*, published in 1885, carried the hype right up to the brink of the cattle era's collapse. It might have been the last such tract, but it didn't lack conviction: "There is not the slightest element of uncertainty in cattle-raising," the author insisted. "No live-stock company has ever failed to pay large dividends after it had been established long enough to begin selling cattle. On the contrary, it is a known fact that many persons have made princely fortunes from this business."

One tip-off that all was not as advertised was a small mathematical error made in a few of these dazzling displays of the compounding numbers of cattle — the erroneous assumption that the calves in these expanding herds would all be born female. As William Thayer noted in *Marvels of the New West*, published in 1887, "To this date, however, by no artifice or persuasion, have stockmen been able to make their cows bring them all heifers [females]. We have no doubt they would if they could."

But forecasts arrayed in elaborate detail on spreadsheets have a way of persuading investors, as witnesses to the era of the dot-com bubble can attest. On both sides of the Atlantic, in the financial centers, in the men's clubs, among the rich and those aspiring to be rich, word of the great American beef bonanza was out. Within a year of Read and Pell's 1879 expedition, twenty companies had been formed, investing $12 million. The British soon became the largest of the foreign cattle investors: in total, thirty-six companies would sink $45 million — or $1.1 billion in today's dollars — into cattle ranches across the West. The historian Lewis Atherton put it succinctly: "Eastern and European aristocrats and commoners alike expected to make money, and many of them expected to make it very fast."

6

Cowboy Aristocrats

O ne of the unemployed young Englishmen who read the articles by "Stalker" in *The Field* — while sitting in a leather armchair at his club, White's, in London's St. James's Street — was a six-foot-two lanky Sussex squire named Moreton Frewen. Coincidentally, he had spent the prior summer, the summer of 1877, as a houseguest of the Scots-Irish financier and rancher John Adair and his wife at their JA Ranch on the Texas Panhandle. Here Frewen had hunted buffalo and heard firsthand about the attractive financial aspects of the cattle trade. He relished his experience in the American West and returned to England intrigued with the business possibilities of cattle ranching. He figured that if Adair could make a fortune in cattle, then he could too.

Frewen came from an old, distinguished Sussex family, a stalwart member of England's landed gentry. The family owned a number of estates, including extensive land holdings in County Cork, Ireland, with property there that for three miles abutted lands owned by the Duke of Devonshire. According to Frewen, his father visited those Irish properties only once in his lifetime. One lineal ancestor, Accepted Frewen, had been a tutor to Charles I and vice-chancellor of Oxford, then later held the exalted position of archbishop of York Minster, the great gothic cathedral. As Frewen would tell his fiancée a few years later, "Next to you I love the name I bear ... more than any earthly thing ... After all we are very much the greatest people of Sussex, at least I was always brought up to believe so." Unfortunately, he was the fourth son in his family. His oldest surviving brother, Edward, had already inherited the family estate at Northiam known as Brickwall, a Tudor manor house surrounded by formal gardens and the obligatory thousand-acre deer park.

Frewen had been tutored at home before attending Trinity College, Cambridge, where he had been master of the drag hounds and president of Athenaeum, a now-defunct gentlemen's sporting club. He wrote his college thesis on the best cures for hangovers. Even before graduation, he had earned a reputation as a great horseman by beating Lord Rossmore in a midnight steeplechase ride. He added burnish to his renown when in January 1877 he became the star of a fox hunt in Leicestershire, which was written up in *The Field*. Frewen rode Shaughraun, a horse that he considered the best he ever owned: "He was fashioned like an ideal polo pony, had wonderful shoulders on very short legs, and while full sixteen hands people took him for a pony. He was the kindest and bravest horse ever foaled; a child could ride Shaughraun with a snaffle — or without."

The article in *The Field* was memorable because its author, Captain Pennell-Elmhirst, leapt some remarkable rhetorical hurdles of his own: "Am I wrong in saying that the grand gallop of Saturday last, Jan. 13th, was as fine a run as has been seen in Leicestershire for years? ... Over the brow tear the hunt in a fever of eagerness, in a whirlwind of excitement ... the man whose heart does not burn and whose brain does not whirl with the glorious extasy is too phlegmatic for fox hunting, and ought to have been born a Bourbon." The hunt lasted an epic eighty-five minutes, but in the end, the fox managed to escape. The author concludes, "So grand a fox as ever faced the open lived for another day. Let us hope he found a warm shelter for his stiffened limbs and wearied frame that night."

All told, Moreton Frewen had jumped two sets of railroad tracks, countless fences and hedgerows, and a wide brook to outride a small army of England's finest riders and best horses, in what came to be called "The Ride from Ranksborough Gorse."

Since graduating from Cambridge, Frewen had been enjoying the social calendar of the English upper class: November to April he spent fox hunting, mostly in Leicestershire, followed by a month of salmon fishing in Ireland; May, June, and July he spent enjoying the London "Season," which included Royal Ascot and, perhaps, Wimbledon, which had begun its championship lawn-tennis tournament in 1877; then came the Glorious Goodwood flat races, followed by Cowes Week, the yacht-racing regatta on the Solent, off the southern coast of England. Next up, grouse hunting, perhaps in Scotland, followed by the flat races at Newmarket, at which point the cycle would begin again.

Although pompous at times, Frewen could be very good company, a charming and witty companion who made friends easily and so was always welcome as a weekend houseguest. He styled himself as something of a ladies' man and once boasted to a relative, "Without a single exception the partners of my pleasure have been either charmed by my evident superiority or completely paralyzed by the vigor of my performance." Among the London beauties of his day, whom he pursued as diligently as the Leicestershire foxes, was Lillie Langtry, a young (notionally married) woman from the isle of Jersey, where, according to Frewen, two British aristocrats in a yacht had first spied her on a beach, "her hair rippling to her waist on the Jersey sands." When she first arrived in London in 1874, she had posed for the illustrator Frank Miles, who leaked to his male friends that "a lady lovely beyond words" might be observed in his studio. Langtry possessed handsome looks in the square-featured, classical Greek mode that was the rage in the 1870s. Frewen taught her how to ride horseback, but in his pursuit of her, it seems he was beaten to the post by the handsome Crown Prince Rudolf, heir to the Austro-Hungarian Empire, who would die at the imperial hunting lodge at Mayerling a few years later, in a murder-suicide pact with his seventeen-year-old mistress, Baroness Mary Vetsera, thus destabilizing the empire.

Chasing foxes and London beauties were expensive pursuits, and Frewen had already squandered a portion of his inheritance by gambling at cards. He had borrowed money from an uncle to offset the losses, only to irritate and alienate this uncle by gambling some more. Compounding these financial pressures, Frewen had developed a taste for expensive clothes and horses; furthermore, he had in his employ an Irish manservant named William MacVittie, or simply Mack, whom he needed to pay: "He could clean breeches and boots to perfection, and proved to be a very speedy and safe loader, always watching the gun breeches and not the birds."

In mid-September 1878, Frewen attended the running of the Doncaster Cup, which was an even-money handicap race between two fine horses, Hampton and Pageant. Frewen had just enjoyed a run of good luck at the card tables. "The great game in those days was écarté. It was a game of some skill but much nerve, and my nerves were excellent." He had also backed two winners at the Goodwood Racecourse earlier that summer and so was feeling flush. He decided to bet his entire summer's winnings — a sum in the thousands of pounds — on the outcome of the cup race. If he won, he would accept the position that had been offered to him to serve as Master of the Kilkenny Hounds in Ireland. Should he lose, he would instead become a cattle rancher in the American West and seek his fortune.

The morning of the race, Frewen strolled into the stables, looking for Fred Archer, Hampton's celebrated jockey, nicknamed "the Tin Man," who was a good friend of his valet, Mack. Archer told Frewen that he liked his horse's chances in the race despite the fact that the course was long — two miles and five furlongs — and Hampton would have a slight weight disadvantage. Ignoring the fact that the date was Friday the thirteenth, Frewen bet everything on Hampton to win. As he wrote in his memoirs late in life, "The dear, handsome little horse ran most gamely, but in the last hundred yards, tired under the weight and just failed to get home. So America was under the lee, and I felt quite excited and bucked up. I went to the weighing room, shook Archer's hand, and I looked and indeed felt so happy he never dreamed I was a heavy loser by the pretty race."

Thus it was decided: no more fox hunting. And no more gambling, either: "I never backed a horse after, nor did I ever again tempt the fates with cards." He went home, packed his bags — or, more accurately, had Mack pack them, and the two soon boarded a steamer for America, where Frewen intended to use what remained of his £16,000 inheritance to buy a cattle ranch. He persuaded his brother Richard, who was off hunting big game in Africa, to join him in the new enterprise. He left London with one last gallant gesture: although he was forced to sell his hunters, he came up with a better plan for his most beautiful horse, an elegant five-gaited park hack named Redskin. "Color, action, symmetry, manners — all alike perfection. The average horse is not a fond but a rather foolish creature, but this one had the nuance and the devotion of your favorite dog . . . I have a hundred times regretted that I never had this horse painted." He gave Redskin to Lillie Langtry as a token of his esteem. It was the horse on which he had taught her to ride. Langtry would remember it fondly — in fact, far more fondly than she remembered Moreton Frewen. She would ride it along Rotten Row, the bridle path on the southern edge of Hyde Park, in the company of her latest conquest and lover: Queen Victoria's son Bertie, the Prince of Wales.

As for Moreton Frewen, he was about to embark on one of the most extraordinarily ill-fated careers of his generation, despite herculean efforts to the contrary. It would be a career so plagued with financial failure and disappointment that it would earn him the nickname "Mortal Ruin." His other nickname, given by those more kindly disposed to him, or those who had not lost a fortune investing with him, was "the Splendid Pauper." Invariably, his zeal, abetted by his questionable business judgment, would lead him deeper into financial trouble as he backed one doomed speculative venture after another. As one director of his cattle company would remark years later, "If I was the devil I would hire Moreton Frewen to write prospectuses for hell explaining that however warm it might be in summer it was quite comfortable in winter!"

And yet his career would put him in charge of one of the West's largest cattle ranches — in fact, the first such cattle company to register on the London Stock Exchange. This career enabled him to marry the beautiful daughter of one of America's richest financiers, a girl so refined, she readily admitted that she had never once tied her own shoes. Through this career, Frewen would discover, while traveling in India, an unknown twenty-two-year-old writer named Rudyard Kipling. He would come to be on a first-name basis with *nine* successive American presidents (Hayes through Wilson) and numerous other heads of state around the world, to befriend famous writers (including Oscar Wilde, Stephen Crane, Henry James, and Joseph Conrad), and to know, personally, virtually every significant peer of the realm in Britain. His final claim to fame was offering counsel to a nephew (Winston Churchill, no less) on how to develop a sonorous prose style.

But all that lay ahead for Moreton Frewen. All he knew for certain in the fall of 1878 was that, at twenty-five years of age, he was about to become a cattle rancher.

The English, Irish, and Scottish aristocrats were not alone in catching cattle fever.

One cold afternoon in January 1883, another twenty-five-year-old, this one a tall, exquisitely dressed French nobleman, sauntered into Thompson & Sons on lower Broadway in Manhattan and proceeded to buy a trunk, a tackle box, a pair of riding boots, and two revolver holsters. He walked with ramrod posture. His handsome face was striking for its hooded, haughty eyes and its long mustache, worn waxed to a pinpoint at each side. His name was Antoine Amédée-Marie-Vincent Manca de Vallombrosa; his title, Marquis de Morès et de Montemaggiore or, simply, the Marquis de Morès. He had just quit his job as an arbitrageur on Wall Street and planned to depart the next morning for the American West.

De Morès's title came down through his father's side of the family. In the fourteenth century the Spanish king had awarded the title, along with two Sardinian villages, for military service to the throne, specifically the conquest and sacking of Sardinia. The maternal side of his family boasted an equally impeccable military pedigree: de Morès's mother's father, the duc de Cars, was a general who helped in the French conquest of Algeria. The marquis was born in a lovely ancient house at 9 rue de Grenelle, in the fashionable Faubourg Saint-Germain section of Paris; while he was still a boy, the family moved to a large villa with a crenelated roof at Cannes, on the Riviera, to improve his mother's health. One neighbor in Cannes dismissively recalled de Morès's father, the duc de Vallombrosa, as "a rather stagy-looking Coriscan [*sic*] with a stagy-castellated villa."

An excellent student, de Morès was privately tutored, mastering four foreign languages by age ten. He graduated from the Jesuit College of Poitiers, where his brilliant academic performance would be remembered, then joined Saint-Cyr, France's equivalent of West Point, where he graduated at age twenty-one, in 1879. He then attended the renowned cavalry school at Saumur. Here too he performed remarkably. Wrote his biographer, Donald Dresden, "As a one-man army, he was practically invincible, for he combined the coolness and courage that were essential to the aggressive handling of broadsword, épée, and pistol, and his superb coordination never failed." Assigned to garrison duty in a succession of French provincial towns, he quickly grew bored with peacetime military service. He resigned his commission in 1882, but not before he had fought and won two duels of honor — killing both opponents — though the details of these events remain sketchy.

That spring, in one of the Paris salons, he met and fell in love with an American girl named Medora von Hoffman, whose German-born father, Baron Louis von Hoffman, ran a successful investment firm at 50 Wall Street in New York. A tiny beauty, only five feet tall, she had fine features, pale skin, and long, lustrous dark hair. Medora was an accomplished watercolorist, rode horseback well (sidesaddle), and was an excellent shot. The couple married in Cannes that summer.

Although de Morès's father-in-law went by the title of baron, there is some question as to the title's legitimacy. It appears that Kaiser Wilhelm I awarded a baronetcy to Louis von Hoffman's father, for providing the German royal family with banking services and financial advice, but whether it was intended as a hereditary title is unclear. No such title was found for Louis von Hoffman in the *Almanach de Gotha,* the definitive directory of European royalty and higher nobility. Today he is best remembered for helping to found New York City's all-male Knickerbocker Club, in 1871. He was one of a group of men from the Union Club, the third-oldest club in the country, who quit to found their own club in response to a perceived decline in the Union Club's admission standards.

Von Hoffman offered de Morès, his new son-in-law, a job in his Wall Street–based firm. That fall the newlyweds traveled to the United States and moved into the von Hoffman estate on Staten Island, accompanied by their five servants. From there de Morès began to commute to work on Wall Street.

L. Von Hoffman & Company was one of the earliest and most successful arbitrage firms in the country, trading on the differences between share prices on the stock exchanges in New York and London, a business made possible by the transatlantic telegraph cable, first laid by Cyrus Field in 1858 though not perfected until after the Civil War. De Morès quickly and thoroughly mastered the nuances of arbitrage and other aspects of American finance, so much so that he would later write a respected book on the subject, titled *The Secret of Exchange.* But the endless paperwork and the capturing of tiny spreads that marked the career of an arbitrageur lacked excitement for the former cavalry officer. It wasn't long before de Morès began to feel trapped by office life.

He began to ponder ways to escape and came up with an idea — and a business plan for it. The venture would be nothing if not daring. At first he considered investing purely in cattle and becoming a cattle rancher, but then he was struck by a far grander notion. He would build his own fiefdom in the Badlands, in the northern part of the Territory of Dakota. He had heard of this area from a cousin who, after hunting there, spoke of its abundant game and its proximity to excellent grasslands, which could be used for cattle grazing. The centerpiece of his new town would be a huge abattoir, or meatpacking plant, that would cut out the Chicago middlemen and allow the shipment of dressed western beef directly, and inexpensively, to markets in Manhattan — in fact, to de Morès's own retail stores. He soon purchased an option on a parcel of land, sight unseen, and a collection of buildings known as the Little Missouri Land and Cattle Company, located on the Little Missouri River. Furthermore, he persuaded his father-in-law to back him financially and to play an active role in the enterprise. Medora, the wife of the marquis, somewhat reluctantly embraced the idea. She had married a Frenchman in hopes that they would live in Europe, but moving abroad was now out of the question: she had recently discovered that she was pregnant. She agreed to join her husband in the West, but only after the baby was born and suitable accommodations had been built for her in the Badlands.

The following morning, the marquis, fully outfitted and accompanied by William van Driesche, his personal secretary, or *homme de confiance*, set off by train for the Dakota Territory. As de Morès boasted to a friend, "I shall become the richest financier in the world."

The United States too had its share of young cowboy aristocrats who saw opportunity in the cattle trade and pursued it. One of those was Theodore Roosevelt, a state assemblyman from New York City, also twenty-five years old.

For Roosevelt, a rising leader in the Republican Party, the 1884 Republican National Convention in Chicago had been a colossal disappointment. Despite his efforts, and those of his good friend Senator Henry Cabot Lodge of Massachusetts, to prevent the nomination of former Maine senator James G. Blaine, whom Roosevelt and Lodge considered utterly corrupted by railroad money, Blaine had won the presidential nomination. Disgusted by the direction the Republican Party had taken and unsure what to do next with his political career, Roosevelt decided to take a break from politics and move to the Dakota Badlands, where he had recently purchased a small cattle operation. He hoped to pursue a dual career as writer and ranchman.

Roosevelt was the grandson of an immensely wealthy New York merchant, Cornelius Van Shaack Roosevelt, of Dutch New Amsterdam stock, one of the city's five richest men in his day. Cornelius Roosevelt had shrewdly diversified the family fortune, made through a monopoly on plate glass, into banking and real estate. In addition to owning property throughout lower Manhattan, Cornelius owned two shipping piers along the Hudson and cofounded National Chemical (later just Chemical) Bank. His son, TR's father, Theodore Sr., or "Thee," was an attractive and imposing man, known to be highly moral and philanthropically minded, "a big, powerful man, with a leonine face, and his heart filled with gentleness for those who needed help or protection," according to his son. Thee gave away much of the family fortune when he helped found the American Museum of Natural History, the Metropolitan Museum of Art, and the New York Orthopedic Hospital.

Theodore Roosevelt grew up, by his own description, "a sickly and timid child," the second of four children and the older of two brothers. He suffered from asthma, digestive trouble, migraines, and poor eyesight. Over the course of his childhood, with his father's boundless encouragement and support, he worked to build up his strength and endurance. It helped that the family's new mansion at 6 West 57th Street featured a gymnasium in the basement. Roosevelt's great passion as a boy was natural history, and ornithology in particular. When, as a twelfth-birthday present, his father gave him a 12-gauge double-barrel Lefaucheux Brevete shotgun made in Paris, he began to shoot birds, which—after taking lessons in taxidermy—he then skinned, stuffed, labeled, and added to his own natural history collection. A voracious reader with a terrific memory, he was tutored at home and entered Harvard with a strong background in history, geography, and biology, though weak in the classics and mathematics. After much practice, he became a skilled boxer. A devotee of Charles Darwin, he hoped one day to pursue a career as a scientist or a naturalist.

Although he had been coddled as a child, the young Roosevelt was not spoiled. He arrived at Harvard fully appreciative of what his family had done for him. As he wrote to his father, "I do not think there is a fellow in College who has a family that love him as much as you all do me, and I am *sure* that there is no one who has a Father who is also his best and most intimate friend, as you are mine."

Interest in the natural world was something of a family preoccupation. Roosevelt's father loved the outdoors and personally oversaw the creation of the American Museum of Natural History, approving its charter in the front parlor of the family's brownstone. Roosevelt's uncle Robert kept a menagerie of animals in his home, worked all his adult life to protect New York and New England fisheries from pollution, and wrote a popular book on game fish that was the *Silent Spring* of its day.

When Roosevelt was nineteen and still an undergraduate at Harvard, his father, whom he adored, died suddenly at age forty-six of colon cancer. Roosevelt inherited $125,000, worth about $3 million in today's dollars, which made him one of the richest members of his college class. By 1884 he had already tapped into the principal — twice to invest in a friend's Wyoming cattle operation, and a third time to buy his own cattle ranch, the Maltese Cross, a few miles south of the property acquired by the Marquis de Morès in the Dakota Territory.

Just a few months before the Republican National Convention, Roosevelt had suffered a pair of devastating personal losses. On one horrific day, Valentine's Day of 1884, in the family's New York mansion, he witnessed the deaths of the two women who meant the most to him: his mother, Mittie, and his wife, Alice. At the end he was at each one's bedside. His mother, forty-eight, died first, of typhoid fever. Eleven hours later Alice, only twenty-two, died from Bright's disease, which would now be described as nephritis, a chronic inflammation of the kidney. Just two days earlier Alice had given birth to the couple's first child, a daughter, who would also be named Alice.

The death of Roosevelt's wife occurred exactly, to the day, four years after their engagement announcement, and by all accounts the marriage had been a love match. That night Roosevelt wrote a large "X" in his diary and then added below it, "The light has gone out of my life." He appeared so grief-stricken that his family worried for his sanity. For a time he refused to discuss his loss with anyone. Family members heard him pace incessantly in his room late at night. He later told his ranch manager, Arthur William Merrifield, that the grief was "beyond any healing." For the rest of his life he resolutely avoided mentioning Alice by name, and he could not bring himself to mention her in his autobiography.

A few weeks later, he left the newborn baby in the care of his older sister, Anna, so that he could return to his job in Albany. Once there, to battle his depression, he threw himself into his work as a New York State assemblyman. Despite his youth, he won the position of leader of the New York delegation to the Republican National Convention. But, as he told reporters at the close of that event, he had already made plans to take a break from politics. His recurring asthma may have played a role in this decision — indeed, Roosevelt said as much to friends. As Roger Di Silvestro postulated in his book *Theodore Roosevelt in the Badlands,* the fact that soft coal was starting to be used as fuel in New York City in the 1880s may well have aggravated his medical condition. He had a heavy dose of heartbreak to deal with as well.

In taking up ranching, Roosevelt was following in the footsteps of a much-admired college friend, Hubert Englebert Teschemacher. Two years older than Roosevelt, Teschemacher had initiated Roosevelt into the Porcellian Club at Harvard. Founded in 1791, the P.C. was the oldest, the most selective, and the most secretive of Harvard's social, or "final," clubs. Its members claimed that it was the only organization of its kind that had never changed, because it had been born perfect. Roosevelt's great friend and political ally Henry Cabot Lodge was a member, and so was his closest college friend, Richard Middlecott Saltonstall. Saltonstall first introduced Roosevelt to his comely blond cousin and next-door neighbor in Chestnut Hill, Alice Lee, Roosevelt's now deceased wife.

The P.C. members, or "Brothers," bonded over black-tie dinners and social outings, developing close personal ties that often led to partnerships and joint business ventures after graduation. Embracing and fostering high ideals, the club also inspired many of its members, possibly including Roosevelt, to pursue careers in public service. Somewhere along the way, Roosevelt's ambition to become a scientist changed, as politics beckoned.

It seems that the Brothers had great confidence in Teschemacher. The Scotsman John Clay, who befriended "Teschie" in Cheyenne, Wyoming, described him as passionate about politics and philosophy, "a man of supremely high character and influence" and "an intimate of presidents and princes." Teschie was handsome, debonair, and wealthy — one of those instantly anointed "most likely to succeed." His father had made a fortune in San Francisco real estate and served a four-year term as the city's tenth mayor before retiring to France. Teschemacher's introduction to the West had occurred upon completion of his education at Harvard, during a yearlong trip around the world, a graduation gift from his father. Shortly after his return, while staying at his parents' villa in Paris, he came across an article in *Galignani's Messenger,* the only English-language daily newspaper in Paris at the time. The article described the profits that could be made in cattle ranching on the Great Plains. Recalling the sublime beauty of the western landscape, Teschie knew immediately that he had found the business that suited him.

By the early 1880s some twenty prominent Bostonians and New Yorkers — many of them members of the Porcellian Club and classmates of Teschemacher — had invested the substantial sum of $491,000 (worth $11.7 million today) in Teschemacher's Wyoming ranch. Roosevelt himself had invested $5,000 initially and then added another $10,000 a year later, when Teschemacher expanded and added more stellar credentials to the highly promising enterprise by recruiting a new general partner, fellow Harvard graduate Frederick DeBillier, whose father ran a Wall Street stock brokerage. At this point the ranch's name was changed to Teschemacher & DeBillier Cattle Company. The following year, another friend and classmate of Roosevelt and a fellow Porcellian Club member joined Teschemacher and DeBillier in Cheyenne. Richard Trimble, accompanied by his black standard poodle, Mifouche, would spend the next five years as a co-manager of the ranch. But the influx of Harvard men, money, and influence did not end there. A fourth member of the Porcellian Club, a former music major from Philadelphia named Owen Wister, whom Roosevelt and Trimble had initiated into the club, found his way to Cheyenne a few years after Trimble did. He went at Roosevelt's urging. Drawing on his experiences there, Wister would write the best-selling 1902 cowboy novel *The Virginian: A Horseman of the Plains.* The book not only made Wister famous but also established the western as a major fictional genre, thanks to its iconic cowboy hero. Hollywood would adapt the book into a feature film on five separate occasions.

So by June 1884, Roosevelt was already a knowledgeable investor in the cattle trade, with a handful of good friends in the business. He received periodic updates about how his investment in the cattle business was faring, and no doubt these glowing reports helped spark his own interest in getting more deeply involved. He was not the type to be satisfied with a mere passive investment. Like many young men his age, he was eager to try his hand at the vigorous western lifestyle and the day-to-day activities of cattle ranching. As he had written to his wife, Alice, on his first expedition to the Dakota Territory, "The more I have looked into the matter — weighing and balancing everything, pro and con, as carefully as I knew how — the more convinced I became that there was a great chance to make a great deal of money, very safely, in the cattle business."

Before he left New York, Roosevelt tapped into his inheritance once again to outfit himself for his western adventure. He bought a sterling-silver bowie knife, custom-made by Tiffany & Company; its handle, blade, and scabbard were engraved with hunting scenes and floral scrolls. Today it is considered the finest bowie knife made in the nineteenth century. Similarly, he spared no expense on his pistols. He bought a pair of Colt six-shooters — Frontier Single Actions in .44-40 caliber, with 7½-inch barrels — and sent them to Schuyler, Hartley & Graham in New York in May 1883 without the grips, to have the firm's celebrated master engraver, Louis Daniel Nimschke, embellish the pistols. The new grips were made of ivory. One featured a large "TR" monogram on one side and a bison head on the other — to commemorate the slaying of his first big-game animal. The companion revolver, which he would use as a spare, simply featured his full name engraved in cursive along the length of its grip. The barrels and other major metal parts of both guns were intricately adorned with chased-work scrolls and elaborate geometric motifs. The accompanying leather holsters were finely tooled and lined with chamois. These three beautiful weapons, along with the bespoke fringed-buckskin suit that he ordered from a seamstress in Amidon, North Dakota, would instantly mark Roosevelt as a neophyte cattleman, or "tenderfoot."

He planned to work on the ranch in the mornings and then read and write in the afternoons and evenings. He hoped to get fit too. At five foot eight, slim, bespectacled, and anemic-looking, he weighed only 135 pounds when he arrived in the Dakota Territory. But that would change: over the next few years Roosevelt would add thirty pounds of muscle to his frame. He would participate in the local cattle roundups in the spring and fall and take regular weeklong hunting trips into the Rocky Mountains. Although he would spend a total of only twelve months in the Badlands over the next four years, those periods, usually two to four months at a time, would prove to be the most formative of his young life.

Soon after arriving in Medora, Roosevelt bought his second

ranch, the Elkhorn, and built up his herd to thirty-five hundred head of cattle. In total, he would invest some $85,000 in the cattle business — two-thirds of the inheritance his father left him.

From the moment he arrived in the Badlands, ranch duties and hunting trips apparently kept Roosevelt happily occupied. As it turned out, he did most of his writing back in New York, especially during the winter months, working largely from memory. But little of what he saw in the Badlands was lost on him. Keenly attentive to detail, with near-photographic recall, he seemed to remember everything and everyone. This was not his first foray into professional writing. He had published a pamphlet on bird watching in the Adirondacks before attending college, and at age twenty-three had written a distinguished work of naval history, *The Naval War of 1812*, to considerable acclaim. In all, he would publish some forty books over the course of his life, a level of literary productivity that few politicians, other than Winston Churchill, would ever match — and Churchill lived much longer.

Still a committed amateur naturalist, Roosevelt arrived in the Badlands aware that the wildlife around him was rapidly disappearing. The year before, on his first trip to the Dakota Territory, it had taken him two weeks of long, exhausting trail rides to find and kill his first bison. Very few of the animals were left. The wapiti elk too, once so prevalent, were disappearing. More than once in the months ahead, he came to believe that he had shot the last elk in the Badlands.

Despite his poor eyesight, Roosevelt was an avid sportsman hunter. He subscribed to the prevailing gentleman's code of hunting conduct, largely English in derivation. It stipulated that you didn't shoot certain harmless animals, such as songbirds, for sport, and for the most part, what you shot you should eat. Exempt from this gentlemanly code were the predators — the bear, the cougar, and the wolf. In pursuit of these the hunter need show no mercy.

An outpouring of writings would emerge from Roosevelt's western experiences. His many articles for *The Century Magazine* and *Outing* were later compiled into three books, *Hunting Trips of a*

Ranchman (1885), *Ranch Life and the Hunting Trail* (1888), and *The Wilderness Hunter* (1893). Every page reflects Roosevelt's joy at his encounters with the natural world. Here, for example, he evokes the sounds of the American West:

> Yet in certain moods a man cares less for even the loveliest bird songs than for the wilder, harsher, stranger sounds of the wilderness; the guttural booming and clucking of the prairie fowl and the great sage fowl in spring; the honking of gangs of wild geese, as they fly in rapid wedges; the bark of an eagle, wheeling in the shadow of storm-scarred cliffs; or the far-off clanging of many sandhill cranes, soaring high overhead in circles which cross and recross at an incredible altitude. Wilder yet, and stranger, are the cries of the great four-footed beasts; the rhythmic pealing of a bull-elk's challenge; and that most sinister and mournful sound, ever fraught with foreboding of murder and rapine, the long-drawn baying of the gray wolf.

These works did more than advance Roosevelt's reputation as an author. They started him down a path of ideas and personal encounters that would give birth to the American conservation movement. The Elkhorn Ranch in the Badlands is today appropriately known as the Walden Pond of the American West and the cradle of the conservation movement. As Roosevelt's biographer Edmund Morris has written, "To my mind there is no memorial of marble or bonze anywhere in the country that evokes the conscience of Theodore Roosevelt as powerfully as the Elkhorn bottom and its surrounding hills. It is a crucible of calm, a refuge from the roar of worldly getting and spending. The very disappearance of the ranch TR built here — except for a few foundation stones — emphasizes the transitoriness of human achievement, and the eternal recuperative powers of nature."

Moreover, for Roosevelt, who had led the life of a somewhat coddled rich kid, the Badlands would provide his first real acquaintance with common humanity — the cowboys, the homesteaders, and the immigrant townspeople of the American West. He would emerge from these encounters — and those with the wilderness itself — with his boundless self-confidence intact, perhaps even enhanced. His psychic wounds would be largely healed and his energy and spirits restored. His years as a cattleman, he would later insist, were "the making of him" as both a man and a politician.

Frewen, de Morès, and Roosevelt had more than their youth, their affluence, and their crusading personalities in common. While representative of their respective countries and the role those countries played in the world of that day, each is relevant to the broader story of the cattle kingdom for a specific reason. To start with, they each faced a different challenge: the challenge of recovering from a devastating personal trauma, in Roosevelt's case; the challenge of dealing with the rapid institutionalization and corporatization of the cattle trade, in Moreton Frewen's case; and the challenge of facing off against the rising monopolistic powers of the beef trust, in the case of the Marquis de Morès. Combined, their experiences highlighted the lessons still to be learned from the open-range cattle era.

But ambitious twenty-five-year-olds weren't the only ones seduced into the cattle trade. Once the word got out, celebrated figures began to invest in western ranches. They included the railroad and copper magnate William Rockefeller, brother and cofounder with John D. Rockefeller of the Standard Oil Company; William K. Vanderbilt, a son of the Commodore — his daughter Consuelo would marry the ninth Duke of Marlborough and rescue the Spencer-Churchill family from penury; Marshall Field, who founded the eponymous Chicago department store; Oliver Ames, president of the Union Pacific Railroad and heir to a successful New England shovel company; C. W. Post, the breakfast-cereal magnate; Joseph Seligman, the German-born New York investment banker who funded many of the American railroads; and William C. Whitney, a wealthy New York businessman who made his family's name synonymous with American thoroughbred racing. When the Colorado cattleman David W. Sherwood published a list of the investors in his cattle business, it included the governor of Connecticut, P. T. Barnum, the police commissioner of New York, five presidents of major banks, the president of a railroad, and a professor at Yale University.

In London, investors in the cattle business read like a *Who's Who*, or rather a *Debrett's Peerage* or a *Burke's Peerage*, of the British aristocracy. Their ranks, in order of precedence, comprised various dukes, marquesses, earls, viscounts, and barons. Among them: the Duke of Sutherland (the 1.4 million acres he owned in England and Scotland made him by far the landowner with the largest holdings in Great Britain in his day), the Duke of Argyll, the Duke of Manchester, the Marquess of Tweeddale, several earls (of Aberdeen, Airlie, Alyesford, Dunmore, Dunraven, Ilchester, Lichfield, Mar and Kellie, Rosslyn, Strathmore, and Wharncliffe), and Baron Dunsany, to name only those who invested most heavily.

Some of these American and British men bought their own ranches or acquired a ranch for a son; others invested passively through partnerships or joint-stock companies. But just as herding and trail-driving cattle was a young man's work, it was, for the most part, the sons and heirs of the rich who wound up owning or managing most of the new cattle ranches. It wasn't long before these young men became ubiquitous across the open ranges of the American West. As the cowboy Teddy Blue Abbott observed, "Rich men's sons from the East were nothing new as far I was concerned. The range in the eighties was as full of them as a dog's hair of fleas, and some of them were good fellows and some were damn fools."

Few of these young men fully understood the challenges that they were about to undertake. Few had practical business experience running a ranch or, for that matter, knew anything substantive about the cattle trade or the ecology of the grasslands. The life and work of a ranchman appealed to them because it sounded so easy, so profitable, and so much like good fun. But raising cattle on the open range would not be easy, the profits would prove elusive, and the fun would not last.

This was not the first time that the promise of profit and the lure of adventure had inspired a wave of immigration to the American West. In the late 1840s John Sutter's discovery of gold fired the imagination of tens of thousands of mostly young men, who headed to the gold fields of California in search of a quick score. Now, forty years later, the cattle boom enticed all comers with a new promise of easy money. First, barriers to entry looked low. Second, raising cattle was physically less demanding than prospecting for gold, and seemed to involve less speculation. Third, many people felt they had the qualifications — they had spent time on a farm, knew something about raising livestock, and felt certain that they could learn the rest on the job. Fourth, there was the romance. What a lifestyle! Be your own boss, enjoy riding and hunting, and roam free over an unspoiled landscape.

For a time cowboys, ranchers, bankers, cattle-town builders, railroad men, and speculators (mostly American and Canadian, but also British, French, and German) united in this common pursuit. Few understood the long-term ramifications of the enterprise — the industrialization of agriculture. This development would prove to be beyond the control of any of them, no matter how rich or well connected.

Virtually all the participants of the nascent boom overlooked another important factor. They were rushing into an old-fashioned commodity boom, with all its excitement and fever and blind disregard for risk. What made entry into the business so easy was precisely what would account for its rapid overexpansion: too many participants, too many unseasoned managers making rookie mistakes, and too much money chasing rapidly diminishing returns. The seeds of the era's destruction were, in fact, planted at its outset.

PART TWO

Cowboys and Cattle Kings

7

From Stockyard to Steakhouse

A herd of Texas Longhorn cattle, deposited by trail drivers in the stockyard of a cattle town, faced a grim future, which is to say, little or no future at all. Once weighed and counted and sorted, they were marched through a maze of timber corrals, alleys, and chutes, and then up a wooden ramp onto a crowded railroad stock car, which was soon packed almost solid with lowing cattle.

The earliest stock cars were old open-roofed carriers first deployed in the 1830s or reconfigured railroad boxcars with iron-barred doors that simply enclosed the cattle and left them largely exposed to the elements. To keep the cattle alive on a journey of several days, the cattle cars pulled onto sidings en route and the animals were let out to drink and feed. Every so often, these early stock cars were left parked on the sidings, mislaid or forgotten. The cattle perished. But eventually the railroad companies made improvements; they customized the boxcars, allowing cattle to feed and drink without disembarking. They also built their own stockyards, resulting in fewer casualties, less trauma to the cattle, and, of most concern to the owner, less loss of weight, since weight meant money. Once unloaded into pens and corrals in Chicago, St. Louis, or Kansas City, the cattle were either sent directly to slaughter or purchased by local feeders, who postponed the slaughter in order to fatten them up more, on surplus local corn. A year or two later these bulked-up animals were sold to the meatpackers or put back on the rails for the trip to, say, New York City, where they would be slaughtered for the metropolitan market or boarded onto steamships for sale and slaughter abroad.

Since the early years of the republic, the business of slaughtering animals and packing meat — pork as well as beef — had been pushed westward to spare the major metropolitan areas the unpleasant odors of the packing plants and the difficulty of disposing of offal and other unused portions of the carcass. Pork had long been the dominant meat of the country because it could be preserved in palatable forms — smoked or otherwise cured as bacon or ham and successfully salted and packed for shipment. Beef, which could be canned but was never really popular in this form, was preferred when fresh and so remained more of a seasonal offering.

By the early nineteenth century, Cincinnati was well established as the center of the pork-slaughtering trade. The landscape surrounding the city was well suited to farming hogs, and a confluence of rivers, including the Ohio, allowed for transport of the packed pork, first by flatboat and later by paddle steamer, to southern markets. The Ohio River also served as a giant disposal drain for the enormous amounts of hog offal.

Slaughterhouses for cattle were, by contrast, scattered around the Midwest. They operated only in the cooler winter months, preparing, or "dressing," beef for the eastern markets.

But the Civil War brought change. With the blockading of the north-south Mississippi River trade, the railroads stepped in to transport various commodities, including pork and beef. Chicago, with its confluence of railroads rather than rivers, became a logical site for the buying and selling of meat and, eventually, the slaughtering of pigs and cattle. From Chicago, the meat would be shipped east, then south, to feed the Union army.

To bring order to the chaos of cattle yards scattered around the city, the nine largest railroads banded together to form a single giant stockyard, called the Union Stock Yards, or just the Yards. According to William Cronon, in *Nature's Metropolis,* "Tourists might hesitate to subject themselves to the stench and gore of the place, but all knew that something special, something never before seen in the history of the world, was taking place on the south side of the city."

Completed on Christmas Day, 1865, just in time for the end of the Civil War and the arrival of the first Texas cattle herds, the new stockyard occupied 320 acres of former marshland south of Chicago. Over time the site would grow to 375 acres and include 2,300 livestock pens, which at any given time could accommodate massive numbers of animals: 21,000 head of cattle, 75,000 hogs, and 22,000 sheep. The water trough was three miles long; the feeding trough, five miles long. A city of saloons, hotels, restaurants, and offices quickly grew up around the Yards. By the turn of the twentieth century, the site would process 82 percent of the meat consumed in the country, slaughtering some nine million animals annually.

After investing in a joint stockyard, the railroads now had an interest in fairly dividing up and sharing the cargo of live cattle that was headed to the wholesalers in the East. As part of a pooling agreement, they adopted what they called the "evener system." Cattlemen or wholesale butchers — whoever owned the animals — were offered a fifteen-dollar rebate on every carload of cattle that they shipped through the Union Stock Yards. This rebate gave an instant price advantage to anyone who transported cattle through Chicago. The cattlemen could pocket the additional profit or, better yet, use the rebate to offer their beef at lower prices to the wholesale market and hopefully add to their market share. If McCoy's deal with the Hannibal & St. Joseph Railroad was the first blow against St. Louis, the evener system was the knockout punch. Most of the open-range cattle came to be shipped through Chicago.

But at first only a small portion of the actual slaughtering took place around the Union Stock Yards. Almost all of the cattle were passed on, alive, to wholesale butchers in the East, who could ensure the meat's freshness by slaughtering the animals close to retail outlets, where the meat was actually sold. But it wasn't long before a handful of savvy butchers and grocers began to devise ways to systematize and automate the process of delivering meat to the American public. They would prove to be among the century's greatest business innovators and most rapacious capitalists.

Philip Danforth Armour built the first large-scale meatpacking plant in Chicago with his brother, Herman, in 1867. His company would remain a player in the industry for nearly a century; his meatpacking plant was for a time the largest factory in the world. Two others, George Hammond and Gustavus Franklin Swift, who both had moved west to get closer to the source of the cattle, would make their names by tackling the problem of refrigeration. They realized that if you could slaughter the cattle at the point of purchase in Chicago or, in Hammond's case, northwest Indiana, you should be able to sharply reduce the costs of shipping by rail because you wouldn't be shipping the useless bits — the bone, entrails, horns, hooves, and skin that accounted for some 60 percent of the animal's weight. You also wouldn't be paying to feed and water the animals along the way and losing money as each steer lost valuable weight.

But challenges appeared immediately. If you shipped dressed beef rather than live cattle, you encountered the problem that vexed the steamship exporters — you needed some way to keep the meat fresh. The answer was refrigerated railcars. But the only ones in existence were those few devised to transport fresh fruit. Hammond and Swift began to explore ways of retrofitting railcars in order to pack them with ice. Hammond was the first. His partner, Marcus Towle, had already had some success in shipping dressed meat to Boston, packed with chipped ice taken from the Great Lakes. Hammond's cars quickly proved the principle — refrigeration worked just as well for beef as it did for produce. Gustavus Swift then took this simple idea and ran with it. He hired an engineer named Andrew Chase to build an insulated boxcar, which carried the ice across the roof of the car with the meat packed tightly below, keeping the center of gravity low enough to prevent the cars from derailing on curves.

Swift had arrived in Chicago with thirty thousand dollars in capital from the sale of his share of a successful wholesale butcher business. But more important, he brought with him his Yankee thriftiness as well as a work ethic and general fastidiousness that would prove invaluable. One of twelve children, he had been slaughtering and selling beef since he dropped out of school in the eighth grade, on Cape Cod. Lacking the capital to build the refrigerated railcars himself, he persuaded a manufacturer — the Michigan Car Company of Detroit, owned by the McMillen family — to take a 15 percent down payment on each car, and risk the rest of the payment on the success of the enterprise. The gamble paid off for both parties. Within two years Swift had over a hundred refrigerated cars running between the Union Stock Yards and the rail terminals in the East.

Both Hammond and Swift understood that refrigeration could bring additional benefits — huge ones. If you could ship refrigerated beef around the country and store it in refrigerated warehouses close to your end market, say, Boston or New York, you could deliver beef year-round instead of just seasonally, a development with enormous ramifications for the slaughtering business. You could transform the meatpacking companies into much more efficient enterprises, better utilizing their capital, machinery, and labor, with more predictable results. Furthermore, the companies could benefit from economies of scale.

But even as refrigerated railcars became a reality, a new obstacle arose. The railroads refused to embrace the new technology, and for good reason: shipping live cattle was simply more profitable for them. In addition, the railroads had just invested in stockyards around the country, Chicago's Union Stock Yards being the largest. Furthermore, stock cars heading east with live cattle could be quickly retrofitted to carry other kinds of freight on the return trip, but a refrigerated car invariably returned to Chicago empty. Not surprisingly, the railroad owners dragged their feet and continued to favor their live-cattle customers. They set the rates for dressed beef at five times that of live cattle, roughly the same as for the salted pork that was packed and shipped in barrels. They flatly refused to buy their own refrigerated railcars or to construct ice plants to support them. Perhaps most threatening of all to Gustavus Swift, they refused to guarantee timely shipments, essential for dressed beef to ensure it was delivered unspoiled to the wholesale butcher. A few of the railroads even refused to attach Swift's railcars to their trains.

The entire enterprise looked doomed to failure until Swift discovered the Grand Trunk Railway, a tiny railroad operated out of Montreal and headquartered in London. GTR wasn't shipping live beef to the eastern markets, so it had no vested interest in the status quo. But the company was eager to gain a foothold in the cattle-freighting business. The railroad agreed to carry Swift's dressed beef in refrigerated cars along its route, which was long and circuitous: from Chicago, up along the Great Lakes into Canada, and then down through Buffalo, New York, to the destination cities along the East Coast. Despite the longer trips, this northern route offered one decided advantage: the all-important ice would be easier to procure along the way. Before long the Grand Trunk carried 60 percent of the dressed-beef shipping business, and the other railroads began to capitulate to the meatpackers' demands.

Even when the path was cleared for dressed beef to arrive fresh and in a timely manner in Boston or New York City, new problems cropped up. At first the wholesale butchers saw no reason to accept beef that their customers might perceive as somehow less than fresh. Swift retaliated. He proceeded to build his own warehouses and his own wholesale operations. He ran advertising campaigns extolling the meat's virtues. Where necessary, he and the other meatpackers offered their meat directly to the public, at enormous discounts. The public bought it, ate it, and loved it. In city after city, the wholesalers were forced to surrender. In each market, the first to do so usually received an offer from Swift — he would buy out the business and make it Swift's exclusive local distributor.

Before long Swift had assembled a highly profitable, vertically integrated meatpacking empire — that is, one that merged the different stages of production and distribution in a single enterprise. Swift's company took the cattle from the stockyard all the way to the local restaurant. Eventually this empire would include the shipping of dressed beef to distribution centers in London, Liverpool, Hong Kong, Tokyo, Osaka, Singapore, Shanghai, Manila, and Honolulu, among other places.

What had begun in 1850 as a highly fragmented business, with some 185 meatpacking firms, grew and consolidated until, by 1919, the number had risen to 1,304 plants, dominated by five giant national meatpackers known as the Beef Trust. These five — Swift, Armour, Morris, Cudahy, and S&S — came to employ more workers than any other industry in the country until the auto industry overtook them early in the twentieth century.

Thus it was that Chicago became the place where livestock came to die. The animals faced a death devoid of sentiment. Little real attention was paid to the means of their killing. Indeed, as the panicked cattle entered the slaughterhouse, apparently with a pretty good idea of what lay in store for them, in the eyes of management they ceased to be living things and became a financial commodity. Any notion that a steer was a sentient being, perhaps deserving of compassionate treatment when it came to its execution, would have to wait for a later day and more evolved thinking on the part of the meatpacking industry. The 1958 federal Humane Methods of Slaughter Act and the lobbying efforts, more recently, of animal rights activists such as Temple Grandin helped create a new approach.

In the 1870s the slaughtering of livestock — whether cattle, pigs, or sheep — involved a series of gruesome steps. An animal was rendered unconscious with a blow struck to the head by a two-pointed hammer wielded by hand — not always successfully. The unconscious animal was then dragged into the so-called sticking room. Here, in a process called exsanguination, it was hung upside down from a hook and its throat cut to drain the carcass of its blood — five gallons of the stuff, for an average-size steer. A pig carcass was briefly dipped into a vat of boiling water to soften the skin, remove debris, and loosen the hair. Next the animal carcass was laid on a table. Here, a group of knife-wielding cutters, each with a specialized task, worked to remove the skin and the head, preferably at the first cervical vertebra, all in preparation for the work of the "gutter," who re-hung the carcass and disemboweled it, removing the entrails. The carcass was then split in half down the backbone into two "sides" and then chilled in a cooler called a "hotbox" for twenty hours before the sides were divided into various bulk cuts.

The workers in these plants faced extreme safety and sanitation challenges. Aprons and knee-high boots did only so much to protect them from the spattering of gore and the piles of entrails, and did absolutely nothing to insulate them from the distress of the desperate dying animals. Ultimately, it would take labor disputes and passionate journalistic exposés, such as Upton Sinclair's muckraking 1906 novel, *The Jungle*, before the meatpackers would consider serious reforms to improve safety and sanitation for their workers. Even today, the work remains so unpleasant and dangerous that the annual labor turnover in the industry approaches 100 percent.

For the meat-eating public, the chief concern was, and remains, food safety. The hide of the steer arriving at the plant was often caked with manure, and disassembling the animal required removing its intestines, filled with fecal matter containing toxic microbes. How, then, did you avoid contaminating the meat, especially when your workers were encouraged to work fast while standing up to their ankles in entrails, waste, and blood? No one had a simple solution to this problem, and no federal regulations existed to protect the consumer — just as there were none to uphold the rights of the animal or the safety of the worker.

A large steer weighing 1,000 pounds typically produced 590 pounds of beef, of which about 35 pounds would be porterhouse,

55 pounds sirloin, 50 pounds round steak, 30 pounds rib roast, 25 boneless rump roast, 105 chuck roast, 100 hamburger, and 50 stew meat. The remaining 140 pounds of the original 590 consisted of waste and trimmings.

The meatpackers soon found a variety of uses for the waste and trimmings, as well as for the offal, much as the American Indians had found uses for different parts of the bison. Leather from the skin was one such staple item, along with glue from the hooves, soap and oleo margarine from the lard, fertilizer from the blood, brushes from the hair, buttons from the bones, and violin strings from the serosal layer of the small intestine — the term "catgut" is thought to be an abbreviation for "cattle gut." Entire factories grew up around the processing of glue and hair. As the industry matured, the sale of these byproducts would account for most of the meatpackers' profits.

Automation was the secret ingredient. Overhead wheels were introduced to carry the hog or the steer from one fixed workstation to the next. Before long, this approach evolved into an overhead trolley system driven by steam engines and industrial belts. Specific repetitive tasks were assigned to each worker along what became, in effect, the first assembly line, although the actual work was *dis*assembly. It was from studying this process in the Chicago slaughterhouses that Henry Ford came up with his own method for assembling automobiles — a development that would revolutionize mass manufacturing.

Meat was becoming big business. By the late 1860s the value of meat-animal production amounted to $1.4 billion, or 20 percent of the country's $7 billion gross domestic product. Add in the meatpacking component and you exceeded 22 percent of the GDP, making meat — primarily beef, pork, and lamb — by far the largest industry in the United States at the time. The industry would double in size by 1900, but its percentage of the GDP would shrink to 16.6 percent, a testament to how rapidly other components of the industrializing economy were growing.

Gustavus Swift, driven, obsessive, and relentless, proved to be one of the country's greatest business innovators, earning a place in the American Business Hall of Fame. Not only did Swift give the auto titan Henry Ford the idea for the mass assembly line; the management practices that Swift developed and pursued so ruthlessly formed the beginnings of the American system of business procedures and management practices, which largely accounts for the country's rise to industrial preeminence. As William Cronon has written in *Nature's Metropolis*, "However impressive individuals like Swift or Armour might be, their real achievement was to create immense impersonal organizations, hierarchically structured and operated by an army of managers and workers that would long outlive their founders." These were corporations "on a scale never before seen in the history of the world." Swift was the first to pursue vertical integration and functional specialization and the first to develop a culture that promoted from within and developed managerial expertise. He was also the first to create a national, and then a global, distribution network, and the first to encourage the rapid adoption and deployment of advanced technology. He was, at once, daring in his use of leverage and exemplary at maintaining his good credit. In short, the meatpacking industry, as gruesome, violent, and inhumane as much of the actual work was, became an academy of best practices for business. It was the Harvard Business School of its day, with Gustavus Swift, the thrifty Yankee butcher from Cape Cod, as its first dean.

Once the dressed beef arrived in New York City by rail, it was stored in giant refrigerated warehouses built by the meatpackers or their captive wholesalers. From there it was distributed, by horse-drawn wagon or cart, to butcher's shops and grocery stores.

New York was a bustling and noisy port city in the 1870s and '80s. Its office buildings stood five to ten stories high and had just begun to feature Otis elevators. The cobblestone streets, crowded with clattering horses and carriages, lacked streetlights. The city's population was doubling every sixteen years.

In this heaving metropolis, the best place to try dressed beef, or any other kind of beef — indeed the true popularizer of the great American steak — was the trio of restaurants known as Delmonico's.

The original Delmonico's was the creation of two brothers who arrived in New York City in 1823 from an Italian-speaking canton in Switzerland and opened a chocolate shop on William Street in Lower Manhattan. After their store burned down in the Great Fire of 1835, they turned their attention to "restaurants," employing a new concept of fine dining known as *à la carte* (as opposed to *table d'hôte*), which featured menus and a wine list presented in a formal setting — an approach only recently introduced by the French. The concept was so successful in Manhattan that by 1860 a nephew of the two brothers, Lorenzo Delmonico, had expanded into three superb venues, and these restaurants became internationally renowned. The most impressive was the restaurant at Fifth Avenue and 14th Street, known to the cognoscenti as "the Citadel."

As in most high-end restaurants at this time, women were not allowed to eat at a table unless escorted by a man. But at Delmonico's the prohibitions went further: a couple could not eat alone in a private dining room unless the door to the room remained open at all times. Delmonico's head chef, a Frenchman named Charles Ranhofer, is credited with inventing eggs Benedict — for Mrs. Benedict, a regular patron who requested something new for lunch. His other innovations include lobster Newburg, Manhattan clam chowder, oysters Rockefeller, and, in honor of the country's 1867 purchase of Alaska, the dessert known as baked Alaska.

Private dinners at Delmonico's were hosted in honor of visiting presidents, foreign dignitaries, celebrities, and honorees, from Ulysses S. Grant to Oscar Wilde, Charles Dickens, and Mark Twain. In 1871, the New York Yacht Club hired Lorenzo Delmonico to cater a nautical dinner in honor of the Russian grand duke Alexis Romanov, who was paying a visit on his way west for his widely publicized buffalo hunt. According to Lately Thomas, author of *Delmonico's: A Century of Splendor,* "The Grand Duke assured Lorenzo that never, afloat or ashore, had he been blessed with better cooking."

The Gilded Age robber barons and the Wall Street parvenus competed to outdo each other at private dinners at Delmonico's. Take the case of three men: Leonard Jerome, a Wall Street short-seller; August Belmont, the U.S. representative of the Rothschild banking empire; and William R. Travers, a Wall Street lawyer, who, because he belonged to twenty-seven clubs, was considered the most popular man in New York City. These three gave a series of competing dinners for their friends and fellow horseracing enthusiasts that came to be known as the Silver, Gold, and Diamond dinners. No expense was spared. The party favors included gold bracelets for the ladies, hidden in their napkins and adorned with medallions engraved with the initials JP, for Jerome Park, the racetrack that Jerome and Belmont had recently built in Fordham, on the outskirts of the city. Leonard Jerome's dinner, which featured truffle ice cream for dessert, reportedly took the top honors.

Many of these carte blanche dinners ran to $100 a person, or roughly $2,390 per head in today's dollars. However, as Lorenzo reported to the press, if you spent $20 per person on the flowers and another $20 per person on the embossed menu, "it doesn't take long to run up to $100 in that way."

The most talked about dinner of the day was the Swan Dinner. Edward Luckmeyer, a successful importer celebrating an unexpected tax windfall, threw the dinner in the Citadel's largest dining room, for seventy people, in February 1873. A remarkable oval table was constructed, featuring a thirty-foot freshwater pond landscaped with exotic plants and waterfalls. Floating in the middle were several swans brought in from Prospect Park in Brooklyn. The entire pond was sheathed in a finely wrought gold cage built by Louis Comfort Tiffany; it reached the ceiling. Surrounding the large cage hung smaller matching gold cages filled with chirping songbirds.

The famous Delmonico steak, advertised in its day as "the best steak available," is today mistakenly assumed to denote a New York strip steak or a rib-eye with the bone left in. But the food writer Joe O'Connell, in a fine piece of historical sleuthing, has determined that the truth is otherwise: "The historical fact is that the original, authentic Delmonico Steak is, in modern terms, the *first boneless top loin steak* cut from the front of (anterior to) the short loin."

What was so remarkable about the Delmonico steak — served, incidentally, with Delmonico potatoes, which were whipped, sprinkled with Parmesan cheese, and then browned — was not simply how far removed geographically it was from the western open ranges and the Texas calving grounds. Rather, it was how the beef had been transformed into an abstract commodity, a commercially packaged urban food that few associated with refrigerated dressed beef, let alone with a living, feeling animal. According to William Cronon, "Severed from the form in which it had lived, severed from the act that had killed it, it vanished from human memory as one of nature's creatures. Its ties to the earth receded, and in forgetting the animal's life one also forgot the grasses and the prairie skies and the departed bison herds of a landscape that seemed more and more remote in space and time."

The beef business had been industrialized.

8

The Rise of Cheyenne

The growing popularity of steaks, the Delmonico cut in particular, helped spread the news of the beef bonanza. It also provided a kind of tangible justification for investing in the boom. The allure of the American West and the widely publicized lifestyle of the cowboy were proving irresistible to young men everywhere, whether poor or well-off, as we have seen. The cowboy Andy Adams expressed the sentiment of many who heard the call: "the fascination of a horse and saddle was too strong to be resisted. I took to the range as a preacher's son takes to vice." Young impoverished farm boys, particularly those who grew up in Texas or on the edge of the Great Plains, where they could see developments in the cattle business for themselves, were as eager to get involved as the well-to-do young men of the cities in the Northeast and Europe, who arrived with an eye to the main chance, looking for a financial score, backed by their family's or other people's money. Destiny would set these two groups on a collision course. Their paths first crossed in Cheyenne.

Cheyenne, Wyoming, was rapidly becoming the epicenter of the boom. You went to Cheyenne if you were looking for work as a ranch hand, in the case of the cowboys, or to build or buy your own ranch, in the case of the aspiring ranchers. A trail drive up the Goodnight-Loving Trail would bring you directly to the town. The Western Trail, which ended in Ogallala, Nebraska, was close to Cheyenne by rail. But, as we have seen, the work of trail driving was arduous; only a small percentage, perhaps a quarter, of the trail drivers from Texas had the stomach for a second thousand-mile-long cattle drive — one was more than enough. (Teddy Blue Abbott was an exception: he returned to Texas late each fall and made the trip north repeatedly.)

Most cowboys easily found jobs in Cheyenne, getting work on the newly formed cattle ranches in the Wyoming, Montana, and Dakota territories, where they watched over the scattered open-range herds and waited out the long winters. There were plenty of ranch jobs in Colorado, especially around Denver, a livestock hub, and in those sections of the state that weren't too mountainous, but conditions at the higher altitudes were often harsh, and across the state ranchers faced growing competition from homesteaders. That paucity of ranching jobs north of Texas extended to the other neighboring states and territories: Kansas and Nebraska had been overrun with settlers by the 1870s; much of what would become the state of Oklahoma remained Indian Territory; much of Arizona and New Mexico was too hot and arid to provide suitable forage for cattle; and Utah and Idaho were less accessible, cut off from the trail drives by the Rocky Mountains.

An aspiring cowboy named Reuben B. Mullins arrived in Cheyenne in April 1884 with only fifty cents in his pocket after stowing away in a Union Pacific boxcar for twenty-four hours without food or water. He found hordes of young cowboys and ranchers tramping the streets in full cowboy regalia. The annual stock convention was in session, and all the local ranches were hiring their cowboys for the summer and for the roundups. He found a job at a ranch within an hour.

The roundups occurred twice a year, on prearranged dates in the spring and the fall. On these dates the cowboys from a group of neighboring ranches, or a district, went out to find their dispersed herds, accompanied by wagons and provisions. Open-range ranching meant, of course, that cattle were free to wander where they chose across the vast public lands of the Great Plains and the High Plains. Invariably, the cattle — young and old, male and female — dispersed widely and mixed with those of other ranches, speckling the landscape. The cowboys rode across this terrain to round up the scattered herds and then segregate them, identifying each animal's ownership by the brand seared on its thigh. Depending on the number of cattle, this process could take anywhere from two weeks to a month or more. During the spring roundup, each newborn calf was lassoed, flipped on its side, and held down as the red-hot end of a poker, with the appropriate brand affixed, was applied to its skin. In the fall roundup, the two- and three-year-old steers would be separated from each herd in preparation for their shipment to the slaughterhouses in Chicago.

Just as jobs on a trail drive featured an informal seniority system, a similar hierarchy existed on the ranches. For example, as Teddy Blue's experience as a cowboy grew, he was rewarded with more interesting assignments during the summer months. The best of these was "repping." This job was considered a notch higher than the work of a common cowboy. In effect, Teddy Blue spent his spring and fall going from roundup to roundup as the representative of his district, participating in the branding and sorting exercises but also bringing back any cattle that had wandered out of his district. He traveled with a string of horses and without any supervision. But he needed to know from memory, and be able to identify on sight, the dozens of cattle brands that he might encounter. "As soon as I saw a cow, I knew what outfit owned her, clear down to the Platte," he boasted. For someone like Teddy Blue, who enjoyed the camaraderie of the roundups, repping was the ideal job.

By the early 1870s a business that originated with the small personal investments of individual entrepreneurs like John Wesley Iliff, Charles Goodnight, and John Adair had become subject to a cascade of wealth pouring in through a variety of investment vehicles. The Scottish moneymen of Edinburgh favored the investment trust, which was essentially a private limited partnership. The Dundee investors and the English, by contrast, favored the joint-stock company, a public company floated on a stock exchange — a vehicle that allowed for more leverage because the company could carry debt as well as equity on its books. But both approaches provided incentives to their managers to meet the goals of the passive (general) partners or the stockholders back in Scotland or England. They awarded a share of the profits — up to a third of them — but usually only after the initial investment had been paid back to the investors through dividends or other distributions; this was likely to occur a few years down the road. In the meantime, the manager lived off the dividends from his own investment in the partnership, or in some cases, on a modest salary paid to him on top of his incentive fee. This approach is similar to, and is a direct precursor of, that of hedge funds today.

As the profits from the sale of their beef flowed back to the cattle ranchers, the more foresighted of them began to spend money to improve their stock. They did this by importing bulls from better-quality breeds. Durhams, also known as shorthorns, came in by trail or by rail from Oregon; Herefords arrived by ship from England. The goal was to raise the quality of the beef so that the cattlemen could charge a higher price. Breeding the longhorns to more refined stock resulted in meat more tender in texture, which was easier to chew, and more marbled with fat, which improved the taste. Ultimately, the hearty Hereford proved the breed best suited to the arid conditions of the West. Eventually the Hereford would largely replace the longhorn on the open range.

Soon different parts of the country came to specialize in a certain aspect of the cattle business. For example, Illinois cattlemen stopped breeding cattle and focused on the more profitable niche business of running feedlots, where they took possession of steers from the West, fattening them up on surplus midwestern corn bought on the cheap from grain silos nearby. And the ranches down in Texas became the primary calving grounds — the logical place to breed the cattle. That left the open range of the central and northern plains as the place where trailed cattle, mostly steers, inexpensively grew to maturity by feeding on the free grass.

Many new cattle companies flourished in their first few years. But then, in September 1873, the industry suffered its first hiccup. A sudden financial panic, triggered in part by the failure of the Philadelphia investment firm Jay Cooke & Company, led to the widespread collapse of railroad shares. In the space of three months, fifty-five railroad companies went bankrupt; by the following September another sixty had folded. At first, the cattle industry, like all industries across the country — indeed the developed world — swooned. But fortunately, beef and cattle prices, fueled by the still unmet demand for beef in the urban East, rebounded well before the broader economy recovered. Before long the cattlemen felt flush again. As the boom times resumed, the ranchers began to expand and consolidate their herds and to spruce up their ranches. The most successful ones, as the affluent are wont to do, began to flaunt their wealth.

Cheyenne was the capital of the Territory of Wyoming (organized in 1869; it would become a state in 1890). Unlike neighboring territories, which had profited from mining or timber extraction, Wyoming was all about cattle. In the post-panic prosperity, Cheyenne was the town that seemed to grow the fastest and flourish the most. A place that began as a small cattle depot was already emerging as a young city. Fortuitously located at the center of the open range, with Colorado, Kansas, and Nebraska to the south and the Montana and Dakota territories to the north, Cheyenne was ideally situated for shipping cattle east by rail. By 1880 it could claim three thousand residents, including a remarkable eight millionaires.

Cheyenne boasted a few sheepherders too, such as John B. Okie and Morton Post, and a word should be said about them. Like cattle ranching, sheep ranching could be a lucrative business, thanks to a steady market for fleece, lamb, and mutton, and their prices rarely fluctuated. But far less is known about the sheepherders than the cattlemen of the West, simply because the trade lacked the romance and glamour of cattle ranching, and so the business never caught the imagination of the chroniclers of the era. No doubt the sheepherders of the Old West deserve their own history. A number of them made fortunes and became important citizens in towns scattered across the open range. Eventually, the two livestock trades came to overlap, when cattle barons such as Cheyenne's Francis Warren built sizable herds of both animals. Toward the end of the era, the two groups would come into conflict over the dwindling grass on the open range.

Ten years into the beef boom, the trailblazers of the cattle kingdom had established numerous cattle ranches, and the brokering to buy and sell them was becoming a business unto itself. Between 1880 and 1900, an additional 181 livestock companies — most of them cattle companies — would be incorporated in Wyoming. But countless others simply traded hands. Cheyenne itself, which doubled as a hub for the Union Pacific Railroad, became the primary marketplace for the buying and selling of cattle ranches on the open range. The town's two-mile grid of eighty-foot-wide treeless streets and its rows of red-brick buildings were lined with provisioners to meet the wants and needs of every aspiring ranchman. If you had the time and the money, and your tastes inclined toward outdoor activities and equestrian adventure, shopping in Cheyenne in the late 1870s or early 1880s, to buy or simply outfit a newly purchased cattle ranch, could be the cattleman's equivalent of a Paris shopping spree.

A stroll down Ferguson Street in the early 1880s gave the full flavor of the beef bonanza at its peak. Only a couple of years before, the buildings had been made of clapboard wood, many of them imported by rail from Chicago pre-assembled. But now two-story and even three-story brick buildings, many fronted with awnings, were the norm. The telegraph poles were also new. The town boasted numerous saloons, six churches of different denominations, and a school. Unlike those of many other cattle towns, the streets of Cheyenne were well policed.

An aspiring rancher's first stop might be J. S. Collins & Company, a shop that sold stock saddles, fine harnesses, bridles, quirts, spurs, and lap robes. The interior was redolent with the appealing smell of newly worked leather. A quirt, by the way, is a forked leather stock-whip, much like a riding crop, sometimes used to strike a rearing horse or, in the *romal* version, to goad cattle from horseback.

Western saddles, like most cowboy paraphernalia, had evolved from the equipment first created by the Mexican vaqueros. The frame of a saddle is usually little more than a flat wooden chair, called a tree, wrapped in rawhide, which is then dampened so that the leather shrinks tightly over the wood, strengthening the entire structure. More leather is then stitched over the tree; fancy tooling is added at the end. Most of the saddles in the West in those days were heavy and long and had deep seats, especially compared with the lighter, shallower, and hornless English saddle. This feature not only made the saddle more comfortable, but it allowed cowboys to avoid rising, or "posting," when riding at a trot, which is the convention in English riding. The so-called Cheyenne saddle, invented locally, featured a shallower seat; the thicker saddle horn on the pommel was tilted farther forward, making it easier for the cowboy to loop a rope around it and slide more easily out of the saddle to tie up a calf with a piggin' string. The cantle, or back of the seat, initially was quite high on the fancier Mexican charro saddles, but had shrunk over time, and so had the saddle horn, which was once as wide as a saucer. To strap the saddle to the horse, dual cinching prevailed on the open range, to take the stress of heavy roping. The single-cinch and the so-called center-fire rigs, which were popular in California, were not as secure. A basic saddle might run you forty dollars and up. Expect to pay another hundred for the horse. (For comparison, each U.S. dollar in 1880 would be worth $23.90 today.)

The hooded stirrup, with hard leather covering the toe, was known as a tapadero. Often purely decorative, the tapadero was originally designed to prevent the cowboy from getting his boot caught too deep in the stirrup. It also kept brush from poking through.

You could buy your spurs at J. S. Collins too. In fact, you might buy different spurs for different riding occasions. For leisure riding you might strap onto your boots a pair that featured a small, round spur wheel. For more active riding—say, for roping—you might use larger Mexican-style spurs with a bigger spoke. The choice of spur also depended on the length of the rider's legs. The long-legged needed a shank that tipped upward; the short-legged required just the opposite—a shank that tipped downward, to better reach the horse's belly. Many old-timers who wore these accessories rarely used them to spur their horse at all. Just jangling them was enough to get the steed's full attention.

Chaps, short for *chaparejos,* came in three styles: the slim-fitting shotgun chaps that you stepped into, the wide, fringed stovepipe chaps, and the bat-wing chaps, with a short-strap-around-the-thigh design. J. S. Collins also carried heavy, wooly angora chaps for use in cold weather.

Although halter and bridle designs have changed little since antiquity, bits did vary. Typically they were made of scrap metal from wagon wheels or copper pans. The rein chains were often fashioned from smelted nickel-silver wire.

If you didn't like the selection at J. S. Collins, Frank Meanea's Saddle Shop on 17th Street made everything from saddles to holsters. Their motto was "If it can be made in leather, we do it."

Your next stop on Ferguson Street might be F. E. Warren Mercantile Company, the town's best jobbers in furniture. The owner, Francis Warren, who would later become a celebrated U.S. senator, made his first fortune right here. By 1880 he owned many of the commercial buildings along Ferguson Street and served as the area's territorial governor. A rocking chair in his shop would set you back $2.50, and six bow-backed chairs another $4.50 each.

Next on your to-do list would be a stop at F. Schweickert, which sold hardware, cutlery, tin ware, and stoves. Schweickert did a brisk business in bucksaws, which cost eighty-five cents apiece. The store also sold rope, nails, and pocketknives.

Not far from him, on 18th Street, was Peter Bergersen, the town gunsmith and dealer in firearms. A competitive marksman and by all accounts an excellent shot, he first sold Sharps rifles to the bison hunters, but now dealt in the popular Winchester and Remington rifles and Colt and Smith & Wesson handguns. He was also known to sell a few of the now extraordinarily rare and elaborate single-shot Pope Barreled Marlin-Ballard Custom Schuetzen rifles. These weighed up to fifteen pounds and were used only for target shooting at the Schuetzen (marksmen's) clubs, which were popular at the time.

Draper, Organ & Kelly, a little farther down Ferguson, might be your next stop — for kitchen supplies. Here an aspiring rancher could load up on pots and pans. An eggbeater cost 35¢. A coffeepot retailed for $1.35. Other requirements for every ranch: washboards (40¢) and washtubs ($1.25) — as close as you could get to a washing machine, which wouldn't be invented until 1908.

George W. Hoyt, the druggist and pharmacist, would be happy to sell you your tooth soap, toothbrushes ($1.75 a dozen), lead pencils (65¢ a dozen), Vaseline, mustang liniment oil, pocket combs ($1.50 a dozen), and sarsaparilla. And why not include in your purchase some of Hoyt's own custom-made cough syrup in the event someone in the outfit contracted the croup? Not far away, William Meyers at 301 Ferguson Street would sell you shoes, riding boots, and other "gents' furnishings" such as long underwear and Stetson hats.

The Stetson, known as the "Boss of the Plains," was first made out of shaved animal fur by John Stetson while on a trip panning for gold in Colorado — to prove to a group of friends that a good hat could be made without tanning. He shaved the fur off the pelt and used boiling water to shape and shrink the material — a primitive form of felting — and to his amazement sold the hat to a passing hunter. First mass-produced in 1865 and sold by traveling salesmen for five dollars each (thirty dollars for a later beaver version), the Stetson would become the greatest-selling hat of all time, quickly displacing the trail driver's wide-brimmed sombrero. By 1902, the company, which Stetson had launched with a hundred dollars in capital, was producing two million hats a year out of a massive multistory factory in Philadelphia, which sprawled across nine acres. The standard hat, with its four-inch crown and four-inch brim, remains an important western clothing accessory to this day, and the "ten-gallon" model has always been popular with Texans.

Farther down Ferguson Street, C. H. King dealt in wholesale groceries, tobacco, and cigars. (This was not *the* Clarence King, the geologist and author of *Mountaineering in the Sierra Nevada* who blew the whistle on the diamond hoax of 1872, although he was a regular visitor to Cheyenne.) Here, one hundred pounds of oatmeal would run you $6.50. If you didn't like the prices or the selection, you could try Whipple & Hay, general grocers, or the Union Mercantile Company, the best place in town to stock up on bulk coffee, sugar, bran, and bacon. Union Mercantile was partially owned by Alexander Swan, the cattle baron who used to run the Two Bar with his two brothers, Thomas and Henry, until in 1880 he launched his own ranch: the famed Swan Land & Cattle Company.

Finally, at the far end of town, the blacksmith firm of Brooks & Neil could shoe a new horse for you at fifty cents a shoe.

If you needed to place an advertisement to recruit a couple of cowboys, you might stop in at the offices of the *Cheyenne Daily Sun*. A 1¼-inch classified ad cost $1.25 and would appear in the paper for a month. Nearby, Bristol & Knabe Printing Company would happily make up the letterhead for your new ranching business.

If the aspiring cattleman couldn't find some item on Ferguson Street, a fresh alternative launched at this time provided a solution: the Chicago-based Montgomery Ward catalogue, the equivalent of today's Amazon.com. With the tag line "satisfaction guaranteed or your money back," the catalogue carried dry goods of every conceivable kind, which the company shipped to customers for pickup at the nearest rail station. Montgomery Ward would have the western market to itself until 1896, when one-cent-per-pound postage and the creation of Rural Free Delivery made it possible to send goods by mail directly to rural homes far from a railroad stop. These developments inspired a competitor to Montgomery Ward: the Sears, Roebuck catalogue, sending goods all over the country from the "Cheapest Supply House on Earth."

The best way to enter the cattle business was not by laboriously assembling your ranch from scratch. If you had the capital, it was better to buy a ranch that was up and running and fully furnished: cattle, horses, wagons, and barns, all-inclusive. This is what Hubert Teschemacher, his brother Arthur, and their Harvard classmate Fredrick DeBillier did to jump-start their business. This approach also gave them range rights to acreage they might otherwise have to quarrel over.

Another strategy was to buy into an existing ranch at the partnership level, which Richard Trimble did when he caught cattle fever. He had arrived at Teschie's Duck Bar Ranch at the peak of the boom, with no real intention of getting into the business. But then he and the visiting opera writer Owen Wister had the unforgettable experience of camping out with Teschie during a county cattle roundup—in moonlight—and he was sold on the cattle trade. As he wrote in a letter addressed to "Dear Family" in August 1882, "That night I shall never forget. The camp was on a little point of about ten acres' ground by a bend in the river. Just across the river was a bunch of beef with two men riding slowly around them all night. Round the mess wagon were the beds of the men and within a few steps of each a saddled horse picketed in case of a stampede. At a few rods' distance was the herd of about 125 horses with their night herder riding round them and down on all fell the light of an almost full moon. A few hundred yards from the camp the coyotes formed a circle and from time to time burst out in their agonizing wail."

At first, Trimble hoped to start his own ranch in Montana, where open-range land was more readily available and less settled, but then he heard rumors that the water there was so alkaline that even boiled in coffee, it "affect[ed] the bowels," which made it difficult to find cowboys willing to work there. By contrast, the Teschemacher & DeBillier Cattle Company, which included the Duck Bar Ranch, was already beautifully situated, featured excellent hunting in the neighboring hills, and offered as a bonus the agreeable companionship of other Harvard men.

Teschie, who was eager to raise more capital and expand, offered to let Trimble buy in and become a ranch co-manager. "I am going to think this all over for a day or two but if I decide to go in I think I shall ask father to lend me fifteen ($15,000) at nine per cent (9%). Of course I could give no security but the $25,000 stock. If any of the rest of the family want to go in of course they can but simply as an investment independently of me, for fifteen thousand would be the outside limit that I would borrow on my ten thousand. Nine per cent I find is what Teschie pays his father for some money he borrowed of him."

In truth, Trimble's mind was made up, and he decided to buy in immediately and get down to work. "Although there are several personal matters I should like to attend to," he wrote to his brother, "i.e. [buying a] remedy for baldness etc., I don't think I shall come East." He too was hooked.

Many of the cowboys aspired to own their own ranch too, but most lacked the capital to get started — or they squandered their money as soon as they had earned it. Trapped by a lack of social and economic mobility, a disproportionate number of those who stayed in the trade remained cowboys for their entire working lives. They might move from ranch to ranch, leaving one outfit for another if they didn't like their boss or their foreman, but most were ill quipped to do much more than ride a horse, twirl a lariat, and rope and brand a calf. If a cowboy was laid off for the winter, as most of them usually were, he traveled what was known as "the grub line," moving from ranch to ranch on horseback — on a borrowed horse if he didn't own one, which was often the case. Accepting the hospitality of free meals and a free bunk had become a popular custom and an important perquisite for cowboys wintering on the open range.

But one route to financial independence did remain open for an aspiring cowboy. It required the judicious combination of mavericks and the Homestead Act.

Mavericks were unbranded, and thus unclaimed, large calves that had become separated from their mothers on the open range and had largely weaned themselves. Conventional practice allowed a cowboy who found one of these animals, wandering motherless, to claim it for himself, and this was usually considered a supplemental compensation for his labor. Most would sell the young animals, often back to the rancher who had originally owned them. But an enterprising cowboy might view these calves as the potential foundation stock for a ranch of his own. He could look for an unclaimed well-watered area, stake out 160 acres for as little as $10 under the rules of the Homestead Act, collect a few more mavericks over time, and graze the calves there. Before long, the cowboy had the makings of his own small herd. Naturally, the custom of "adopting" mavericks could easily be abused, and it became one of the great operational loopholes in the open-range cattle industry. The ranchers were willing to look the other way when times were good, viewing the loss of a few calves each year as a minor cost of doing business. But it wouldn't always be so.

As the industry matured, other abuses grew in severity, such as the altering of the cattle brands. These brands were simple in design, and it wasn't difficult to brand over a brand, changing a letter to a number, say, and thereby taking possession of cattle belonging to someone else. The practice was, of course, pure theft and illegal. Any cowboy willing to risk such theft needed to exercise great caution, especially because the penalty for rustling, or cattle or horse stealing, was typically death by hanging, often without benefit of a judge, jury, or trial. Still, given the prevalence of absentee ranch owners, there was opportunity to cheat, and incentive too, in light of how few options the cowboys had for advancement and how little they made in wages. Some weighed the risk against the potential reward and chose to rebrand cattle when they could.

. . .

For Wyoming cattlemen, Cheyenne became the place to escape the solitude and tedium of their remote ranches, especially during the long winter months. The more affluent hired architects to build large brick-and-clapboard homes along upper Ferguson Street, which came to be known as "Cattlemen's Row," or along 17th Street, a neighborhood that years later would come to be known as the Rainsford Historic District, named after the popular architect George D. Rainsford. He moved to Cheyenne from the East in the 1870s to breed Clydesdales and Morgans and soon found himself designing gabled Victorian homes, with generous front porches, for his local friends. Among those commissioning homes were five sets of brothers, all active in the cattle business: William and Thomas Sturgis, Hubert and Arthur Teschemacher, Charles and Henry Oelrichs, Philip and James Dater, and, of course, Richard and Moreton Frewen. Hubert Teschemacher built a house large enough to share with his brother as well as his business partners Frederick DeBillier and Richard Trimble; it was appropriately dubbed "the bachelor quarters."

When Richard Trimble's father, a successful New York banker, expressed some skepticism about having two headquarters for a ranch, Richard took offense. "I am sorry thee has so little confidence in my ability to judge whether it is for my advantage to stay at the ranch or in Cheyenne. There are two sides to the cattle business, the theory and the practice, one is learned better in Cheyenne where cattle men conjugate and the other on a ranch." Just such rationalizations for lax habits and spending would get the cattlemen into trouble.

By some estimates, Cheyenne by the mid-1880s had the highest median per capita income of any city in the world. This is hardly surprising, given that the entire investment in the cattle industry in Cheyenne alone totaled some $15 million by 1886. At times the streets, particularly 16th Street, were crowded with speculators, "like a young Wall Street," according to the *Laramie Boomerang* newspaper, which added, "Millions are talked of as lightly as nickels and all kinds of people are dabbling in steers."

It is worth remembering that in 1880 nothing resembling a Securities and Exchange Commission existed to regulate the U.S. financial industry; Congress would not create the SEC until 1934. And nothing in a cattle-company prospectus warned an aspiring rancher that past performance was not indicative of future results. Aspiring cattlemen would learn the hard way the meaning of the old Latin adage *caveat emptor,* "buyer beware."

Although the Scottish investors initially showed the greatest financial creativity in funding the cattle boom through limited liability companies and joint-stock companies, enterprising American financiers on the ground in the West would now take up the mantle. One opportunity they seized on was to become cattle commission agents — in effect, middlemen. They brokered the sale of entire herds and ranches. More important, they appeared early every spring to negotiate advance commitments with the cattle ranchers to buy their stock upon its arrival in Chicago in the fall. The contracts always stipulated that no runts and no blind, injured, or diseased animals be included, and often Mexican cattle were prohibited. Payment was due upon receipt of the cattle in Chicago, for whatever prices prevailed at the time — that is, whatever the meatpackers were prepared to pay for the steers, plus a modest commission for the agent added on, usually fifty cents a steer, or 1 to 2 percent of the gross sale.

But the commission agents soon began to serve as more than brokers for the cattle barons. They often lent money to the cattle companies when they faced a liquidity squeeze. Or if the commission agents couldn't afford to lend the money, they would broker a loan, again for a 1 to 2 percent commission. In many cases, the commission agents took a financial stake in a ranch, aligning their interests with those of the cattle barons. In other cases they helped New York insurance companies or Scottish bankers to invest fresh capital in ranches or in the underlying real estate. In short, they acted much like merchant bankers, bringing to the fore in American finance much of the financial creativity that would come to distinguish U.S. bankers and financial markets in the generations to come.

The town of Cheyenne soon sported recreational facilities, such as tennis courts and a horseracing track known as the Wyoming Fair Association Park; by 1882, Cheyenne had its own thousand-seat opera house. Locals had founded a bicycle club boasting twenty members, each of whom owned his own big-wheeled penny-farthing; members of the town's Schuetzen gun club traveled to compete in sharpshooting contests across the West. The Knights of Pythias launched a local fraternal order there in 1870, and by 1884 had built their own ornate building on 17th Street. The Oelrichs brothers, Henry and Charles, built a polo field and soon imported the ponies to go with it. Horse-drawn carriages of all types — phaetons, landaus, broughams, tallyhoes, and gigs, as well as the big-wheel bicycles — began to fill the city streets, among the first anywhere to boast electric streetlights (1882); the streets would not be paved until the 1890s. Henry Oelrichs owned a covered yellow-and-black park drag carriage, built in London at a cost of $4,000 ($95,600 in today's dollars) by Peters & Sons in 1874; it was drawn by a team of eight horses. Able to carry twelve passengers easily, it was the stretch limousine of its day. It is now displayed at the Old Town San Diego State Historic Park.

Many of the early cattlemen were not just rich — they were sophisticated men of the world, not ashamed to show off their wealth. DeBillier, for example, owned a villa in France. The Oelrichses were one of the two most prominent German American families in New York, along with the Havemeyers, to whom they were related by marriage and with whom they would cobble together the Great Sugar Trust. The older Oelrichs brother, Herman, who ran the family shipping business in New York, was known for, literally, swimming with sharks, which he naively maintained were harmless, and for marrying an heiress to the Comstock Lode. In Rhode Island he would build one of Newport's great mansions: Rosecliff.

In 1880 a dozen of these Cheyenne cattlemen decided to build the city's first social club for gentlemen. William Sturgis, who helped organize it and became its first secretary, noted in a letter to prospective members: "We do not propose doing anything extravagant but hope to have a quiet social club where members can live instead of going to a hotel . . . in short a good club on an Eastern basis . . . the Somerset [Club] moved West and barring Beacon Street and [Wedgwood] India china."

The club's original name was the Cactus Club, but it was soon changed to the more approachable Cheyenne Club. It would prove far more extravagant than Sturgis perhaps intended. Suddenly, up out of the sagebrush on an empty lot rose a large two-story Victorian clubhouse topped with a mansard roof. The club boasted two tennis courts in back; inside there were two grand staircases, a large dining room, a bar, a smoking room, a reading room, a billiard room, and a wine vault, and upstairs, six bedrooms for guests and visiting members who hadn't yet built their own Cheyenne mansions. The building cost some twenty thousand dollars to construct — financed by a bond that paid 10 percent interest. Fifteen hundred dollars purchased the building's state-of-the-art furnace. Situated in the basement, it heated the entire structure through steam radiators, which were still a novelty. Encircling the building on three sides was a large porch where members could tie up their horses at nineteen separate hitching posts and then relax in one of the wicker rocking chairs, an ideal spot to enjoy a cigar.

The décor featured a variety of memorable touches. The tiles around the fireplace grates bore Shakespearean quotations. In the dining room hung an engraving of the painting *In the Heart of the Bighorns,* presented to the club by the artist himself, the landscape painter Albert Bierstadt. A portrait of a prize bull by the Dutch artist Paulus Potter hung over the main bar, but it was soon defaced. A member named John Cobble, in his cups, mumbled something to the effect that such effete foreign livestock was inappropriate for Wyoming, drew his .45-caliber revolver, and fired a bullet through the canvas.

A handful of Canadian-trained servants staffed the club, along with a French chef named Alexis; a steward named DePrato supervised them all. The initial membership was limited to 50 men, although that number soon widened to 150. The initiation fee was set at fifty dollars; annual dues were thirty dollars; both amounts rose over time. Late in 1882, a fire broke out in the club and caused extensive damage. The membership, now up to 170, roughly half of them residents of Cheyenne, used the event as an excuse to expand the dining room, increase the number of bedrooms to fourteen, and add electric lighting. The members believed the club to be as good a gentlemen's club as any in New York, Boston, or perhaps even London. No less a confirmed clubman than Owen Wister admired it and soon became a regular visitor. "No wonder they like the club at Cheyenne," he remarked. "It is the pearl of the prairies." The new clubhouse was open all year. A visitor, proposed by a member, could buy six-month guest privileges for thirty dollars, or the equivalent of the annual dues for a member. Meals were reasonably priced: twenty-five cents for lunch, fifty cents for dinner.

The steward and the club's secretary, William Sturgis, upheld the highest standards. In one exchange of letters, Sturgis chastised the high-end grocers Park & Tilford, located at 919 Broadway in New York City, for the quality of their Havana cigars. "We wired you last week to omit one shipment of cigars to this club. We wish now to say that there has been for some time past a general complaint among members about the cigars rec'd from you. Either that the brands we use have depreciated or else that the selection is not carefully made. Please send for your shipment of Monday next something in different brands — a complete change — something better in each grade if it costs a trifle more." In another letter he complained about the Garvey sherry: "It lacked almost entirely the bouquet of our earlier purchases and was by no means clear."

Over the next fifteen years, the Cheyenne Club became the locus of political and economic power for the open-range cattle industry. Here, over lunch or cocktails in the bar or boozy dinners, much of the insider business of the trade was conducted with the commission agents, accompanied by the casual swapping of stories and gossip. John Clay recalled discussing business with the local bank president and cattle baron A. R. Converse over a bottle of champagne at lunch. "Converse was one of the few men I have met in my life who could get hilarious three times a day and still do business without a single mistake."

It comes as something of a shock to historians of the era to discover that, in the Territory of Wyoming in the 1880s, a group of cattlemen in Cheyenne were dressing for dinner in black tie, smoking Cuban cigars, and quaffing French champagne and grand cru vintages. The food they enjoyed was nothing to sneer at either — not up to Lorenzo Delmonico's standards, but fine cuisine just the same. It rivaled anything served west of the Mississippi in its day.

The menu for one dinner, thrown by member Francis Warren, the territorial governor, listed four courses, starting with Russian caviar on toast and followed by fresh salmon with hollandaise sauce, each course accompanied by a fine wine. The meal concluded with a selection of exotic liqueurs. On another occasion the British members of the club threw a dinner party for the American members. The forty-one attendees consumed sixty-six bottles of champagne and twenty-two bottles of red wine, which comes to two bottles per person.

It wasn't long before Cheyenne, Wyoming, had become one of those haunts of the wealthy — like Florence or Capri in Italy, Heiligendamm on the Baltic Sea, Nice on the French Riviera, or the hill stations of India, where the nineteenth-century idle rich freely indulged in their privileged lifestyle. Among this select group, the Cheyenne Club soon became famous — far more so than its more modest rivals, the Denver Club in Denver or the Montana Club in Helena.

To be fair, many members of the Cheyenne Club might be confirmed hedonists, but they were far better behaved than the wife-swapping Marlborough House set in London of that day or the dissolute Happy Valley set that would gather in Kenya a few years later. And they did mix some actual business with the pursuit of pleasure.

But the club was not without its moments of saloon-like behavior. All the usual sorts of disputes arose that occur when willful men and alcohol are mixed. Both Oelrichs brothers, for example, were ultimately expelled from the club, Henry for striking a waiter — in some accounts it was for kicking him down a flight of stairs after the waiter refused to hold his horse for him; his brother, Charles, for the use of "dictatorial and disrespectful language." John Clay, who kept a room at the club for years, described the membership as "a motley group full of ginger and snap, with more energy than business sense." Elsewhere, Clay described what a typical day in Cheyenne was like for Hubert Teschemacher and his partners, Fred DeBillier and Richard Trimble. They employed an elderly manservant at the ranch's so-called bachelor quarters, who served them coffee and rolls when they awoke in the morning. The partners then "made a pretense at business" before heading up the street to the Cheyenne Club for lunch. In the afternoon they played tennis on the club's courts, followed by a lengthy dinner at the club and "a lively evening" afterward.

Women, of course, were excluded from the premises, which meant that men could pursue them only outside the confines of the club. More than a few of the young members were ardent playboys. Henry Oelrichs is said to have followed Lillie Langtry across America when she toured in 1883, running up five hundred dollars in bills just for the flowers he bought for her in New York City. He eventually persuaded her to visit him at his Cheyenne ranch so that she could perform at the Cheyenne opera house. Hubert Teschemacher, who would become the third president of the Cheyenne Club and remain a board member, was known to be "a sailor who had a girl in every port." Many of the older cattle barons were married, but their wives rarely came west with them, preferring to spend summers in the seaside resorts of Newport, Rhode Island, or Southampton, New York, or among the horseracing set in Saratoga, or even more extravagantly, at Nice on the French Riviera. As women were excluded from most of the activities that transpired on a cattle ranch, their absence is hardly surprising.

Would the Cheyenne cattlemen's behavior have been any less objectionable if their club had not been a single-sex institution? The same question might be asked of the entire cattle kingdom community, which was a kind of giant bachelor redoubt where women, if present at all, played only a subsidiary role. It is true that the macho culture of the Cheyenne Club, combined with the members' lack of judgment and practical business sense, ultimately proved self-destructive. These traits ultimately drove the membership headlong into a testosterone-fueled conflict that resulted in murder and disgrace.

Cheyenne, and its Cheyenne Club in particular, reflects the highly aspirational nature of western cattle and mining towns. The town's leading citizens wanted more than anything else to be like their eastern counterparts — in Boston, New York, or Philadelphia — or, for that matter, their European counterparts in London and Paris. And for a short time the town, thanks in part to the Cheyenne Club, would achieve that objective. It had more of everything that a western town aspired to: more merchants, more churches, more saloons, more fancy homes, and more millionaires. Even so, Cheyenne could not escape what the historian Howard R. Lamar has described as the classic bimodal existence of a boomtown. It seemed to exist in two worlds, "one centered on relaxation and the other on the struggle to make a living." Cheyenne nevertheless had more money, more talent, more initiative, and more competition than most cattle towns, in part because the opportunities in front of it looked so large.

In addition to the dreams it sold to newcomers in the mid-1880s, the town of Cheyenne sold another essential product (for eight cents a pound). This product, or more specifically, this technology, would play a pivotal role in the cattle era and the literal appearance of North America: barbed wire.

9

Barbed Wire: The Devil's Rope

O ne hot, quiet afternoon in July 1874, three men — a farmer, a hardware dealer, and a lumberman — stood in the "Ag" section of the DeKalb, Illinois, County Fair. They were staring at a display of primitive cattle fencing. Titled "Wooden Strip With Metallic Points," the fencing was the work of one Henry Rose, who had filed and been granted patent number 138769 for his invention the year before. Originally, Rose conceived of the device as a short board studded with metal prongs, to be hung on the forehead of a "breachy" cow and poke it in the forehead every time it attempted to escape through a fence. In the displayed version, which was Rose's second iteration, the board with the prongs hung over an existing fence made of wire or board, a visual and physical discouragement to any cow contemplating escape.

That day no one bothered to record the words, or the laughter, of the three men, Joseph Glidden, Isaac Elwood, and Jacob Haish, but the general drift of their conversation seems clear. "Wouldn't it make far more sense to put the barbs on a wire instead of on a board?" one of them must have said aloud. That was what all three were thinking. Each one's business faced a similar need for improved fencing.

The observation — and the ensuing innovation — was simple enough, but its repercussions could hardly have been more far-reaching, not just for the future husbandry of cattle but for the fate of the cowboy as well. And considering the fact that barbed wire would be used to incarcerate people as well as livestock, most notably in concentration camps, this chance encounter at a county fair would have a surprisingly significant impact.

Within six months all three men had filed for patents on barbed wire. The three, along with a fourth man named John W. Gates, who entered the business soon after, would get credit for launching a giant, highly profitable industry. By 1884 over one hundred companies engaged in the manufacture of barbed wire, some thirteen of those in the vicinity of DeKalb. Eventually, as was the case with the meatpacking business, a single U.S. corporation would come to dominate the industry, an enterprise that could mass-produce the wire at the lowest possible cost.

The fact that these events happened in DeKalb in the year that they did is one of those accidents of history that in hindsight seems almost foreordained. The town stood on the edge of the great prairies, a land largely devoid of timber and stone — the traditional fencing materials in the East. Simple wire fencing, in various grades, was both inexpensive and widely available, the fencing of choice in the West. But it did not effectively contain cattle. The animals simply pushed through it, as the three DeKalb entrepreneurs well knew. Attempts to use various alternatives had failed; Osage orange, a thorny shrub that had seemed promising, was difficult to handle and took time and effort to transplant and grow.

The situation cried out for a better technology. Homesteaders needed some way to keep the open-range cattle and the herds of trailed Texas cattle from wandering onto their acreage, devastating their crops or infecting their livestock with contagious diseases. The open range was "fence out" land; it was the responsibility of the landowner, or homesteader, to build a fence that would keep out other people's livestock. By contrast, in the East and the Midwest the law mandated that the livestock owner fence livestock in or be held liable for damages on other people's property. The railroads needed a similar deterrent to keep bison and elk off their tracks. Barbed wire was the obvious answer. Its time had arrived.

Conception, of course, was one thing, execution quite another. Glidden went home and in the ensuing summer evenings began to tinker in his kitchen, trying to devise a way to make wire barbs that could be fixed not to a board but to the plain twelve- or fourteen-gauge mild steel wire itself, the flimsy, pliable wire sold by the spool in hardware stores. His eureka moment came when he removed the coffee grinder from the kitchen wall and, on a whim, ran a strip of wire through the gears. Turning the grinder twisted the wire into two neat little coils, each roughly a third of the circumference of a coffee bean. Using a pair of wire clippers, he easily trimmed each end and produced a spooled wire barb. He made a few more ex-perimental barbs and then threaded them, one by one, down a strip of wire. He quickly realized that he would need a way to hold the barbs in place or they would all bunch up at one end. The solution: he added a second clean thread of steel wire, running parallel to the first one. This one could be twisted around the first wire both before and after each barb to hold the barbs in place.

This coffee-grinder configuration of a wire barb became the pro-totype for what Joseph Glidden would appropriately name and pat-ent as "The Winner." It would dominate barbed-wire sales for a gen-eration. Pleased with his invention, Glidden hung his demonstration wire between two posts at the front gate to his property. A few days later, Isaac Elwood, who by then had come up with his own barbed wire, rode out in his buggy with his wife to see what Glidden had come up with. He swore in dismay when he saw what Glidden had done, recognizing instantly that it easily surpassed his own crude version. He went home, and after sleeping on it for a night, admit-ted defeat and approached Glidden about forming a partnership to patent and commercially develop the new wire. Glidden agreed.

Jacob Haish, the German lumberman, had been busy too. In fact, in the race to patent barbed wire, his "S" version single-loop barb would actually beat Glidden to the patent office by a week. In fact, Haish would receive three separate patents before Glidden had one. The two competing camps and their emerging companies would fight it out in patent court in the years to come. Patent suits would also become their preferred method for fending off other entrants into the field. Haish's suit against Glidden finally reached the U.S. Supreme Court in 1892, where it lost.

But credit for truly commercializing the technology goes to a young twenty-one-year-old from Illinois named John Warne Gates, who in 1876 took Elwood and Glidden's product down to San Antonio, a mecca for the Texas cattle business. There one night, while sitting in a Mexican chili parlor and staring out the window at a snake-oil salesman peddling his wares in Military Plaza, Gates had his own epiphany. What he needed, he realized, was some dramatic way to sell the world on the virtues of barbed wire. So why not build a corral in the center of town made entirely of barbed wire? Why not fill it with the most ornery longhorn bulls he could find and demonstrate that the barbed wire could contain them? With the town's permission, he set to work on his publicity stunt, constructing a wire corral the likes of which no one had ever seen before. The mystery surrounding his project created its own sensation, and a huge crowd turned up on the day of the demonstration. Much like the snake-oil salesman, he began to bark out his pitch to the crowd: "This is the finest fencing in the world. Light as air. Stronger than whiskey. Cheaper than dirt. All steel, and miles long. The cattle ain't born that can get through it. Bring on your steers, gentlemen!"

At this point, a group of longhorn bulls — historical accounts put the number anywhere from 25 to 135 — were herded into the enclosure. Gates then let the technology speak for itself. Provoked by the crowd, the irate bulls took turns charging into the wire fence, only to retreat, stung by the barbs. Even when two men carrying lit torches stirred up the bulls, they failed to escape. Eventually, chastened by their painful encounters with the sharp prongs of the wire, they began to mill unhappily at a safe distance from the fencing.

According to most accounts, by nightfall Gates had sold hundreds of miles of the product at eighteen cents a pound and made his first small killing in wire. Later, he would argue with Elwood and his partners over his share of the profits, quit, and move to St. Louis to start a firm of his own. Using his extensive contacts from his years as a salesman—and willfully violating the patents of others in the industry—he built up his own company and then systematically bought out his competitors. He created the great monopoly of the wire business, American Steel and Wire, which he sold in 1901 to U.S. Steel. Not satisfied, he went on to build and sell railroads and helped develop the city of Port Arthur, Texas. A compulsive gambler who had grown up playing poker in a West Chicago railroad yard, Gates once participated in a weeklong marathon poker game on a slow train from Chicago to New York. In 1900 he reportedly won $600,000 on a $70,000 bet on a horse race in England. Perhaps most memorably, he was said to have bet $1 million on which of two raindrops on a windowpane would reach the sill first—history fails to record whether he won. When "Bet-a-Million" Gates died of throat cancer in Paris in 1911 at age forty-six, a funeral was thrown for him at the Plaza Hotel in New York.

Thanks to Gates's promotional boost, barbed-wire sales began one of those accelerating "rapid adoption" curves that make Wall Street investors giddy and rich. The business quickly grew to gigantic proportions: 2.8 million pounds of the wire were produced in 1876; 12.8 million pounds in 1877; 26.6 million pounds in 1878; 50.3 million pounds in 1879; and 80.5 million pounds in 1880. And that was just the beginning: in 1950 some 482 million pounds would be made and sold. Different styles of barbs emerged, such as the "spur-wheel" or the "chain-link," and the once brittle and uneven mild steel improved in tensile strength and went from being painted to being galvanized.

Eventually the area around DeKalb, Illinois, would become a sort of Silicon Valley of barbed-wire innovation where, at one point, some thirteen companies launched factories engaged in manufacturing the wire.

Glidden's simple modification of plain wire fencing proved to be a surprisingly transformative piece of technology. Initially it was popular among homesteaders and the railroads, but it wasn't long before cattle ranchers found uses for barbed wire too. Bulls let loose on the open range typically had five times the mortality rate of cows. The cattlemen could better protect their bulls, which were more expensive than cows, by fencing them in and, at the same time, they could better control the breeding process. Barbed wire had other advantages: it helped cut costs. Yes, you faced the upfront expense of buying and installing the wire, but you then no longer had to worry about your cattle wandering off and mixing with other herds, with the ensuing problems of altered brands and stolen mavericks. The fencing also reduced losses from predation — wolves being a particular problem. If your ranch was fenced with barbed wire, you no longer needed to participate in labor-intensive roundups twice a year, which meant you needed fewer cowboys, which in turn meant lower labor costs and improved profitability. You could also use the fencing to keep homesteaders out and to section off watering holes or the best grassland for your exclusive use — at least that was the new thinking, and it would prove controversial. The economics were crystal clear: the bigger the ranch, the greater the return on investment from barbed-wire fencing. This largely explains how the XIT Ranch in Texas, on a strip of land some thirty miles wide that ran irregularly through ten counties on the Panhandle, came to encompass some three million acres, the largest fenced cattle ranch in the world.

But barbed wire did have a few notable drawbacks. For example, in a blizzard it trapped cattle against the fences, where in some cases they froze to death; without the wire they could drift downwind safely before a storm. The wire also gouged holes in the animals' skin, leading to screwworm infestations; screwworm flies would lay their eggs on the open wounds. That problem was solved with the development in the mid-1880s of "obvious" wire, with shortened prongs. But whatever the drawbacks, barbed wire proved irresistible.

The cattle barons' adoption of barbed wire marks the moment when their interests began to diverge from those of their smaller counterparts in the cattle business — and from the cowboys and the homesteaders — which would lead to small-scale conflict, such as episodes of fence-cutting, then ultimately escalate into the range wars that arose late in the cattle-boom era.

Other factors would contribute to these conflicts, such as drought, rising unemployment among cowboys, and the fear of monopolies. But much of the controversy came down to who was using the new wire and in what manner.

The barbed wire that so many seized upon as a useful new tool had other sweeping effects on the history and culture of the open range. It removed forever any chance of widespread rehabilitation of the bison herds or the numerous Plains Indian tribes who had once depended on them for their livelihood. The open range could now be divvied up into ranches and homesteads. In this sense the development of barbed wire slammed the door on one culture and opened it to another.

10

Frewen's Castle

Moreton Frewen and his brother Richard became early members of the Cheyenne Club. They, like Hubert and Arthur Teschemacher and the Teschemachers' Harvard friends, were among the wealthy young men who went through the exhilarating exercise of arriving in Cheyenne, buying a ranch, and shopping locally to equip it. And like the Teschemacher and Oelrichs brothers, they soon built a house in Cheyenne in order to maintain a local presence, for purposes of business and pleasure.

When the Frewen brothers first arrived, they spent the summer of 1878 in the company of three Cambridge University friends, hunting game in western Wyoming. The men shot elk, mule deer, pronghorn, and bighorn sheep, and camped at night in tiny two-man alpine tents with socket poles. They rested tucked up in sleeping bags made of opossum fur, lined with the soft pelts of bobcat and lynx. Late in the year, after their friends returned to England, the brothers began to search in earnest for a suitable location to launch their cattle operations.

Heading out from what is today Cody, Wyoming, and accompanied by two guides, the brothers picked their way through the Bighorn Mountains to inspect some land in a distant valley, now devoid of Indians, which they had heard might be appropriate for cattle ranching. They traveled through countryside teeming with game—a sportsman's paradise, as idyllic as anything they had seen, other than in East Africa. Along the route they encountered friendly but impoverished Shoshone Indians armed with nothing but bows and arrows and a single worn-out Springfield rifle. The Indians asked them to shoot some buffalo for them, to use for the tribe's winter rations; the brothers happily complied. A few days later, while crossing a pass at a higher elevation, a heavy snowfall stymied their progress. The drifts were impassable until their guide conceived of the idea of using a nearby bison herd as a snowplow. Galloping their horses at the herd and whooping and shouting, they succeeded in driving the animals before them like a herd of long-horns. The bison trampled a trail for five miles through the snow and clear over the top of the pass. The lead bulls, Frewen recalled, rose and fell through the deep snow like porpoises through waves. A day later the four men rode down out of the mountains into a wide, long basin, two hundred miles long and one hundred miles wide that, amazingly, was free of snow. The valley was named after the Powder River, which they could see wending its way down the middle, bordered by cottonwood trees. A few minutes later they found themselves cantering through tawny autumn grass seemingly as thick and luxuriant as fox fur.

They were struck by the serenity of the area and by the smooth, undulating landscape, almost sensuous in its contours. Even with their limited knowledge of the cattle business, the brothers understood that this land was ideally suited for grazing. For one thing, water was plentiful. Indeed, according to the historian John W. Davis, who took the trouble to count, thirteen deep streams flowed off the eastern slopes of the Bighorn Mountains into what would come to be called Johnson County, providing ample crystal-clear water—and ample water usually meant ample grass. Most of these streams flowed into the Powder River or the Tongue River, both of which flowed north into Montana. Furthermore, the gentle terrain was easily navigated on horseback.

The Frewen brothers had stumbled onto some of the most pristine, fertile grazing land in the American West. If such a thing as a cattleman's Shangri-la existed, this was surely it. Others who came later would feel much the same way, and it seems no accident, in hindsight, that it would be here in the Powder River Basin that the battle over land would be most hotly contested — and where the open-range cattle era would come to its bitter close, in a battle between cattle barons and cowboys. Then, a generation later, this basin would become the epicenter of the U.S. coal industry, the site of its richest deposits and largest mines. Moreton Frewen never forgot the moment when he discovered it. "Not a human habitation was in sight," he recalled in his memoirs. "No cattle, nor could we make out any buffalo . . . How amazing the idea that for five hundred miles at least this immense area was destined to fill up with settlers and their cattle during the next five years." But for that one giddy moment, the valley was open range and all theirs, free for the taking.

By the following spring the brothers had begun to build what would amount to a large hunting lodge to use as their headquarters. They would name the structure Home Ranche, but the building was so large by the standards of the American West at that time that it quickly came to be called Frewen's Castle. They wanted to build a structure impressive and comfortable enough to lure their aristocratic friends over from England on annual hunting expeditions. While entertaining these people on the banks of the Powder River, the brothers hoped to induce them to invest with them in the cattle trade.

The house was built of sheared pine logs and plaster and situated on an elevation overlooking a bend in the Powder River. It bore a distinct resemblance to Brickwall, the Tudor manor house in Sussex where the brothers had grown up, although on a far smaller scale. The first floor included an office, a drawing room, a kitchen, a pantry, and a great hall. The drawing room featured an upright piano purchased in Chicago, along with all the furniture, the bulk of it shipped out to Rock Creek by train. From there the piano had been carried the last two hundred miles to the ranch on a bouncing buckboard hauled by oxen. Today it resides at the Jim Gatchell Memorial Museum in Buffalo, Wyoming, along with a slab of siding from Frewen's Castle and a black-and-white photo of the lanky Moreton Frewen himself, dashingly dressed in custom-made buckskins.

The great hall, some forty feet square, was dominated at either end by stone fireplaces constructed of river rocks worn smooth by spring torrents. The stripped-pine log walls of the room were soon adorned with Native American spears and feathered war bonnets, beaver skins, elk antlers, and the mounted heads of bison, deer, and bighorn sheep. A walnut staircase, imported from England, led up to a small mezzanine balcony where the brothers envisioned an orchestra one day performing for their guests. The house was every bit as grand as the brothers' ambitions. Boasted Moreton Frewen, "Twenty of us can dine in the hall comfortably, and after we can move out and lounge on the piazza and watch the great purple shadows stealing down over the prairie from the mountains."

The drawing room bookcase held a copy of Tocqueville's *Democracy in America,* Draper's *Intellectual Development of Europe,* and works by the historians James Anthony Froude and Thomas Babington Macaulay and the popular novelist of the day, Lord Lytton. Over the piano hung a colored engraving of a painting by George Earle called *A Polo-match at Hurlingham,* depicting three of Moreton Frewen's close personal friends, Charlie Fitzwilliam, John Brocklehurst, and Sir Charles Michael Wolseley, all of whom would visit the ranch. In the colored print the men are seated on horseback on the field where British polo was first formally established, in 1869, at the legendary Hurlingham Club on the banks of the Thames River, on the outskirts of London.

The hunting in the Powder River Basin and in the neighboring Bighorn Mountains was exceptional. Fearful that word would leak out and the English hunting establishment would overrun the area,

Frewen wrote a letter to *The Field* wildly exaggerating the danger of Indian attacks. "I feel a proprietary right to these mountains, and 'we' will keep the game for our friends," he wrote to his fiancée.

The Frewens acquired their first herd, the "76" brand, from a rancher on the Sweetwater named Tim Foley. According to local lore, Moreton Frewen paid twice for the cattle. As Foley marched the cattle past the Englishman so he could count them, Foley had them pass around a hill and back into the corral — so that they went by twice. In his memoirs Frewen vehemently denied the veracity of this tall tale, insisting that they were "stories without a vestige of truth." The actual methodology he used to purchase the herd, he claimed, was the standard one of the day: he looked at the average number of calves produced by the herd over the prior three years and then multiplied it by five to estimate the total size of the herd. But such "book count" methods of estimating the size of herds, as opposed to actual inventories, were suspect, one of the accounting problems that would come to haunt the open-range cattle industry.

Other acquisitions followed, and the Frewen herds would eventually swell to seventy thousand head. But before the first cattle arrived, the brothers put out the word in Cheyenne that they needed cowboys. Soon they had gathered a crew of twenty or so, along with a foreman, an Englishman named Fred Hesse, to oversee them. Hesse would play a major role in the range wars to follow. The cowboys were housed in a bunkhouse a few miles south of the ranch headquarters so that their branding activities, broncobusting, games of horseshoes, and general rowdiness did not disturb the tranquility of Frewen's Castle and the steady stream of hunting houseguests arriving from England.

In its early years, the remote location of the Big Horn Ranche Company, the name of the Frewens' business, presented real risks. It was not easy to get sufficient provisions — let alone a piano — in or out. That first October, Moreton nearly lost his life attempting to walk the last forty miles to the Rock Creek train station after his horse went lame. For the final ten miles of the journey he had to fight his way through three-foot drifts of deep and crusty snow. In all it took him twenty-six hours to walk the forty miles, fighting off sleep and an insatiable desire to simply quit. "Never in my life was I in such peril," he would recall.

In order for the ranch to function in such a remote outpost, the brothers needed additional infrastructure. First they built a general store and a post office at the Powder River crossing, twenty miles downstream from their ranch. To communicate with the store they erected one of the first telephone lines in the area — and then proceeded to confound the Indians at the trading post with the new technology. Moreton also began the construction of a refrigeration plant on Sherman Hill, the highest point along the Union Pacific in the Territory of Wyoming. Here he hoped to run a beef storage and packing plant without the use of real refrigeration — taking advantage of the year-round cold weather on the hilltop to preserve the meat. And not long after, he took the lead role in helping to organize Johnson County into a bona fide county in Wyoming, gathering the necessary signatures, even from men he suspected were outlaws.

From the beginning, the ambitious brothers were game for any venture of a speculative nature. Almost immediately they explored the possibility of buying a coal mine in southern Idaho, on the theory that coal could be shipped cheaper from there to San Francisco than from Pennsylvania. Next, they took a flier on some bat caves in Texas, hoping to export the guano to England either as a source of saltpeter to make explosives or as garden fertilizer. They borrowed the money to purchase the caves, only to discover that their partner was an incompetent charlatan with a gambling problem. The business collapsed when the first shipment of guano delivered to England killed their friends' gardenias. The bungled venture was an omen of far greater failures to come.

When fall arrived, the two brothers headed back east. Like many of the wealthy cattle barons of the day, they would become seasonal ranchers and largely absentee landlords — another factor that contributed to mismanagement in the nascent industry and a distrust between the cattle ranchers and their hired cowboys.

In New York, Moreton made it a point to visit his former Leicestershire neighbor and childhood friend W. B. Duncan, who now lived in the brownstone at One Fifth Avenue. That fall, at a dinner party around Duncan's "poem" of a dining room table, a lovely oval made out of Honduras mahogany "lacquered with age and care," Frewen first met and befriended the men of New York's emerging horseracing establishment, a group that included two especially close friends and business partners: Leonard "Larry" Jerome and William "Bill" Travers, two of the three Wall Street millionaires who had thrown the celebrated Gold, Silver, and Diamond dinners at Delmonico's. The popular Travers was a great wit despite his pronounced stutter. Moreton once heard Jerome tease him, "Really, Bill, you stammer much more here in New York than at home in Baltimore."

"H-h-have to," replied Travers. "New York is a much larger town."

Moreton was particularly fond of Travers, who enjoyed carousing at night with the younger crowd, but it was the walrus-mustached Leonard Jerome who soon would become his father-in-law. Jerome had made a fortune as a short-seller on Wall Street, much as Joseph P. Kennedy would do a generation later. He had built an enormous five-story mansion at 32 East 26th Street overlooking Madison Square Park; it featured a six-hundred-seat theater, its own ballroom, and an attached three-story stable for horses and carriages. During the draft riots of 1863, Jerome had manned a Gatling gun in a window of the *New York Times* building at 41 Park Row, determined to protect the young newspaper, in which he had an investment, from rioters. Short-selling, however, was and is a perilous Wall Street activity. Jerome made a large fortune during his early years on Wall Street, lost everything in 1856, made most of it back in the 1860s and the 1870s, but now was in the process of losing it all over again.

In addition to his love of racing, Jerome had an eye for the ladies. He was allegedly the father of the celebrated opera singer Minnie Hauk, whose career he would dutifully nurture. His long-suffering wife, dismayed by his infidelity and by her own inability as an arriviste to crack the top echelon of Manhattan society, presided over by Mrs. Astor and her chosen Four Hundred, eventually moved to Paris with the couple's three attractive young daughters. Paris was still a city and a royal court where the nouveaux riches from around the world were welcomed and included in the proceedings. The eldest Jerome daughter, Clara, debuted at the court of Empress Eugénie, and all three girls quickly befriended members of the French nobility. Once at home in the French court, Mrs. Jerome set about trying to engineer brilliant marital matches for her daughters among the European aristocracy. But before that could happen, the four women were forced to flee to London at the outbreak of the Franco-Prussian War. They narrowly escaped the Prussian siege of Paris, boarding the last train to leave the city.

In London the four women took up residence at Brown's Hotel in Mayfair. Soon the daughters joined the list of the hundred or so wealthy American debutantes singled out for marriage by those members of the British aristocracy and landed gentry who were desperate to restore their dwindling fortunes.

The first to the altar was the middle daughter, a regal beauty named Jennie. At a ball in honor of the future Czar Nicholas II and his wife on board the guard ship *Ariadne* during the Cowes regatta week, Jennie met Lord Randolph Churchill. The two fell instantly in love. Churchill was the third son of the seventh Duke of Marlborough, whose family ranked highest among the peerage after the members of the royal family. Leonard Jerome made the marriage possible by providing the couple with a dowry of ten thousand dollars annually. Even with that money, the young couple would live beyond their means, as did the rest of the Churchill family, which, despite possessing the fantastically grand Blenheim Palace and enormous landholdings, struggled to stay solvent. Salvation would come in 1895 in the form of an arranged marriage between the ninth duke and Consuelo Vanderbilt, the only daughter of the railroad magnate William K. Vanderbilt, a good friend of Leonard Jerome.

Consuelo brought with her a $2.5 million dowry and $100,000 in annual income for life, rescuing the Marlborough fortune.

Clara Jerome, the oldest of Leonard's daughters, was fair-skinned, blond-haired, and blue-eyed. Chronically late for everything, she possessed a dreamy, romantic nature that stood in sharp contrast to the steely ambition of her sister Jennie. Lord Essex, an English earl, had courted Clara, and she had "more or less accepted him" when her father happened to introduce her to Moreton Frewen in the late fall of 1879, in New York City. Entranced by Clara, Moreton turned on his loquacious charm. After an initial and perhaps perfunctory rejection, she accepted his marriage proposal. The only hitch in the proceedings occurred when Leonard Jerome insisted that, as far as he was concerned, there had been no understanding that he would provide a dowry for Clara. Moreton, flabbergasted, protested and the engagement nearly unraveled.

"Now there was no understanding of the sort," Moreton sputtered to Clara in a letter from London. "There was no such folly on your side or mine!" Then he hastened to add, "You understand, darling, that I am very far from complaining that I am to take you with nothing."

In the end Moreton was appeased when Leonard gave Clara an exquisite thirty-diamond necklace — presumably the one that Leonard had bought for his wife for thirty thousand dollars at Tiffany & Company some years before. Although the diamonds would come in handy, no cash would be forthcoming to the newlyweds, and that would prove to be a problem.

The couple was married at Grace Church in Manhattan in June 1881 — but only after Clara arrived late for the ceremony, panicking the bridegroom. A reception followed in the ballroom of the nearby Jerome mansion on Madison Square, although the family no longer occupied the property. Baron Bagot, an aide-de-camp to the governor-general of Canada, was Moreton's best man, and among those in attendance at the packed church ceremony was Lord Stafford, the son of the third Duke of Sutherland, England's wealthiest man and owner of more property than anyone else in the realm, and

Pierre Lorillard IV, a close friend of Moreton and a fellow racing enthusiast.

The previous day Lorillard, standing beside the stock ticker in the Union Club in Manhattan, had learned that his horse Iroquois, sired by the great stallion Leamington, had won the prestigious Epsom Derby, the first American horse ever to win a classic European flat race. Moreton Frewen's friend Fred Archer, the jockey from the Doncaster Cup, was the winning jockey. Frewen and Leonard Jerome joined Pierre Lorillard at the club to celebrate the victory. In the years to come, Lorillard, the heir to a fortune in tobacco and snuff and the man who founded the exclusive community of Tuxedo Park, just north of New York City, would prove to be a loyal friend to Moreton, lending him money for a number of his ill-fated ventures.

The newlyweds honeymooned at West Point, and then Moreton took Clara out to Wyoming to visit Frewen's Castle for the first time. He hoped the trip would become their annual summer pilgrimage. At first, all went according to plan. Clara wrote her sister Leonie rapturous descriptions of the landscape: "This is our *real* honeymoon. Moreton is the greatest darling *sur terre* [on earth] . . . the air is perfectly delicious and the scenery so beautiful with the snowcapped Bighorn Mountains in the near distance and troops of antelope come by our house going down to the river to drink." That summer a steady stream of houseguests arrived to try their hand at the local big-game hunting, among them Moreton's great friend the ostentatious and spendthrift Hugh Lowther and his wife, the former Lady Grace Gordon. A year later, with the death of his brother, Lowther would become the Earl of Lonsdale and heir to the Cumberland coal mines. He would earn the sobriquet the Yellow Earl for his penchant for dressing his liverymen in yellow, for his fleet of yellow automobiles, and for the yellow gardenias that he always wore as boutonnières. Other guests included Major General Brocklehurst, a future equerry to Queen Victoria, his wife, and the polo player Charley Fitzwilliam. Guests in future years were no less remarkable: the seventh Earl of Mayo, whose father, the assassinated fourth viceroy of India, had been stabbed to death by a mentally ill man at a penal colony on the Andaman Islands; the fifth Earl of Donoughmore, whose incompetent Irish Hunt Contingent would become the laughingstock of the Boer War; the Marquess of Queensberry, described by Oscar Wilde, with whom he feuded, as "drunken, déclassé and half-witted"; Sir Maurice de Bunsen, who shot the ranch's only milk cow, somehow mistaking it for a bison; and the Bakers — Sir Samuel Baker, an explorer, naturalist, and big-game hunter, and his wife, Lady Baker, whom Sir Samuel had acquired at the Vidin slave market in Bulgaria.

Cattle ranching took a back seat to hunting and fishing with this set. One entry in the visitors' book read, "A big bear which measured eight feet six by eight, came near being the end of Hanna [a hunting guide]. Lovat Wise [a houseguest], at fifteen feet, killed the brute on him. Hanna badly mauled but will live." Trout, weighing one to three pounds, were caught by the bushel in the Powder River.

In August, Clara discovered that she was pregnant, and the couple announced the news to their assembled houseguests, who responded with toasts and cheers. Then, in early October, while on a hunting trip, Clara became ill and needed to be rushed to a doctor in Cheyenne — a day's journey south. There she suffered a miscarriage. Chastened by the experience, she headed back east. She would never again return to Frewen's Castle or, for that matter, to the American West. Her three children would all be born in London.

This was the official beginning of Moreton Frewen's troubles.

Not long after, Moreton and Richard, equal partners in the Big Horn Ranche Company, began to feud. "We had a fearful row and shame to say I had to lay hand on him," Moreton recalled. Richard was cranky and quarrelsome, and Moreton was self-centered and impractical, but the differences amounted to more than style and temperament. They mostly concerned Moreton's free-spending ways and the absence of any profits from the cattle business, as well as the high cost of maintaining Frewen's Castle. Finally, Richard announced that he wanted out of the partnership. Moreton, who possessed even less money than Richard, lacked the funds to buy his brother out. It looked for a time as though the ranch would have to be sold just as the business was starting to achieve scale. Then Moreton concocted a plan. He would turn the ranch into a proper cattle company, creating and selling shares, much as he heard the Scots were doing in Edinburgh and Dundee. The brothers would sell their ownership in the business to the company in return for shares. With the additional capital thus raised, the business could be expanded rather than folded. Ideally, Moreton would stay on as the manager.

He set off at once for London, determined to make the deal work.

To create a joint-stock company required at least seven investors. That part would not be a problem. But Moreton wanted a few prominent people to serve on his board of directors. The latest trend in the City of London was to include peers on the board of a company, to add aristocratic cachet. They became known as "ornamental" or "guinea pig" directorates. Fortunately, an American friend of Clara's named Consuelo Iznaga, the daughter of a wealthy Cuban diplomat and sugar baron, had recently married the son of the seventh Duke of Manchester. The duke, fifty-nine, had just returned from a business trip to America and reportedly was shopping for investment opportunities. Frewen hurried over to see him at his London office and signed him on as the titular chairman. Once the duke was in place, other investors, such as the Earl of Wharncliffe, a Yorkshire rail and coal baron, and Lord Henry Neville agreed to subscribe to the shares. There would even be one Dundee director, Andrew Witton, who served on a number of cattle-company boards and managed the estates of the Earl of Wharncliffe.

The Companies Act of 1862 required that joint-stock companies with twenty or more shareholders incorporate, and that in turn meant that the London Stock Exchange recognized the entity as a public company. In late 1882 Moreton Frewen's new Powder River Cattle Company became the first British cattle company to achieve this status.

In all, a total of £300,000 in capital was raised: ten thousand preferred shares were sold for £10 each and forty thousand common shares at £5 each. Frewen was paid £12,000 in cash and given eight thousand shares of the common stock in return for surrendering the lands that he had acquired under the Homestead Act and the Desert Act, 160 acres and 640 acres respectively, and a herd of cattle that now numbered forty thousand. He successfully contracted to be manager of the company until November 1, 1887. His salary would consist of one-third of all surplus annual profits, but only after a 10 percent dividend had been paid to shareholders. The property would be appraised at the end of his contract term in 1887, and if the value of the company exceeded the initial £300,000, he was to receive one-third of any surplus over that amount — the so-called deferred incentive. Only the most sought-after hedge funds and private-equity partnerships today can negotiate such a generous compensation plan. Moreton had significant incentives to make the company succeed.

And yet, as with every prospectus, the devil resides in the details. By agreeing to a preferred stock issue, Frewen not only gave the preferred shareholders first dibs on the annual dividends, but also preferential treatment if and when a liquidation might be necessary, a detail he either overlooked or conceded to too readily. The preferred shares could be repurchased, but only after five years. Apparently Frewen viewed this repurchase as a virtual certainty and thus did not concern himself with the provision, although that too would prove to be a mistake. This group of preferred shareholders knew full well that they would have effective control of the company if something went seriously wrong.

Prophetically, Moreton's brother Richard expressed his skepticism from the outset. "I tell you plainly, you can not run this . . . They are all good schemes but you can't run them." Undeterred, and thrilled with what he accomplished, Frewen returned to Wyoming. With the cash raised from the sale of shares to the public, he began to buy up neighboring cattle herds. He wrote a letter to his wife, urging her to spend freely: "Do not stint yourself in any way darling little wifie, we are making money so fast it is no imprudence to spend freely and enjoy; I hope you have succeeded in getting a footman. Has the new carriage been finished?" In another letter to her he wrote, "Dear vulgar money. Don't laugh at my enthusiasm if I say the dream of diamonds may be near."

A month or so later, he wrote a circular to his shareholders, a lengthy dissertation in which he hoped to show off his deep understanding of the cattle business and his command of its every nuance. First, he dismissed outright and as virtually impossible the threat of overgrazing. Next, he brushed aside any risk of a collapse in beef prices, remarking, "Nor is it reasonable to anticipate any fall in the price of beef, on the contrary it is a problem of great perplexity how, at any price, the population of the United States is to be supplied." In fact, he argued, beef sales would need to grow by 25 percent each year just to meet the current demand, and that demand was growing as rapidly as the U.S. population. Gaining steam, he then blithely dismissed the dangers posed by poor weather: "I may also fairly claim for Powder River a local exemption from snowfalls, which is well-known throughout the territories, and it was this tradition, during the winter of 1878, that first directed my attention to that range." He concluded by deploring the practice of buying western land to secure legal rights to the open range — it was money that would come straight out of dividends, and he saw no reason for it: "I can imagine no more mistaken policy than to pay money for land which you can possess for nothing . . ." After professing a reluctance to predict investment returns, he then contradicted himself by stating that he saw no reason why a £10,000 investment in the company couldn't double in four years and pay 15 to 20 percent annual dividends in the interim.

Alas, within a short period of time he would prove to be categorically wrong on every single point.

The Frenchman, the Marquis de Morès, meanwhile had arrived in the Badlands of the Dakota Territory with an option to purchase a parcel of land and a handful of buildings. But on inspection the buildings proved worthless and the land not worth the price that was being asked. He tore up his option, crossed the Little Missouri River on horseback, found a parcel that he liked much better, and bought the new property instead. After deciding to dedicate the area, soon to become a cattle town, to his pregnant wife, Medora — and naming it in her honor — he and his private secretary, William van Driesche, smashed a bottle of champagne over a tent pole to commemorate the occasion.

It wasn't long before the marquis had dispensed with the tent. He bought a lavishly furnished railroad car from the Northern Pacific Railroad and had it moved off the tracks to a site near Medora. There he lived comfortably as he began to assemble his empire. He immediately bought up twenty-four thousand acres of surrounding land, hired more than 150 carpenters and staff, and began to construct the headquarters for his company, which would soon become the largest abattoir west of Chicago, incorporated as the Northern Pacific Refrigerator Car Company. He also launched construction on his own residence, high on a bluff overlooking the Little Missouri River. The locals would call this twenty-six-room clapboard house, with its wide veranda, "the Chateau." But the word does not do justice to what was essentially a large hunting lodge, containing eight small bedrooms spread over two floors, a maid's quarters, and a wine cellar. Although huge for the American West in its day, it was modest in comparison with the stately villas with their crenelated roofs that the marquis and the marquise were accustomed to in the south of France. With his home under way, the marquis organized the construction of the new town's first buildings, including its church and its general store. He proceeded to literally, and almost single-handedly, put Medora on the map.

Not content with that, he bought, for $300 apiece, four lightly used Concord stagecoaches, which each retailed for $1,050 when new. The Abbot-Downing Company, based in Concord, New Hampshire, had built these gorgeous conveyances. De Morès outfitted them with 160 horses and prepared to run a triweekly coach service between Medora and Deadwood, 215 miles south, a trip that would take thirty-two hours and cost the ten or eleven passengers $21.50 per person.

The coaches were lovely to look at because each had received an extraordinary amount of custom attention and handcrafting. Built out of white kiln-dried ash and hand-tooled poplar, with hand-forged Norwegian-iron axles and tires, they received multiple coats of exterior paint. The paint was then pumiced and layered with double coats of varnish. The design innovation that distinguished the coaches from the British stages, which preceded them by 140 years, was their suspension system. The British steel springs had been swapped for four-inch-wide, six-ply belts made of steer leather, which more gently cradled the carriage over the bumpy western terrain. You might get seasick from the swaying, but you weren't likely to get catapulted out of your seat. The least bumpy place to sit was with your back to the driver, also known as the reinsman, or "whip."

How to behave on a stagecoach journey? Rules of etiquette had evolved in consideration of fellow passengers and personal comfort. The *Omaha Herald* advised the following:

Bathe your feet before starting in cold weather, and wear loose overshoes and gloves two or three sizes too large. When the driver asks you to get out and walk, do it without grumbling. He will not request it unless absolutely necessary. If a team runs away, sit still and take your chances; if you jump, nine times out of ten you will be hurt . . . Don't growl at food at stations; stage companies generally provide the best they can get . . . Don't smoke a strong pipe inside especially early in the morning; spit on the leeward side of the coach. If you take anything in a bottle, pass it around; a man who drinks by himself in such a case is lost to all human feeling . . . Be sure to take two heavy blankets with you; you will need them. Don't swear, nor lop over on your neighbor when sleeping. Don't ask how far it is to the next station until you get there . . . Don't discuss politics or religion, nor point out places on the road where horrible murders have been

committed, if delicate women are among the passengers. Don't linger too long at the pewter wash basin at the station. Don't grease your hair before starting or dust will stick there . . .
Don't imagine for a moment you are going on a picnic; expect annoyance, discomfort, and some hardship. If you are disappointed, thank Heaven.

Driving a stagecoach was no simple matter. The reinsman held the three sets of reins between different sets of fingers in both hands, taking the slack for each rein in and out with the thumbs and thus effectively controlling each of the six horses independently, while simultaneously operating the brake by means of a foot pedal. It took practice.

But the Medora stagecoach operation was a fiasco from the outset. The horses, bought at a hundred dollars a head, were broncos and had not been trained for the harness. Just to get them into the breast straps and traces at the front of the stagecoach entailed blindfolding them and pushing and pulling them into place. Roosevelt's biographer Hermann Hagedorn described what happened next:

"Ready?" asked the man at the head of the near leader.
"All set," answered the other helpers.
"Let 'er go!" called the drivers.
The helpers jerked the blinds from the horses' eyes. The broncos jumped into their collars as a unit. As a unit, however, they surged back, as they became suddenly conscious of the horrors they dreaded most — restraint. The off leader made a wild swerve to the right, backing toward the coach, and dragging the near leader and the near swing horse from their feet. The off leader, unable to forge ahead, made a wild leap from the off swing horse, and fairly crashed him to earth with his feet, himself tripping on the harness and rolling at random in the welter, his snapping hooves flashing in every direction . . . The near wheeler was bucking as though there were no other horse

within a hundred miles; the off wheeler had broken his single-tree and was facing the coach, delivering kicks at the melée behind him with whole hearted abandon and rigid impartiality.

That was not how it was supposed to work.

Compounding the problem, the marquis could not find a manager capable of running the operation. The first manager quit; the second, a local saloon owner, proved incompetent; the third, Arthur T. Packard, was the editor of the local newspaper, the *Cow Boy*. He too knew nothing about running a stagecoach service. Even if he had, he had little chance of succeeding: de Morès had never secured the government contract to carry the mail, the most lucrative aspect of any stagecoach business. Furthermore, the placer-mining business in Deadwood was soon replaced by deep-vein mining, which required far fewer miners. And when a silver strike was made in Coeur d'Alene, Idaho, most of the miners moved on, leaving de Morès with a virtually worthless stagecoach company serving a ghost town.

Much like Moreton Frewen and Theodore Roosevelt, de Morès was as interested in the local hunting opportunities as he was in his cattle and meatpacking venture. He and his wife would travel into the Rocky Mountains for a month at a time, accompanied by guides and numerous horses and wood wagons loaded with provisions. At night they slept in a custom-built hunting wagon, modeled on the one built for Napoleon's Russian campaign of 1812. Fully provisioned with table linens, china, and silver, it included folding tables and a bed. There is some question as to which of the pair was the better shot. Both were excellent marksmen. The marquis, for example, had been known to use a rifle to successfully take pigeons and sage grouse on the wing. But on one trip, the marquise took credit for killing three bears, compared to his two.

The marquis, however, soon grew jaded with hunting bears with a rifle. He announced to the *Bismarck Tribune* his intention to kill a grizzly bear with a bowie knife. He achieved the feat not long afterward. He set a bait trap along a riverbank not far from the Chateau, using the carcass of a horse. Then, hiding on foot in the shrubbery, he waited until a large grizzly arrived. He allowed the bear to claim the carcass and begin feeding before he stood up and showed himself. The bear, furious, charged him. De Morès held his ground until the last moment, when the bruin rose onto its hind legs and began swiping at him with its front paws. The expert fencer and swordsman sidestepped the attack and plunged the blade of his eight-inch hunting knife into the bear's heart, killing it instantly.

Barbed wire and the meatpacking cartel would prove to be de Morès's true undoing.

His problems first arose when he elected to fence his enormous new property with the newly available wire. Although in Europe it was perfectly normal to fence your property, and this is apparently why de Morès did it, the fences that he erected closed off access to the old Indian trails used by local commercial hunters. Given the topography of the Badlands, its tight mix of often-impassible buttes and coulees and plateaus, navigating from point to point was difficult enough without having to circumnavigate pastures or acreage now enclosed by barbed wire. The hunters were soon forced to rely on local roads and lost access to some of their best hunting grounds. While no one disputed that de Morès had the legal right to enclose his land — he had bought it outright — the fences were still an affront to the hunters, and they began to cut the wire surreptitiously. Also, the local nesters — settlers with no legal right to the land they occupied — now found themselves dispossessed squatters on de Morès's property, which infuriated them. The marquis had already raised the hackles of the locals with his aristocratic hauteur; he delivered orders to his hired men in a high-handed, peremptory manner. His conceit simply rubbed people wrong. As he told the local rancher Howard Eaton, "My plan is altogether feasible. I do not merely think this. I know it. My intuition tells me so. I pride myself on having a natural intuition. It takes me only a few seconds to understand a situation that other men have to puzzle over for hours. I seem to see every side of a question at once. I assure you, I am gifted in this way. I have wonderful insight."

But not enough insight, it would seem, to stay out of trouble.

Three local hunters, irate about the new fences and emboldened by alcohol at a local saloon, threatened to shoot the French nobleman the next time they encountered him. Word of their threats got back to de Morès. After confirming with the local justice of the peace that he had every right to defend himself, he decided to take preemptive measures, especially after the threats escalated and he narrowly avoided one attempt on his life. De Morès and two of his men set an ambush on the outskirts of the town for the three disgruntled hunters. A shootout ensued. One hunter was shot through the neck and killed, a second escaped, and the third took a bullet in the thigh but managed to hobble off to safety. De Morès and his men emerged from the skirmish unharmed.

A handful of enraged townspeople vowed to convict de Morès of murder. They brought suit against him and managed to have him arrested and jailed. Over the next three years, in a case of not double but *triple* jeopardy, he was acquitted three times of the same murder by three different justices of the peace. His reputation with the neighboring townspeople would never recover.

But de Morès's fundamental problem didn't involve barbed wire at all. His gigantic abattoir was simply ill conceived. Five months after laying the foundation, he had the operation up and running. In the first year it processed eighty steers a day. But the second year, 1884, was a dry year and the cattle never reached the desired weight and thus couldn't be slaughtered. He soon realized that he needed a year-round supply of beef to run an efficient, cost-effective meatpacking operation, and he simply didn't have it and wasn't likely ever to have it, given the severity of the winter weather and the grazing methods of the local cattlemen. He attempted to remedy the problem by launching a new feeding operation, shipping in grain from Chicago to fatten up penned cattle during the off-season. But beef prices had become a problem too, and he began to suspect that the Chicago meatpackers, fully apprised of what he was up to, had decided to make things difficult for him by keeping their prices inordinately low. Apparently he was unaware of the discounts that meatpackers and the railroads were offering to those who shipped their live cattle directly through to Chicago. Still, he continued to build out the operation, adding cold storage and ice stations along the rail route between Helena and Chicago. On more than one occasion those ice stations were not staffed and his freshly butchered meat soon spoiled. On a whim, he began to ship fresh West Coast salmon in his half-empty refrigerated railcars, and for a time he did so profitably.

In one final attempt to bypass the middlemen and thus increase the margins earned on his beef, the marquis opened his own retail butcher shops, first in St. Paul and then in some of the poorest sections of New York City. This latest initiative had his rich Wall Street bankroller and father-in-law, Louis von Hoffman, rolling his eyes. Von Hoffman is said to have remarked, "My God, de Morès has got that retail butcher's apron on me at last!" The Frenchman managed to open six stores in Manhattan, but the local butchers picketed them, smashed the plate-glass storefront windows, and spread rumors that the meat the shops sold was diseased. Worse, when de Morès attempted to float the shares of the retail company, capitalizing it at $10 million and projecting a possible three to four hundred outlets, the initial public offering flopped. Wall Street's moneymen showed their shrewd understanding of the power of Gustavus Swift and the beef-packing trust. They handicapped de Morès and refused to back him. One early venture partner in the operation, Sumner Teal, head of the Western Dressed Beef Company in Kansas City, had advanced de Morès seven thousand dollars for his expenses; he felt compelled to sue the marquis when the bill came in at fifty thousand.

By the fall of 1886, little had gone as de Morès had hoped, but he remained determined to prevail, convinced that he would finally have the abattoir fully operational and running profitably by the following spring. "There was something gorgeous in the Marquis' inability to know when he was beaten," wrote Hermann Hagedorn. "His power of self hypnotism was amazing." Dead ahead lay the Big Die-Up and the worst winter the Badlands had ever seen. De Morès's grand scheme was doomed.

11

The Nature Crusader

While Frewen and de Morès almost immediately encountered headwinds in the West, twenty-five-year-old Theodore Roosevelt seemed to thrive from his first days as a rancher.

The unusual geological features of the Dakota Badlands make it far different from the open plains of Montana or the pristine prairies of Frewen's Powder River Basin. In the Badlands, serrated bluffs give way to gorges and steep drainages where the hillsides have dissolved over time into carved ravines and twisted riverbeds, often dry in the summer, that eventually find their way to the Little Missouri River. From an airplane, the landscape resembles the deep fissures of a careworn face. At ground level, sandstone pinnacles, chimney rocks, and stone escarpments, streaked in purples and grays, reds and blacks, browns and yellows, jut into the air. Theodore Roosevelt described it as a landscape suitable for a story by Edgar Allan Poe. Where the Badlands end and the Montana prairies begin, the rolling land suddenly unfurls into a carpet of swaying grasslands, which stretch across a landscape so vast, under a sky so blue, they make a rider on horseback feel humble and small.

Roosevelt loved the area. "I have been having a glorious time here. I feel as absolutely free as a man could feel," he wrote in a letter to his sister Anna. In another letter to her in September he wrote, "So I have had good sport; and enough excitement and fatigue to prevent over much thought; and moreover I have at last been able to sleep well at night."

After the grievous personal loss that he had suffered earlier in the year, he surely lived through periods of anguish and loneliness, but he was not one to complain. The only clues to his stifled despair are borne out in his descriptions of the landscape: "Nowhere, not even at sea, does a man feel more lonely than when riding over the far-reaching, seemingly never-ending plains; and after a man has lived a little while on or near them, their vastness and loneliness and their melancholy monotony have a strong fascination for him . . . Nowhere else does one seem so far off from all mankind."

Although he missed his deceased wife, he didn't lack for company. William Merrifield and Sylvan Ferris, the brother of Roosevelt's favorite hunting guide, helped him manage the Maltese Ranch, and he saw them daily. Soon, to get even farther away from civilization, he bought his second ranch, the Elkhorn, a day's ride from Medora and some fifteen miles from his nearest neighbor. To help him run it, he recruited two of his favorite Maine guides whom he knew from his youth: William Sewall and his nephew Wilmot Dow. Before long the three men were building an eight-room ranch house in a grove of aspens with a view of the Little Missouri River. Roosevelt grew in confidence that he could succeed as a rancher, and he continued to invest heavily in cattle: "I regard the outlook for making the business a success as being very hopeful . . . I shall put on a thousand more cattle and shall make it my real business."

From the first he was something of a man apart to his colleagues in Medora, including his hired cowboys and his hunting guides, all of whom were instructed to call him "Mr. Roosevelt." But these men, and the others he met, quickly realized that Roosevelt was un-usual. Although he might not be physically bigger or stronger than they were, and at best a decent shot with a rifle, an average rider, and a distinctly poor roper, he nevertheless was every bit as tough and rugged as any of them. Already known as a staunch crusader against political corruption, Roosevelt was quite possibly anyone's equal in virtue.

Time after time he displayed resilience. In letters to friends he described being bucked off half-broken horses, slammed to the ground by a horse when it fell over backward onto him, and twice getting thrown off when the horse that he was riding tripped in a prairie-dog hole and sent them both somersaulting. He boasted of working as hard as any of the cowboys, and indeed, during one roundup, which featured a stampede during a thunderstorm, he was in the saddle for over eighteen hours and wore out five horses.

And yet the cowboys were not above challenging the newcomer. One night in the bar of Nolan's Hotel in Mingusville, an intoxicated local man, knowing Roosevelt was rich, made the mistake of calling him "Old Four-Eyes" and demanding that Roosevelt buy everyone in the bar a round of drinks. Waving a pair of revolvers, he taunted Roosevelt, but then stepped a little too close to him. Roosevelt seized the opportunity.

He was foolish to stand so near, and, moreover, his heels were close together, so that his position was unstable. Accordingly, in response to his reiterated command that I should set up the drinks, I said, "Well, if I've got to, I've got to," and rose, looking past him. As I rose, I struck quick and hard with my right just to one side of the point of his jaw, hitting my left as I straightened out, and then again with my right. He fired the guns, but I do not know whether this was merely a convulsive action of his hands or whether he was trying to shoot at me. When he went down he struck the corner of the bar with his head. It was not a case in which one could afford to take chances, and if he had moved I was about to drop on his ribs with my knees; but he was senseless.

Nobody in Medora taunted Roosevelt after that. The Medora cowboys didn't know that Roosevelt had been an avid boxer in college. He lost in the featherweight division of the Harvard College boxing championships — a bout that, according to Owen Wister, he might well have won had it not been for a late blow he received after the bell had sounded to end a round. The punch reportedly bloodied his nose. When the crowd began to boo, Roosevelt waved them silent and announced that it was an understandable mistake on his opponent's part. Bleeding badly and soon virtually unable to see, Roosevelt soldiered on through the remaining rounds, forced to flail blindly at his opponent, who proceeded to pummel him. Roosevelt lost the fight but won the admiration of his classmates, both for his good sportsmanship and for his astounding resilience. Owen Wister, to whom we owe this perhaps somewhat fanciful account, was sitting in the audience. The freshman music major took note of Roosevelt's gutsy display and soon sought out the older classmate as a friend. Roosevelt would continue boxing recreationally until, during his presidency, he was permanently blinded in one eye by a blow to his face, a detail withheld from the public and still not well known today.

After Roosevelt returned to the East Coast in the fall of 1885, others closer to home saw their own version of that toughness. During a fox hunt at the Meadow Brook Hunt Club on Long Island, Roosevelt took a bad fall that broke his arm. He described the event in a letter to his good friend Henry Cabot Lodge: "A great many men had falls, and about half way through I came to grief. Frank [Roosevelt's horse] is stiff and the company was altogether too good for him, I pounded the old fellow along pretty well up with the first rank, but he was nearly done out. Then we came to a five-foot fence, stiffer than iron, that staggered the best. My old horse, completely blown, struck the top rail, didn't make an effort to recover, and rolled over on me among a lot of stones. I cut my face to pieces and broke my left arm (which accounts for my super-ordinarily erratic hand writing)."

But Roosevelt, of course, finished the race: "I looked pretty gay with one arm dangling, and my face and clothes like the walls of a slaughter house. I guess my hunting is over for the season." When questioned about the accident by a reporter for the *New York Times*, Roosevelt remarked, "It's a mere trifle. I am always willing to pay the piper when I have a good chance; and every now and then I like to drink the wine of life with brandy."

With the loss of his wife and his parents, Roosevelt had over-come painful psychic trauma. The physical ones were not trivial either, and he continued to rack them up for the rest of his life, including an accident in Pittsfield, Massachusetts, when his open horse-drawn presidential carriage collided with an electric trolley car, badly wounding his left leg and killing one of his Secret Service men. In a famous episode during his campaign for the presidency as the candidate of the Progressive (Bull Moose) Party, he was shot in the chest by a mentally disturbed saloonkeeper — despite the pain and bleeding, he went on to give a one-hour speech.

Roosevelt's courage was as unimpeachable as his physical tough-ness. Once, riding alone, he was approached by what looked like a hostile band of Indians, who galloped toward him across the plains, their rifles drawn. He dismounted and stood his ground, rifle in hand. "I waited until they were a hundred yards off, and then threw up my rifle and drew a bead on the foremost." That brought the Indians to a halt. After a brief conversation with their leader, dur-ing which Roosevelt warned them not to come closer, the Indians thought better of attacking him. He later learned that they were a group of Sioux warriors.

In a well-publicized incident, after Roosevelt's boat was stolen from his ranch on the Little Missouri River in March 1886, he, Wil-liam Sewall, and Wilmot Dow set out to apprehend the thieves. It took them four days to build a new boat and then two days of trailing the thieves downstream before they located the three men, surprised them at gunpoint, and made their citizen's arrest. It took another week to deliver the thieves to the authorities in Dickerson, 150 miles away. For the last stretch of the journey, Roosevelt had the men loaded into a wagon, which he followed on foot, guarding them at gunpoint with his Model 1876 Winchester carbine. He went without sleep for the better part of thirty-six hours. Arriving in Dickerson, he delivered the thieves to the local sheriff and received, for his efforts, a bounty of fifty dollars — and badly blistered feet. The event made national headlines. TR was, as his Badlands friend Jack Reuter described him, "a fearless bugger."

Roosevelt had one memorable run-in with his neighbor the Marquis de Morès, which could easily have ended badly. The two had disagreed over property boundaries and, in another case, over the price that de Morès had verbally agreed to pay Roosevelt for his cattle. Thinking Roosevelt might be behind the effort to jail de Morès, he wrote Roosevelt a letter from his jail cell, effectively challenging him to a duel. "If you are my enemy I want to know it. I am always on hand as you know, and between gentlemen it is easy to settle matters of that sort directly." The letter dumbfounded Roosevelt, who considered de Morès a friend. He shared the letter with William Sewall, whom he asked to be his second, should the duel come to pass. Roosevelt, nearsighted and considerably less than a crack shot, decided to write back equally yet forcefully, without backing down yet leaving room for the matter to be dropped. Informing Sewall that he would not allow the Frenchman to bully him, he flipped the letter over and wrote his reply.

Medora, Dakota, September 6, 1885

Most emphatically I am not your enemy; if I were you would know it, for I would be an open one, and would not have asked you to my house nor gone to yours. As your final words, however, seem to imply a threat, it is due to myself to say that the statement is not made through any fear of possible consequences to me; I too, as you know, am always on hand, and ever ready to hold myself accountable in any way for anything I have said or done. Yours very truly,

Theodore Roosevelt

At this point the Frenchman reconsidered and wrote a conciliatory reply, stating that gentlemen could always find a way to settle a misunderstanding "without trouble." A duel would have been fatal for Roosevelt. De Morès, an experienced dueler and an expert shot, would easily have killed him.

In Medora, Roosevelt continued to amaze and amuse the locals. During a roundup he would yell to a cowboy, "Hasten forward there," in his nasal, patrician falsetto, reducing everyone to hysterics. "Dee-lighted to meet you!" he would exclaim upon being introduced. It seems he won over everyone who spent time with him — and this is not retrospective hagiography. Roosevelt simply impressed people, and the folks out west were not easily impressed. He seemed to burn more brightly and live life more fully than others, savoring every detail and every challenge.

Throughout his life Roosevelt would use his insatiable appetite for new experiences to quell what he described as his "restless raged wolf feeling." Some have speculated that this trait is evidence of mania, or perhaps manic-depressive disorder — and he certainly endured periods of depression, an affliction that ran in his family. His brother Eliot, lacking TR's gumption and drive, regularly succumbed to bouts of depression; grieving after the loss of both his wife and daughter to diphtheria, he drank himself to death at age thirty-four, in 1894. Yet it seems equally likely that Roosevelt, who struggled with ill health early in life and was warned that because of his dickey heart, he had better take it easy, transformed these setbacks into opportunity: assuming that his life would be short, he resolved to pack into it as much adventure, human interest, and physical activity as possible. Joe Ferris remembered overhearing Roosevelt on their exhausting two-week buffalo hunt, wrapped in blankets one night before nodding off to sleep, murmuring to himself, "By Godfrey, but this is fun!" Even during his White House years, Roosevelt enjoyed skinny-dipping in the Potomac in the dead of winter.

This behavior had a philosophical component to it, a mix of advice from Roosevelt's father and their wealthy clan's version of noblesse oblige. It upheld the vigorous life as the best life to live. It not only helped combat depression and overcome discouragement, but also could lead to great things. As TR said in his speech "The Strenuous Life," delivered in Chicago in 1899, "It is hard to fail, but it is worse never to have tried to succeed. In this life we get nothing save by effort." He went on to argue that there were two kinds of success. The first came from genius, and here he cited Abraham Lincoln authoring the Gettysburg Address; the second kind, like his own, came from simply doing what others didn't dare to do—in his case, taking on political corruption or abandoning politics to gamble on a career as a writer and a ranchman. He advocated this latter approach for everyone. Passivity was, in his mind, a crime against humanity. The same theory applied to the country at large: the United States needed to step forward onto the world stage. It should never shy away from conflict. To realize its great destiny, the country needed to act boldly and courageously, to take the world by the reins and spur it forward. Thus was born the interventionist and imperialist foreign policy that would come to characterize the Roosevelt White House.

When TR wasn't busy ranching, he was busy hunting.

His first grizzly bear provided a memorable encounter. Led by his guide William Merrifield, Roosevelt had tracked the animal into a dense pine forest, strewn with fallen timber. Roosevelt carried his best rifle, the Winchester Model 1876, custom-made to his strict specifications. The frame was embellished with exquisite engravings of elk, deer, buffalo, and pronghorn. The historian R. L. Wilson described this as "a spectacular gun, one of the finest Model 1876 Winchesters known—and certainly the most historic." Roosevelt posed with this weapon for the frontispiece photograph in *Hunting Trips of a Ranchman*, the first book he wrote about his experiences in the West.

> Cocking my rifle and stepping quickly forward, I found myself face to face with the great bear, who was less than twenty five feet off — not eight steps. He had been roused from his sleep by our approach. He sat up in his lair and turned his huge head slowly toward us. At that distance and in such a place it was very necessary to kill or disable him at the first fire, doubtless my face was pretty white, but the blue barrel was as steady as a rock as I glanced along it until I could see the top of the bead fairly between his two sinister looking eyes; as I pulled the trigger I jumped aside out of the smoke, to be ready if he charged; but it was needless, for the great brute was struggling in the death agony, and, as you will see when I bring home his skin, the bullet hole in his skull was as exactly between his eyes as if I had measured with a carpenter's rule. This bear was nine feet long and weighed over a thousand pounds.

Roosevelt always tipped his guides handsomely. When Merrifield helped him bag that first grizzly, Roosevelt offered him a choice: $150 in cash or a gold pocket watch. Merrifield opted for the watch. Roosevelt bought it for him at Tiffany & Company, with its eighteen-karat-gold case engraved with this saying: "If it's a black bear, I can tree him; if it's a grizzly I can bay him." When Joe Ferris helped him shoot his first bison, Roosevelt handed him a hundred-dollar bill. When Roosevelt shot his first pronghorn, he offered the guide his rifle. But most amazing to the guides was Roosevelt's childlike delight at each killing. He whooped and skipped and danced around the carcass, rubbing his hands together in sheer glee. "I never saw any one so enthused in all my life," wrote Joe Ferris after Roosevelt killed his first bison. As another guide put it on another occasion, "He fairly danced with joy."

Like many big-game hunters, Roosevelt set out to bag at least one of each of the great mammals of the American West. The hardest to find and slay was the mountain goat. True to form, Roosevelt tracked down the best-known hunter of these white goats and talked him into letting Roosevelt and Merrifield accompany him on a hunt. The climbing and hiking were so arduous that Merrifield grew crippled by blisters and had to abandon the pursuit. Roosevelt soldiered on until he bagged his goat.

His most dramatic hunt may well have been his tracking of a cougar with a pack of dogs in Colorado, in January 1901. Repeatedly, the treed mountain lion leapt off a high branch and fled, with the dogs in pursuit. When the dogs finally succeeded in encircling the big cat between trees, Roosevelt, fearful for the dogs' safety, leapt in to kill the cougar by hand. As he wrote to his son Theodore Roosevelt Jr., "I ran in and stabbed him behind the shoulder, thrusting the knife you loaned me right into his heart. I have always wished to kill a cougar as I did this one, with dogs and a knife."

This bloodthirsty slaughtering of animals — wild animals that, as a devoted naturalist, Roosevelt professed to appreciate and love — comes as a jolt to today's reader. But in the nineteenth century, an appreciation for the wilderness and a love of hunting went hand in hand, and loving animals and killing them were not contradictory concepts. A reasonable amount of hunting was thought to be compatible with the preservation of nature. Hunting might even serve the useful purpose of regulating certain animal populations. Furthermore, male identity at the time was colored by the desire to dominate nature. Demonstrating prowess in hunting harked back to some deeply ingrained concept of man as hunter-gatherer. It also tapped into the idea, current at the time, that Americans needed to tame their continent's wilderness to make room for civilization. But these widely accepted notions were about to change. In fact, Roosevelt lived through the period during which Americans, and arguably humanity as a whole, would start to transform their attitudes toward animals.

It all began with Charles Darwin's theory of evolution. As the idea of natural selection spread, it knocked humans off their pedestal, putting us more on a par with other animals. No longer was the human simply assumed to be some creature assembled by God from the dust of the earth. If the human had actually evolved from apes, then apes — and the rest of the animal kingdom — were a whole lot more like us than previously credited, and thus more deserving of humane treatment. As Darwin himself put it, in *The Descent of Man,* published in 1871, "There is no fundamental difference between man and the higher mammals in their mental faculties ... Even the lower animals ... manifestly feel pleasure and pain, happiness and misery ... Only a few persons now dispute that animals possess some power of reasoning."

Simultaneous with the spread of Darwinian thought, perhaps even prompted by it, a group of writers emerged to produce stories about animals that shared the feelings and even the thoughts of humans. These authors included Ernest Thompson Seton, William J. Long, and Charles G. D. Roberts. One of the most celebrated of these stories, "Lobo — The King of the Currumpaw," by Seton, depicts a massive alpha male wolf as hero. In this tale, the wolf is pitted against a rancher bent on its extermination. The general public developed a new sympathy for wild animals, recognizing that, in many cases, the advancement of civilization threatened the existence of these creatures.

Eventually this anthropomorphic depiction of animals devolved into outright sentimentality; the portrayals strayed so far from actual animal behavior in the natural world that people protested. In what would be called the "nature fakers controversy," scientists and dedicated amateurs pushed back against the sloppy science and overly anthropomorphic depiction of animals that they perceived in these stories. Roosevelt would take part in this controversy during his presidency. In 1907 he wrote an article for *Everybody's Magazine* titled "Nature Fakers." By siding with the scientists, he effectively brought the controversy to a close after six years of debate.

In the meantime, the new treatment of animals in fiction and the gradual acceptance of Darwinian evolution were changing popular attitudes toward wild animals. The public accepted the argument that it made sense to protect species like the bison from extinction. Roosevelt, who took the study of wild animals and their behavior seriously, would play an important role in advancing this argument.

Roosevelt finished writing the first of his hunting books, *Hunting Trips of a Ranchman,* in March 1885. A few months later, G. P. Putnam's Sons, a publishing house in which Roosevelt had a personal financial stake, printed five hundred calfskin-encased volumes for the first edition, which sold for the extravagant price of fifteen dollars a copy. The reviews were generally favorable. The *Saturday Review* described it as "one of the rare books which sportsmen will be glad to add to their libraries." The *New York Times* opined that it would assume "a leading position in the literature of the American sportsman." However, one unfavorable book review particularly irked Roosevelt. It appeared in the much-admired outdoor magazine *Forest and Stream.* The magazine's editor, George Bird Grinnell, scolded the author for perpetuating some now scientifically discredited theories pertaining to a number of western mammals, and he described Roosevelt (accurately) as no more than a knowledgeable amateur when it came to natural history. Stung by the criticism and unable to sit still, Roosevelt marched over to the magazine's Manhattan offices, stormed in, and demanded an audience with its editor.

Grinnell, a small mustached man with a long face and big ears, invited Roosevelt into his office and proceeded to critique the book for him, chapter by chapter, pointing out the numerous errors. Grinnell, nine years older than Roosevelt, had grown up on the thirty-seven-acre estate of John Jay Audubon in northern Manhattan. Audubon's widow had been his teacher, in classes held in the Audubon mansion. Grinnell had graduated from Yale and earned a PhD there in zoology. A lifelong collector of fossils, he was at the time of this meeting the country's leading expert on the ethnology of the Plains Indians.

It was instantly clear to Roosevelt that the man sitting across from him knew far more than he did about almost everything having to do with the natural world and the American West. Further-more, the kindly editor had been accurate and fair in his criticism. The men began to talk more generally about the disappearance of big game across the West, and over the next few hours they formed a firm friendship that could hardly have had more profound impli-cations: it would launch the nation's conservation movement.

Grinnell confirmed Roosevelt's own observations concerning wildlife across the West: it was in a highly precarious state, and some Rooseveltian form of aggressive action was needed. "No doubt it had some influence in making him the ardent game protec-tor that he later became, just as my own experiences had started me along the same road," Grinnell wrote some years later. The bison, of course, was by now virtually extinct, but the situation facing other western animal species was also dire. The populations of wapiti elk and pronghorn had dropped by 98 percent since the early decades of the century. White-tailed deer had declined in number from some twenty-four million to 500,000. Beaver were entirely gone east of the Mississippi and were becoming rarer across the West. In the prior dozen years, some notable eastern and western species and subspecies had been lost completely or were on their way to being lost, most notably the Carolina parakeet, the heath hen, the great auk, the eastern elk, and the Merriam's elk.

By December 1887, Roosevelt had a plan. Following in the foot-steps of his uncle Rob, who had lobbied for the protection of North-east fisheries for the benefit of sport fishermen, Roosevelt devised a way to champion big game. He organized a club, the Boone and Crockett Club, named after two of his childhood heroes, Daniel Boone and Davy Crockett. The club was restricted to one hundred members, with no more than fifty associate members; membership was limited to those men who had shot and killed at least one of the country's big-game animals in a "fair chase" with a rifle. "Fair chase" meant the hunt must exclude trapping, shooting an animal while it was swimming, fire-hunting (using lights at night to hunt game), or "crusting" animals by chasing them over deep snow, each of which gave the hunter an unfair advantage. Each member would swear to a code of hunting conduct and adhere to covenants and bylaws that encouraged geographical exploration, wildlife preservation, and inquiry into the world of nature. But preservation became the club's forte.

Its first meeting took place in the living room of the cramped Manhattan townhouse belonging to Roosevelt's sister, Anna. Present were a dozen men, all avid outdoorsmen and nature lovers, among them Roosevelt's brother Eliot, his cousin J. West Roosevelt, and George Bird Grinnell. Roosevelt made certain that many members were wealthy and well connected. It was the first such environmental organization of its kind. Among those later recruited were the landscape painter Albert Bierstadt, the geologists Clarence King and Raphael Pulmelly, the Civil War generals William Tecumseh Sherman and Philip Sheridan, and the capitalists E. P. Rogers, Archibald Rogers, J. Coleman Drayton (son-in-law of John Jacob Astor), Thomas Paton, and Rutherford Stuyvesant. Roosevelt also brought in his good friends and Porcellian Club "Brothers" the U.S. representative and future U.S. senator Henry Cabot Lodge and the writer Owen Wister.

Roosevelt asked Grinnell to be the club's cofounder. (Just a few months after his first meeting with Roosevelt, Grinnell had helped launch the Audubon Society to protect birds and their habitats.) Roosevelt served as the Boone and Crockett Club's first president, a position that he held until 1894. And he would remain "the sheet anchor and the soul of the organization" until his death in 1919.

The club threw its considerable clout behind the Forest Reserve Act, which became law in 1891. This milestone legislation gave the president of the United States the power to set aside and protect from development or exploitation any wooded or partly wooded countryside. Roosevelt, when he became president, would exploit this power to the fullest. Later the club promoted the passage of the Lacey Act of 1894 to protect wildlife in Yellowstone National Park from the ravages of hunters, trappers, and poachers, who had been rapidly depleting the park of its animals, including its bison. The club's members would also create the New York Zoological Society, now known as the Wildlife Conservation Society, to found and operate the Bronx Zoo.

Here, then, was the ideal marriage of a man and a mission. The values inherited from his father's generation, TR's own childhood hobbies of bird watching and collecting animal specimens, his adventures as a cattle rancher and hunter in the Badlands, and his experience in politics worked in concert to produce the perfect nature crusader. And once Roosevelt found himself in the White House, he accelerated the work of the Boone and Crockett Club, doubling the number of national parks from five to ten. He would create eighteen national monuments and conserve an astonishing 230 million acres of American soil as wilderness preserves and protected areas. Roosevelt's conservation achievements stand out as the single greatest legacy of the open-range cattle era, despite the fact that most cattle barons were unsympathetic — and their actions largely antithetical — to its ideals.

PART THREE

The Boom Busts

12

Teddy Blue and the
Necktie Socials

The year 1884 would mark the apex of the cattle boom. By now some twelve million cattle grazed over an area comparable in size to all of western Europe. As Edward Everett Dale explained it in *Cow Country*, "The cattleman's empire of grass seemed rich, powerful, and prosperous. Cattle [prices] were high, profits great, and it appeared to be entering upon a golden age of still greater prosperity and wealth." But, as is often the case in a speculative bubble, few saw what was actually happening: the industry had peaked.

In March 1884, Teddy Blue Abbott was involved in the suppression of a minor Indian revolt. It began when a pair of off-duty hands at a ranch near Lame Deer Creek thought they would have some decidedly dangerous fun at the expense of a Cheyenne chief named Black Wolf, whom they found napping on the porch of the ranch house after a big lunch. "I'll bet you a dollar I can shoot a hole through his hat without hitting his head," said one of the cowboys, a Kentuckian name Sawney Tolliver, to the other. Tolliver proceeded to shoot off the chief's black stovepipe hat, grazing his head and nearly killing him. The next day the tribe, offended by the callous prank, retaliated by burning down the ranch house and shooting the owner's dog. Teddy Blue was part of the posse sent from Miles City to arrest the Indians for vandalism; he was hoping to somehow avoid a bloodbath.

Teddy Blue was sympathetic to the plight of the Plains Indians. He could see that the federal government was mistreating them: "After I got some sense in my head and saw the way things really was in that country, I was sorry for the Indians and ashamed of the deal they got at the hands of the white man . . . They can't show a place in history where the Indians ever broke a treaty. The white men always broke them because they always made a treaty they couldn't keep and knew they couldn't keep it." And Teddy Blue had a particular fondness for the Cheyenne, whom he considered especially upright and moral, unlike the Apache, whom he considered vicious.

A band of seventeen Cheyenne men eventually surrendered peacefully to the posse, and Teddy Blue found himself guarding a tall, slim warrior of about his own age whose name was Pine. Over the next few days, the two slept side by side, ate together, and soon struck up a genuine friendship. Teddy Blue visited him in jail every day before the trial, sneaking him cigarettes and candies. In return Pine gave him a silver ring engraved with a shield and an insignia that read C CO 7 CAV. Teddy Blue realized it was a signet ring once worn by a member of Custer's cavalry — probably an officer — who died at the Battle of the Little Bighorn in 1876. Pine, just fourteen at the time, had fought in the battle. The ring was no doubt a trophy taken off a dead finger.

Ultimately, four of the Cheyenne men involved in the ranch burning were tried, convicted, and sentenced to a year in a penitentiary. Pine, however, was released. He and Teddy Blue would remain lifelong friends. For years the cowboy wore the ring around his neck for luck, like a Saint Christopher medal.

By late spring of 1884, Teddy Blue Abbott was working for Zeke Newman's N Bar Ranch just outside Miles City. One day, while "repping" during a roundup, his horse reared and fell on him, pinning his back to a log. The ranch sent him to Miles City for rest and medical treatment, all expenses paid. He was in town for eight days and took full advantage of it. The moment he recovered enough, he was carousing in the local saloons and brothels.

Miles City, in eastern Montana, was flush with cattle money and humming with activity, like the rest of the cattle kingdom. The town's excellent stockyards provided direct access to the Northern Pacific Railroad. It was convenient for Montana cattlemen, but also for many of the northern Wyoming stock growers. They could trail their herds up the Powder River Basin and avail themselves of the good water and long grass along the Tongue River for the last hundred miles to Miles City.

Among the citizens of Miles City at that time was a photographer named Layton Alton Huffman, who left an indelible record of the period. He arrived in 1878 to work as the post photographer at Fort Keogh. He tried his hand at cattle ranching before opening his own photography studio on the main street of Miles City in around 1880. Recognizing that the open-range era would not last, he set about recording it in photographs. Initially he used a homemade camera set up on a tripod and wet plates that had to be coated and sensitized on location, then exposed and developed before the emulsion dried. Each exposure took fractions of a minute. Despite these handicaps, L. A. Huffman left a first-rate collection of candid images — buffalo hunters skinning hides, cowboys working at roundups, cabins of homesteaders, individual portraits of Native Americans, and many more. Remarkable for their documentary quality and historical interest, the photographs capture their subjects in elegant compositions suffused with pathos and nostalgia.

Teddy Blue would remember the spring and summer of 1884 as perhaps the most fun period of his life: "Oh, boy, but life was good." He had been around Miles City long enough to have many friends among the cowboys, the local girls, and the saloonkeepers — he knew the ins and outs of the cattle town. For example, he knew that Charlie Brown, who ran the Cottage Saloon, kept a bowl of mulligan stew on the stove for the cowboys to help themselves to. He knew that you didn't have to pay fifty cents for a room at night; you could take your blanket roll and bed down on Charlie's saloon floor after closing. And he knew about the spacious park on the outskirts of town, shaded by cottonwoods, where the cowboys and the buffalo hunters and the bullwhackers (drivers of ox wagons) could sleep out in the open air, free of charge.

When Teddy Blue failed to reappear at the ranch after a week, Zeke Newman rode into town to track him down. "A man who can drink sixty-five dollars' worth of whisky while he is eating sixteen dollars' worth of grub is well enough to work," he remarked. He ordered the cowboy back to the ranch.

A few weeks later, Teddy Blue and a friend shirked their duties and slipped back into town to resume carousing. When Teddy Blue bumped into Newman in a saloon, his boss looked at him suspiciously and asked, "Teddy, what guard are you standing tonight?"

When he responded evasively, Newman asked him if he had been drinking.

"Mr. Newman, the boys told me you said in Ogallaly that a man who wouldn't take a drink didn't have no snap."

Newman scowled at him. "You have too much snap."

A week or so later, Teddy Blue broke a cardinal rule by sneaking a bottle of whiskey into the camp. When the foreman John Burgess objected, Teddy Blue deposited the bottle out in the sagebrush, exactly one hundred feet from the camp. He knew that, by definition, a camp could have a radius of only a hundred feet, so technically he was no longer breaking any rules. Then he taunted Burgess: "Sweetheart, your camp ends a hundred feet from the fire."

Burgess laughed and the bottle stayed out in the sagebrush. The cowboys took turns sneaking off for swigs. The whiskey didn't last long.

Teddy Blue was pushing his luck and he knew it, but he was also highly confident of his value to the outfit. "If I say it myself, I was a hell of a good cowhand." He could do everything required of a cowboy and do it efficiently and well. Although he weighed only 135 pounds, he was an expert at calf wrestling. He performed so much rope work at roundups over the course of his career — repeatedly scarring his palms with rope burns — that later in life he would lose the use of all but two fingers on each hand.

That fall, when the ranch owner Newman began laying off cowboys for the winter, he asked Burgess why he wanted to keep the troublemaker Teddy Blue on the payroll. The foreman's reply: "Well, he can sing."

The cattle baron exploded. "If you think I'm going to pay forty dollars a month for a music box for you fellows all winter, you're crazy!"

"That's all right," said Burgess, defending Teddy Blue. "The night never gets so dark nor the river so deep that Teddy isn't with the herd."

Instead of firing him, Newman ordered Teddy Blue to help Burgess move a large herd of Texas steers, which were grazing down on the Powder River, up some three hundred miles to the mouth of the Musselshell River, where the N Bar outfit hoped to establish a third ranch.

The day before he departed, Teddy Blue had one last hurrah in Miles City. On a dare, he strutted up Main Street dressed in drag, wearing the prostitute Cowboy Annie's ruffled drawers pulled up over his jeans, her necklaces and scarves hanging from his neck and decorating his hat. The townspeople poured out of the shops to witness the spectacle and to cheer him on. According to Teddy Blue, no doubt deep in his cups at this point, "It turned the place upside down."

He left town on horseback the following morning, carrying a flag made out of Cowboy Annie's ruffled drawers. Tied around his arm like a badge of honor, he wore the silk stocking of his favorite whore.

There were four thousand head of cattle in the N Bar herd that needed to be trailed to the mouth of the Musselshell. At one point the cowboys had to swim the herd across the Yellowstone River not far from Miles City. When they arrived on the near bank, the water was icy cold and flowing swiftly. In fact, it was so cold that mush ice had formed in the shallows. Teddy Blue dismounted and began to undress. One of the Texas cowboys teased him. "What are you taking your clothes off for? Hell, it's nothing but a crick."

"You'll think it's the Atlantic Ocean before you get to the other side," Teddy Blue replied, continuing to disrobe. Somehow the cowboys managed to cross the wide river without losing a single steer. Teddy Blue's big Oregon horse, Jesse, swam with its tail high up out of the water, but the small Texas ponies, who were new to deep water, tried to touch the river bottom with their hind feet, and bobbed under, causing all the Texas cowboys to get soaked. "When we got to the other side, they were all sitting on their horses, shivering, the water running off them, and a fellow said, 'That's colder than any ice water I ever drank in Texas.'"

A week later, as they approached the flats at the mouth of the Musselshell, the cattle at the head of the herd spooked and began to panic. It was all the cowboys could do to keep the entire herd from stampeding. Later that night, sitting around a campfire, the boys tried to puzzle out what had disturbed the cattle. Although the timbered breaks in the area were heavily populated with bear — both grizzly and black — there had been no sign of any bruins.

It wasn't until later that winter, holed up in a cabin nearby, that Teddy Blue learned the reason for the cattle's restlessness. A cowboy riding the grub line pointed out that the herd had passed directly over the shallow graves of a group of horse thieves who had been hanged there that spring by the cattle baron Granville Stuart and his vigilante group, known as Stuart's Stranglers. The smell of dead bodies had spooked the cattle.

Death by hanging, the so-called necktie social, was becoming commonplace on the western frontier by the 1880s. Even where jails and a judiciary existed, a posse made up of members of the community, mostly men, would often invade a jail to remove a suspected rustler and hang him from a telegraph pole, without benefit of a trial or due process of law. These hangings did not always go smoothly. To be effective, the noose had to be fastened snugly along the left jaw, just off the shoulder, so that the knot pressed against the carotid artery and instantly cut off blood to the brain, rendering the hanged person instantly unconscious. If there was too much slack in the rope and the drop was too far, the victim's head could easily rip off. This happened in the case of the train robber Thomas "Black Jack" Ketchum, who was beheaded by the noose before a large crowd in Clayton, New Mexico, in April 1901. Conversely, with too little slack, the hanged person might not die.

In 1894, an issue of the *St. Louis Globe-Democrat* carried a detailed description of the ordeal of a hanging victim. Dr. D. S. Lamb, a former army surgeon, explained the three stages of the process, when properly administered:

> In the first stage the victim passes into a partial stupor lasting from thirty seconds to two minutes, but this is generally governed by the length of the drop, the weight of the body, and the tightness of the constriction. There is absolutely no pain in this stage; the feeling is rather one of pleasure. The subjective symptoms described are intense heat in the head, brilliant flashes of light in the eyes, deafening sounds in the ears and a heavy numb feeling in the lungs. In the second stage the subject passes into unconsciousness and convulsions usually occur. In the third stage all is quiet except the beating of the heart. Just before death the agitation is renewed, but in a different way from that in the second state. The feet are raised, the tongue has a peculiar spasm, the chest heaves, the eyes protrude from the orbits and oscillate from side to side, and the pupils dilate. The pulse can, in most cases, be felt ten minutes after the drop.

Another remarkable example of a bungled hanging was that of "Big Nose George" Parrott, a well-known wanted train robber, rustler, and murderer. In August 1878, Big Nose George and his crew had planned to rob the Westbound No. 3 train, owned by the Union Pacific Railroad. They sabotaged the tracks in order to derail the train near Medicine Bow, Wyoming, but an alert railroad foreman, retrieving some forgotten tools, noticed the damage to the tracks, averting the accident and the robbery. A local sheriff's deputy named Robert Widdowfield and a railroad detective named Henry Vinson tracked down the Parrott gang at a campground on Rattlesnake Creek. There they attempted to arrest the men for the crime. But both lawmen were shot and killed and their horses stolen. Two years later, after stealing a herd of horses in Canada and selling it at Fort Benton, Parrott got drunk in a saloon in Miles City, boasted of his exploits, and was finally arrested. He was transferred for trial to Rawlins, in Carbon County, Wyoming, near the location of the two murders. When Parrott attempted to escape by clubbing the jailer with his handcuffs, a posse of local men decided to deal with him in a more unilateral fashion. Wearing masks, they stormed the jail.

The jail's logbook has an entry for George Parrott under the heading "How Discharged": "Went to join the Angels via hempen cord on telegraph pole in front of Fred Wolf's Saloon." The specifics were far grislier: Parrott had to be hanged twice. In the first attempt, the posse had him stand on an empty kerosene barrel while the noose was slipped around his neck. Unfortunately, when the barrel was kicked out from under him, the rope stretched just enough for his feet to touch the ground. He choked but didn't die. The rope was then restrung higher up, and this time Parrott was forced to climb a ladder propped against a telegraph pole before the noose was again secured around his neck. When he threatened to jump in order to end the proceedings quickly, someone responded by kicking the ladder out from under him. Somehow Parrott was able to free his hands and grab the pole halfway up. Clutching it to his chest, he pleaded for someone to shoot him and put him out of his misery. No one did. Eventually, he tired and his grip on the pole began to slip. He died in convulsions, in a prolonged strangulation. His death mask revealed that both ears were missing — the hangman's rope may have rubbed them off during his death throes.

Adding to the ignominy of the lynching, the local coroner, Dr. John E. Osborne, took a large swatch of skin off Parrott's chest and torso during the autopsy. He then had the skin tanned and made into a medical bag and a matching pair of shoes. He also sawed off the dead man's skullcap and gave it to his assistant to use as a door-stop. The remaining body parts were loaded into a whiskey barrel filled with saline solution and buried in an unmarked grave not far from Osborne's medical office. Osborne would go on to become the third governor of the state of Wyoming, the first Democrat to hold the job.

In 1950 a construction crew unearthed an old whiskey barrel containing a human body. It was identified as the remains of "the pickled Parrott," and the skeleton was reunited with its long-lost skullcap. Today, the buckskin-style human-leather shoes are on display at the Carbon County Museum in Rawlins, Wyoming.

The mouth of the Musselshell, where Teddy Blue and a pair of fellow cowboys settled in for the winter, was an eerie, desolate place, still largely devoid of settlers. The surrounding area, known as the Missouri Breaks, contained a series of white cliffs that slid down to the banks of the Missouri River. Some of the canyons descended deep into the countryside. It was territory so rough that, in the words of the cattle baron Granville Stuart, "the magpies' wings got broke flying over it."

The Sioux used the flat area at the mouth of the Musselshell as a spot to ford the upper Missouri. Today the place is buried under a body of water created by the Fort Peck Dam. Over the years the landing became the site of some thirty altercations between the white men and the Sioux. In one instance, a white woman named Jenny Smith survived her own scalping by feigning death. The area had once been the site of a trading post, abandoned long before Teddy Blue arrived. The surviving ramshackle structures included a dilapidated corral and a couple of decaying cabins, including a two-room structure, with a warped countertop, a storage area, and a rotting puncheon floor, that had once functioned as a general store. Until Granville Stuart came along with his Stranglers, the place had served as a hideout for escaped convicts and horse thieves. One of those who had taken refuge there was "Big Nose George" Parrott, in the days when a twenty-thousand-dollar reward was offered for arresting him, together with his gang.

Teddy Blue had only one indirect interaction with Stuart's vigilantes. During the spring roundups earlier that year, he had taken a side job as a so-called telegraph man for the Stranglers. His tasks included carrying messages back and forth and alerting the Montana Stock Growers Association to the appearance of horse or cattle thieves on the open range. While working on one roundup near Buffalo, Wyoming, Teddy Blue encountered Rattlesnake Jake and Long-haired Owen, known and wanted thieves. Teddy Blue duly sent off his telegraph to Granville Stuart to tip him off that the thieves were headed his way. But before Stuart's Stranglers could track them down, the two men died in a shootout in a saloon in Lewistown, Montana, over the Fourth of July weekend. Teddy Blue boasted to his cowboy friends that he worked for the "Montana Assassination"—and they knew exactly what he meant.

The idea for a vigilance committee had been hatched at the second meeting of the Montana Stock Growers Association in Miles City, in April 1884, with 429 stockmen present. The association was modeled on the Wyoming Stock Growers Association, founded in 1872, which had grown into a potent political force and the de facto territorial government of Wyoming. Many of its rules and regulations had become law. The WSGA's original purpose was to organize the seasonal roundups, schedule cattle shipments, and track and publish lists of brands. But it wasn't long before the association began to hire professional detectives whose job was to police the range and chase down cattle thieves. These range detectives were given plenty of latitude to deal with rustlers as they saw fit, and that usually meant hanging them or shooting them on the spot. Many association detectives were former scouts, gunslingers, hunters, or marshals.

The new Montana Stock Growers Association put "the rustler problem" on the agenda for its second meeting. But from the outset it planned to address the problem in secret, so as not to tip off the thieves. Granville Stuart claimed he had lost at least 3 percent of his herd to rustlers the prior year. During the public portion of the meeting, an outright war on the rustlers was proposed, seconded, and voted down. According to Teddy Blue, the meeting then went into a more secretive executive session, where a plan was hatched to divide the territory into three sections. In each section a vigilante committee would be formed, as needed, to pursue rustlers. These subcommittees were called executive committees, but they might as well have been called *execute* committees.

Granville Stuart, in charge of the Maginnis section, would prove the most ardent enforcer of the new "no tolerance" policy. This was hardly surprising, given his experiences as a member of the Vigilance Committee of Alder Gulch in 1863 and 1864, when the placer gold miners hanged a group of twenty road agents, known as the Plummer gang, without bothering to try them.

When a stallion and thirty-five of Stuart's best steers were stolen not long after the second meeting, Stuart gathered fourteen men at his ranch and set out on horseback to mete out the Montana version of frontier justice. Without due process of law, Stuart's Stranglers proceeded to shoot and hang dozens of men. After each execution they pinned a card to the dead man's chest that read HORSE THIEF or CATTLE THIEF.

Both the Marquis de Morès and Theodore Roosevelt had been present at the Montana Stock Growers Association's initial meeting, and both had argued strenuously in favor of aggressive action. Both volunteered for Stuart's vigilance committee, but Stuart rejected them, worried that their well-known names would attract publicity and remove the element of surprise. One can only speculate what impact Roosevelt's participation in the group would have had on his subsequent political career; it might well have disqualified him from holding public office. (Roosevelt went on to organize the Little Missouri Stock Growers Association, which he chaired for a number of years. This association never engaged in vigilante activities. Some have speculated that serving as chairman of the cattle association rekindled Roosevelt's interest in politics, though he stated that he preferred his association work to serving in the New York assembly.)

Stuart's Stranglers quickly became controversial. Some claimed that many of the slaughtered men were simply innocent settlers whom Stuart wanted to remove from his grazing areas. Others defended the vigilantes, arguing that no formal system of justice had evolved to deal with local thievery and that the stealing was getting out of hand. In all, the vigilantes hanged some thirty-five men, without a trial. Teddy Blue heard a woman accuse Granville Stuart of hanging thirty innocent men. Stuart raised his hat to her and said, "Yes, madam, and by God I done it alone." One thing is certain: these actions set an unfortunate precedent for the infamous events that were to follow in Johnson County, nine years later.

The charge that Stuart had targeted innocent settlers may have had some validity. Settlers had begun to encroach on the open range, carving out bits of land along waterways, which hindered the movement of the cattle herds. The cattle barons, not very tolerant of change, were beginning to fear this encroachment. Only a few years before, the idea that the open range could actually become crowded had seemed inconceivable. But now it was indisputably true, not only in Wyoming but in southern Montana and Colorado too. "It was getting settled up," according to Teddy Blue. "There was ranches every few miles."

One factor that made settlement possible across such an arid landscape was the new technology for pumping water. A Vermont engineer named Daniel Halladay had in 1854 created the first self-regulating wind pump for farms. These wood or steel structures automatically turned to catch the wind and had a fail-safe mechanism that prevented their spinning too hard, and thus self-destructing, in heavy breezes. They could suck up water from a well one hundred meters deep, saving the farmer or rancher considerable time and physical effort. A well serviced by such a wind pump might produce water for as many as three hundred cattle, once steel storage tanks were added. The windmills became an iconic emblem of homesteads across the rural American landscape.

Some of the newcomers brought sheep too, which proceeded to shear the already overgrazed grass down to its roots, leaving barren desert in their wake. The cattle ranchers came to loathe the sheep ranchers, although, as mentioned, some, such as the Wyoming senator Francis Warren, kept both animals. Conflicts between the two groups would continue for another twenty years. The most memorable, the Pleasant Valley War in Arizona (1882–92), was essentially a feud between two families, the Tewksburys and the Grahams. It resulted in thirty-five to fifty deaths, annihilating almost all the men of both families.

Rustling, overcrowding, Texas fever — the various state and territorial stock growers' associations dealt with these matters, and by 1884 they had their hands full dealing with complaints. "We were blamed for everything that happened but the good weather," remembered Granville Stuart, but he wasn't entirely surprised — nor was he deterred from his strong-arm tactics. Assets needed to be protected: $35 million had been invested in cattle across Montana's seventy-five thousand square miles of open range.

The formation of the various associations and the hiring of range detectives were evidence of the rapid maturation of the open-range cattle business and its growing complexity. Organizing the semiannual roundups became a key responsibility of the new associations. Because cattle wandered free, crossing rivers and meandering onto other men's ranges, strict rules and codified cooperation were the only hope for sorting and separating the herds when it came time to brand calves or sell steers.

Furthermore, somewhat surprisingly, beef prices began a steady decline. As the number and size of the cattle herds proliferated on the open range, the meatpackers in Chicago exerted more power and leverage over the cattlemen. With the business suddenly neither as profitable as it had once been, nor as profitable as the many newly incorporated and publicly listed cattle companies had hoped it would be, the ranchers began looking for ways to save money.

The new associations helped immeasurably in these tighter economic times. They allowed the cattlemen to negotiate group freight rates, to share in the otherwise prohibitive costs of policing the range for thieves and wolf predation, and to work together to lobby for legislation at the state or territorial level that would favor their businesses.

Labor costs were an easy target, and in a number of places cowboys' wages were cut. Horace Plunkett, the Irish rancher in the Powder River Basin, was one such cattle king arguing for reduced wages, and the local cowboys never forgave him for it. Treasured cowboy perquisites began to disappear too, such as the availability of ranch horses for a cowboy's personal use. Then one day, the winter grub line was no longer free. Cowboys now had to pay for their meals if they chose to spend the winter months wandering from ranch to ranch. And perhaps most significant, cowboys were no longer allowed to collect maverick calves on the range, which had long been a means of supplementing their wages or building stock to start their own ranch. In fact, according to a new rule adopted by associations in Wyoming and Montana, cowboys were forbidden to own any cattle at all. Granville Stuart, to his credit, made a speech strongly opposing this new edict, arguing that 99 percent of the cowboys were honest and deserved a chance to get ahead in life; moreover, permitting cowboys to own cattle would align their interests with those of the cattle barons. Stuart was overruled. Even if he hadn't been, a cowboy would have found his prospects diminished. If he had been able to procure cattle, because of overgrazing on the open range, he would need to buy his own land to make a go of raising cattle. And land prices were soaring.

In short, the average cowboy's standard of living was eroding and his opportunities for advancement were dissolving — and he knew it.

A cowboy was lucky to net a hundred dollars in wages for participating in a four-month cattle drive, and twenty-five to forty dollars a month for his work on the range in the summer. He might pride himself on his horsemanship and his skills with a lariat and consider himself a tier above most other western workingmen, but in reality he was paid poorly to do an unglamorous job. Wallace Stegner, the western novelist and essayist, once described the cowboy as "an overworked, underpaid hireling, almost as homeless and dispossessed as a modern crop worker, and his fabled independence was and is chiefly the privilege of quitting his job in order to go looking for a another just as bad." Or, as the historian Lewis Atherton put it, the cowboy was "a hired hand on horseback."

It was not the cowboy but rather the cattle that held all the economic value on the open range. The cowboy was a cost — not a source of profit — to the rancher or the joint-stock company. As would become painfully apparent, the cowboy was little better than an indentured servant. As the ranches began to be fenced in, in response to overgrazing, the demand for cowboys decreased; a rancher needed fewer to operate his outfit. As mentioned, fenced ranches eliminated the need for twice-annual roundups because the cattle could no longer stray; they were collected and herded much more quickly and efficiently. Most of the cowboy's work became seasonal in nature. Those employed full-time found that a portion of their time was spent irrigating fields and fixing barbed-wire fences. The latter, a chore that entailed stringing the wire tight between posts and digging new post holes where needed, was laborious and unpopular. The other new activity was the growing, cutting, and bailing of hay to feed the cattle through the winter months. New barns were being built with haylofts to hold it.

The cowboy looked at these changes — most of them imposed by a stock growers' association to which he could not belong — and soon realized that his job description had changed without his being informed or receiving any compensation for the loss. Ranch work was becoming commoditized and corporatized. Working conditions and pay were not improving, despite the boom on the ranges. In fact, forced to pay for his horse and his winter meals, the cowboy found he had not only higher expenses, but also less interesting work to do—and it offered even less opportunity for advancement. It wasn't long before the trust between the cowboys and the cattle barons began to fray.

The rise in cowboys' discontent inevitably led to labor unrest, which took the form of cowboy strikes. The idea at first seems at odds with the cowboy's much-vaunted independence. Indeed, the average cowboy generally saw himself as a sole practitioner, not as a potential member of a union where he might engage in group activism or collective bargaining. Nevertheless, the first cowboy strike occurred on the Texas Panhandle in March 1883. Here three cowboys, each heading a crew for a different ranch, presented their bosses with an ultimatum signed by twenty-five other cowboys. Among their demands: pay for regular cowhands and cooks needed to rise to fifty dollars a month; range bosses should receive seventy-five dollars a month. The cowboys issued a strike deadline and threatened consequences if their grievances were not heard. The ranchers responded with a few minor concessions, which the cowboys rebuffed. The strike commenced, and the offending cowboys were promptly fired.

At its peak, the walkout involved as many as three hundred cowboys, but this group of men was less than fully committed. Needing money, many crossed in and out of the boycott as other work presented itself. The ranch owners, in disbelief that the cowboys would refuse to work for them, held all the cards from the outset. They had the support of the local press, for the simple reason that for the most part, they owned the newspapers, or the papers were beholden to them for advertising. The ranchers also knew that a surplus of available cowboys existed around the state, and thus the strikers could be easily replaced. Meanwhile, the cowboy boycotters lacked money, a strong class-consciousness, and the discipline to keep the strike going. Too many retreated to the neighboring cattle town of Tascosa, where they squandered their money in saloons and brothels, drank up their strike funds, and then were forced to return to work. The strike lasted two and half months and ended in ignominious failure for the cowboys.

The strike had one serious aftershock. Soon after the walkout ended, the Panhandle suffered a rash of rustling incidents attributable to disillusioned cowboys venting their frustration and seeking revenge.

The second and more successful cowboy strike occurred the following spring (1884) in Johnson County. This one was far better orchestrated. Led by Jack Flagg, who would play a central role in the Johnson County War, the cowboys picked with great care the moment to launch their strike: just at the outset of the spring roundup, which was expected to be the largest in Wyoming history. The cattlemen, in this case the foremen (few of the owners participated in the roundups), had no choice but to capitulate to cowboys' demands for higher wages. However, this victory would be short-lived. Without his knowledge, Jack Flagg's actions had earned him a position high on the Cheyenne cattlemen's list of political enemies. The settled strike made a deep impression on the cattle barons and would help shape the events that followed.

During the ensuing long winter, while he was holed up on the banks of the Musselshell, Teddy Blue first heard about Granville Stuart's daughters. A grub-line rider reported that there were as many as six pretty girls on Stuart's DHS Ranch, three of them Stuart's own daughters. "We talked them all over for days," recalled Teddy Blue. At one point he and the visiting wrangler each settled on one of the girls to be his wife, then grabbed their hats and announced that they were heading off seventy-five miles south to the ranch to claim their brides. "We were joking of course. We went about ten feet in the snow and came back—concluded we'd wait until spring."

It was not the first time Teddy Blue had contemplated marriage. A few years before, he had encountered a demure Cheyenne woman whom he found so fetching that he asked the local chief, High Walking, for her hand in marriage. The chief ignored him and nothing ever came of it, but so far as Teddy Blue was concerned, marrying an Indian was nothing to be ashamed of. "We were starving for the sight of a woman, and some of these ... were awful good-looking, with their fringed dresses of soft deer or antelope skin that hung just below their knees — that was all they wore, just the dress — and their beaded leggings and wide belts. Oh, boy, but they looked good to us. But I was always that way. I always wanted a dark-eyed woman." And Granville Stuart himself had married a twelve-year-old Shoshone named Awbonnie Tookanka.

The following spring John Burgess asked Teddy Blue to dig some post holes for a barbed-wire fence so that the N Bar Ranch could create a hay field. When he failed to dig them, insisting he had been given a hoe to perform the work instead of a proper shovel, Burgess felt he had no recourse but to fire him. Teddy Blue gathered his belongings, which is to say his bedroll and his few articles of clothing, and headed south to Granville Stuart's DHS Ranch. A week or so later he was hired.

"It was a wonderful outfit, very well run, and the best I ever knew for a cowboy to work for," he wrote in his memoirs. The ranch was known for serving the best food among all the local ranches; the cowboys were fed canned tomatoes and peaches, while at most outfits they were lucky to get dried apples and prunes.

As far as a cowboy's career went, Teddy Blue had done as well as one could hope for. He had lived the wild cowboy life, trailing and roping and branding cattle; he had repped for a number of ranches, befriended a Cheyenne Indian, and enjoyed boisterous times carousing in the cattle towns. Still only twenty-five years old, he worked for the DHS Ranch, perhaps the best known and best managed on the entire open range. Not only that, his boss was an enlightened employer who took the welfare of his cowboys seriously. You couldn't do much better than that as a cowboy — unless, of course, you hoped to one day settle down and get married.

As luck would have it, at the DHS Ranch Teddy Blue first laid eyes on Granville Stuart's second daughter, Mary, only fifteen at the time: "The Stuart girls were [half Indian and] pretty, well-dressed, good dancers and very much sought after." Stuart, who had a library of some two thousand volumes, had made sure that his daughters were properly educated and brought up as polite young ladies. He had a school built on the ranch and hired a full-time teacher. The girls attended parties at Fort Maginnis and in Lewistown, always accompanied by chaperones. "The Stuart girls had prettier and more expensive clothes than any of the others in that country and was always dressed in the latest style, and it drove the white girls wild," Teddy Blue recalled.

Mary was the smallest of these girls but also the prettiest. She was Teddy Blue's ideal of a dark-eyed beauty, all right, and it wasn't long before she was his favorite. "I was so damn in love with her that instead of a DHS [brand] on a cow I'd see Mary." In his diary he wrote, "She is sure enough a Daisy Dipped in Dew."

Immediately, Teddy Blue set about trying to make himself useful and popular by offering to do errands around the kitchen, such as fetching wood and water for the cook and drying dishes. He and the other hands, keenly aware of the presence of young women — the Anderson family who lived on the ranch had three attractive daughters as well — began to spruce up to impress them. They tried to keep as clean as they could and wore their best and brightest white shirts and their "twelve dollar California pants" (Levi blue jeans) even when out branding calves.

Teddy Blue knew that he was likely to face plenty of competition for Mary's hand in marriage — from other cowboys and from soldiers at the neighboring forts. If he was going to win her, he realized that he would have to make a few changes of a personal nature: give up drinking, chewing tobacco, and the small amount of gambling that he engaged in. Next, he needed to pay more attention to his personal hygiene, stay out of barroom fights, and no longer waste his paycheck on prostitutes. Perhaps hardest of all, he would have to save some money. Much like Huck Finn at the end of his adventures, it was time, as Teddy Blue put it, that he "reformed" and "got civilized." In short, he would have to grow up. And one day soon that would mean no longer being what he was best at: a cow*boy*.

In addition to marking the peak of the boom, 1884 stood out as a pivotal year for the open-range cattle industry for another reason.

In that year, yet another twenty-five-year-old made his mark in the West. An aspiring epidemiologist named Theobald Smith began work on the cattle industry's greatest mystery and most expensive problem: Texas fever.

Smith had grown up in Albany, New York, the son of German-born parents — his father was a tailor. Gifted in mathematics, highly musical, fluent in both French and German, Smith won a scholarship to Cornell College, where he was able to pay for much of his education by playing the organ during services at the university chapel. His undergraduate career was so brilliant, in all subjects, that he had trouble deciding which occupation to pursue. When he failed to find a job as a math teacher immediately after graduating from college, he opted to attend medical school instead.

In late 1883, the young graduate of Albany and Cornell Medical schools was invited to Washington, D.C., by Dr. Daniel E. Salmon to work as his lab assistant in the newly formed Bureau of Animal Industry.

A dignified and austere man, Theobald Smith proved to be exceptionally hardworking and devoted to his research. Clearheaded and honest, he lacked humor and was far too reserved to achieve much intimacy with his colleagues or his pupils. Many of them nevertheless came to revere him. Although Smith is largely forgotten today, his contemporaries fully understood the importance of his achievements. "The influence which he exerted on the development of our science in our own country was greater than that of any other individual," wrote Hans Zinsser in a biographical memoir for the National Academy of Sciences in 1936.

When he arrived in the nation's capital and began to study the infamous cattle disease, Smith knew nothing about bacteriology, a new science that Louis Pasteur and Robert Koch were exploring, separately, in Europe. Not only did Smith have no training in the subject, but the science was so new that no books or journals devoted to the topic were available. Fortunately, thanks to his language proficiency, Smith could read in their native languages the papers that Pasteur and Koch published on anthrax and bacillus. And that is what he proceeded to do. He taught himself the science of bacteriology from scratch. Then, once equipped to do his job, he set about solving the mystery of Texas fever. His discovery would emerge as one of the great medical breakthroughs of the nineteenth century — it would save the lives of countless cattle and those of humans as well.

13

Mortal Ruin

In the 1884 annual report of the Powder River Cattle Company, the board of directors expressed its unhappiness in no uncertain terms: "The Directors regret that Moreton Frewen, the manager of the company in America, has been unable to make a more satisfactory realization of the Stock."

It had quickly become clear, as it should have been from the outset, that the weather in the Powder River Basin was far more treacherous and fickle than Moreton Frewen had projected. Nor was the area "exempt" from snow. In 1881 a drought occurred and the cattle lacked enough grass to bulk up to a weight appropriate for slaughter. In the following year more rain fell, but the arrival of other herds meant far more competition for the grass. Soon prices for beef were not rising, as he had forecast they would, but instead had begun a protracted decline. The *Dundee Advertiser*, a Scottish daily newspaper, summed up the problems a few years later: "When the winter has been good, the summer has been bad. When the drought has been on its best behavior, the blizzard has been violent all over the plains. The one thing that has not varied has been the downward run of prices." Many cattlemen responded to the lower prices by adding to the size of their herds, hoping to make up in volume what they lost in price per steer, leading inexorably to overgrazing. Adding to the financial distress, as beef prices declined, freight rates on the railroads continued to rise.

Moreton Frewen looked at his cattle business and understood early on that the economics were not going to be what he had promised his investors. In 1883 the company dividend was only 6 percent. Now, a year later, it was far worse: only 4 percent, which ranked near the bottom of the list of all the public cattle companies. The number of calves born on the Powder River Cattle Company ranches would decline every year the company was in existence — a phenomenon that Frewen was never able to explain. After the first couple of years, the size of the herd shrank too. Was it ever as large as Frewen claimed it was, using the controversial "book count" methodology, when he created the company and sold the first herds to investors? He was hardly alone in making this mistake: no one had come up with an effective way of counting cattle in herds that now regularly numbered in the tens of thousands. It was a logistical and costly nightmare to gather them and tally them one by one — and too wearing on the cattle.

Looking for ways to improve his profit margins, Frewen came up with two new strategies. The first was to remove the middleman, the so-called feeder, who bought the cattle from the rancher to fatten them up for a year or so before slaughter. Frewen could do the feeding himself. All he had to do was trail his cattle north and establish his own feedlot in Superior, Wisconsin, across a bay of Lake Superior from the city of Duluth, Minnesota. Here the plentiful inexpensive surplus grain could be used as feed. In fact, if Frewen used the lower-quality grain rejected at the grain elevators, the cost to fatten up his cattle would be virtually nothing. Second, he could remove from the equation the railroads, whose high shipping fees had cut deeply into his profits. Instead he would ship his cattle east by steamship from the new port at Superior — a big savings because transport by steamship was much cheaper. The plan had all the hallmarks of a grand Frewen scheme.

He had one further insight: if he could get Parliament to repeal the Contagious Diseases of Cattle Act, which required the slaughtering of all U.S. cattle on their arrival in British ports, he could further fatten up his cattle on that side of the Atlantic. Then he would have all the elements in place for a fully integrated beef export business. He later refined this plan to include the rather convoluted shipping of his cattle to Canada by steamship to the port of Sarnia, on Lake Huron, then their transport by rail to Montreal, from which point they could be shipped by steamer down the St. Lawrence River and across the Atlantic to London or Liverpool. All he needed was the repeal of a pesky law. He set off for London to lobby Parliament.

He launched a one-man public relations campaign replete with newspaper editorials, the arm-twisting of politicians in Ottawa and London, the relentless name-dropping at which Frewen was consummately skilled, and various verbal sallies in which he "gaily libeled his opponents." Despite his effort, the scheme failed. The entrenched cattle interests in Britain and Canada, seeing the U.S. cattle as a competitive threat to their respective interests, stonewalled him.

No one could fault Moreton Frewen for a lack of ingenuity or initiative. One longtime observer would say of him, "You might sometimes — especially if you differed from him — put him down as a bit of an actor but you never could describe him justly as a bore." He was forever hatching new schemes to improve or salvage some aspect of his business. But he simply could not refrain from spending money in the process. He was profligate. When he threw a dinner party in Cheyenne for some visiting titled British friends, he went to great expense to order gardenias for the women and have them delivered from Denver by train. Instead of under-promising and overdelivering, he habitually overpromised and underdelivered.

With two more years of toil in the cattle business behind him and little to show for it, Frewen's personal finances were becoming a problem. He had borrowed forty-five thousand dollars from Pierre Lorillard and even more from the Post Bank in Cheyenne. When, in 1883, his father-in-law bought Clara and him a townhouse in London (18 Chapel Street, later Aldford Street) — that is to say, bought a long lease for the use of the house from the Duke of Westminster — Frewen promptly mortgaged it. Clara then went on a spending spree in London to fix the house up, leaving the couple even deeper in debt. Before long he owed money in London, New York City, and Cheyenne.

Moreton's brother Richard had launched a smaller cattle company of his own in the Dakota Territory, with the Earl of Dunraven as chairman, but by now Richard was in similar financial straits and spoke of having no money at all. The brothers had recently wrapped up their failed efforts in the bat guano business by selling off their cave in Texas. The business had been a complete flop; Moreton personally lost sixty-three hundred dollars on the venture. Late in the year, he admitted in a letter to his wife that money was getting tight: "I shall have to plot and scheme so much, darling, to pay our way this winter."

Then, almost as though a sluice gate had been opened, more and more cattle began to pour into the Powder River Basin. Inevitably these herds competed with the Frewen ranches for use of the open range. It wasn't long before there was talk of overstocking across the entire Wyoming Territory and complaints that the grass was too short and the cattle too thin. Settlers also were homesteading the region now, and the barbed wire that they used to enclose their 160-acre plots complicated matters for the neighboring cattle operations, which could no longer freely move their cattle across the landscape. Starting in the summer of 1885, federal law forbade the ranchers from using barbed wire on public-domain lands, and all existing wire on those lands was ordered removed, which meant the rancher had no way to keep the new cattle herds together, and no way to keep the arriving homesteaders out. A collision between cattlemen and homesteaders looked inevitable.

Moreton Frewen wrote his neighbor, the Irish rancher Horace Plunkett, in desperation in May 1884. "We have got to face this invasion of fresh Texans boldly and at once. I am going to war." The fresh Texans he spoke of were often newly arrived cowboys who hoped to establish themselves as small-time ranchers and homesteaders. To address the problem, the Powder River ranchers formed a new league, with Frewen as secretary. They wrote letters to newcomers, discouraging them from settling in the valley: "I have now to inform you that if you insist on moving [in] we shall oppose your interest by every legal means." Privately, Frewen wrote to his English-born manager Fred Hesse concerning one such new neighbor, a man by the name of Robert Tisdale, "As to this hound Tisdell [*sic*], split him like a rail . . . pull his fence all over the place and have the wire cut in short lengths. He is the kind of man to make an example of."

Frewen himself began to explore the possibility of moving a portion of his herd up into the cattle lands of Alberta, Canada, north of Montana, where reportedly good open range, still largely undiscovered by cattle ranchers, could be found. This new initiative took on urgency when President Grover Cleveland, shortly after his inauguration in early 1885, ordered the removal of cattle herds — totaling some 200,000 head — from the huge Cheyenne and Arapaho Indian Reservation in the Indian Territories where they infringed on the tribes' legal right to the land. When Frewen arrived back at the ranch in the spring of 1885, his foreman, E. W. Murphy, approached him and said gloomily, "Boss, can we clean get out of Wyoming before the fall and save our beasts in Alberta? . . . You will have these southern cattle here in five months and if you lose those five months you had better advertise for skinning outfits." He was right: the overgrazing was about to get far worse.

Frewen telegraphed his directors in London for permission to move the first eight thousand head up to Alberta. But the directors, caught off guard and alarmed at this sudden shift in strategy, balked. It was the beginning of a power struggle for control of the company that would last for the next two years.

By now many of the directors felt they had been hoodwinked

when they first bought into the company. The question, however, was how to minimize their losses. Moving eight thousand head of cattle up to Alberta seemed like a drastic step, but if eight thousand should be moved, then why not all of the cattle? And who should manage this new operation? And what about the existing investment in the Powder River Basin, not just in cattle but also in infrastructure? Or should the new feedlot operation on the banks of Lake Superior, across from Duluth, become the focus? Frewen, ever impatient, finally acted unilaterally and managed to move the eight thousand head fifteen hundred miles north into Canada by the end of that summer. He grazed them there and sold them at a respectable profit. In London, the directors, still unsure how to proceed, hired an expert to review the entire ranch operation.

The expert happened to be the Irishman Horace Plunkett, whose cattle outfit, the EK Ranch, was northwest of Frewen's, on Crazy Woman Creek. At the Cheyenne Club, Plunkett was known for simultaneously playing a set of tennis against one opponent and a chess match against another, calling in his chess moves from the baseline between points. Eton-educated but frail-looking and weighing only 130 pounds, with a limp handshake, Plunkett had arrived in Wyoming, also at age twenty-five, largely for health reasons: he had what he termed a weak constitution. In better times Frewen had tried unsuccessfully to acquire Plunkett's EK Ranch in order to expand the Frewen herd. Moreton griped that Plunkett was hardly an objective outsider and unlikely to treat him fairly. Nevertheless, Plunkett had a better record than Frewen did in delivering dividends to his investors and was thought to be a more experienced manager. Plunkett made the trip up to the city of Superior to view the new feedlot. Badly bitten there by mosquitoes, he hated the area and wrote a report critical of the feedlot scheme. Other parts of the operation struck him as ill conceived as well. For example, privately, he referred to the refrigeration plant on Sherman Hill as "the monument of Frewen's folly & British investors' gullibility."

By now it was apparent to the board and to outsiders that the entire company was poorly organized, with far too little focus on managing costs. There were three separate ranches to manage — four, if you included Alberta. Then the company had its office in Cheyenne, which was over 250 miles from the three main Powder River cattle outfits. Frewen's Castle required a thousand dollars for annual maintenance and thus was proving to be a white elephant. And although Frewen continued to defend the refrigeration operation on Sherman Hill, which he had sold to the company for ten thousand dollars, it had been a financial drain and not the windfall he had promised. Even the feedlot operation would prove to be a long-term money loser. The meatpackers — Gustavus Swift no doubt leading the charge — had responded to Moreton's initiative in Superior by cutting in half the price for which they were willing to sell their prime dressed beef in neighboring Duluth, undercutting Frewen's sales to the local community.

Moreton, who could see that the company was beginning to unravel, wrote a barrage of letters questioning the motives of the directors, arguing his own brief, dishing dirt on his opponents on the board, obfuscating, blaming, refusing to own up to his own fallibility and mistakes, and ultimately suing the directors over the allocation of the preferred dividends. He clashed and fell out with his fellow directors, one by one. The first was the Duke of Manchester, whom he had persuaded to be the first chairman of the company. The duke was by all accounts a stodgy if well-intentioned bore. Frewen described him as "a nice old gentleman" who had "no natural business aptitude."

When Frewen ran into the Duke of Manchester on a London street, the disgruntled noble had a few pointed words for him: "I hope things may now go smoothly with you, even though you have given me really a lot of trouble. I am grown old in the ways of the world, and I joined your Board to oblige you. Let me offer you this word of advice. You are a young fellow and you will find as you travel through life that there are other ways of dealing with elderly men in responsible positions than by running clear over them once a week."

The following year, Manchester's successor as chairman of the board, the Earl of Wharncliffe, the Yorkshire railroad baron, had similar struggles with the impetuous Moreton Frewen and ultimately resigned in disgust. "The board have been very much irritated this year, and set against you by what you call your 'want of discipline' and my efforts have all been directed to peacemaking so far as my sense of duty allowed to do this." Wharncliffe, whose full name was Edward Montagu Stuart Granville Montagu-Stuart-Wortly-Mackenzie, had the dubious distinction of being the man who had introduced Lillie Langtry into London society.

William Beckett Denison, a banker from Leeds and a large shareholder, expressed the view now held by the entire board when he wrote, "I have wished a thousand times that I had never been fool enough to allow myself (mainly from the wish to please my son) to listen to your story in the summer of '82."

Even Frewen's most loyal and devoted friend, the fifth Earl of Rosslyn, a published writer of sonnets and a well-known raconteur, was compelled to remark, "For myself I wish that I had never heard of a horned beast. I'll tell you a story. I telegraphed my factor [stockbroker], 'Buy all horned beasts.' The message arrived, 'Bury all horrid beasts.' I wish we could."

As Frewen freely admitted, "My relations with a lot of good fellows went hopelessly from bad to worse." One news report of the board proceedings that appeared in the financial press read, "Mud was thrown freely by the directors at the manager, and by the manager at the directors." Eventually, to appease the board, Moreton surrendered the position of manager and the thousand-dollar annual salary that went with it — to a new manager of his choosing, a rancher named Thomas Peters. Frewen fully expected to remain in control behind the scenes. Peters, however, did not prove to be up to the job, and he too objected to Frewen's plan to focus on the Superior feedlot operation. Another full-fledged board battle ensued. The directors demanded Frewen's resignation; he refused. The latest acting chairman, William Mackenzie, the Scottish stockbroker and a cofounder of the Dundee Stock Exchange, who represented the preferred shareholders, wrote to Moreton's brother Edward

Frewen in desperation: "Your brother's action absolutely paralyzes us and this is really more than I can bear at a time when I feel very despondent as to my ability to pull the thing out and when I certainly require all the assistance I can get."

At about this time, desperate letters from the foreman in Superior arrived in London, addressed to the company's secretary: "I think you will admit that it is not a very pleasant position to be placed in, to have 1,500 head of cattle forced on me at the last moment, with Winter on us, and no preparations made whatever to take care of them. They are now in the open yard with snow up to their bellies, with the account at the bank overdrawn, and no money to either buy feed or pay the freight on them . . . Unless there is a very radical change made in the manner the Company has of doing business, it must certainly come to grief."

With the help of his brother Edward, who was still the single largest shareholder in the company, Moreton eventually succeeded in electing a new board of directors. Moreton and Edward were granted directorships but only on the condition that Moreton give up his ambition to be reinstated as the manager. Instead, the board chose Horace Plunkett to take over the managerial duties — and Plunkett had the good sense to keep Moreton and his brother Richard, who had once been Plunkett's close friend, but now was his sworn enemy, at a safe distance. But Moreton continued to foment chaos. He stood up at a board meeting and attacked Plunkett, questioning his managerial skills, calling him weak, ineffectual, and overextended. He quarreled with the current strategy and generally made a nuisance of himself. He would ultimately come to believe that it was impossible to run a joint-stock cattle company efficiently five thousand miles away from its directors in London. This was surely true if he himself was involved. His excuse for his overbearing behavior: "I had a very great interest at stake; I had been in a condition of highly strung emotional alarm for two years, and it did really eventuate that the skies were about to fall."

In late 1886 the board floated a plan to reorganize the Powder River Cattle Company. The key provisions were to remove the preferred shareholders and raise more capital. Frewen vehemently opposed the reorganization because he soon realized that if the preferred shareholders accepted debentures in return for their shares, a key feature of the plan, the preferred holders were, if anything, in a stronger position in the event of a liquidation. They would have a higher claim on the company's assets relative to the common shareholders, which included him. "If we are forced to repay the £120,000 in lump sums between now and 1889–90, infallibly we common shareholders will get nothing whatsoever. Our capital is wholly gone," he wrote to Mackenzie. "Your preference people having milked the cow dry, are now anxious to kill her for beef!"

The Powder River Cattle Company had been Moreton's pet project, his first great chance at a financial windfall. Now it was slipping away. He couldn't bear to cede control, nor could he stand to have his judgment questioned. He was terrible at the compromise and accommodation that are at the root of committee work. His letters and circulars were inflammatory, contradictory, polemical, even libelous — but rarely helpful. He threatened and then initiated lawsuits against the company. He sought injunctions on the sale of company property. He conspired with the bank's lenders against the company. He relentlessly lobbied board members outside the meetings and got under the skin of everyone.

There were extenuating circumstances that the board was unaware of: by 1886 Frewen's personal financial condition had grown desperate. His $45,000 debt to Pierre Lorillard had swollen to $50,000, and he was able to pay only a small portion of the interest due on it. He owed the Stebbins & Post Bank in Cheyenne $96,000. This would grow to $100,000 and never be paid off; the bank would go belly up first. He owed his friend Charles E. Lyon £4,000. Lyon too would declare bankruptcy before he was paid off. Finally, Frewen owed £4,000 more to other friends scattered around the world. Late in the year, realizing how dire his circumstances had become, he wrote a frantic letter to his wife from Portland, Oregon, where he was traveling on business.

Get the house sold if possible but don't stick at price. Then about your diamonds, what have you done about them? Try & get Jennie [Churchill] to take them, if you have not; in any case . . . do your best to sell them somewhere. Every hundred is of such importance just now. In six months if things go well we may be all clear . . . Don't you get down in the Blues. Things will come out all right. It will be a lesson to me not to hand the control of my business over to others, whether company directors or false friends like Peters and Plunkett. The fact is there are very, very few people in the world one can trust . . . God Bless you sweet thing. M.

Not long after this he wrote to her again from New York City. Reading the newspaper while dining alone at Delmonico's the night before, he had come across the obituary of Fred Archer, the celebrated jockey who had won the Epsom Derby on Iroquois for Pierre Lorillard, on the eve of the Frewens' wedding day. The death, Moreton was shocked to read, was a suicide. Archer, a tall jockey at five foot ten, was forced throughout his career to crash-diet to keep his weight down. Delirious from one such regimen and depressed following the death of his wife during childbirth, Archer wrested possession of a revolver from his sister and, before she could stop him, shot himself through the roof of the mouth. Acknowledged as the finest jockey of the Victorian era, with 2,748 race wins, including a remarkable 246 in a single season, he was only twenty-nine at the time of his death. "Poor Archer," Frewen wrote in the letter. "What a loss he will be to the riding of our turf. He made a whole school of keen lads & his dash [death] will spoil the future of racing." Frewen made no mention of the fact that his bet on Archer to win on Hampton at the Doncaster Cup race had first launched him on his feckless crusade in the American West.

As yet another disappointing year for the Powder River Cattle Company drew to a close, the new manager, Plunkett, threatened to tender his resignation: "I am shortly to resign the management of the Powder River Cattle Company because I find it a position compared with which the throne of Bulgaria is a bed of roses." He was persuaded to stay on, despite Frewen's constant quibbling with his decisions. At year's end, the company owed ninety thousand dollars and had only twenty-five thousand in cash on hand. Plunkett admonished the board, "Raise all you can. We are in a mess."

The trip that Frewen made to Wyoming in August of that year would be his last. He was struck by how quiet things were in Cheyenne. Collapsed beef prices and overcrowding on the range had resulted in a swift contraction of the industry. Furthermore, the cattle trails between southern Texas and the northern ranges — such as the Western Trail that went straight up to Cheyenne — had been closed that year, permanently, it would seem, by the Kansas legislature, fed up with the spread of Texas fever. Cheyenne was suddenly a cattle town with no cattle arriving. Frewen wrote again to Clara, "Well whatever happens if we do pull our Co. out of its troubles, the rest are all broke, the gang of them; no one in Cheyenne has got a bob left. I never saw such a depressed place. Much love, sweet thing. Your M." He might as well have been describing his own financial condition. He continued, as a postscript, "I dread the coming winter; if it is a severe one half the cattle in Wyoming will die for sure." For once he was right.

The winter of 1886–87 was fast approaching — one that would bring the final curtain down on the Powder River Cattle Company and many of its joint-stock-company compatriots. Moreton Frewen later characterized the board's turmoil over the previous five years: "Had we but known it we were really quarreling over a corpse."

14

Poker on Joint-Stock Principles

Moreton Frewen was not alone in his travails, as the suddenly subdued state of business in Cheyenne in the fall of 1886 suggested. Hubert Teschemacher, operating the Teschemacher & DeBillier ranches, had also tried to move cattle out of Wyoming Territory and had similarly shocked his investors. Teschemacher compounded his problems by announcing that his ranches (his company owned three, scattered around Wyoming) could accommodate five thousand more head of cattle, only to suddenly reverse himself the very next day, stating that the herds must be moved instantly to new grazing areas. To meet his dividends, Teschemacher had borrowed against future earnings by leveraging the company and using the cash raised to meet the annual dividend, a recipe for disaster if business didn't improve — and it didn't. One irritated investor, John Bigelow, a former editor of the *New York Post* and U.S. consul to Paris, scolded Teschie for not keeping the directors better informed: "I now learn for the first time that the pasturage on our ranges was insufficient and that you were driving your stock into neighborhood states. I think this necessity and

the occasion of it should have been communicated to stockholders."
Bigelow asked to see the accounts, but it is doubtful that Teschemacher ever provided them. If he had seen them, Bigelow would
have been shocked at the sloppy records — even the handwriting
was barely legible.

One aspiring British cattle rancher had proved far more feckless than even Moreton Frewen. The Earl of Aylesford failed to get
his operation off the ground. Aylesford's wife, a onetime mistress
of the Prince of Wales, had run off to Paris to live with Randolph
Churchill's brother, the Marquess of Blandford, heir to the Marlborough dukedom and the magnificent Blenheim Palace, where Winston Churchill was born. This new affair had caused a scandal, and
the Prince of Wales cursed Blandford as "the greatest blackguard
alive." That in turn brought Lord Randolph Churchill (Winston's father) to the defense of his brother, brandishing letters revealing the
affair between Aylesford's wife and the Prince of Wales and threatening to release them to the public, an act that might have doomed
the prince's chance of becoming king. Furious, the Prince of Wales
challenged Randolph Churchill to a duel on the dueling grounds of
northern France. Prime Minster Benjamin Disraeli intervened to
negotiate a rapprochement. Randolph and Jennie Churchill would
remain out of favor with the Prince of Wales for a decade. Aylesford's
wife remained with the Marquess of Blandford in Paris, where she
gave birth to an illegitimate son. Aylesford himself sought solace in
the American West but seemed to find more of it in the bottle.

Aylesford bought himself a ranch in Big Spring, Texas, not far
from Midland, paying forty thousand dollars for an unknown quantity of cattle on "range delivery," which is to say, sight unseen. He
arrived accompanied by twenty-five horses, thirteen hunting dogs,
five servants, and an Episcopal clergyman to serve as his private
secretary and spiritual counselor. He soon added a pair of purebred
basset hounds to the menagerie, for hunting the local cottontail
rabbits. From the outset he was more interested in hunting than in
ranching, and even more interested in drinking. His ability to con-
sume alcohol became legendary. He reportedly drank half a gallon

of whiskey daily, occasionally chasing it with a fifth of gin. Known as "Judge," he endeared himself to the cowboys by purchasing both the local hotel and the local saloon and regularly treating everyone there to free drinks — one afternoon he reportedly bought seventeen rounds for the house. He showed up at his first spring cattle roundup with a ten-gallon keg of whiskey and promptly brought the proceedings to a halt as the cowboys got riotously drunk, delaying the work by a day. It was said that heaps of empty liquor bottles piled up outside his ranch house and that he would always open a new bottle for anyone who dropped by. "He don't stop at one, neither," reported one cowboy to the local newspaper. "I've been to the ranch many a time to stay all night and woke in the mornin' to find the bottles lyin' around as thick as fleas, the boys two deep on the floor snorin' like mad buffalo and the Judge with a bottle in each hand over in the corner."

It didn't end well. Aylesford died of alcohol poisoning in Big Spring on January 13, 1885, at age thirty-six. His embalmed remains were shipped by rail to New York. From there the casket was returned to England by a British warship at the request of the Prince of Wales, one of the two men who had cuckolded Aylesford in his homeland. Something must have been amiss with the Aylesford range count because the cattle herd that he bought for $40,000 was valued at and sold posthumously for $750.

The New Yorker Thomas Sturgis, who had run a ranch with his brother William and served as the first secretary of the Wyoming Stock Growers Association, caught the expansionist bug and floated a cattle ranch called the Union Cattle Company on Boston money in 1883. His directors included distinguished Bostonians and Harvard men, such as the copper baron Alexander Agassiz, son of the scientist Louis Agassiz; the stockbroker Henry L. Higginson, who founded the Boston Symphony Orchestra; and Quincy Adams Shaw, a scion of the distinguished Shaw family, once among the richest of the Boston Brahmins. (Shaw was also Francis Parkman's friend and companion on the trip recounted in *The Oregon Trail*.) The three men were related by marriage: Higginson and Shaw had both married sisters of Alexander Agassiz. Capitalized at $2 million, with sixty thousand head of cattle, the Union Cattle Company had delivered 8 percent dividends for its first two years before going into a tailspin from which it never recovered. Like so many others, the company struggled to respond to the problems of low beef prices, overgrazing, and the need to acquire land and a feed station. By the fall of 1886, on the eve of the winter of the Big Die-Up, the company had taken on $1.6 million in debt and, unbeknownst to its Boston shareholders, was nearing bankruptcy.

A similar story could be told about the Swan Land & Cattle Company. The operation began as three ranches started by the brothers Alexander and Thomas Swan in 1881, but it became a joint-stock company floated in Scotland in 1883, with a capitalization of £600,000, or $3 million ($71.7 million in today's money), with Alexander Swan staying on as the manager, for better or worse. Swan was once quoted as saying, "In our business we are often compelled to do certain things which, to the inexperienced, seem a little crooked." Through further acquisitions the ranch became the largest cattle company on the open range, owning or controlling a swatch of land as large as Connecticut. Somehow it delivered dividends of over 20 percent right up until 1886. But it was highly leveraged, and worse, its herds were purchased based on inflated book counts. Here, too, its shareholders were in the dark that the company was about to unravel.

With the proliferation of these joint-stock companies, consolidation had become the norm, and the larger ranchers acquired many of the smaller outfits. By the mid-1880s the average ranch was ten times the size it might have been a decade earlier, the herds numbering in the tens of thousands instead of the mere thousands. Bigger was perceived as financially better for the economies of scale that it allegedly offered. And of course, a bigger ranch meant more prestige for the cattle baron. By late 1886, nearly thirteen million cattle grazed on the open range.

The huge growth extended well beyond the open range. In California, a former San Francisco butcher named Henry Miller had assembled a mammoth cattle ranch, owning 1.4 million acres and controlling some 22,000 square miles of land in California, Nevada, and Oregon. Most of these holdings were located in the San Joaquin Valley, today known as the food basket of America for the amount and variety of fruits and vegetables it grows annually. In Texas, Richard King, a former steamboat captain of Irish extraction, assembled 614,000 acres and a herd of fifty thousand cattle, thirty thousand sheep, and six thousand hogs before he died of stomach cancer in 1885. His widow and son-in-law would more than double the acreage until the ranch extended across four Texas counties.

The Texas Land and Cattle Company, a Dundee syndicate with the famed Scottish financier Robert Fleming as a shareholder, owned thirteen ranches and owned or leased a parcel of land that was larger than all of Long Island, New York. Another Scottish syndicate put together the Matador Land and Cattle Company in 1882 near Lubbock, Texas, with leased land of 1.8 million acres. Today the remnants of this ranch, a mere 130,000 acres, are operated as a subsidiary of Koch Industries.

The largest of them all, the XIT Ranch, was backed by Chicago money as well as the Marquess of Tweeddale and the Earl of Aberdeen. At its peak it boasted three million acres of land covering parts of ten Texas counties. There were 325 windmills and 10 dams scattered across its vast property. Over 150,000 cattle grazed behind fifteen hundred miles of barbed wire.

Virtually every big ranch was overseen by a board of directors and a shareholder syndicate whose financial expectations had to be met *consistently,* and this meant a much greater focus on how to manage costs and ensure growth. The territorial stock associations, such as the Wyoming Stock Growers Association, created new regulations, mostly designed to protect the entrenched interests of the cattle barons, and these entailed new and more expensive ways of conducting business. No longer was a cattle ranch the product of the ambitious individual efforts of a trail driver like Charlie Goodnight or Granville Stuart, though both men remained active ranch owners. No longer could a ranch be run loosely, according to the founder's whims. No longer could the manager count on the cooperation of like-minded cowboys who shared origins similar to his own. With greater investments now at stake, the demand arose for a more professional approach to the business. This meant the hiring of professional managers, many of them experienced cattlemen from Scotland who could actually run cattle companies. A few of these, Murdo Mackenzie and John Clay in particular, would earn stellar reputations in the business — especially in the aftermath of the catastrophe that was brewing. The widespread corporatization of the cattle trade had taken hold. It happened so quickly and so seamlessly, in response to emerging financial pressures, that even the cattle barons were slow to understand the changes that were transforming their enterprises, once highly lucrative and highly entrepreneurial in nature.

Between 1865 and 1890 no fewer than fifteen hundred British companies, many of them cattle companies, had been formed to invest in the trans-Mississippi West. Between 1879 and 1888 alone, the British formed thirty-three limited companies to invest in cattle. Of the total $169 million ($4 billion in today's dollars) initially invested, some $45 million, or roughly a quarter, went into cattle companies. The Anglo-American outfits were the largest, most visible cattle companies on the open range.

As gigantism took hold, corruption became more prevalent. Even if you were wary of book counts and wanted to count your cattle in person, you could still get scammed. The two McWatty brothers came over from Scotland to buy a herd in 1885 at the peak of the boom, after fellow countrymen had warned them not to trust book counts. They had the misfortune to run into a clever rancher named Charlie Williams on Sand Creek in Carbon County, Wyoming. Spotting a pair of greenhorns, Williams insisted that the high altitude of Wyoming didn't agree with him, compelling him to retire. The McWatty brothers arranged to buy his herd of fifteen hundred head of cattle after Williams offered to throw in his ten saddle horses for free. The brothers were convinced they had found a bargain, but insisted on counting the cattle in person. What they didn't know was that Williams owned only five hundred head. But his neighbor on Sand Creek, who owned a much larger herd, happened to use a brand very similar to his own. Williams borrowed a thousand head of his neighbor's cattle and drove them over to his ranch, where he corralled them with his herd. The *Cheyenne Sun* of August 31, 1889, reported what happened next: "The Scotchmen arrived on time, and taking a seat on the fence near the corral proceeded to count the cattle as they passed out of the corral gate. Charlie took good care to keep the cattle moving and plenty of dust flying, and along with his 500 head the borrowed stock went through the gate and were counted without a suspicion of the difference in the brands. Soon the whole herd had passed out on the prairie and were scattered everywhere. The Scotchmen, after an inspection of the buildings and the horses, expressed themselves well satisfied, paid over their money and took receipts."

Then Charlie Williams vanished with his ill-gotten gains.

In hindsight it is easy to see that the big cattle companies had taken on huge risks that they poorly understood. They had grievously misjudged the environment of the open range, assuming the weather to be tolerable for their cattle and not factoring in the role that a drought or vicious winter weather might play, or how overgrazing might make it impossible for the grasslands to provide feed for such gigantic herds. They had founded their operations on the use of public-domain land, overlooking the fact that U.S. land laws favored the small settler, who could claim legal title to 160-acre parcels on the same public land (and 640 under the Desert Land Act), in places that might constrain ranchers' ability to freely graze their herds or supply them with water.

As these joint-stock-company cattle ranches grew bigger and bigger, their size, visibility, and bureaucracy began to work against them. Before long they incurred the resentment of small ranchers and the rush of arriving settlers, who complained to their congressmen and to the press about the self-regarding behavior and bullying tactics of the big ranches.

A classic example of the cattle barons' overreach lay in the leasing or purchasing of railroad lands, which ran in a checkerboard pattern along each side of the tracks; every other square remained in the possession of the U.S. government. The cattle companies, notably the acquisitive Swan Land & Cattle Company, leased or bought (at a dollar per acre) the alternating squares not claimed by the government and then ran fences along two adjoining sides of each of their squares. At the point where four squares of the checkerboard met, the cattle barons left eight inches fenceless, where they crossed the government's property, before resuming the fence along the perimeter of their next square. This had the effect of enclosing twice the acreage that the ranchers were entitled to. This highly controversial strategy was successfully defended in court until 1895, when such enclosures were finally declared illegal.

Suddenly the big cattle interests found themselves unpopular, viewed as an overbearing political and economic force not averse to flexing its muscles to exploit whatever advantages it could find on the open range. The Wyoming Stock Growers Association was quick to pick up on this. In the minutes of its annual meeting in April 1885, the remarks of its secretary, Thomas Sturgis, reflected the cattle barons' new defensiveness:

> Among the new questions arising, one imperatively demands attention, namely the use of government lands for grazing. The eastern public who gladly hailed our production of cheap beef ten years ago, and welcomed us to the use of the barren plateaux where we risked our lives daily against the Indians, has now no milder term for us than bullock barons and aristocrats of the plains. Every possible misrepresentation is made in the public prints. Though we have built up the only industry practicable on these arid and sandy prairies and created millions of taxable property, Congress is daily urged to crusade against us as though we were a class whose business was a byword and reproach and whose destruction would be a commendable one.

Just how much of this anti–cattle baron criticism was deserved is debatable. Unquestionably the WSGA, representing the only viable industry in Wyoming, had a stranglehold on the territorial legislature. Indeed, it had largely created that legislature. Furthermore, at that time corruption in politics was widespread at both the local and national levels; abuse of the land laws, in particular, presented an ongoing problem. Much of the public backlash focused less on the WSGA, per se, and more on the growing tide of foreign investment in the United States, in the cattle business and elsewhere. To the most vocal critics, this looked like a problem that could be addressed through legislation.

The British, in particular, were ripe targets for criticism. Great Britain in the late nineteenth century still stood at the pinnacle of world power, blessed with huge capital surpluses available to invest in the New World. With an empire that stretched across a quarter of the world's landmass and encompassed a fifth of its people, the British were the power to be feared most — especially their prodigious wealth and acquisitiveness. As colonizers they were fast becoming unpopular, and the patronizing attitudes of men like Moreton Frewen didn't help their cause. "If I laugh at Americans, it is the laughter of affection — as of one who laughs not at, but with them. What a people!" he would remark in his memoirs. "When I am in the Great United States I want to move about amongst its people and laugh at them. I yearn to pull legs. I want them without resenting it to let me regard them as children — not yet half through the schools — children who play with all the fire-crackers of a vast continent; who are strangely irresponsible in their ways." He professed to be "absurdly fond of this strange people," but in a confidential letter to his wife, Clara, he wrote, "These western men, at least some of them, are the most impracticable, aggressively independent people possible, and I often long to thrash one or two but for the want of dignity in such a proceeding." Other Brits were even more scathing: "I did not like the cowboys; they impressed me as brutal and cowardly, besides being utterly devoid of manners or good feelings," wrote Lady Rose Pender in her book *A Lady's Experience in the Wild West in 1883*.

The ill will was mutual. Aristocratic hauteur, in particular, did not play well among the egalitarian-minded American cowboys. "Of all the English snobs of great pretensions who flew so high and sank so low, probably the Frewens are the chiefs," the *Cheyenne Daily Sun* stated in 1887, the year of Queen Victoria's Golden Jubilee. A letter to the *Castle Rock Journal* in Douglas County, Colorado, that same year spelled out the anti-monarchal sentiments of the average American: "We want no caste, no upper classes, no 'lower orders.' We should unite in trying to stamp out feudalism and flunkyism." American farmers too were growing restive. Suffering from low prices for their commodities in the 1880s, they began to resent the powerful railroads, which were gouging them on freight costs. But they harbored even more ill will for wealthy foreigners, who appeared to be buying up vast tracts of railway grant lands, depriving Americans of access. "Together, big corporations and 'titled aliens' were accused of filching the patrimony of the people," wrote Peter Pagnamenta in his book *Prairie Fever: British Aristocrats in the American West, 1830–1890*.

The wave of Irish immigration, which added Irish (and Scottish) cowboys and homesteaders to the ranks of workers in the American West, contributed to this growing distrust. These Irish immigrants deeply resented the English for the decades of mistreatment they had received in their home country. Absentee landlords, men like John Adair (Charlie Goodnight's partner) and the Duke of Sutherland, were especially unpopular. Both men, along with many of the great British landlords, had forced many thousands of Irish farmers and Scottish crofters off their estates because of failure to pay rent or because the landlords wanted to pursue large-scale sheep farming or game hunting. The so-called Highland Clearances, which had been going on for nearly a century, had devastated Gaelic culture and impoverished tens of thousands of small tenant farmers, who were forced to the coasts or put on ships bound for Australia or North America. In Adair's case, the evictions were meant to clear his lands of tenants so that he could build a castle and convert twelve thousand acres of former farmland into his personal hunting grounds. In one memorable episode in 1861, he forcibly removed from their homes forty-seven families, which included 150 screaming children, despite the fact that these folk had no place to go. Between 1813 and 1913 the area covered by salmon-fishing estates and deer forests in Scotland alone went from a few hundred thousand to 3,599,744 acres, creating the largest human-made "wilderness" in Europe, for the exclusive private use of the sporting class. Over in Ireland, as part of the so-called land wars of the 1870s, '80s, and '90s, Irish agitators and the National Land League fought to get land redistributed and to evict absentee landlords, further poisoning relations between the Irish and the English. The last thing that Irish and Scottish immigrants to the United States wanted to see was the same crowd of landlords asserting themselves in their new country. As voting Americans, these groups lobbied for legislation to limit the amount of British investment allowed in the western territories.

The British did not seem to realize that they had a public relations problem. For example, the Duke of Sutherland, who already owned vast western ranch holdings in addition to his incomparable acreage in England and Scotland, didn't do the British any favors when he and his son (Moreton Frewen's friend Lord Stafford) decided to add to their American holdings. The largest landowner in Great Britain, the duke owned a castle in northern Scotland, known as Dunrobin, that was so enormous, imposing, and magnificent that Queen Victoria upon visiting it exclaimed, "I have come from my House to your Palace!" In the spring of 1881 the duke and his son embarked on a well-publicized rail trip through the American West, with a view to buying even more land. Newspapers chronicled their lavish spending and extravagant lifestyle, from their private railcars to their crates of champagne. "Through the ornamental windows of the coaches the open-eyed and expansive mouthed population of Lathrop caught glimpses of white aproned and sable hued waiters filling silver coffee pots. The cooking carriage was sending up a volume of smoke as if the Duke were arranging a barbecue for his 24,000 tenants," reported the *San Francisco Chronicle*.

Newspapers and vote-seeking politicians picked up on the negative sentiment. "It is impossible to exaggerate the gravity of the danger that threatens the Republic if the seeds of absentee landlordism, so plentifully planted by the British aristocracy, be allowed to grow and bring forth their legitimate fruits of poverty and degradation," grumbled the *Chicago Daily Tribune* in early 1885. These criticisms suggested that unless such subversive action was checked, the outcome of the American Revolution, no less, might be overturned in Britain's favor, as Americans lost their land by selling it back to colonial overlords. This, of course, was a gross overstatement.

The British had roughly $45 million invested in the range and the cattle ranches in the mid-1880s. If we assume that they got what they paid for when they bought in, a dubious supposition, and if the value of all the cattle on the open range and in Texas, combined, was valued at roughly $340 million (16.5 million cattle at twenty-five dollars a head), then the British investment likely accounted for, at best, 13 percent of the entire investment in this portion of the industry. Theirs was not a dominant share, but the prominence of a handful of large ranches and the visibility of their managers and owners made them seem more powerful. Incidentally, that $340 million made up only 28 percent of the value of all the cattle in the country in 1884; much of the remaining investment was in midwestern feedlot cattle, dairy cattle, or cattle on small ranches and farms, which were never intended for commercial beef markets.

An 1886 report compiled by the Department of the Interior, at the behest of a group of congressmen, revealed for the first time how much land the British actually owned: 21 million acres, an area slightly larger than the state of South Carolina. (By comparison, Wyoming has 64.1 million acres.) The foreign owners of the largest tracts were the Marquess of Tweeddale (1.75 million acres), the Duke of Sutherland (425,000 acres), Lord Dunmore (120,000 acres), the Earl of Dunraven (60,000 acres), and Lord Houghton (60,000 acres). Foreign syndicates owned millions more, but even in aggregate, the foreigners hardly presented a significant threat to the American way of life.

In the summer of that same year, after three years of legislative maneuvering, it looked as though Congress would pass legislation to restrict foreign investment. A bill was designed to limit aliens and companies more than 20 percent owned by non-Americans from buying land in the western territories, where land speculation was most rampant. Congressman Lewis Payson of Illinois made the case: "We are at present permitting the coining of immense private fortunes in the hands of foreign nobility and gentry." The House voted and passed the bill, but the Senate delayed passage, pushing the final vote into the next session. Finally, in February 1887, the federal Alien Property Act passed Congress. On March 3, President Grover Cleveland signed it into law. It did not affect foreign holdings already in existence, but it greatly limited new foreign investment in land.

It proved to be something of a moot point. The British press had grown skeptical of the value of investment in the western cattle trade. Why, if the business was so good, one publication asked, were the Americans so eager to sell their herds to the British? The *Edinburgh Courant* went so far as to call American cattle ranching "only poker on joint-stock principles." The consensus was that the Americans were asking 20 percent more for their herds than they could sell them for domestically and that the book counts inflated the size of those herds by another 25 percent. Such practices had put British cattle investors in a deep hole from the outset. The price of shares in existing cattle companies declined sharply, making it impossible for new cattle syndicates to be formed or for existing ones to raise more money. Furthermore, the mediocre investment returns of recent years were about to turn into outright losses. In fact, in the months immediately following the bill's passage, the British would lose so much money on their cattle investments that they would never again pose a serious threat as landlords, or cattle barons, in the United States.

A bison skull pile in the mid-1870s waiting to be ground up for fertilizer. Hunters, in collusion with the military, the railroads, and the telegraph companies, slaughtered the great bison herds that once numbered in the millions. By 1884, only 325 of the animals survived south of Canada.

Bison skinners in Montana Territory, around 1881. A good skinner could strip thirty to forty bison hides a day.

The chuck wagon, invented by Charles Goodnight, became ubiquitous across the open range. Here a crew of cowboys enjoy such delicacies as son-of-a-bitch stew.

Joseph G. McCoy, founder of Abilene, Kansas, the first cattle town — "one of the great single ideas of the nation's history," according to historian Paul Wellman. After failing to make a fortune in the cattle trade, McCoy would try his hand at selling refrigerated railcars and barbed-wire fencing and counting cattle for the U.S. Census Bureau.

McCoy's Drovers Cottage in Abilene. Built at a cost of $15,000, or $359,000 in today's money, the hotel featured a saloon and a billiards parlor. It could sleep 80 and feed 240.

Cowboy Teddy Blue Abbott at age nineteen, in 1879. His account of life on the open range is unsurpassed in its accuracy and piquancy.

Rye whiskey was the drink of choice in western saloons. Mixed drinks included such concoctions as Cactus Wine and Mule Skinner. Also on sale were various medicinal tonics to cure every conceivable ailment. Note the brass cuspidor on the floor, also known as a spittoon or a gaboon.

Bat Masterson, one of the few gunmen to survive the era and live a long life. He spent his later years as a New York sportswriter and died of a heart attack at his office desk in 1921.

James Butler "Wild Bill" Hickok. An early marshal of Abilene and known to have killed eight men, he was shot in the back of the head in a Deadwood saloon. His poker hand at the time, two black aces and two black eights — "the dead man's hand" — earned him a place in the Poker Hall of Fame.

Meatpacker Gustavus Swift, whose groundbreaking business practices helped set the course for American corporations.

The Union Stock Yards outside Chicago, about 1880. The gigantic facility covered 375 acres and included 2,300 livestock pens. By the turn of the century, 9 million animals were slaughtered here annually.

IN THE SLAUGHTER HOUSE.

Knife-wielding gutters and cutters in a Chicago slaughterhouse, 1892. These workers faced extreme safety and sanitation challenges, and no regulations existed to protect the meat from contamination.

New York's world-famous Delmonico's restaurant at Fifth Avenue and 14th Street, circa 1873. Here at "the Citadel," French chef Charles Ranhofer invented eggs Benedict, lobster Newburg, and baked Alaska, and helped popularize the American steak.

Many cattle barons made Cheyenne, Wyoming, their headquarters and built grand houses and bachelor quarters there. By the 1880s, the town purportedly had the highest per capita income of any city in the world.

Modeled on the Somerset Club on Beacon Hill, Boston, the Cheyenne Club offered its all-male membership superb food, French champagne, Cuban cigars, and a discreet venue to conduct cattle business. At one dinner given by the British members for their American counterparts, 41 attendees in white tie consumed 66 bottles of champagne and 22 bottles of red wine.

Five gentlemen in formal evening dress in Wyoming in the 1880s. Wealthy Ivy Leaguers and British aristocrats alike caught cattle fever.

Scotsman John Clay. The savvy ranch manager witnessed every major event in the cattle business for fifty years and was one of the few cattlemen to emerge from the era with his fortune, if not his reputation, intact.

Owen Wister, author of *The Virginian: The Horseman of the Plains*, published in 1902. His iconic cowboy hero became the model for the western genre.

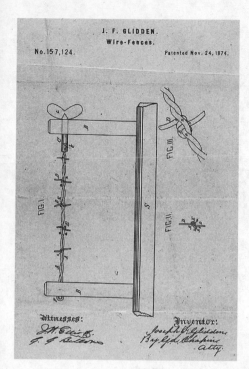

Joseph Glidden's original patent for barbed wire, which he named "The Winner." His kitchen coffee grinder made the creation of the barb possible.

Theodore Roosevelt in 1885, posing in his bespoke buckskins and holding his favorite Winchester rifle, engraved with western animals and scrollwork. The bowie knife was custom made for him by Tiffany & Co. His Colt six-shooters sported ivory grips monogrammed and engraved by master engraver Louis Daniel Nimschke.

Theodore Roosevelt in the Badlands. His experiences there following the deaths of his wife and his mother would be crucial to his formation as a man, a politician, and a conservationist.

The dour epidemiologist Theobald Smith, circa 1890, when he solved the riddle of cattle fever — one of the great medical breakthroughs of the nineteenth century.

English entrepreneur Moreton Frewen wearing his buckskins. In 1882 his Powder River Cattle Company became the first cattle company to be listed on the London Stock Exchange. A succession of business failures would earn him the nickname "Mortal Ruin."

Frewen's Castle, on the Powder River in Wyoming, was used to lure British aristocrats out to the American West on hunting junkets. The structure included a walnut staircase imported from England and a mezzanine balcony where it was hoped one day an orchestra would perform.

Clara Jerome at the time of her marriage to Moreton Frewen in 1881. She was dreamy, romantic, and chronically late for everything, including her own wedding ceremony. At the time of her trip to Wyoming she had never once tied her own shoes.

The Marquis de Morès, the son of a French duke, quit his job as a Wall Street arbitrageur to build a doomed meatpacking empire in the Badlands. A superb shot and a deadly swordsman, he became, in Morton Frewen's words, "a lightening rod for any local ructions."

The marquise, the former Medora von Hoffman, was the daughter of Baron Louis von Hoffman, a financier best known for cofounding New York's Knickerbocker Club. She was an accomplished rider, sharpshooter, and watercolorist.

The Chateau, the eight-bedroom hunting lodge built by de Morès in the Badlands. His other ventures included a stagecoach service and the shipping of fresh northwestern salmon to eastern markets in his refrigerated railcars.

Onetime gold miner Granville Stuart became the largest cattle baron in Montana. Stuart's Stranglers killed thirty alleged rustlers and used vigilante tactics that set the precedent for the Johnson County War.

"Big Nose George" Parrott, a notorious train robber, rustler, and murderer. He had to be hanged twice — an indignity compounded when the coroner, future Wyoming governor Dr. John E. Osborne, skinned his corpse to make a pair of shoes and matching medical bag. Osborne is said to have worn the shoes to his gubernatorial inauguration.

Vigilante justice on the open range. There were 326 known vigilante movements in the United States between 1767 and 1909, but many were ineffectual and fewer than half resulted in a lynching.

Alleged cattle rustler Cattle Kate was actually Ella Watson, a kindhearted Kansas newlywed falsely accused of theft and prostitution. She and her husband, Jim Averell, were hanged side by side from a tree branch.

Frank Canton, a stock detective hired to find and punish cattle thieves and the man who did more than anyone to instigate the Johnson County War. Unbeknownst to his Cheyenne cattle baron bosses, his real name was Joe Horner, an escaped convict who had once clubbed a man to death with a wooden neck yoke.

Nate Champion, a cowboy and cattle foreman who fell out with the Cheyenne cattle kings. Trapped in a cabin, he single-handedly held off fifty gunmen for almost a day — and managed to record details of the encounter in his diary. "By God, if I had fifty men like you I could whip the whole state of Wyoming," said one of his killers.

The captured Johnson County invaders. The Cheyenne cattlemen hired twenty-five professional gunmen from Paris, Texas, and headed north with them by train. The sheriff of Buffalo, Wyoming, his deputy, and all the county commissioners were targeted for assassination as the invaders tried to drive homesteaders and small cattle ranchers off the open range.

Teddy Blue Abbott as he looked later in life, rolling a cigarette. He ultimately became what no cowboy ever wanted to be: a farmer.

A wolfer's cabin. Gray wolves were the real rustlers in Johnson County. When the cattle industry contracted, the cattlemen could no longer afford to pay for wolfers, and the wolf population exploded. By 1960 federal bounties would drive the animal to the brink of extinction.

Hubert Teschemacher, the urbane Harvard man, cattle baron, and former president of the Cheyenne Club. He would help to write the Wyoming state constitution, then violate it by participating in the Johnson County War.

Theodore Roosevelt reading in Colorado in 1905. Historian Stephen Ambrose would write of TR, "He was one of America's first conservationists, and he is still her greatest."

15

The Big Die-Up

E very fall, two out of three cowboys in an outfit on the open range were laid off and had to fend for themselves during winter. But the best ones, like Teddy Blue Abbott, were kept on the payroll so that the ranch, by retaining a strong skeleton staff, could be up and running quickly in the spring.

For the cowboys kept on payroll, there were two forms of winter accommodations. If you were assigned to work at the home ranch, you boarded in the bunkhouse, often known as the Dog House or the Dive, along with the other cowboys who remained on staff. This form of lodging at least guaranteed you some company during the long winter months. Bunkhouses were often joined to a mess hall and cookhouse by a breezeway where a cowboy could store his saddle and other tack, so even when you were snowed in, you had some room to move around.

If, alternatively, you were assigned to line duty at a line camp on the boundary of the ranch, perhaps for a few weeks at a time, then you might well live alone in a cabin of, at best, two hundred square feet. This poorly insulated structure was usually equipped with a potbellied stove or a stone fireplace to keep you warm and, needless to say, had no running water. Here your work involved preventing the cattle from getting into trouble of various kinds, keeping the gray wolves at bay, and ensuring that the river ice was broken somewhere nearby so that the cattle could drink. Wood needed to be collected and cut, water boiled, food prepared, dishes somehow washed. The horses had to be fed and watered, and their stalls, if there were any, shoveled. On the coldest days of winter, each trip to the outhouse became an ordeal; frostbite was a distinct possibility. Weeks might go by without seeing another person. You had to be happy in your own company or risk losing your mental bearings. Cabin fever could become potentially life-threatening. As Teddy Blue said, "They tell a story about a fellow down in Texas who was stuck out in a horse camp by himself all winter, and when they went and hunted him up in the spring, they found he had his hat and coat draped on a stump and was shooting at it. He said: 'I'm going to get the son of a bitch before he gets me.'"

Back at the home ranch, the cowboys crowded around the fireplace in the ranch house and tried to keep themselves amused with dominoes, card games such as Auction Pitch, or singing songs and telling stories—all of which they had heard many times before. Whittling and quirt making were also popular hobbies. Gambling and alcohol were forbidden, as they were on trail drives and roundups. As Teddy Blue pointed out, "There wasn't anything to do except talk, and the talk soon ran out. We told each other everything we knew in a week. I knew about ten songs, and I sung them until everybody was sick of them. After that nobody had much to say. It's not that men get to fighting when they are holed up together, unless there is some reason for it, but they get kind of surly and quit talking." More often than not, reading matter consisted of mail-order catalogues, picture magazines, and farm journals. No one could escape the deadening monotony of bitterly cold days, which were short on sunlight and spent mostly indoors. Stories have been told of cowboys who took to memorizing the ingredient labels on food cans. Even the food itself became boring. When the cowboys grew sick of the taste of beef, they would hunt for deer during the day, but it wasn't long before they grew sick of deer meat as well. "So after that it was nothing but sowbelly and beans, three times a day," Teddy Blue remembered.

Reuben B. Mullins, a cowboy who worked in Wyoming on the open range from 1884 to 1889, recalled two cowpunchers in his outfit who, one winter, seized on the idea of writing to a matrimonial magazine called *Heart and Hand* in search of mail-order brides. They wrote letters stating that they were each looking for "some young lady who would be willing to come out to the big, open spaces and share their cabins and wages." To their utter astonishment, a gunnysack arrived a few weeks later, packed with letters addressed to the two cowboys. For the next fortnight, according to Mullins, the ranch was the quietest on the Cheyenne River as all the cowboys in the outfit read each and every one. "All the noise to be heard was the rustle of paper, perhaps a snicker, and occasionally a good hearty laugh."

According to Mullins, a cowboy named Frank began a correspondence with a very literate letter writer, a woman from Arkansas, and the two quickly became amorous pen pals. In due course, he rode into Cheyenne in his best clothes, had his picture taken in a photo studio, and sent it off to his new sweetie. Weeks passed with no response, and the cowboy grew despondent. Finally, a month or so later, a reply arrived, also with a photo enclosed. To Frank's dismay the smiling woman in the photo was black. Mullins describes how the cowboys fell silent, and "none could decide wither to laugh at Frank or mourn with him." Given the social mores of the time, it is not surprising that the photograph brought an end to this intriguing correspondence. It wasn't long before the cowboys grew bored with letter writing and resorted to "former sport," to put it euphemistically, for diversion.

Even if you had the money to afford creature comforts, like good rocking chairs, which Hubert Teschemacher did, the long winters still presented an endurance test, in the northern ranges especially.

Teschie and his brother Arthur holed up their first winter along with Frederick DeBillier and, a year or two later, with Richard Trimble, at their ranch near Laramie, when they weren't at their bachelor quarters in Cheyenne. Richard Trimble had his poodle to keep him company, although the best winter companion in these circumstances, by all accounts, was a cat, if you could find one, because a cat was cheaper to feed than a dog and didn't require exercise. Teschemacher had a box of paperback literary classics, all in French, to keep him occupied, as well as a piano, a guitar, and two banjos, and a banjo instruction manual. He also kept sheet music on hand, such as Geo. von Kameke's *Musical Library*, which included the scores and lyrics to popular melodies such as "O Maiden Mine I Sing to Thee," "Spring Gentle Spring," "Goodbye Charlie," "Won't You Tell Me Why Robin?" "O! Give Me a Home by the Sea," and "Home Sweet Home," a lineup that may have accentuated the Harvard men's homesickness. Hubert's brother Arthur made it through just one winter in Wyoming, then hung up his spurs and returned to the comforts of Paris, where he soon became romantically entangled with a Russian princess.

But whether winter lodgings consisted of a bunkhouse or a cabin, the space was soon likely to be pervaded by the stench of sweat, tracked-in manure, dirty socks, chewing tobacco, and smoke from lamps that burned coal oil or tallow. Such close quarters were none too tidy either: clothes were "hung on the floor so they wouldn't fall down and get lost," as one wag put it.

If a young man had enlisted in the ranks of cowboys for what he thought was a glamorous life, one winter on the open range was usually more than enough to disillusion him. The work was hard, dirty, and monotonous — hardly the exciting version depicted in the dime novels and the eastern press. As the cowboy Reuben Mullins noted in the preface to his memoir, "Many writers of fiction portray this wild and romantic life of cowboys, yet through the years of my experience while engaged in the actual work, the romance supposed to be a part of such a life failed to show up. However, I did find such a life and work a continual round of drudgery, exposure, and hard work which beggar description, and in no case is the departed cowboy deserving of the obituary given him by commercialized writers."

Needless to say, the winter of the Big Die-Up, in 1886–87, presented unique challenges for the men as well as the animals. The big storms and record-breaking cold spells never let up. Nearly three feet of snow covered the ground in Moreton Frewen's "snowless" Powder River Basin by mid-January, and the temperature sank to twenty degrees below zero Fahrenheit. The snow and cold were followed, relentlessly, by more snow and even deeper cold. Even to those holed up in Cheyenne or Medora, where saloons and brothels broke the monotony, the winter seemed interminable. And when the Big Die-Up was over, it wasn't just the loss of cattle that staggered the imagination. Some 320 people were dead as well, cowboys and settlers trapped by the huge snowfalls, lost in snowdrifts while on foot or on horseback, or starved and frozen to death in remote cabins and line camps.

For cattle investors the outcome was catastrophic. "Something dreadful always happens to these soft, sure things," H. Norman Hyatt wrote in his biography of an early Montana settler. And such was the case. "As the South Sea bubble burst, as the Dutch tulip craze dissolved, this cattle gold brick withstood not the snow of winter," wrote the Scotsman John Clay. "It wasted away under the fierce attacks of a subarctic season aided by summer drought. For years, you could wander amid the dead brushwood that borders our streams. In the struggle for existence the cattle had peeled off the bark as if legions of beavers had been at work."

News of the calamity was remarkably slow to filter out of the territories, even as the horrendous winter, with its wholesale slaughter, drew to a close. Many of the local newspapers were organs of the cattle industry — and in the habit of obfuscating, misrepresenting, or exaggerating the facts — so for a considerable time no one knew quite how bad the damage was. Journalists did not want to report the truth and thereby risk further hurting the already depressed cattle business, which the success of their papers largely depended on. Even when the truth did leak out, they tried to make light of it. The *Yellowstone Journal,* for example, assumed a jocular tone: "It is told of one untruthful manager in an adjoining county that he reported a loss of 123%, 50% steers and 73% cows." Many papers were determined to underreport the destruction.

Poor records make it impossible to know the exact extent of the losses. Some historians insist it was not all that bad—as low as 15 percent in the Wyoming Territory, although admittedly much higher in the Montana and Dakota territories. But even if the lower estimates were true, the surviving cattle were so emaciated that tax assessors reduced the value of the entire cattle inventory in the Wyoming Territory by 30 percent the following spring.

By the time of the spring roundup—and in many areas, roundups were canceled—the scope of the disaster became fully understood. None put it better than the rancher James A. Jackson, who wrote succinctly to Thomas Sturgis, the secretary of the Wyoming Stock Growers Association, in July 1887: "Times hard. Money short. *Loss 50%,* no calves. Cattle credit *played out."*

The businesses of Sturgis and Alexander Swan, the two best known Cheyenne cattle kings, immediately foundered. Swan had reported to his shareholders in Scotland during a February visit that the winter appeared to be a mild one. He was flat wrong. A year later his company went into receivership and he was relieved of his duties. The company ultimately took a $1.6 million write-down of its assets.

In addition to his cattle ranch, Swan, a born gambler, had tried to build a financial empire on the side by cofounding a local bank, the First National Bank of Cheyenne. It now faced a run on its deposits and collapsed, which in turn panicked investors from Wall Street to Scotland. To run the Swan Cattle & Land Company, the Scottish board of directors hired an interim manager and then turned to their countryman John Clay, who, over time, successfully reorganized the business. Clay blamed Swan's downfall on hubris: "He was vain and loved to do big things, with a jealous disposition and a somewhat overbearing manner with his neighbors and associates.

Sycophants in abundance buzzed round him and he was swept off his feet by hero worship." But the real causes went deeper: when the company's herd was finally counted, it was estimated that Swan's original book count was off by thirty-two thousand head of cattle, meaning that he had swindled the Scots out of at least $500,000. He had also borrowed against the company without informing anyone and used the money for personal expenses, a clear case of embezzlement. Swan declared personal bankruptcy and quickly sank into poverty and obscurity, from which he never recovered. He died in Ogden, Utah, in 1905.

Thomas Sturgis, whom John Clay considered "intellectually head and shoulders above them all," was forced to write his Boston stockholders the "frightful" news that, of the fifty-five thousand head of cattle on the books, only thirty thousand had survived. Their value had plummeted from sixty dollars a head in 1883 to twenty dollars in 1887. Liquidation soon followed, but even this process seemed ill-fated: the feedlot station the company had purchased in Gilmore, Nebraska, caught fire and burned to the ground. Sturgis abandoned the West and returned to New York City to pursue a career in the construction business.

Theodore Roosevelt too had trouble comprehending the extent of his losses. Roughly a third of his herd had survived. He rode out day after day, trying to survey the damage. As he wrote in his second book on the West, *Ranch Life and the Hunting Trail*, "The land was a mere barren waste, not a green thing could be seen; the dead grass eaten off till the country looked as if it had been shaved with a razor." His net loss: $23,556.68, although this sum fails to include the additional $7,500 or so that he likely lost by investing in Hubert Teschemacher's ranch.

Others fared worse. One was German-born Carsten Conrad Kohrs, one of the deans of the industry, who had begun life as a ship's cabin boy, then sold sausages, worked in a distillery, ran logs down the Mississippi, and mined unsuccessfully for gold at Grasshopper Creek in western Montana before entering the cattle trade, first as a butcher. He reportedly salvaged only three hundred head of cattle from a herd of thirty-five thousand. He would, however, prove to be a survivor. Somehow, he persuaded his banker to lend him $100,000 in the aftermath of the disaster, and with this money and the help of his half brother, he started over. This time he embraced new methods of ranching, such as using barbed wire to fence the range, creating feedlots to fatten his herd, growing hay to feed the cattle in the winter, and constantly improving his stock with shorthorns and Herefords. He was able to pay off the loan in four years.

In Montana, Teddy Blue's boss, Granville Stuart, was so badly wounded financially that he never recovered. His Shoshone wife died the year after the Big Die-Up, and he remarried, this time wedding a young schoolteacher. He moved to Butte, where he became the local librarian. From there he pursued a career as a writer and speaker and eventually secured a three-year political appointment as the U.S. State Department's chief diplomatic representative to Paraguay and Uruguay. Once the largest cattle rancher in Montana, he would leave his second wife with so little money at the time of his death that she was forced to take a job as a cook. Nearby, Zeke and Henry Newman, who ran the N Bar Ranch, where Teddy Blue had refused to dig fence posts, lost 60 percent of their cattle and sold out to a gold miner and sheep farmer named Tom Cruse.

Horace Plunkett, returning from a winter spent in Ireland, arrived in the Powder River Basin in the spring of 1887 and expressed stupefaction at the extent of the damage: his EK Ranch had lost half of its cattle. Moreton Frewen's Powder River Cattle Company, which Plunkett now managed, had lost 75 percent of its cows and 10 percent of its steers. The calf crop came in at only 1,200, down from 6,485 the year before. He estimated that a herd that once numbered 33,000 had been reduced to 12,000. The company, already mortally wounded by Moreton Frewen's mismanagement, had been walloped once again. Plunkett began to liquidate the business, but, as was the case for many of the cattle companies, the liquidation took a great deal of time. The business struggled on for a few more years as Plunkett tried to sell off the herds and holdings. The French cattle baron Pierre Wibaux ultimately bought much of the remaining herds, and did so at a big discount: seventy-four hundred head of cattle for $139,000. Plunkett sold off the refrigeration plant on Sherman Hill for the value of the building's used lumber. Even after the liquidation, handfuls of lost cattle carrying the Powder River Cattle Company "76" brand kept reappearing on the open range. It took until 1891 to finally close the books on the enterprise.

Wibaux had arrived late to the cattle boom. In fact, he arrived so late that he was the inadvertent beneficiary of perfect market timing. He was in Paris, raising money to expand his herd of ten thousand head of cattle, when the Big Die-Up occurred. When he returned to eastern Montana in the spring of 1887, he had $500,000 of new capital. He could buy cattle when the rest of the cattle kings were selling, and that is what he proceeded to do, buying as many as he could lay his hands on. Even better, he got the hardy animals that had withstood the horrendous winter. While everyone else was going belly up, he built a herd of sixty-five thousand head and became one of the major cattle kings in the West, his wealth built on his opportunity to exploit other men's misfortune. His ranch house, one of the showcases of the West, was variously known as the White House or the Palace. He went on to similar success as a banker (State National Bank in Miles City) and gold miner (Clover Leaf Mining Company). He was the rare rancher from that era who was able to sell his ranch and retire on his own terms, which he did in 1904.

Moreton Frewen lost his entire investment in the Powder River Cattle Company: "My own unissued shares, representing my sale price to the company, locked up for the five whole years by my contract with the company, I never even saw. What had destroyed us was the magic growth in settlement and prosperity of the Great West—that and a bull-headed President." In truth, it was much more than the arrival of settlers and the actions of Grover Cleveland that had brought his company to its knees. The closest Frewen ever came to owning up to his limitations as its manager was admitting to a "want of discipline." None of his shareholders would argue with that.

Certain herds in certain valleys fared better than others. Up in Alberta, where ample grass still grew, the cattle sustained fewer losses. On the Panhandle, where the weather had been much worse the year before, the damage was minimal. Outside Laramie, Hubert Teschemacher fared marginally better than his Cheyenne brethren: his ranch lost only 10 percent of its herd. But due to the leverage he had assumed—at high interest rates—to expand and to pay dividends, his business was mortally wounded. He had already announced plans to liquidate, although he too would take his time doing so. Many of his shareholders, like many others in the East and overseas, now wanted out of cattle investments and were prepared to sell their shares at a substantial loss. Teschemacher & DeBillier Cattle Company dividends had never lived up to expectations. They began at 5 percent in 1882 and trailed off to 1.5 percent in 1890 and 1891. Teschemacher's ranch would not be fully liquidated until the fall of 1892. His investors would lose 47 percent of their capital, plus whatever interest they might have earned on that capital if they had simply left their money in a bank.

For these young men, the ignominy of failure was unforgettable. Many rightly felt that they had wasted the first five to ten years of their business careers. Worse, many of them, Teschemacher included, had borrowed heavily from their father or had been entrusted with his funds to launch their operations at the outset. To lose their investors' money was bad enough; to lose a father's was mortifying. From Denver, Teschemacher's partner Richard Trimble telegrammed his father the bad news that the company stood on the verge of bankruptcy. Trimble had borrowed heavily from his father to buy a management role in the company, and his father had invested a modest sum alongside him. Merritt Trimble, Richard's father, a banker who had just assumed the job of president of the Bank for Savings, New York's oldest savings bank, founded in 1819, replied with a letter that was rare for its compassion and understanding.

Dear Dick,

Your telegram from Denver was an awful wet blanket. I
am heartily sorry for your disappointment . . . I want you to
look the situation over carefully to see if there is any adequate
reason or inducement for your remaining West longer. Of
course, if by staying you can do anything to save the investment
you and your friends have made in the Cattle Co, I think you
are bound to do all you can for that object, but if you can do
nothing in that direction and don't see any other occupation
there that will do more than give you a temporary support with
[nothing] leading to better, then I think it is time to consider
whether there are sufficient reasons to keep you away longer.
I do not ignore the fact that you may have private reasons for
reluctance to come back to N.Y. but don't know enough about
them to say . . . [other] than that, so far as they influence you, I
should feel no right to question any decision you may come to.
I understand perfectly, too, that it will hurt to come back, so
far as that may imply a confession of defeat in what you have
undertaken. But I can't doubt that a man of your character &
ability will soon find something worthwhile to do. And as soon
as you find that and you are doing good fruitful work, you will
let the past go.

Then, having advised and consoled his son, Merritt Trimble went
a step further and offered his unequivocal support:

I shall be only too glad to do all I can do to help you in anything
you may decide to undertake — either here or elsewhere . . .
I should have no hesitation in furnishing you with whatever
money you would be willing to take for any new enterprise that
seems to you reasonably promising. We are looking forward to
your coming for a visit next month, when all these matters can
be discussed.

Affectionately, MT

As it happened, Merritt Trimble's faith in his son's "character & ability" was not misplaced. Or perhaps such faith and such parenting enabled Richard Trimble, like Theodore Roosevelt, another product of model parenting, to not only survive his cattle ordeal but go on to far greater things. He returned to Manhattan with his poodle in tow and found a job in investment banking. He eventually won the confidence of the banker J. P. Morgan, and later in life was appointed the secretary-treasurer (one of the top three officers) of U.S. Steel, which in its day was the largest corporation in America. Trimble thus engineered an extraordinary comeback from the painful folly in his youth.

Not all the fathers — or fathers-in-law — were so understanding. Take the case of the Marquis de Morès. When he left Medora in the fall of 1886 on the eve of the Big Die-Up, his entire operation was in jeopardy. He knew it, others knew it, but he flatly denied it. An editorial in the *Bismarck Tribune* noted that "the Marquis de Morès has gone to New York, and expects to visit France before he returns to Medora in February. He denies all reports of financial troubles. He has a steady income from an estate that can not be encumbered. Financial embarrassment is an absolute impossibility." If these public denials were part of a public relations effort, they failed utterly. A few weeks later the *New York Tribune* wrote that it had received word in a cable dispatch from Paris that an argument and a falling-out had occurred between de Morès and his father-in-law, Louis von Hoffman. The financier had reportedly withdrawn support from all his son-in-law's western ventures. Unlike the statement in the *Bismarck Tribune*, this one happened to be true.

The Medora abattoir would never reopen for business. The refrigerated railcar business was sold off and the stagecoach business folded. The shell of the abattoir, a sprawling, deserted wood-frame structure, stood empty until 1907, when a fire scorched it to the ground. The multistory yellow-brick chimney stands to this day in a public park on the outskirts of Medora, a would-be obelisk that nicely commemorates the era's financial follies.

The article about de Morès said that his estate "can not be encumbered," apparently meaning that his father, the duc de Vallambrosa, no doubt furious over the financial losses, brought a court action to have his son's remaining property put under the supervision of a trustee. According to de Morès's biographer, Donald Dresden, the two had become involved in "legal skirmishes over money in business deals." Those deals almost certainly concerned the marquis's collapsed cattle operations in Medora, which had cost his father some $250,000. De Morès, whose anti-Semitism was on the rise, insisted he had been the victim of "a Jewish plot"; he alleged that the meat dealers of Chicago were dominated by Jews.

In all, de Morès had lost over $1 million ($23.9 million in today's money), $250,000 for the construction of the abattoir alone. How much of it was his family's and how much of it belonged to Louis von Hoffman is not known. Compounding de Morès's money problems were the rumors that his wife was unhappy. In fact, according to a smug report in the *New York Tribune*, she was suing for divorce. The couple must have patched up their differences because they spent the next few months tiger hunting in the Far East — on foot in India and by elephant in Nepal. Moreton Frewen would encounter the couple as he traveled through Nepal on a business trip and reported that their hunting party included more than eighty elephants. Both husband and wife bagged their tigers; she shot three and he took credit for four.

In an interview shortly before de Morès departed for the tiger hunt, he came close to acknowledging his mistakes: "It is necessary for me to make some money, for I cannot let my house fall. Unfortunately, for five hundred years we have been soldiers. It is hard to change the old instincts of the race. I am profoundly worried by these financial losses; I blame myself for believing that I was stronger and better than others — but, patience! Every lane has a turning. A man without ambition is good for nothing. There must be an aim in life, always higher. I am 28 years old. I am strong as a horse. I want to play a real part. I am ready to start again."

The part he played next would cause his father to go one step further and publicly disown him.

16

The Fall of Cheyenne

T he bursting of a commodity bubble is one of capitalism's most brutal and indiscriminate destroyers of wealth. On the open range in the years following the Big Die-Up, financial pressures tore at the fabric of the cattle industry. Beef prices continued to fall as the big cattle outfits struggled to downsize by slaughtering more cattle, which only added to the glut of beef in Chicago and kept a downward pressure on prices. Dudley H. Snyder, of Georgetown, Texas, summed up the situation in testimony before a Senate select committee: "I do not think I ever saw a business that was as prosperous as the cattle business up to 1884 and 1885 that went down as quick and fast, with no confidence left in it at all." The trade newspaper *Rocky Mountain Husbandman* echoed that sentiment: "Range husbandry is over, is ruined, destroyed." It placed the blame on "the insatiable greed" of the cattlemen.

As wealthy investors withdrew support, a succession of big ranches folded. "The big guns toppled over," reported John Clay. "The small ones had as much chance as a fly in molasses." No doubt in the eastern and British financial capitals investors were second-guessing themselves, asking how they could have been so foolish — to invest so heavily in nothing more than a commodity business! Worse, they had placed their trust in twenty-five-year-old neophyte managers.

The folding of ranches and loss of fortunes had an immediate knock-on effect. Membership in the once all-powerful Wyoming Stock Growers Association collapsed, from 416 members in 1886 to 68 in 1890. Letters of resignation poured in. "I find that my cattle most all died last winter and I think I will withdraw from the association," wrote one member.

The loss of membership fees meant it was harder to pay for cattle detectives and stockyard inspectors. In response to these harsher economic realities, the cattlemen drafted a new law, the Maverick Law, and rammed it through the Wyoming legislature without much thought to the consequences. Drafted by the WSGA, the statute was printed in a small blue pocket-size booklet and quickly became notorious, its constitutionality questioned. The new law required that all the mavericks found during roundups and at other times be collected and handed over to the WSGA, which would then sell them to pay for the all-important inspectors who monitored the stockyards for regulatory compliance and kept an eye out for evidence of disease. It also stipulated that cowboys employed by the big ranches could not own their own cattle — and threatened to blackball them from work if they tried. Although the big cattle interests viewed the law as a logical revenue-raising scheme to help the industry, it had immediate unexpected consequences. It marked the absolute end to the ambitious cowboy's favored path to advancement. As John Rolfe Burroughs wrote in his history of the WSGA, *Guardians of the Grasslands:* "Ambitious cowboys, and others intent on getting a foothold in the cattle business, felt that they had been run over by a legislative steam roller operating on behalf of the big outfits."

Other problems emerged as well. All the U.S. land laws had been written by eastern lawmakers who had no understanding of the cattle industry and its massive land requirements. Small parcels of

242 | *Cattle Kingdom*

80 to 640 acres were thought to be all that was necessary for the average American settler to establish a profitable farm, which might have been true in the East but wasn't in the arid West. For years the cattlemen had responded by exploiting the Homestead Act and the Desert Act to their advantage. In an effort to assemble larger parcels that they could actually hold title to, they had encouraged their cowboys to file claims under the acts, which the big cattlemen, based on secret agreements, then bought from the cowboys. But the tactic was only so helpful, as they had only so many cowboys, and by the late 1880s the homesteaders were arriving in growing numbers. For years the cattlemen had watched in dismay as their best grazing land was taken away from them in those same 160-acre increments.

Cowboys' wages had been cut before the Big Die-Up. Now their jobs were disappearing rapidly. The harsh economic realities brought home to them the limits of their chosen profession. A cowboy might lay claim to his cowboy code of honor, his tight-knit outfit of fellow cowhands, his courage, independence, and ruggedness, but when times turned tough he became a tragic figure — at least by today's standards. His career rarely lasted more than seven years and always carried the risk that at any time work or disease might break his health. With little opportunity for advancement, he might find himself a broken-down old cowboy dependent on the charity of his ranch owner — and if so, he might be heard to praise his benefactor as the finest man he had ever encountered, a claim with a certain irony.

The cowboy Reuben B. Mullins, who went on to become a dentist, recalled in his memoir, *Pulling Leather,* the conversation he had with his ranch foreman the day he quit working as a cowboy, in 1889. "I said, 'Any young man who will punch cows for an extended number of years isn't normal. I have worked six years in cow outfits and am fed up on cow punching, so I am quitting. In punching cows there is absolutely nothing to look forward to, other than monthly wages, doing top work, and riding good horses. Probably in the far distant future one might become a foreman, yet that is problematical as the cow business is headed for the bow-wows, and there is not long to go, so why wait for the deluge?'" His foreman did not argue or try to dissuade him but instead wished him well.

By the late 1880s, wherever the ambitious cowboy turned, his path was obstructed. He had only three real options once the heyday of the open range was over. He could become a butcher — but the meatpackers destroyed the careers of countless small-town butchers with their monopolistic practices and the ubiquitous marketing of dressed meat and, after the turn of the century, of meat that was frozen (by means of a process pioneered by the Russians). He could enter the livery trade — but before long the automobile would obliterate that business, too. That left becoming a farmer, the one profession he had scoffed at throughout his career as a cowboy. "I reviewed my past life as a cowboy from every angle," said the trail driver F. M. Polk, "and came to the conclusion that about all I had gained was experience, and I could not turn that into cash, so I decided that I had had enough of it, and made up my mind to go home, get married and settle down to farming."

This was precisely Teddy Blue's train of thought after he became engaged to Granville Stuart's daughter, Mary. Like most of his cowboy brethren, he had no money: "I had never saved a dime or owned any cattle in Montana until I was engaged. I had always blowed my money as fast as I made it or a lot faster, but now I made up my mind to get enough for a start in life and a nice little home of our own." In his diaries he exhorted himself to spend less and save more. First, he took a job pushing a coal car in a coal mine, a job that he hated. Next, he took work as a night watchman at a gristmill and as a deliveryman, bringing bullion to the railroad. He quit to try his hand at moving cordwood until a log fell off a wagon onto his foot and laid him up for ten days. In the end, he accepted what he saw as the inevitable. He became a farmer, the very profession that he had fled as a boy. He began to look for a farmhouse to rent. He would still volunteer to help on the local roundups, but, as he admitted, "from now on I wasn't a cowpuncher any more."

Mary sewed her own wedding dress — out of red velvet bought in

Helena. One day she, Teddy Blue, the Anderson girls, and one other neighbor rode in a wagon to the town of Alpine so that she and her intended could get married before a justice of the peace.

The cattle barons made two final attempts to reclaim their glory days. In 1887 they tried to create a giant cattle trust. This was hardly an original idea. There were trusts launched in the 1880s in meat-packing, whiskey, tobacco, copper, railroads, steel, and oil. Rock-efeller's Standard Oil was by this time a towering, well-established trust known to everyone. Even sugar companies, such as H. O. Havemeyer's Sugar Refineries Company (later the American Sugar Refining Company), were doing something similar in 1887, in re-sponse to overcapacity and shrinking profits. The theory behind the cattle trust was that it would allow the big cattle ranchers to wrest control of pricing back from the meatpackers in Chicago. The ranchers hoped to create a kind of cattle-trade cartel, modeling the organization, including the documents used to draw up the trust, on Standard Oil.

The idea itself was sound — and not yet illegal, as it would be-come in 1890 with the passage of the Sherman Antitrust Act. But the actual implementation proved to be a nightmare. Many cattle barons embraced the plan, understanding the logic behind the en-terprise. But others — willfully independent westerners accustomed to acting alone — thought they had better ideas. They could not be persuaded to join the effort and surrender so much control over their own enterprises. Nevertheless, the trust went forward. At one point it owned 218,000 head of cattle and its own packing plant, as well as offices in four states, but it never achieved the scale needed for real success. As prices continued to languish, it lost momentum and ranchers defected; it was liquidated in 1890.

The cattlemen's second last-ditch effort to reverse their fortunes was their proposal to create the National Cattle Trail. They aimed to persuade Congress to approve a six- to twenty-mile-wide per-manent cattle trail, on land attained by means of eminent domain. The trail would run from Texas through the Oklahoma Panhandle,

Colorado, Nebraska, South Dakota, Wyoming, and Montana, up to the Canadian border. The ranchers had high hopes: trailing was still cheaper than shipping by rail, and a dedicated trail would eliminate the threat posed by quarantines, so often issued locally due to fear of cattle disease. Alas, the whole idea was unrealistic; the plans did not adequately address who would be forced to give up land to the trail or how the cowboys would graze and water the cattle en route without trespassing off the trail. But worse, it provoked opposition in those states and territories terrified of Texas fever. The following year, in 1885, in retaliation for the initiative, the legislatures in Colorado, Kansas, Nebraska, New Mexico, and Wyoming passed new, stricter quarantine laws, which largely closed the old cattle trails altogether. The National Cattle Trail proposal made it as far as the U.S. House of Representatives in January 1886, but the House Committee on Commerce blocked it, under pressure from the northern cattle interests, who feared further overstocking, and the Texas railroads, whose owners wanted the business of moving cattle all to themselves.

Unbeknownst to the state and territorial legislatures, the young epidemiologist Theobald Smith was homing in on the cause of the cattle disease known as Texas fever, and his work might well have made stricter quarantine laws unnecessary.

Smith, along with other close observers of cattle, suspected that ticks were somehow involved in transmitting Texas fever, but they weren't sure just how. Smith, working with the veterinarian F. L. Kilbourne, designed a series of experiments that exposed isolated disease-free cattle to various pathogens, including those known to be carried by ticks. In other cases, they injected blood from infected cattle into healthy cattle.

They identified a protozoan parasite, *Babesia bigemina,* as the culprit in Texas fever. The tick transmitted the parasite, causing the disease. When the tick consumed blood from a sick cow, it passed the parasite on to its own eggs; thus its young carried the parasite, and through the saliva of their bites they passed it on to more cattle.

Smith's field experiments provided the proof, which was confirmed under the microscope, where the protozoan could be seen wiggling in the actual eggs of the ticks. Smith recorded this landmark discovery in a laconic diary entry of July 1890: "Probably discovery of Texas Fever parasite in tick eggs this afternoon. Mrs. Egleston [Smith's mother-in-law] returns from North. Finished reading *Lorna Doone* this week. Using hose on grass almost every night."

Close to this date, a twenty-year-old botanist named David Fairchild was working late one night in his laboratory down the hall from Theobald Smith's at the Bureau of Animal Industry. Suddenly Smith walked in and asked him if he would like to see, in the blood of a tick, the organism that caused Texas fever. "He was in the first exciting moments of his discovery and spoke brilliantly of it and its bearing upon the transmission of blood-infecting parasites. Of course I was thrilled! It was the first time that I had been in the presence — actual presence — of an epoch-making discovery."

The discovery that a blood-sucking arachnid could transmit disease was a new idea, and it turned out to have enormous medical importance. Within a few years, similar breakthroughs followed. Researchers found that insects transmitted many diseases, including sleeping sickness (by tsetse flies), malaria, yellow fever, and dengue fever (these three by mosquitoes). In the wake of this new understanding came ways to protect and immunize against these diseases, making Smith's discovery a towering contribution to human health.

Unfortunately for the cattlemen, Smith's great breakthrough, published in medical journals in 1889, did not arrive in time to prevent the closing of the cattle trails. Happily, the understanding of the cause of Texas fever made way for its eventual elimination, although sadly, it didn't entirely benefit the environment. Texas ranchers began to sprinkle arsenic across their pastures to eradicate the ticks. Later they took to spraying insecticides over their land and dipping cattle in vats of arsenic solution. By the 1950s they had largely eradicated the disease, a boon to the cattle industry achieved at great cost to the environment. The Texas ranchers had inadvertently nearly wiped out a dozen species of birds from southern Texas, including the crested caracara and the chacalaca, which only today are making a comeback. Some have argued that the poison also drove the last of the jaguars and jaguarundis from areas of Texas south of San Antonio.

Theobald Smith was far from done. Over the course of a long and productive career, which included posts at Harvard University, the Massachusetts State Board of Health, and Rockefeller University, he discovered the bacterium that causes salmonella poisoning and was the first to identify the causes and characteristics of the severe allergic reaction that came to be called the anaphylactic response, also known, appropriately, as "the Theobald Smith phenomenon." He contributed to improved laboratory production of vaccines and was the first to develop a way to test for the fecal contamination of water. Outside the laboratory, he became a leading advocate for food and water sanitation. In a letter to colleagues in 1933, he spoke of the rewards of scientific research: "To those who have the urge to do research and who are prepared to give up most things in life eagerly pursued by the man in the street, discovery should come as an adventure rather than as the result of a logical process of thought. Sharp, prolonged thinking is necessary that we may keep on the chosen road, but it does not necessarily lead to discovery. The investigator must be ready and on the spot when the light comes from whatever direction . . . The joy of research must be found in the doing since every other harvest is uncertain."

When he died a year later of colon cancer, at age seventy-five, he was cremated, per his request, clad in a pair of green cloth trousers custom-made for him long ago by his father, the Albany tailor.

The closing of the cattle trails proved financially devastating to many struggling cattle towns. In another blow, the railroads, now competing for the cattle trade, had extended their southern lines deep into Texas, to towns like Fort Worth, making the trails obsolete. The Kansas cattle towns lost their primary function as cattle depots, and their rowdy times came to an end. A few of them, like Tascosa, became ghost towns and then vanished altogether. "It is useless to look on a modern map for Tascosa because the town is not there," according to the historian Prescott Webb. "It died so long ago that the map makers have forgotten it."

The collapse of the cattle towns, like that of the mining towns, highlighted the shockingly transitory nature of the economic foundations of American society. The pace of change in business was, and remains, extraordinarily swift; opportunities can shift almost overnight, as old industries fall to new ones. Merchants, liverymen, ranchers, and bankers could suddenly lose their status because of any number of events: a recession, the winds of political change, the sudden obsolescence of a previously thriving business, or the arrival of a disruptive new technology like barbed wire.

Dodge City, the last and largest of the cattle towns, endured for over a decade, but it too faltered. On a cold night in November 1885, a kerosene lamp exploded on the second floor of the Junction Saloon. Flames destroyed a barbershop, a second saloon, a restaurant, a law office, and a real estate office, then spread to a furniture store, a mercantile store, a drugstore, two jewelry stores, two more saloons, a billiard hall, and a "fireproof" warehouse, before they were finally contained. Ten nights later, a second fire broke out, this time in the chimney of a brothel. Three neighboring homes, a stable, a boot-and-shoe repair shop, a paint shop, a dry goods store, and a grocery store burned. The town was rebuilt but never fully recovered.

Of the five major Kansas cattle towns, only Wichita achieved the status of a metropolis in the decades to come.

Abilene, Kansas, survived, albeit in greatly reduced circumstances. On the main street four-fifths of the stores closed, rents collapsed, and hotels folded. Recalled the town's founder, Joseph G. McCoy, "Property became unsalable. The luxuriant sunflower sprang up thick and flourished in the main streets, while the inhabitants, such as could not get away, passed their time sadly contemplating their ruin. Curses both loud and deep were freely bestowed on the political ring. The whole village assumed a desolate, forsaken and deserted appearance."

Most of the town of Medora was disassembled and moved by rail to bigger and better towns elsewhere, farther down the rail line. Across the river, the village of Little Missouri disappeared completely.

The gunmen who had worked as sheriffs and marshals in these towns didn't fare much better. Wild Bill Hickok, who had worked in Abilene and other cattle towns, was already dead. After leaving Abilene, he began a long descent into vagrancy and alcoholism before coming to a violent end in Nuttal & Mann's saloon in Deadwood City, in the Dakota Territory, one afternoon in August 1876. He sat with his back to the saloon door, violating his own rule about always keeping his back to the wall while playing cards. A gunman approached him from behind. His assailant, a disgruntled saddle tramp named Jack McCall, claimed Hickok had shot and killed his brother, but more likely he had simply taken umbrage at a condescending remark that Hickok made to him during a poker game earlier in the day. He shot Hickok through the back of the head, using a .45-caliber revolver, a handgun powerful enough to take down a large grizzly bear.

Hickok sprawled face-first onto the poker table, his poker hand reportedly spilling open: two black pairs — aces and eights. It came to be known as the Dead Man's Hand. In 1979 this poker hand earned Hickok a place in the Poker Hall of Fame. The gun Hickok was carrying at the time of his death, a No. 2 Smith & Wesson revolver, went up for auction at Bonhams in November 2013, with a presale estimate of $300,000 to $500,000, but failed to sell. By contrast, the Colt .45 that Wyatt Earp used during the shootout at the OK Corral sold at auction for $225,000 in April 2014.

The three Masterson brothers fared slightly better. James died of consumption at age thirty-nine; Ed died in a gunfight in 1878. Only Bat, the best known of the three, lived a long life, finishing his varied career as a sportswriter for the *Morning Herald* in New York

City, where he died of a heart attack at his office desk in 1921, at age sixty-seven.

Like many of the cattle towns, Cheyenne, Wyoming, was already in recession before the Big Die-Up. Now it experienced a full-blown depression. As the Irishman Horace Plunkett wrote in his diary after a visit in 1888, "Cheyenne dull and doleful. Surely the glory has departed. The cattle kings are gone and Cheyenne must settle down to the humdrum life of a farmer town." Indeed, Cheyenne had become "a town of many shattered hopes." Numerous once-bustling businesses along Ferguson Street folded. Many of the great mansions built for the cattle barons now stood deserted, available for sale or rent. One of the largest was converted into the Keely Institute for the treatment of drunks. It did not lack for occupants.

Still, the citizens were determined that Cheyenne not end up as another fly-by-night boomtown that stumbled and then, almost overnight, became a ghost town — like Tascosa, on the Texas Panhandle; Atlantic City, Wyoming; Caribou, Colorado; or Silver Reef, Utah, to name only a few of the many towns that flickered out like candles. In a sense, its merchants, its cattle barons, its politicians, and its ordinary citizens succeeded, because Cheyenne indeed survived, bruised and humbled but still alive.

For a time the only significant construction project in Cheyenne was the building of the capitol. The cornerstone of this impressive structure was placed on May 18, 1887, after which work began in earnest; the city held a parade and a barbecue to celebrate the occasion. Many former cowboys would join the construction crews.

The Cheyenne Club, once bustling with social activity, lost most of its members, to say nothing of its international luster. The club's trustees asked the city to reassess the club's property taxes at a lower level, but that was not enough to save it. The club struggled on for a few more years, underwent a financial reorganization, then folded. The building was sold to the city and became, for a time, the Industrial Club and then the Cheyenne Chamber of Commerce. In 1936 the building was leveled. Thomas, the popular longstanding steward of the club, continued working there until the restaurant closed.

He never found a better job, ending up in a single-occupancy room in Pueblo, Colorado, where one day, a few years later, he put a bullet through his head.

The tough times in Cheyenne in the late 1880s had dire consequences. In the aftermath of the Big Die-Up, a group of lucky, high-living Cheyenne cattlemen who had briefly stood atop the business world in the West were left so drastically reduced in circumstances that many became deeply embittered. They were no longer young men. They had lost much, or all, of their personal fortunes. Their decades of effort had amounted to nothing. Furthermore, their popularity as community leaders was in steep decline, particularly among the smaller cattle ranchers, the cowboys (disgruntled over reduced wages), and the newly arrived settlers. Though they still wielded significant political power — cattle remained Wyoming's only real industry — nonetheless they felt they were under siege.

In a desperate attempt to reverse their fortunes, a band of these Cheyenne cattlemen made a series of rash decisions. They began to look for scapegoats and for ways to take revenge. They plotted to evict cowboys and homesteaders from the open range, launching what came to be known as the Johnson County War, the most famous of the so-called range wars.

Other range wars had occurred in the years leading up to the Johnson County invasion — conflicts over cattle thefts in Mason County, Texas (1875–76); over mining claims and water rights in Castaic, California (1890–1916); over the ownership of the Maxwell Land Grant in Colfax County, New Mexico (1873–88); and over cattle and horse rustling in Pleasant Valley, Arizona (1882–92). Many others would follow, such as the mostly nighttime attacks launched by gunnysack-hooded cattlemen, challenging the sheep ranchers over the use of grazing land. Some of these civilian conflicts took many human lives over many more years, but none could match the paramilitary scope, or the sheer harebrained nature, of the Johnson County War.

Of the characters whose careers in Cheyenne we have traced, only a few now remained there: Hubert Teschemacher, his partner

Frederick DeBillier, and the Scotsman John Clay. Each would play a central role in the events that followed.

The Johnson County War — a term that overstates the scope of the conflict while capturing the intense feelings of those involved — would be the last gasp of the cattle kingdom era. Pitting the big cattle barons against the cowboys, it brought the two main classes of men responsible for the cattle boom to a final, perhaps inevitable, clash — a gunfight over their industry's dwindling resources.

Only in the past twenty years has an accurate account of this conflict been properly pieced together. Justice was so deliberately and thoroughly perverted, and the truth so vigorously obfuscated, that the facts of the episode remained in dispute for generations. The distorted record of the Johnson County War illustrates how easily, even in a democracy, those in power can doctor the truth.

Two unlikely amateur historians, George W. Hufsmith and John W. Davis, the former an opera composer and the latter a small-town lawyer, changed all this. Their respective books, *The Lynching of Cattle Kate, 1889,* and *Wyoming Range War: The Infamous Invasion of Johnson County,* prove through exhaustive scholarship that this range war could be characterized as the Watergate of Wyoming — a criminal enterprise followed by a criminal cover-up. In this conflict, ill-conceived vigilantism escalated to the abuse of political power and even murder.

But even Hufsmith and Davis overlooked one wider cause of the conflict and the larger role played by one important culprit.

PART FOUR

Nails in the Coffin

17

The Rustler Problem

O n the afternoon of July 20, 1889, six armed men on horseback rode up to the two properties owned by a storekeeper
named Jim Averell and his wife, Ella Watson. Five of these
men were members of the Wyoming Stock Growers Association,
and two, including the local rancher Albert John Bothwell — who
kept wolves as pets — were members of its executive committee,
responsible for overseeing the policing of the open range. They
loaded Watson, and later Averell, into a buggy and drove them to
a nearby gulch, where the vigilantes found a tree appropriate for a
hanging. The couple were forced to climb up onto a large rock, side
by side, while the men strung nooses from the tree branch overhead
and then placed the loops around their necks.

An out-of-town friend visiting Averell, by the name of Frank Buchanan, learned of the abductions, hurried to the scene, and tried to
intervene, firing his revolver from a distance as he approached and
apparently wounding one of the vigilantes in the hip. But Buchanan
could not get to the couple fast enough to save them. The two victims, whose hands and feet had not yet been tied, were pushed off

the rock. It is said that Bothwell shoved Averell. He and his wife were left to struggle wildly, clutching at the rope with their hands and kicking frantically as they strangled to death.

Despite newspaper accounts to the contrary, neither victim was guilty of any serious crime, let alone of cattle rustling or, for that matter, prostitution, the charge leveled against Ella Watson, whom the papers falsely identified as Cattle Kate. In any case, prostitution was not illegal in Wyoming at the time. The charges were a fabrication, dreamed up by a reporter for the *Cheyenne Daily Leader*, Edward Towse. This newspaper was part of the Cheyenne cattle barons' "kept press" and a mouthpiece for the Wyoming Stock Growers Association. All three of the local papers at some point were owned by cattlemen — and two remained so at the time of the lynching. Towse would later become city editor for the *Cheyenne Daily Sun*. His complicity in this and later cover-ups, and his frequent fabrications, stand out as one of the worst press abuses of the era. He was perfectly willing to smear and libel victims and invent phony justifications for their murder.

At first the *Cheyenne Daily Sun* disputed Towse's account of the "Cattle Kate murder." But then the newspaper's owners called the *Sun*'s editor, Edward A. Slack, on the carpet. The newspaper reversed its position and printed its own sensational story, a version that supported and embellished Towse's version. Slack described the event as "a question of life and death between honest men and cut-throat thieves" — another phony contention. The couple's only real crime had been to offend the neighboring cattle baron Bothwell, who viewed their homestead as a threat to his water supply.

Within a few weeks, the primary eyewitness to the lynching, Averell's visiting friend Frank Buchanan, disappeared. Rumors persisted that he had been whisked abroad to Great Britain, where he lived comfortably off the money that he was paid to remain silent. It is far more likely that he was assassinated, or "dry-gulched," as the locals described it, and his corpse buried. Soon after, another witness to the abduction, eleven-year-old Gene Crowder, also went missing. Finally, the twenty-two-year-old nephew of Averell, Ralph Cole, at work at his uncle's store at the time the lynching occurred, was poisoned to death, perhaps as a warning to others who might want to testify against Bothwell and his fellow cattlemen.

This scenario, whereby the perpetrators easily escaped prosecution for their crimes while the Cheyenne newspapers threw up a smokescreen to hide their culpability, created a template for future lynchings. And it may have emboldened the cattlemen into thinking that they could easily get away with murder. Indeed, they would deploy this strategy in the far larger "lynching bee" known as the Johnson County War.

A few months later, the Cheyenne newspapers began a new campaign of misinformation. They wrote stories stating that Johnson County had a rustler problem. This was curious because the county was actually among the safest and quietest in the American West. Minor cases of petty thievery occurred—the odd steer stolen for food by the starving or the indigent—but far less crime occurred than one might expect. As noted earlier, this was true of most cattle towns, despite their reputation. Other parts of the West and Wyoming had real rustling problems—often the disgruntled actions of disaffected cowboys; however, Johnson County was not one of them.

Johnson County did have one serious problem: a particularly dangerous gunman, a man living under an alias to hide the fact that he possessed a long criminal record. And this individual would do more than anyone else to instigate the conflict that followed.

His name was Frank Canton. Thomas Sturgis, secretary of the Wyoming Stock Growers Association in Cheyenne, had hired Canton as a range detective. His assignment was to patrol Johnson County at a monthly salary of $150. Detectives had roamed the range since the WSGA formed its first detective bureau at a special meeting in July 1883. Many of the bureau's activities had a shadowy, extralegal aspect, or, as the WSGA put it, "Much of their work is of such a nature as cannot be properly discussed in detail." After two years, at the urging of the executive committee of the WSGA, Canton decided to run for the higher-paying job ($250 a month) of sheriff of Buffalo, the largest town in Johnson County, with a population of one thousand. He won the election and served two consecutive two-year terms, taking credit for hanging a murderer named Bill Booth and capturing a horse thief named Harvey Gleason, alias Teton Jackson. But in his run for a third term as sheriff, Canton lost to Red Angus, a former bartender and brothel operator. Angus, a worthy political opponent, had proved an effective president of the town council and a popular chief of the town's fire department. By all accounts Canton was dismayed and disgruntled by his loss. He was forced to devote himself to ranch work, specifically to building up his own cattle herd, a task that did not suit him temperamentally. Then, after failing at ranching, he returned to part-time work as a detective for the WSGA, but at reduced wages, a fact that may well have contributed to the events that followed. Forced to police the open range without benefit of the deputy sheriff's badge that he wore during his early years as a range detective, he lacked the authority to make formal arrests. Apparently, he felt that he deserved better.

What Sturgis in Cheyenne and the locals in Buffalo did not know was that Frank Canton's real name was Joe Horner. Born in 1849 in Harrison Township, Indiana, Horner served as an orderly for a Union officer during the Civil War (he was too young to enlist), and then took a job as a teamster, transporting government supplies by oxen-drawn wagon to Fort Leavenworth, Kansas. During an altercation with his boss, he lost his temper and clubbed the man to death with a wooden neck yoke. Horner appeared before a military tribunal but was acquitted of murder. He then drifted down to Texas, where he joined a succession of criminal gangs around San Antonio. He went up the Chisholm Trail to Abilene on a cattle drive in 1868 — the trip during which Osage Indians stole the cowboys' horses, forcing them to complete the journey on sore feet. In February 1876 Canton was imprisoned for bank robbery in San Antonio but managed to escape, along with three other convicts, after sawing through their shackles and boring through two-inch oak planks and a stone wall. Captured not long afterward, Horner was convicted for a second time — this time for robbing a stagecoach. Once again, he got away — escaping from a work crew assigned to chop wood outside the Huntsville Penitentiary. Horner fled north into Wyoming, where he assumed a new identity as Frank Canton. After working as a cowboy for two years, during which time he ingratiated himself to men like Moreton Frewen, he managed to get his name brought to the attention of Thomas Sturgis at the WSGA. He depicted himself as a tough-minded gunman who was willing to do whatever the circumstances required to eliminate cattle thieves.

It was Canton, in pursuit of the bounties awarded by his bosses in Cheyenne, who began the phony drumbeat of reports about cattle rustling in Johnson County and the failure of juries in the county to prosecute those rustlers who were caught. This news had the effect of pouring lighter fluid on smoldering embers, and the furious, financially embattled cattle barons apparently gave the green light to Canton's subsequent killing spree. Canton was involved in the murder of at least three men, each of whom he falsely accused of being involved in cattle or horse rustling, but whose only real crime had been to fall out of favor with the cattle barons. Canton did not operate alone. He had at least four accomplices, each a current or former detective with the Wyoming Stock Growers Association. These men became a de facto assassination squad, executing death warrants discreetly issued to them by the cattle barons in Cheyenne.

The first to die at the hands of this hit squad was Tom Wagoner, a horse dealer who the range detectives had come to believe was no better than a common horse thief. Wagoner was taken from his house and hanged from a cottonwood in a gully a few miles away. His body was not found until twelve days later:

Special to the Wyoming Derrick , June 19, 1891. Lynched: Tom Wagoner Dragged From His Home And The Bosom Of His Family And Put To Death.

The town is thrown into a state of great excitement over the report which reached here of the fiendish lynching of Tom Wagoner, a ranchman living with his wife and two children about 40 miles northwest of Newcastle. The murdered man was found hanging to a cottonwood tree, the hands pinioned at his back, his toes touching the ground and the body having the appearance of a man kneeling as if in prayer.

To the amazement of the range detectives, who had hoped for a big bounty, a posthumous investigation into Wagoner's operation revealed that not one of his eleven hundred horses was stolen. His business was entirely legitimate.

Next on the hit list was Nate Champion, a highly respected cowboy and roundup foreman who had once managed Horace Plunkett's Bar C Ranch. Champion had assembled a tiny herd for himself, just two hundred head of cattle. Along the way, he had quarreled with a local cattleman whose own herd — some of the old "76" outfit once owned by Moreton Frewen — kept interfering with Champion's small herd and mistakenly absorbed some of his cattle, which were then trailed north to the stockyards in Montana. When Champion had the temerity to stand up for himself, he unknowingly earned a Cheyenne death warrant. In his case, however, the hit squad underestimated its opponent.

In the middle of the night on November 1, 1891, four men, including Frank Canton, stormed into the tiny cabin in the Hole-in-the-Wall area of southern Johnson County that Champion was renting along with another cowhand, Ross Gilbertson. The intruders announced their presence and ordered the two men out of bed, shouting, "Give up, boys. Give up!" But Champion, pretending to stretch as he roused himself, snatched a revolver from its holster at the head of his bed, at which point both sides opened fire. One of the shots was fired so close to Champion's head, it left powder burns on his cheek. The intruders were forced to retreat, but not before Champion coolly took aim and shot one of the fleeing men in the stomach. The wounded man was Billy Lykinds, the first man hired as a stock detective by the Wyoming Stock Growers Association. Lykinds stumbled from the cabin, nearly doubled over in pain. He would die of his wounds a few weeks later, but not before being hustled out of Wyoming to avoid capture and prosecution. A Winchester rifle that Champion found abandoned outside the cabin was identified as Frank Canton's.

At first the citizens of Buffalo, Wyoming, failed to link these attacks to the cattle barons in Cheyenne. As the *Buffalo Bulletin* reported on November 5, 1891, "The attack on Nate and Ross is shrouded in considerable mystery, for there is not the least known cause for any such attempt at murder."

Two other murders followed in quick succession. Orley "Ranger" Jones and John A. Tisdale were small-time cattle ranchers and cowboys who happened to be friends of Nate Champion. They may have been perceived as threats to Canton and his fellow assassins — and by association, the executive committee of the WSGA — because both Jones and Tisdale had witnessed the confession that Nate Champion had forced, at gunpoint, from a member of the hit squad a few days after the attack at the cabin.

Jones was the first to be killed. A twenty-five-year-old cowboy and homesteader, he had a reputation as an accomplished broncobuster. Engaged to be married and hoping to upgrade his cabin before his wedding day, he had driven his buckboard wagon into town in late November to buy a stack of wood floorboards. He wanted to install a proper floor over the dirt floor for the benefit of his new bride — further proof, if any was needed, of his homesteading ambitions. His assailants lay in wait for him, hidden under Muddy Creek Bridge just south of Buffalo. When his buckboard clattered across the bridge on his return trip, his assailants, two or three in number, jumped out the instant he passed, took aim, and shot him three times in the back.

Next to die was John Tisdale, thirty-six, a onetime foreman of

Theodore Roosevelt's Elkhorn Ranch and the brother of the home-steader Robert Tisdale, whom Moreton Frewen had asked Fred Hesse to "split like a rail." On the afternoon of December 2, while riding to his homestead in a buckboard wagon loaded with provisions that included Christmas gifts for his children, among them a new black Labrador bitch and its singleton puppy, Tisdale was ambushed. As he passed along the brow of a hill, two shots were fired. The six-shooter at Tisdale's waist deflected the first shot, but the second severed his spinal cord. The bullet exited through his chest wall and wounded one of his horses in the neck. Tisdale collapsed in his seat, dead.

His assailant then raced forward, grabbed the reins of the horse-drawn wagon, and pulled it down into a gully, out of sight. He shot through the head the two horses and the black Labrador. The puppy, later found at the crime scene, was cowering in the back of the wagon, wrapped in an overcoat. The groceries and Christmas presents were drenched in blood.

No witnesses saw either murder, but one neighbor did recall seeing Canton lead Tisdale's wagon into the gully. Terrified, and perhaps threatened by Canton, the neighbor refused to testify to what he had seen. To cover his own tracks, Canton quickly provided witnesses willing to testify that he had been in Buffalo at the time of the Tisdale murder. Still, Canton was the chief suspect, and soon a warrant was issued for his arrest. He fled Buffalo, traveling by rail to Chicago, where presumably he met with one or more of his bosses, and from there to Cheyenne to meet with others in the WSGA. It appears that he persuaded sixteen of the leading cattlemen, most of them members of the WSGA's executive committee, to literally bail him out of trouble. Through a lawyer, they negotiated and arranged payment of his bail bond of thirty thousand dollars, a huge sum in those days.

After reading the sensationalized reports of anarchy and lawlessness in Johnson County, the Buffalo townspeople began to understand that these murders were not random acts of violence. Incredible as it seemed, certain members of their community were being singled out for assassination. The motive, according to the Cheyenne newspapers, was that Johnson County had become the epicenter of cattle rustling on the open range, an assertion that the Buffalo sheriff and the townspeople knew was patently false. To compound their concern, rumors began to circulate that the cattlemen of Cheyenne were now contemplating actions far more draconian than a series of one-off lynchings — possibly a full-fledged invasion of the territory to eliminate those they perceived as cattle thieves and thereby restore order.

But the residents of Buffalo failed to grasp the real motives of the leading cattlemen in the territory, who in the wake of the Big Die-Up had allowed their financial distress to escalate into desperation and paranoia. Stopping the predation of their herds, though important, was not at the top of the list for them. Rather, their first priority was to eliminate homesteaders from the Powder River Basin and the surrounding areas; the increasing numbers of settlers and ex-cowboy small cattle ranchers, like Jim Averell and Ella Watson, presented a direct threat to their financial well-being and their control over the open range.

As each homesteader, for a token fee of ten dollars, claimed another 160-acre parcel of the best grassland — or potentially as much as 640 acres at twenty-five cents an acre under the Desert Land Act of 1877 — the open range shrank, and, as noted earlier, the cattlemen lost access to the creeks and streams they needed for watering their herds. The grossly exaggerated problem of rustling provided the perfect excuse for the cattle kings to send their proxies in to "rectify the situation." First dreamed up by the cattlemen in the discreet confines of the Cheyenne Club, the plan took shape as an actual invasion, a desperate last-ditch effort to salvage the large-scale cattle business. If they could clear the land — first Johnson County and then other counties — of the small settler and the aspiring cowboy rancher, much as the government had once cleared the same land of Indians and the buffalo, the cattle barons could preserve some of the finest grazing land in the state for their herds and at the same time discourage any future homesteaders who might be thinking of Johnson County, or its neighboring Wyoming counties, as a place for permanent settlement.

The Cheyenne cattlemen believed that they had done much more than build a few large ranches. As they saw it, they had helped construct a new industry, a significant town, a prominent social club, and a new way of life. Indeed, they would argue that they had helped foster the entire cowboy culture, with its own privileges, hierarchy, and leadership. Proud of what they had accomplished, they were prepared to defend it.

On April 4, 1892, the day before the invasion, a meeting of the Wyoming Stock Growers Association took place at the opera house in Cheyenne, as it did every year. No one knows what was discussed because the agenda and the minutes of that meeting no longer exist — which is curious, because the WSGA generally kept excellent records. The WSGA subsequently claimed that no executive committee meeting took place that year. That too seems odd and improbable. More likely, the leadership met in "executive session" in order to avoid leaving any written record of what was discussed.

What is known is that forty-five men attended the annual meeting, each representing a large cattle outfit. By no accident they were the same men who would lead the invasion north into Johnson County. They were among the most prominent citizens of Cheyenne.

Historians of the three commissioned histories of the Wyoming Stock Growers Association have attempted to depict the WSGA as a toothless tiger at the time of the Johnson County War, insisting that the association had by then virtually dissolved, after the membership had shrunk to fewer than a hundred men in the wake of the Big Die-Up. There seems little doubt that this claim, and the other irregularities, formed part of the WSGA's rigorous attempt to whitewash the events for posterity. And it is worth noting that the *Cheyenne Daily Leader,* the one Cheyenne newspaper that was trying to take a more populist bent — at the costly expense of most of its print advertising, because the cattle interests immediately blackballed the publication—perceived the WSGA as anything but toothless on March 23, 1892, less than two weeks before the invasion. As the editor wrote that day, "We regret . . . the revival of the old spirit of intolerance in the Wyoming Stock Growers' Association. An un-American spirit of dominance which would ride roughshod over the weaker elements and force them to immigrate or crawl, cowed and subdued, at the feet of a fierce and implacable oligarchy."

The man credited with conceiving the idea of the invasion of Johnson County was a former U.S. marshal and Union cavalry major named Frank Wolcott. John Clay gave a vivid description of this short, portly man: "He was a fire-eater, honest, clean, a rabid Republican with a complete absence of tact, well educated, and when you knew him a most delightful companion. Most people hated him, many feared him, a few loved him." Wolcott, like many of the cattlemen, was struggling with insolvency. He tended to live beyond his means and had borrowed twice, fifty thousand dollars in 1885 and then an additional thirty thousand right on the eve of the Big Die-Up, to expand his herds and his VR Ranch, which was beautifully situated on Deer Creek in Converse County and staffed with Chinese servants. He then lost a third of his cattle during the winter of 1886–87, and now faced financial ruin. He soon would be forced to surrender his magnificent ranch to his Scottish creditors.

Although ultimately some one hundred of the big cattlemen would contribute a thousand dollars each to fund the invasion, not every member of the WSGA approved of it. No doubt the members who were smaller cattlemen were kept out of the loop—after all, they might well wonder whether they would be next on the hit list. The plan for the invasion was clearly a conspiracy of the strong against the weak. Even so, some of the cattle barons chose not to participate. The rancher George T. Beck, ill and hospitalized at the time, upon hearing of the plan from Frank Canton, begged him to convince the cattlemen not to pursue the foolish venture, as it was sure to end in disaster. The shrewd John Clay, now working to rescue the deeply troubled Swan Land & Cattle Company and only recently elected president of the Wyoming Stock Growers Association, claimed in his biography that when he first heard of the plan, from Major Wolcott in the summer of 1891 during a long walk on Wolcott's ranch, he proclaimed the scheme "impossible" and "strongly advised against such action." Whether that is true or not, Clay found himself traveling abroad when the invasion occurred and thus escaped implication in the scandal that followed. When it all went wrong, he would rush back from Europe to help his colleagues in every way he could. According to Clay, "The men who took the leading part in this class of work were Major Wolcott, ex-Governor Baxter, and H. B. Ijams, secretary of the livestock board. They were backed by every large cattleman in the state, and behind them they had the moral influence of two [U.S.] Senators, Warren and Carey. The acting Governor, Dr. Barber, was also friendly."

Meanwhile, up in Buffalo, the locals read with growing amazement the latest articles in the Cheyenne newspapers. They alleged that Sheriff Red Angus, who had replaced the range detective Frank Canton, was in cahoots with all the rustlers. But what rustlers? Before long, many men in Buffalo began to carry rifles wherever they went. By now the local newspaper (the *Buffalo Bulletin*), the Johnson County district attorney (Alvin Bennett), and Sheriff Angus had deduced that the leading stockmen of Cheyenne were somehow behind the killings of Orley and Tisdale. In editorials and in public statements, these three parties made it clear that they intended to place the responsibility for the string of murders where it belonged and to see that justice was done—they claimed that they had the evidence to do so. Unfortunately, when their assertions reached Cheyenne, they provided one more motive for the Cheyenne cattlemen to act.

The final catalyst for the invasion was a decision made by the small northern cattlemen of Johnson County to conduct their own roundup a month or so before the one sanctioned by the WSGA and the newly formed Wyoming Livestock Commission. The small cattlemen of Johnson County, most of them former cowboys, were worried that the big cattlemen's roundup would result in their fences being knocked down, their gardens being trampled, and, inadvertently or not, their calves being swept up with the cattle barons' herds. Better to have their own roundup and get their own calves branded first. But this was heresy to the WSGA. In response, the association retained the services of a clever Cheyenne lawyer, Willis Van Devanter, who worked almost exclusively on behalf of the two biggest business enterprises in Cheyenne: that of the U.S. senator Francis Warren and the once brazenly corrupt Union Pacific Railroad. On behalf of the WSGA and the new commission, Van Devanter drafted an injunction to stop the cowboys' "rustler roundup." By then, of course, the cattle barons of Cheyenne had already completed preparations for the invasion of Johnson County. But here, in their minds, was one more unforgivable provocation.

The invaders, or "regulators," or "white caps," as they would variously come to be called, had drawn up a "dead list," relying heavily on the recommendations of Frank Canton. The Johnson County men targeted for assassination were all innocent yet allegedly rustlers; and like those already dead, their only real mistake was to offend, often unknowingly, the big cattlemen of Cheyenne or, just as likely, Frank Canton. The list included the Buffalo sheriff Red Angus and his deputy sheriff; all three of the Johnson County commissioners; Joe DeBarthe, editor of the *Buffalo Bulletin;* Robert Foote, the most successful merchant in town; the reviled Nate Champion; the rancher provocateur Jack Flagg, who had led the successful cowboy strike a few years earlier; and the names of all the cowboys and small cattlemen of the Northern Wyoming Farmers and Stock-Growers Association, for having the temerity to organize their own roundup. The Cheyenne cattleman had progressed from their earlier lynching-bee tactics to a bigger goal: a full-fledged paramilitary invasion and campaign of assassination.

There were precedents for this vigilante-like approach. Granville Stuart had done something similar in 1884 with his Stuart's Stranglers. Stuart not only accomplished his goal — killing some thirty-five men — but also was rewarded for it; he was elected president of the Montana Stock Growers Association the following year. Stuart, however, had proceeded in a discreet fashion, refusing, for example, to allow the high-profile ranchers Roosevelt and de Morès to join his vigilante group. In its early days, the city of Cheyenne had organized its own secret vigilance committee. In 1868 this committee, formed with the knowledge of local officials and numbering perhaps two hundred at its peak, hanged seven men over a three-month period before it finally went too far, killing a brewer over a debt to a saloonkeeper. Local outrage forced the group to disband.

Even more celebrated was San Francisco's Vigilance Committee of 1856. With its eight thousand members, this group had an agenda that went well beyond restoring order to the city's streets, where criminals had in fact threatened the locals. Its other mission was to wrest political control of San Francisco from the Irish Catholics. The urbane Cheyenne cattleman Hubert Teschemacher had firsthand experience with the San Francisco Vigilance Committee for a significant reason that has not been reported before: his father had been one of its ringleaders. Teschie's father not only helped orchestrate those lynchings, but also parlayed his ensuing fame into career advancement. He campaigned for the office of mayor of San Francisco, on a law-and-order platform, and won. Later he retired to France, a wealthy man. Perhaps Teschie hoped that Cheyenne's new vigilance committee would have a similar effect on his own fading career prospects.

Now, admittedly, the legal system in Wyoming as it existed in 1892 was a shadow of what it is today. Nor should we apply twenty-first-century notions of justice to the nineteenth-century American West. The legal system was in its infancy, which is to say that life was cheap and the law was weak. And the tradition of vigilante activities had made this extralegal approach, if not commonplace, at least somewhat familiar. According to Andrew Karmen, in *The Encyclopedia of Crime and Justice,* at least 326 vigilante movements were known to exist in the United States between 1767 and 1909, but only 141, or less than half, actually killed anyone. Those that did took 729 lives. Many more, of course, would follow, once the Ku

Klux Klan achieved nationwide scale in the 1920s and launched its widespread lynchings — primarily of blacks, but also Catholics and Jews.

But the West by 1890 was a much different place than it was in the 1860s, when the first cattle towns sprang up in Kansas and when effective lawmen were in short supply. For one thing, Wyoming was no longer a territory. It had just achieved statehood and possessed a court system with a formal set of laws strictly forbidding just the kind of extralegal actions the Cheyenne vigilantes were about to undertake.

In fact, in September 1889, a convention to ratify the state constitution allowing for the creation of Wyoming as the forty-fourth state in the Union took place in Cheyenne. Among the delegates drafting the constitution were the cattlemen Charles W. Baxter of Cheyenne (the first governor of Wyoming), William C. "Billy" Irvine of Converse County, and none other than the ubiquitous Hubert E. Teschemacher of Laramie County and Cheyenne, who participated in the debate preceding the adoption of the constitution. And among the articles that these men helped write and pass into law, voting to approve the constitution 37–0, was Article 19, which read, "No armed police force, or detective agency, or armed body or unarmed body of men, shall ever be brought into this state, for the suppression of domestic violence, except upon the approval of the legislature, or executive, when the legislature cannot be convened."

The three aforementioned cattle barons and their accomplices would now knowingly violate that article.

Late in the afternoon of April 5, 1892, the day after the WSGA's annual meeting, twenty-five of the meeting's attendees made their way down to the Cheyenne stockyard near the towering red-brick station of the Union Pacific Railroad, each taking care not to be observed. Once they reached the stockyard, they ducked out of sight into a barn and sat down on bales of hay to wait.

Before long, a private train operated by the Fremont, Elkhorn & Missouri Valley Railroad and nicknamed "the Elkhorn," rolled into

Cheyenne from Denver, hauled by a chuffing ten-wheeler locomotive. Clanging and rattling and blowing steam through its blast pipe, the train came to a screeching halt on the stockyard sidings. Seated on board, in a Pullman car with all the blinds drawn, were twenty-five men from Texas, all reputedly top gunmen. The WSGA range detective Tom Smith had gone to Paris, Texas, a few days earlier to hire these gunfighters.

Paris, a town of only a few thousand, served as a commercial and railroad hub for the northeast section of Texas. It was known at the time as something of a hangout for gunmen and law enforcement officers. The local courthouse boasted an astonishing seventy-five men who had been deputized in some capacity. Every morning, a crowd of aspiring bounty hunters would gather on the courthouse steps, each hoping to receive a warrant to go after a wanted man or to perform other part-time work in law enforcement. Paris was the logical place to start for anyone looking to hire a gunman.

But though they hailed from the courthouse steps of Paris, Texas, not all of the men Tom Smith recruited turned out to be experienced gunfighters. Some were simply hard-up unemployed men who badly needed money and who had weapons. George Tucker, a former lawman with experience as a sheriff and a town marshal, thought the gunmen a motley crew: "There were some good men, and some who were worse than no men at all." Among the six or so whom he considered no better than "saloon bullies" and "more dangerous than helpful" were two Texans named Jim Dudley (alias Gus Green) and Alex Lowther. They would prove Tucker accurate by accidentally shooting themselves. Dudley was so obese that the conspirators had trouble finding a horse that would willingly carry him.

Working in the dusk as quietly as possible, the men began to load the train. Onto six empty stock cars they loaded three brand-new Studebaker wagons stacked with tents, food, and other provisions, including new rifles and ammunition. Then they led the horses on board, a remuda of seventy-five animals bought in Denver specifically for the invasion. Robert S. Van Tassell, one of the earliest cattlemen to settle in Cheyenne and a founder of the WSGA, had purchased them. Married to the daughter of Alexander Swan, of the now-crippled Swan Land & Cattle Company, Van Tassell had lost everything in the Big Die-Up and was $150,000 in debt. Although he would not accompany the expedition, he had once organized a vigilante group out of his own livery stable.

The plan was to get to Buffalo as fast as possible to kill the sheriff, his deputies, and every one of the Johnson County commissioners, thereby removing all county governance, which would give the invaders free rein to pursue other assassinations.

Up in Buffalo no one suspected that the Cheyenne cattle barons and their hired gunmen were en route to murder them.

18

Nate Champion and the Johnson County War

With darkness descending, the Elkhorn chugged out of Cheyenne and headed north over sagebrush prairie toward some of the loveliest and most fertile cattle land in Wyoming, the area first occupied by Moreton Frewen when it was still a cattle Shangri-la.

Of the twenty-five men who joined the Texas gunmen on the train in Cheyenne, seven were stock detectives. Two were Englishmen and one was a Scots-Canadian. Most were prominent cattlemen from Cheyenne; eleven were members of the executive committee of the Wyoming Stock Growers Association; two were former presidents of the Cheyenne Club. Prominent among these men were Hubert Teschemacher, Frederick DeBillier, and a third Harvard man, Richard M. Allen, the assistant manager and a co-owner of the Standard Cattle Company. According to Davis, "Their education and wealth were repeatedly trumpeted by the newspapers who supported them, especially after the invasion, as if such status conferred a special privilege to kill other human beings."

Teschemacher left no account of his participation in the Johnson County War, which is a shame because it would be interesting to glimpse his thinking. He had a nine-year involvement with the WSGA executive committee, including serving as its chair, and as such was its longest-serving member. As a member of that committee, he may well have authorized the killing of rustlers by range detectives in the past. Let's give him the benefit of the doubt and assume that Frank Canton had deceived him as to the nature and severity of the rustling problem in Johnson County. But it is still puzzling why he, a man considered to possess "an unwavering sense of responsibility," would have agreed to join a cockamamie scheme to kill the sheriff and county commissioners of Buffalo. We know Teschie didn't have ranch land in Johnson County. Nor could he accurately be described, as others on the expedition were, as "angry and excitable."

And yet here he was, one of the best connected and best informed of the cattle barons, about to make a disastrous misjudgment that would reveal deep flaws in his character. Of all the cattle barons, he had the most advantages — socially, intellectually, and financially. Early in the boom he had benefited from superb connections in Boston and New York City and a fortunate first-mover advantage when it came to buying up cattle ranches. He had lured Roosevelt and others out to the cattle kingdom by extolling its financial virtues and its promise of pure fun. In addition, he had served as president of the Cheyenne Club and had helped author the constitution of the state of Wyoming. His fall from grace would be precipitous.

Also seated on board was a surgeon, Dr. Charles Penrose, who had joined up as a favor to his friend and fellow physician Governor Amos Barber — in fact, Penrose carried with him Barber's medical bag. Also tagging along were two journalists, the disreputable Ed Towse, now working for the *Cheyenne Daily Sun,* and an ambitious young journalist named Sam Clover from the *Chicago Herald,* who in the stockyards of Chicago had heard rumors about a possible invasion. Filling out the ranks of the invaders were three teamsters hired to drive the new Studebaker wagons.

Edward T. David, the foreman of U.S. senator Carey's CY Ranch, had proceeded ahead of the expedition and clipped the telegraph lines between Douglas and Buffalo just outside Douglas, cutting off communication to and from Buffalo. Meanwhile, Governor Barber had sent orders to the presiding officer at Fort McKinney that specifically forbade troops from being mobilized except on direct orders from him. He did not want the troops rallying to the side of the Buffalo citizenry or its sheriff, which the law allowed under most circumstances.

The train arrived in Casper at 4 a.m. The invaders unloaded the wagons in the dark. Wolcott's plan was to muster the fifty men, present them with new weapons, assign them horses, and then head out of town before the citizens of Casper awoke. However, problems arose immediately. Fifteen of the horses broke loose and stampeded away. Soon thereafter, the wagons got stuck in mud caused by melting snow. Then one of the wagons crashed while crossing a narrow bridge. Wolcott, who had argued repeatedly with Frank Canton, now ceded control of the expedition to the former sheriff in the interest of harmony. The range detective Tom Smith took charge of the Texans, who were mostly his recruits. Then, just as the operation was beginning to make progress, it began to snow, first scattered flakes, then a blinding, freezing storm, which slowed the column's progress to a crawl.

It would take the invaders an exhausting two full days just to reach the ranch they had picked as their headquarters. Here they learned that a group of so-called rustlers were holed up at the nearby KC Ranch, a group that included Nate Champion. A dispute broke out over how to proceed and whether to detour to target these men or head straight to the town of Buffalo before the townspeople were alerted to their presence. After a vote, the invaders decided to pursue Champion, the man whom Frank Canton had earlier tried to murder.

Riding four hours through near-blizzard conditions in the dark, they arrived at the KC Ranch a little before dawn. They silently took up positions surrounding the small ranch house; a handful of armed men stole forward and occupied the stable. Knowing how dangerous Champion was with a handgun, the men opted to wait for him to emerge.

The first to leave the house that morning was a cowboy-trapper named Ben Jones, carrying a water bucket and headed in the direction of the river. As he passed the corner of the stable, the men seized him at rifle point. Next to appear was his younger partner, Billy Walker, who came out looking for Jones, whittling a stick as he walked. Failing to find Jones down by the river, he wandered over to the stable, where he too was grabbed and subdued. As the invaders soon learned, this left just two men in the cabin, Nate Champion and a man named Nick Ray. Soon Ray, a large man, stepped out the door, frowning and squinting suspiciously into the frigid morning air, concerned that something was amiss. The best shot among the invaders, C. D. Brooke, nicknamed "the Texas Kid," waited patiently for Wolcott's whispered instructions, then fired a single rifle shot. Ray fell to the ground, wounded. At that point the others opened fire, unloading a barrage of nearly one hundred rifle shots at the wounded man. Almost immediately the door to the cabin opened; a smallish man appeared and began to return fire. It was Nate Champion. One of his shots grazed the cheek of the Texas Kid. Champion grabbed Ray by an arm and dragged him back inside the cabin.

Me and Nick was getting breakfast when the attack took place. Two men here with us — Bill Jones and another man. The old man went after water and did not come back. His friend went out to see what was the matter and he did not come back. Nick started out and I told him to look out, that I thought that there was someone at the stable and would not let them come back. Nick is shot but not dead yet. He is awful sick. I must go and wait on him.

Champion, who happened to be a terrific shot with both a pistol and a rifle, managed to keep up an effective counterfire, eventually wounding three men, two of them seriously. The invaders riddled the cabin with rifle fire, but no one was able to hit Champion.

> It is now about two hours since the first shot. Nick is still live, they are still shooting and are all around the house. Boys, there is bullets coming in like hail. Them fellows is in such shape I can't get at them. They are shooting from the stable and river and back of the house.

More gunfire. Finally, realizing that they were wasting valuable ammunition, the regulators resorted to taking the odd pot shot at the cabin.

> Nick is dead, he died about 9 o'clock. I see a smoke down at the stable. I think they have fired it. I don't think they intend to let me get away this time. It is now about noon. There is someone at the stable yet; they are throwing a rope out at the door and dragging it back. I guess it is to draw me out. I wish that duck would get out further so I can get a shot at him. Boys, I don't know what they have done with them two fellows that staid here last night. Boys, I feel pretty lonesome just now. I wish there was some one here with me so we could watch all sides at once. They may fool around until I get a good shot before they leave.

At one point early that afternoon, a local rancher rode up on horseback. It was Jack Flagg, whose name was high on the invaders' dead list, accompanied by his stepson Alonzo Taylor, who was driving a wagon. The two men were on their way to the Democratic State Convention in Douglas. They arrived at the KC Ranch planning to spend the night, not realizing that a shootout was in progress. But almost immediately, seeing the number of invaders, they sensed that something was wrong. Not waiting to ask questions, Flagg spurred his horse, his stepson whipped the reins of the wagon, and they headed back down the drive in the direction they had come. A handful of invaders scrambled to mount their horses and give pursuit. As soon as Flagg and Taylor were clear of the ranch, they stopped to cut the tugs of the harness, freeing one of the horses from the wagon. Then both escaped on horseback, galloping away in the direction of Buffalo, intent on alerting the locals to what was happening and spreading the alarm.

It's about 3 o'clock now. There was a man in a buckboard and one on horseback that just passed. They fired on them as they went by. I don't know if they kill them or not. I seen lots of men come out on horses on the other side of the river and take after them. I shot at the men in the stable just now, don't know if I got any or not. I must go and look out again. It don't look as if there is much show of my getting away. I see 12 or 15 men. One looks like [here the name Frank Canton has been scratched out]. I don't know whether it is or not. I hope they did not catch them fellows that run over the bridge towards Smith's. They're shooting at the house now. If I had a pair of glasses I believe I would know some of those men. They are coming back. I've got to look out.

The invaders were so furious at the escape of Flagg and his stepson that arguments broke out. They couldn't agree on whether to stay and kill Champion or hurry to Buffalo before Sheriff Angus and his men could organize a team to come after them. Wolcott, once again in charge and showing his signature poor judgment, was adamant that they do one thing at a time. He insisted that they stay and eliminate Champion first, and only then head north to Buffalo.

The invaders dragged Jack Flagg's abandoned wagon back to the KC Ranch and hid it behind the stables. They began to fill it with freshly split pitch pine and layers of dry hay gathered from the corral until the wagon was loaded "wide and high." At this point Wolcott lined up six of his men with rifles. While they took turns firing through the cabin window, he and four other men seized the tongue of the wagon and began to wheel it backward toward the cabin. Once the wagon rested against one side of cabin, Walcott lit the pile of hay on fire.

At first Champion didn't realize what was happening:

Well they have just got through shelling the house like hail. I
heard them splitting wood. I guess they are going to fire the
house tonight. I think I will make a break when night comes if
alive. Shooting again. I think they will fire the house this time.
It's not night yet. The house is all fired. Good bye boys, if I never
see you again.

— Nathan D. Champion

Forced to escape the blazing cabin, Champion leapt out a back
window in his stocking feet and ran south over the snow, carrying a rifle and a revolver and trying to stay hidden in the dense
smoke from the fire. He made it to a ravine about fifty yards from
the house before the two invaders stationed there confronted him.
They opened fire, striking him in the arm and chest. He tried to
keep running, stumbling onward as they continued shooting. At
last he collapsed.

The invaders gathered around the dead body, stunned that one
man, operating alone, had been able to put up such a protracted
fight against so many adversaries. He had single-handedly kept the
invaders occupied for the better part of a day, dooming any hope of
keeping their Buffalo invasion a surprise. One of the invaders later
recalled Major Wolcott staring respectfully down at the corpse and
muttering, "By God, if I had fifty men like you I could whip the
whole state of Wyoming."

Sam Clover, the correspondent for the *Chicago Herald,* wrote a
warning on a piece of paper — THIEVES BEWARE — and pinned it
to Champion's chest, a touch that would add a little color to his
newspaper report of the events. While pinning it to the corpse,
he noticed a diary sticking out of the dead man's breast pocket. It
contained a firsthand account of what had just transpired. Clover
handed the diary to Wolcott, who read the entries aloud. A week
later the *Chicago Herald* published the version of the diary that appears above. Clover may well have embellished this account for the

newspaper's audience, although the substance and the cool-headed tone seem close to accurate.

Although Clover showed a knack for landing the big story, he was every bit as dubious a newspaperman as Ed Towse, the cattlemen's flack who wrote for the *Cheyenne Daily Sun*. Charles Penrose described Clover as "a fresh [rude] young man with a disposition to take other people's things. The next day he took my bridle — an unusually fine one — and never returned it."

The journalist Ed Towse, also one of the party of invaders, had other problems. Unaccustomed to riding, he was suffering from an acute case of hemorrhoids. "He had to be lifted on and off his horse several times during the journey to the ranch," according to Dr. Penrose, who gave him something to relieve the pain.

With Nate Champion at last eliminated, the invaders downed a quick meal, mounted their horses, and continued north. They were still some sixty miles south of the town of Buffalo. They rode late into the night, in advance of their wagons, and covered about half the distance, stopping to replenish their horses at a ranch owned by a former Wyoming territorial governor, Charles Baxter.

It was here that the obese Texan, Jim Dudley, tried to mount a fresh horse. He had slung the scabbard containing his rifle over the pommel before attempting to heave his immense frame up into the saddle. The horse bucked in protest, flipping the rifle loose from the scabbard. The rifle hit the ground butt-first and discharged a shot into the Texan's knee. Dudley was sent off to Fort McKinney, where the infected leg would require amputation. The operation failed to save him; sepsis set in and he became delirious. Just before dying, according to the *Cheyenne Leader*, which relished the drama, he sat bolt upright in bed and called out for his wife, who was back in Texas. "Gypsy! Gypsy!" he cried, according to the paper, and then "fell back on the pillow dead."

The expedition continued north, stopping to rest and water the horses at the TA Ranch, located just off the main road fourteen miles south of Buffalo. Here, a rider from Buffalo galloped up with the news that Jack Flagg and his stepson had indeed warned the townspeople of the invasion. Sheriff Angus was assembling an armed posse of 250 men to counterattack.

With their horses exhausted and supplies running low, the invaders realized that their plan would have to be aborted. They were hungry and low on provisions and the Studebaker wagons containing their food supplies remained miles behind them. The problem now was how to stave off a complete disaster. The answer: go on the defensive. The invaders opted to dig in at the TA Ranch and prepare for a siege. They found a set of house logs intended for a new cabin and used them to fortify the buildings and construct breastworks. They built a small fort on a rise to protect the barn and stables. This work took most of the night.

When someone found some potatoes and some beef, he carried them into the main ranch house, along with three barrels of water. The invaders also sent word to their allies in Cheyenne, including the two Wyoming senators, Warren and Carey, that the men were in urgent need of assistance. They hoped that the senators could in turn alert the local troops at Fort McKinney, and the cavalry could then be sent to the rescue — forgetting, of course, that Governor Barber had specifically instructed the troops there not to respond to any crisis unless specifically ordered by him to do so. Further complicating matters was the fact that the invaders themselves had cut the telegraph lines outside Douglas, Wyoming.

Early the next day the men of Buffalo began to arrive in large numbers. Before long they had completely surrounded the TA Ranch at a safe distance. The man designated to lead them, Arapahoe Brown, who operated a lumber mill, displayed a distinct understanding of military strategy and procedure. Recognizing that he held a positional advantage, he proceeded with patience and caution, stationing his men at intervals and beginning the construction of his own trenches and breastworks. He had other experienced men to help him, among them a veteran of Ulysses S. Grant's long siege of Vicksburg. They quickly established a supply chain between Buffalo and the besiegers.

The first shots were exchanged later that first morning, but the only casualties were five of the invaders' horses and two heifers that had wandered up to the ranch buildings, looking to be fed. Intermittent rifle fire would continue during daylight hours for the next two days.

Early on the first afternoon of hostilities, the three new Studebaker wagons rolled up, driven by the astonished teamsters. They were easily captured. The contents of the wagons proved a revelation to the Buffalo townspeople: under tarpaulins lay three thousand rounds of ammunition, two cases of dynamite, and, tucked into a valise belonging to Frank Canton, a copy of the official dead list containing the names of the targeted men. It made a mockery of the claim that the invaders were pursuing cattle rustlers.

In the town of Buffalo, the white-bearded merchant Robert Foote, who operated the largest mercantile store, threw open his doors to the townspeople and allowed them to freely arm and provision themselves with weapons, ammunition, and other goods. He rode up and down Main Street on his white horse, exhorting the people to take a stand against the invaders. By late in the second day, three hundred men manned the breastworks and siege lines surrounding the fifty or so invaders at the TA Ranch. Word of the situation was sent north to Sheridan, which soon sent recruits of its own.

When help failed to arrive for the invaders, they realized that the telegraph line must still be down. They desperately needed to get word directly to the governor, or they had little hope of being rescued. Hubert Teschemacher drafted a new telegram to Governor Barber, which Wolcott signed. One invader volunteered for the mission and, carrying the telegram, managed to escape through the lines that night by posing as one of the besiegers. He stole a horse and rode into Buffalo to the telegraph office. Finding it inoperable, he continued nearly a hundred miles south, on the same exhausted horse, to Douglas, Wyoming. Here he finally found a telegraph operator who could send the message.

Conditions deteriorated rapidly for the surrounded invaders. But despite all the gunfire, no one had yet been killed on either side. At one point Billy Irvine warned Teschemacher not to stand in front of a window in the ranch house. Teschie obeyed and moved away — a moment before a bullet whirred past him. Another invader's pipe was knocked out of his mouth by a slug, and a third took a bullet through his hat. One attempt to escape failed when a group of men tried to saddle their horses in the corral, only to find gunfire raining down on them, forcing them to seek shelter. The invaders hatched a plan to make a midnight escape, but once again the weather worked against them. That night the skies were clear and a full moon shone brightly, reflecting off the snow. An attempt at escape would have been suicidal.

The invaders had roughly fifty mouths to feed, and by the third day both ammunition and food were running low. When the last rations of raw potatoes were consumed, the only food left was one loaf of corn bread and the hindquarters of a calf. "I don't care how good a fighter a man may be, he simply can't do his best on such a diet," recalled the invader George Tucker.

As for the besiegers, their numbers continued to grow, eventually reaching more than four hundred men. Many were armed with primitive weaponry, including the old Sharps rifles designed to shoot bison. Their large slugs traveled slowly and, having penetrated a wood wall, caused little more damage than a bad bruise. For example, Billy Irvine, sitting outside on guard duty, recalled feeling something sharply strike the ball of his foot. "When I took off my overshoes and boot I found the bullet in the boot, which had passed through the soles of both shoes but did not break the skin of the foot. It bruised it, however, so that in thirty minutes it was much swollen, and the next day the front end of the foot was as black as my hat." The rancher John Tisdale was standing in the ranch house when a bullet that had passed through a pair of wood doors struck him in the back. He sank to the floor, thinking he was mortally wounded, only to discover the bullet had not penetrated his skin.

The first serious injury of the conflict occurred when the Texas cowboy Alexander Lowther, crawling out of the house to take up a position at one of the fortifications, failed to take the precaution of removing a bullet and leaving only "five beans in the wheel" of his six-shooter. As he crawled along, he accidentally knocked the fully loaded revolver out of its holster. The gun went off and discharged a slug into his stomach. He would die of the accidental self-inflicted injury a few days later.

At about this time Arapahoe Brown conceived of a use for the three captured Studebaker wagons. He tied two of them together and fortified the fronts with pine logs, creating a kind of rolling barricade known as an Arc of Safety or a Go-Devil. The idea was to wheel this device close enough to the ranch house for dynamite to be hurled onto the building.

The invaders in the ranch house could see the Go-Devil being constructed, and they heard a distant cheer go up when it was completed, late on the second day of the siege. Recalled Edward T. David, manager of Senator Carey's CY Ranch, "Each man gave up hope in his heart that day. Each knew the impossibility of rescue, and all understood the ruthlessness and vindictiveness of some of the most active of the besiegers. There was absolutely no hope of life beyond the following daybreak."

When Teschemacher's telegram finally arrived at Governor Barber's office and the severity of the situation became clear, a frantic scramble ensued to rescue the cattle barons. The governor sent off a pair of his own telegrams to President Benjamin Harrison at the White House, requesting immediate military support. The wording was deliberately ambiguous. They stated that "an insurrection exists in Johnson County, in the State of Wyoming, in the immediate vicinity of Fort McKinney, against the government of said state." Barber notably left out of the telegram the fact that his personal friends were leading the insurrection and the county authorities were simply attempting to quell it. He requested that troops from Fort McKinney be sent to "suppress the insurrection, restore order, and protect both life and property." When it became clear that these telegrams were not reaching the desk of the president, he sent similar ones to Wyoming's two U.S. senators in the Capitol, Carey and Warren.

By late evening a few of these telegrams finally got through, and the two Wyoming senators, in the company of Lewis A. Grant, assistant secretary of war, rushed to the White House and roused the president from bed. President Harrison, either confused or deceived as to the actual circumstances, or perhaps simply willing to play along, sent out the order for a military intervention "to protect the state of Wyoming against domestic violence." He had it exactly backward, of course: it was not the state that needed protection from domestic violence at this point but the group of Cheyenne cattlemen that had attacked the state. Some have argued that Harrison's intervention was an abuse of presidential power. If so, it was an understandable one, given the late-night confusion surrounding the events.

Moreton Frewen wrote in his memoirs that he was lunching in Washington, D.C., at the home of former Maine senator James G. Blaine, then secretary of state, when Frewen received a telegram from Teschemacher. It read: "We are held by the rustlers. Can possibly hold them off for three or four days but unless relieved we shall certainly all hang. There are twenty of your old friends. Can you help us with the President?" Frewen showed the telegram to Blaine, who read it and said, "We will do all that is humanly possible. Where are the nearest troops?" Frewen answered that they were at Fort McKinney on Clear Creek. "Mr. Blaine got a message through at the moment of time, or I suppose they would have hanged in the cottonwoods at the KC crossing."

In the darkness before dawn on April 12, eleven officers of the Sixth Cavalry and ninety-six enlisted men from Troops C, D, and H, led by Colonel J. J. Van Horn, left the fort on horseback and headed toward the TA Ranch, some fifteen miles away. Sheriff Red Angus, the Chicago journalist Sam Clover (who had abandoned the invaders and slipped into Buffalo after the killing of Nate Champion to file his news reports), and Governor Barber's personal representative, Justice of the Peace Carroll H. Parmelee, accompanied the cavalry. The governor specifically requested that the invaders besieged at the TA Ranch be safely taken into custody and given the protection of Fort McKinney.

At daybreak the following morning the besiegers began to roll the Go-Devil slowly eastward in the direction of the ranch house, determined to rout the invaders. Behind it, pushing the movable barricade, were fourteen men armed with rifles. They carried one of the two boxes of dynamite.

Then, remarkably, in an example of the kind of theatrics that would become a staple of Hollywood westerns, a bugle sounded in the distance, and the cavalry arrived just in time to intervene, saving the Cheyenne cattlemen and their hired gunmen from a near-certain death by dynamite.

Colonel Van Horn rode up to the ranch house to negotiate with Major Wolcott for the surrender of the invaders. But Wolcott demanded more information. He shouted, from the safety of the ranch house, "Colonel Van Horn, to whom do we surrender — to the United States army, or are we to be turned over to the civil authorities of this county? If the former, we will surrender; if the latter, we will *not* surrender." Van Horn assured him that they would not be handed over to the civil authorities or to Sheriff Red Angus. At this point Wolcott and his men readily gave in.

Forty-five men and forty-six horses were soon taken into custody. The men turned over all of their rifles and revolvers. Only one man was missing. A hired gunman from Idaho, George Dunning, lay hiding under hay in the loft and thus escaped arrest. He would later supply a damning confession to the besiegers, which implicated Governor Barber, the two U.S. senators, a local judge, and others. He also outlined how much the hired gunmen expected to be paid and the additional reward they were to receive for each man murdered in Buffalo: five dollars per day, with a fifty-dollar bonus for each person killed whose name was on the dead list.

Back on horseback, but guarded now by the infantry, the invad-

ers embarked on the three-hour ride to Fort McKinney. There the
captives were temporarily housed in a brick bathhouse, where cots
had been set up for them. Here they nervously awaited their fate,
knowing full well that they might subject to the same lynching-bee
justice that they themselves had so heavily relied upon.

Willis Van Devanter, the Cheyenne lawyer who was the lead attorney for the big cattlemen, as well as state chairman of the Republican Party, leapt into action on behalf of the invaders, throwing up legal roadblocks to their prosecution. By cleverly keeping
them confined together, out of reach of the prosecuting attorneys,
his defense team was able to prevent any of the Texans from turning state's evidence against the Cheyenne cattle barons in return
for immunity from prosecution. Given the fact that the Texans had
been misled as to the nature of the invasion, they might well have
followed that course; they thought the Cheyenne cattle barons had
warrants for the arrest of the so-called rustlers, which of course
they did not. Van Devanter also shrewdly insisted that the invaders
all be put on trial together, a great burden for the court.

Next, witnesses were made to disappear. The two witnesses to
the murders of Ray and Champion — the trappers Ben Jones and
Billy Walker, who had spent the night in the KC cabin and been captured that morning before the gunfire began — were hurried out of
state by friends of the invaders. These friends took the trappers on
a circuitous train route to Westerly, Rhode Island, dodging efforts
to arrest them. Here the two were put up in a hotel for the next two
years, all expenses paid. Each was promised a bonus of $2,700 for
keeping his mouth shut and staying out of sight. Fittingly, perhaps,
these checks bounced when the time came to cash them two years
later.

A press battle continued for months after the event. The Cheyenne papers willfully misrepresented what had happened and
why, always defending what one article called "The Long Suffering
Ranchmen." An anonymous article appeared in the popular East

Coast periodical *Frank Leslie's Weekly* on June 2, 1892; according to John Davis, Ed Towse or Ed Slack may well have written it. It grossly distorted the facts of the invasion, extolled the sterling character of men like Wolcott and Irvine, and commended Governor Barber for "manfully" doing his duty. As Davis said, "This article, though profoundly misleading, neatly encompassed what the big cattlemen wanted the people of Wyoming and the United States to believe."

On the other side of the debate stood the *Northwestern Livestock Journal,* a tiny newspaper run by an educator, author, and editor named Asa Mercer, a onetime supporter of the cattleman who, in light of the invasion, had switched his allegiance. In October 1892 Mercer published a confession by the lone gunman among the invaders who had eluded arrest by hiding in the hayloft of the TA Ranch. George Dunning's firsthand report laid out the events in a far more accurate fashion. Mercer used it as an excuse to launch a diatribe against John Clay, the chairman of the WSGA, calling him a coward for having sent one of his employees, Charles Campbell, on the expedition to fight for him. Campbell, a former president of the Cheyenne Club, responded by storming into Mercer's office and slugging the editor squarely in the face, smashing his glasses and nearly knocking him senseless.

Van Devanter attempted to refute the published confession. With Ed Slack out of town, the lawyer took control of the *Cheyenne Daily Sun,* printing denials from Governor Barber and others and writing an editorial that accused the *Northwestern Livestock Journal* of slander. According to some accounts, he filed a suit against Mercer that closed the *Journal*'s printing operations; he even had the Cheyenne postmaster halt the distribution of the offending issue, on grounds that it carried obscenities. Finally, when Mercer arrived in Chicago as a commissioner to the 1893 World's Fair, Van Devanter and Clay had him arrested, twice. On the second occasion he was jailed overnight for criminal libel. A year later, Mercer would follow up his inflammatory article with a book, *The Banditti of the Plains, or The Cattleman's Invasion of Wyoming in 1892* (later retitled *The Powder River Invasion*), which laid out the story from the point of view of the besiegers — and not without a few biases of its own.

There were other more serious aftershocks to the invasion, most notably a succession of murders committed in Johnson County in a kind of vengeful tit-for-tat.

By July 1892 the captured invaders, charged with first-degree murder, had been moved twice and were now housed in a dance-hall in Laramie City. At this point they were legally remanded into the custody of Johnson County, so that the county would have to cover the expenses associated with housing and feeding them. John Clay and Willis Van Devanter devised this strategy, meant to bankrupt Johnson County with legal expenses before a trial could take place. Eventually the judge who had jurisdiction over John-son County ordered that the trial be held in Cheyenne — the only town in the state with enough potential jurors to convene a trial — and scheduled an arraignment for August. The forty-four men were moved once again, this time back to Cheyenne, to a large au-ditorium known as Keefe Hall, across the street from the old man-sard-roofed Laramie County Courthouse, where the trial was to take place. Here they were allowed to come and go as they pleased, and most of the Cheyenne cattlemen began to resume their nor-mal lives. When the day for their arraignment arrived, the men ap-peared in the dreary courtroom and sat on its heavy oak benches to enter their pleas of not guilty. They posted bond of forty thousand dollars each and were released on their own recognizance. The trial was set for January 2, 1893. But for all practical purposes the invad-ers' legal worries were over.

Four months had passed since the launch of the invasion. The Texas gunmen, finally freed on bail, prepared to leave for home. Before sending them on their way, the cattlemen hosted a party for them at the Cheyenne Club. They presented commemorative rings to each of the Texans, and champagne was served. Most of the gunmen had never tasted champagne before, and they quickly grew intoxicated. "They drank it as they drank water, and you can imagine the result," recalled Billy Irvine. George Tucker elaborated: "I started out taking the champagne at gulps. I expected a breaking spell but every time I emptied my glass, some flunky would fill it up again. Pretty soon things began to go around." According to Charles Penrose, the Texans grew rowdy: "They soon, or at least many of them, wanted to fight, and as no one but themselves seemed so disposed, they commenced to fight among themselves; and all the experiences ever a set of men had, we had it. We had a bunch in the café, another in the reading room, still others upstairs; and it was no easy matter to quiet them; it took hours." At one point guns were drawn, and it required time and effort to confiscate the weapons. Major Egbert, a guest of honor along with Governor Barber, became so drunk, he fell out of his chair.

The cattlemen then presented engraved loving cups to a group of their fellow cattle barons, presumably those who had contributed the most money to pay for the invasion and the ensuing legal expenses. One cup went to Fred Hesse, Moreton Frewen's former ranch foreman. The inscription read, FRED HESSE, IN GRATEFUL REMEMBRANCE OF UNTIRING DEVOTION ON OUR BEHALF DURING THE TRYING TIME OF THE WYOMING INVASION OF 1892.

The next morning, the Texans, nursing hangovers, left Cheyenne by rail, never to return. When the train reached the Oklahoma border, each of them was duly paid $750: $150 for each of the four months of incarceration, $100 ($50 each) for killing Champion and Ray, plus $50 for incidentals. Not one of the men bothered to return for the trial.

When the trial date arrived, the effort to convene a jury soon turned farcical; the *Cheyenne Daily Leader* reported gleefully, on January 7, 1893, that "Mr. Baxter was called but had been a juror in the May term, which freed him. J. Johnson, like Mr. Riner, had an opinion which disqualified him. Fred Boehnstedt could not write English; Mr. Geary had an opinion and J. Slown on general principles, as well as the former two was dismissed. Colin Hunter was sick, A. H. Reel was physically disqualified and C. G. Coutant was the victim of opinion . . . The game will continue this morning at ten o'clock."

In all, 1,064 venire men were examined. After weeks of voir dire, eleven of the twelve jurors had been selected, but the sheriff had exhausted the rolls of eligible county citizens. The stalled proceedings were racking up bills for Johnson County, which was forced to pay the living expenses of the defendants for most of the prior year. The money spent on lawyers' fees, court transcripts, judgments, and interest alone came to $10,482.46. The county still owed $17,295.92 for housing the invaders in Laramie and elsewhere. As John Clay and Willis Van Devanter had intended, the amounts were high enough to bankrupt the northern county. Realizing that he was beaten — his coffers exhausted, his best witnesses shanghaied — Alvin Bennett, the lawyer for the prosecution, finally moved to have the case dismissed. Van Devanter opposed the motion, knowing full well that dismissing the case in that manner would leave open a window for later prosecution. The two attorneys convened with the judge to devise a plan. Shortly thereafter, a courtroom spectator was persuaded to take a seat in the jury box, completing the stalled jury selection process. When Bennett then moved for a dismissal, Van Devanter entered a token objection, which the judge then overruled — thus dismissing the case and eliminating the double-jeopardy threat of a retrial.

In this manner the Cheyenne cattlemen escaped prosecution — and got away with murder.

Although most of the Cheyenne cattle barons had shown up for the trial, two of their most prominent had not: the Harvard men Hubert Teschemacher and Frederick DeBillier. While under house arrest in Laramie City in July, DeBillier had apparently experienced a complete nervous breakdown. Exhausted by the endless proceedings, distraught over what had transpired in Johnson County and his own role in it, and fearing for his safety, he "snapped over," as the cowboys termed it. He leapt out of bed one morning, shouting that someone was out to get him. "Do you hear that noise? There is someone up there going to poison us," he exclaimed, pointing to the ceiling. When it became clear that he was hallucinating, Tesche-macher sent an urgent telegram to the banker and WSGA trea-surer Henry Hay in Cheyenne: "Come at once, bring [Governor] Barber, Fred very ill." Barber, who was a medical doctor, examined DeBillier and determined that "his mind was unbalanced." With the judge's permission, Henry Hay accompanied the deranged cat-tle rancher by train back to his family in New York City, where he could receive proper medical attention. When DeBillier recovered, he made no effort to return to Wyoming. Instead, he spent the next three years traveling around Europe and then went to work for his father's Wall Street stock brokerage firm. He subsequently joined the U.S. Foreign Service.

Hubert Teschemacher too was absent from the trial. He left Cheyenne, reportedly to attend, in Paris, the funeral of his brother Arthur, who thirteen years earlier had endured only one long win-ter in the West before quitting the cattle business. Arthur had ap-parently committed suicide in December, a month before the trial, in the wake of an aborted romance with a Russian princess. Teschie too would never return to Wyoming. The remaining 4,113 head of Teschemacher & DeBillier cattle were sold hastily to Senator Fran-cis Warren. The ranch land and the buildings themselves were signed over to the ranch's foreman.

No amount of rationalization and distorted press coverage could mask the shame these two men must have felt. They had disgraced themselves and surely knew it. Frederick DeBillier would at least manage to salvage something of his professional life with his career in the Foreign Service, which he spent at various diplomatic posts in Iran, Greece, Bolivia, Rome, and Peru. He died in 1935 in Nice, France. But Hubert Teschemacher, the Harvard man of glittering promise, blessed with personal magnetism, handsome looks, erudi-tion, money, and nearly universal popularity, would spend the next twelve years, the prime years of his life, looking after his parents — and living off their wealth — on the banks of Lake Geneva in Swit-zerland, traveling back to the United States once a year to attend the Harvard commencement. Only after the death of his parents did he move back to Boston, his birthplace. From then on he gave the Somerset Club on Beacon Hill as his mailing address. Three years later, in 1907, he died of pneumonia in Boston, at age fifty-one. According to his good friend John Clay, the Scotsman who was now the last man left standing in Cheyenne with his dignity somewhat intact, Teschie "died alone and single, ever a dreamer."

Blamed for what had happened during the Johnson County War, the Wyoming Republican Party took a rare beating in the elections of November 1892. The recent financial panic, during which many western mining interests had gone broke, did not improve its prospects. Fortunately for the Republicans, only three statewide offices — those of governor, congressman, and justice of the Wyoming Supreme Court — were on the ballot. The Democrats won all three and routed the Republicans across the state at the local level, virtually sweeping Johnson County. The new Democratic governor was none other than John E. Osborne, the coroner who had made a pair of shoes out the skin of "Big Nose George" Parrott. According to many accounts, he wore those shoes to his inauguration.

A few years later Senator Francis Warren, who would become a powerful chairman of the Senate Appropriations Committee, saw to it that Willis Van Devanter was repaid for his loyalty and legal work — he became an assistant attorney general at the Department of the Interior in Washington, D.C. From there, President Theodore Roosevelt would nominate him to the Eighth Circuit Court of Appeals; President Howard Taft in turn appointed him to the U.S. Supreme Court. Van Devanter, as a Supreme Court justice, held deeply conservative views. When he was well into his eighties, he chose to remain on the Court rather than accept a comfortable retirement, simply to obstruct the passage of President Franklin Delano Roosevelt's New Deal legislation. He opposed every one of FDR's efforts to regulate business. As one of the so-called Four Horsemen, Van Devanter so infuriated FDR that the president took the rash step — unsuccessfully — of trying to stack the Supreme Court by adding one new judge for every justice over the age of seventy. Van

Devanter's dirty tricks on behalf of the cattle barons early in his career, specifically his role in the Johnson County War cover-up, had been long forgotten. Later in his life Van Devanter destroyed many of his papers dealing with his years in Wyoming.

Many of the Texas gunmen fared poorly in the aftermath of the invasion. For example, C. D. Brooke, the Texas Kid, who took the first well-aimed shot at Nick Ray on Major Wolcott's command, killed his wife in an argument when she criticized him for participating in the Johnson County War. On the gallows in Fort Smith, Arkansas, he expressed remorse for his role in the invasion, insisting that if he had known that the Buffalo townspeople were not rustlers, he would never have participated. Tom Smith, the stock detective who had recruited the gunmen outside the courthouse in Paris, Texas, died in November 1892, shot in the forehead while attempting to enforce liquor restrictions in the "colored" compartment on a train traveling between Texas and Oklahoma. Elias W. Whitcomb, the oldest of the invaders, nicknamed "Paps," died when struck by lightning while riding along the banks of the Belle Fourche River.

Frank Canton, the ex-convict and range detective perhaps most culpable for what had happened, went on to work as a bounty hunter and a gold prospector before serving as adjunct general of Oklahoma after it achieved statehood. In fact, he was in charge of the Oklahoma National Guard for a decade. Late in life he wrote a self-serving memoir titled *Frontier Trails*, published posthumously; in it he depicted himself performing heroic acts as a lawman. Naturally, he exonerated himself of any possible wrongdoing in Wyoming.

The Wyoming Stock Growers Association rebounded from its years of depleted membership. It continued to hire controversial men like Canton to police the range. An even more dangerous figure appeared on the scene almost as soon as Canton vanished: the former Pinkerton detective and gunman Tom Horn. In January 1902 Horn would make the remark that helped ensure his conviction and subsequent hanging in Cheyenne for the murder of a fourteen-year-old boy: "Killing men is my specialty. I look at it as a business proposition, and I think I have a corner on the market."

Entire books have been written on the Johnson County War that slant the truth in favor of one side or the other. So many reports are subjective, or allege guilt without proving it, that the story has remained enveloped in the proverbial fog of war. It was further confused, deliberately, by what George W. Hufsmith has called "a century of obfuscation" on the part of the invaders.

The truth of what happened is best expressed by the former lawman George Tucker, who participated as one of the Texas invaders and years later remarked, "We were in Wyoming as paid assassins of the big ranchers. We were brought there to murder men in violation of the law. Let no one mislead you by saying that we had the law on our side—we had politics and the money, but not the law. We were not convicted of our crimes because we had the politics and the money with us."

One reason why the wider ambitions of the invaders, their farfetched plan to drive the small ranchers and homesteaders out of the Powder River Basin, puzzled observers at the time and American historians ever since is that the events are not placed in a large enough historical context—specifically, the context of the British Isles. The idea of forcibly removing small farmers from an area in order to convert the land to other purposes—for raising sheep in the case of Scotland and the Highland Clearances, or a hunting preserve in the case of John Adair in Ireland—had been a recurring phenomenon in both Scotland and Ireland for over one hundred years. The Duke of Sutherland, the largest British landowner of the day, had ruthlessly evicted ninety families between 1811 and 1820 to pursue sheep farming and other more profitable ventures on his estates. Similarly, in Ireland, between 1847 and 1856 the relatively enlightened Fitzwilliam family evicted 5,995 "surplus" tenants, at least offering them free or assisted passage (usually ten shillings) on ships bound for Canada; thus the family successfully reduced the estate's population from twenty thousand to fourteen thousand.

Although a controversial practice, one devastating to the evicted farmers, who were often reduced to starvation, it worked to the benefit of the landowners. The clan chiefs who first initiated the clearances defended their actions as necessary for their economic survival — and thanks to their patronage, they often had the support of the Church of Scotland. Those who tried to act as enlightened landlords, treating their crofters beneficently, often paid the price with bankruptcy. In Scotland the clearances came to an end only with the passage of the Crofters Act in 1886.

Is it so surprising that the Cheyenne cattle barons would deploy a similar strategy just a few years later? Many of them, like John Clay, A. D. Adamson, and Charles A. Campbell, were Scottish by birth or ancestry; Fred Hesse and Richard M. Allen were English, and others like Major Frank Wolcott worked for Scottish landlords, some of them the very men guilty of these practices. Like the Scottish and Irish landlords, the cattle barons believed that they could get away with their ruthless actions. Moreton Frewen, whose family held large estates in Ireland, had espoused just such an approach years earlier when he advised Fred Hesse to take Robert Tisdale, a homesteader-cowboy, and "split him like a rail." You can almost hear the aristocratic, highhanded chairmen of the Scottish and English cattle companies in Edinburgh, Dundee, or London ordering their distant ranch managers in America to remove the homesteaders in the way they disposed of troublesome crofters.

A number of historians have placed the blame for the Johnson County War on human nature and the corrupting influences of capitalism. As the Scottish philosopher and economist Adam Smith rightly observed, and he was hardly a Marxist, "People of the same trade seldom meet together, even for merriment and diversion, but the conversation ends in a conspiracy against the public, or in some contrivance to raise prices." The evidence would suggest that the Cheyenne cattlemen, who met for merriment and diversion in the Cheyenne Club, followed Adam Smith's maxim to the letter. Ida Tarbell, a muckraking journalist of the era, made a similar point when she wrote, "Human experience long ago taught us that if we allow a man or a group of men autocratic powers in government or church, they use that power to oppress and defraud the public."

From another perspective, the Johnson County War looks like a case of the newly popular notion of social Darwinism run amok. If survival belonged to the fittest, then surely it belonged to the cattle barons, or so they believed.

Finally, the Johnson County fracas shows how easily a struggle over dwindling natural resources can turn violent — even on American soil.

There is a coda to the Johnson County "war story." Let's pause for a moment to consider that the cattlemen had one legitimate grievance: they were, in actuality, losing calves. And if the rustlers did not exist as a problem in Johnson County, the question that lingers is this: who *was* stealing their calves? As it happens, one likely culprit has never been mentioned as a possible villain, and considerable evidence exists to support its guilt: the gray wolf.

The wolf packs of the American West once trailed the great bison herds, living off the meat of their calves. When the herds disappeared at the hands of the buffalo hunters, the effect must have been cataclysmic for the western wolf population. However, when cattle herds began to replace the bison herds in significant numbers, a plentiful new food source had arrived, and evidence suggests that the wolf population began to recover.

When there is ample food available, a wolf bitch will give birth to as many as nine pups, allowing for rapid population growth, although there is usually only one pup-bearing bitch per pack. But this new post-bison wolf population was different: it had evolved, and not only in its choice of prey. In the late 1880s, astute observers of the animal's behavior noticed a major change. Wary of humans as it had *not* been of the bison, the gray wolf had become nocturnal. A nocturnal wolf might be heard but it is rarely seen, and not seen, it can be easily overlooked as a factor in herd attrition.

One other important change allowed the wolf to play a greater role in cattle predation. By 1890 the WSGA and many of the big cattlemen, struggling in the wake of the Big Die-Up, could no longer afford to pay their cowboys to shoot or trap wolves or to dig their puppies out of burrows and exterminate them, as they once had done. Nor could the cattlemen afford the services of a dedicated wolfer. There simply was no longer the money for it.

Anecdotal reports suggest that the wolves were everywhere. As Theodore Roosevelt wrote during the year of the Johnson County invasion, in *The Wilderness Hunter,* "In the present winter of 1892–93 big wolves are more plentiful in the neighborhood of my ranch than they have been for ten years, and have worked some havoc among the cattle and young horses." Ben Jones and Billy Walker, the two trappers who witnessed the deaths of Nick Ray and Nate Champion, reported that they had trapped two gray wolves the day before the invasion despite the fact that wolves were difficult to trap, suggesting that the lobos must have been abundant in the neighborhood. In 1886 in northern Montana, the Sun River Round Club used a hunting pack of greyhounds and deerhounds to kill 146 wolves over the course of one summer. And let's not forget that the rancher Lincoln Lang, only a few years earlier, had managed to poison a record number of wolves — fifteen dead on a single steer carcass — using strychnine during the winter of the Big Die-Up.

Furthermore, on September 19, 1890, in Laramie County, Wyoming, roughly two hundred miles south of Johnson County, the local stockmen, through the Laramie County Protective Association, found it necessary to create a Wolf Fund "for the purpose of devising ways and means to prevent the continual and alarmingly increasing ravages of wolves upon the livestock grazing in this county." They agreed to assess a levy of one cent per head for each cattle or horse and half a cent for every sheep in the county in order to add a five-dollar bounty to the three-dollar bounty already offered by the county for each exterminated wolf. Clearly, a serious wolf problem now existed wherever herds of cattle grazed on the open range, and by 1892 the situation was getting out of hand.

The eating patterns of the wolves may also account for why they were overlooked as a culprit in losses of cattle in Johnson County. A wolf will gorge itself on its kill and then hide the remains of its prey in shrubbery, where vultures — or, for that matter, cowboys on horseback — are less likely to spot it. And much like a dog, a wolf will bury bones. When its prey is a calf, a wolf leaves little evidence of its predation except the distressed mother cow, with her swollen udder — which is just what a rustler would leave behind if he stole the calf. By no accident, forlorn cows with swollen udders are precisely what the big cattlemen of Wyoming complained about.

How much predation can wolves alone account for? A great deal. Today as much as 10 percent of the elk population in Yellowstone National Park is culled each year by wolves. Something similar was happening across the Powder River Basin. No wonder Moreton Frewen's calf counts never came in as high as his forecasts.

A precedent existed for this kind of problem. In Dickens County, Texas, at the Spur Ranch, wolves were such a pestilence that a Wolf Bounty Account was established, which offered a five-dollar reward to anyone who brought in a lobo scalp. The giant XIT Ranch faced a similar costly wolf problem higher up on the Texas Panhandle — so much so that it furnished each wolfer with a wagon, saddle horses, and camp supplies and offered him a bounty of five to ten dollars per lobo. A few years after the Johnson County War, in 1896, one of the XIT wolfers, Allen Stagg, working alone, killed eighty-four wolves over the course of a single winter.

At least a few of the Cheyenne cattlemen likely suspected the truth, that wolves were the real problem in Johnson County and not rustlers, yet they presumably kept their suspicions to themselves. Among these were none other than John Clay and Hubert Teschemacher, who served, respectively, as the president and vice president of the Laramie County Protection Association, the organization offering the hugely stepped-up wolf bounties a little over a year before the Johnson County invasion. But even if the truth about the wolves had been better known, it would hardly have changed the course of events. Rustling provided an excuse for a range-clearing invasion that wolf predation did not.

And if the gray wolf did in fact get away with murder in Johnson County, much as the invaders did, it would not be for long. With the active encouragement of the federal government, states throughout the West began offering a five-dollar bounty for each wolf pelt. In 1906 the U.S. Forest Service empowered the Bureau of Biological Survey to clear the cattle ranges of wolves, making it a de facto wolf-extermination unit of the federal government. By 1960 the animal, a keystone species required for a healthy ecosystem, had been driven like the bison to the brink of extinction across the lower forty-eight states.

19

The Cowboy President

T he Johnson County War may have tarnished the cattle barons' reputation at the end of the open-range era, but the cowboys' reputation survived unscathed — in fact, the cowboy was revered more than ever. And Theodore Roosevelt, a veteran of the cattle boom, was first to seize on that idealized image and use it for a political purpose.

The heroic image of the cowboy had attracted him from the outset, and he was smart enough to realize that it appealed deeply to many Americans. Back in New York City, dressed in his buckskins, he posed in photography studios for expensive memorial photos on cabinet cards, even restaging for the camera some events in the West that he had recorded in his writings. He understood that cultivating a cowboy image would mitigate the fact that he was a patrician New Yorker who had attended Harvard College and inherited his wealth. From this point forward he did not let anyone take his picture when he played tennis, a game that he enjoyed but that could be perceived as elitist.

Despite the financial losses he had suffered, Roosevelt had been reinvigorated by his time in the West, and he had healed from the loss of his first wife. He was ready to put the trauma firmly behind him. One day in New York at his sister Anna's townhouse, the year before the Big Die-Up, Roosevelt had watched as a lithe young woman with considerable sex appeal sashayed down the front stairs to greet him. She was a close friend of the family named Edith Kermit Carow, who many years earlier had been his childhood sweetheart and remained an intimate of his other sister, Corinne. As children, Teddy and Edith had watched President Abraham Lincoln's funeral procession together from the window of a Roosevelt townhouse on Union Square. Now the attraction between them was rekindled.

After keeping their engagement secret for nearly a year, the couple slipped off to London, where they married at a church on Hanover Square in December 1886 — during the winter of the Big Die-Up. They would have five children together. But this happy second marriage would not for a moment quell Roosevelt's adventuresome spirit. On his first honeymoon he had climbed the Matterhorn; on his second, he led an expedition to the summit of Mont Blanc, the highest mountain in the Alps, an accomplishment that earned him membership in the Royal Society of London.

Although Roosevelt returned to the Badlands for brief periods, he now focused on wildlife conservation and politics, and much less so on cattle ranching. Still, he felt a lasting debt to the men he had met in the West and to the professions of cattle rancher and cowboy. On a campaign swing through the Badlands in 1900 — he was by then the vice presidential candidate on what would prove to be the winning GOP ticket, with William McKinley — Roosevelt remarked in a speech to the locals, "I had studied a lot about men and things before I saw you fellows. But it was only when I came here that I began to know anything, or measure men rightly."

The rich city boy with Ivy League credentials would become the cowboy president. And he would not be the last politician to cultivate that image of rugged independence to improve his standing with the American public. Presidents Lyndon Johnson, Ronald

Reagan, and George W. Bush similarly reshaped their public image. For Lyndon Johnson, the cowboy boots, the Stetson hat, and a herd of registered Herefords made a tall, lanky kid from the rural hill country of Texas look like a respectable western cattle baron. Ronald Reagan, a former lifeguard from a small town in Illinois who had acted in B-movie westerns, bought a Santa Barbara ranch and styled himself a twentieth-century cowboy. Ivy Leaguer George W. Bush, scion of a patrician family from Greenwich, Connecticut, which had deep roots on Wall Street, donned cowboy boots, a cowboy hat, and a cowboy swagger to help shed his image as a spoiled, rich preppy who had attended Andover, Yale, and Harvard Business School. Not surprisingly, the public persona of the cowboy proved to be more politically palatable — and more marketable — for these men than the one they had been born with.

At the time of the speech in Medora, Roosevelt's political career was on a meteoric rise. Although he lost a bid for New York City mayor in the fall before his second marriage, he had been appointed to a position with the U.S. Civil Service Commission in Washington and then became president of the board of the New York City Police Commission. In 1898 he left a job as assistant secretary of the navy to form his cavalry regiment, the famous Rough Riders, a group comprising Roosevelt's friends and other cowboys, frontiersmen, Ivy Leaguers, athletes, tradesmen, and sheriffs, many of them from the Southwest, which had a climate similar to Cuba's. Roosevelt led these men on the celebrated charge up San Juan Hill (actually Kettle Hill) in the Spanish-American War, an event that he would describe as "the great day in my life." Alone on horseback, within an easy rifle shot of the Spanish, yelling at his foot soldiers to follow him, Roosevelt, naturally, led the charge. "No one who saw Roosevelt take that ride expected he would finish it alive," reported the journalist Richard Harding Davis, who had thrown journalistic objectivity to the wind, grabbing a rifle during the battle and joining the Rough Riders. "He made you feel that you would like to cheer." According to Roosevelt, "Every man behaved well; there was no flinching. The fire was very hot at one or two points where the men around me went down like ninepins." At one point, two Spaniards shot at him in close quarters, and both somehow missed. Roosevelt kept his cool and fired back, killing one with a shot through the left breast. The ensuing victory earned Roosevelt national recognition and popular adulation, which led him, after only a two-year stint as governor of New York, to join the winning McKinley ticket as the candidate for vice president.

Then, just a year after the speech in Medora, President McKinley was assassinated by an anarchist's bullet, and Vice President Roosevelt, only forty-two years old, was sworn in as the youngest-ever president in U.S. history. His progressive agenda, to secure "a square deal" for all Americans, would feature trust-busting and increased business regulation (not a goal associated with Republicans today). In all, he would launch forty antitrust suits and successfully break up the country's largest railroad and its largest oil company, a feat of considerable political courage. It meant taking on the powerful corporate interests of his day, members of his own party, Wall Street, and railroad magnates like J. P. Morgan and E. H. Harriman, who soon came to despise him. But, as historians have noted, Roosevelt was perfectly willing to be called a traitor to his class — the wealthy business elite — thanks to his independence of thought, his cowboy credentials, and his progressive politics. Roosevelt stood out as an iconoclast, seemingly belonging to a party, and perhaps a social class, all his own.

The progressive-era writer and editor William Allen White, who had met Roosevelt when he was assistant secretary of the navy, vividly recalled him as "a tallish, yet stockily built man, physically hard and rugged, obviously fighting down the young moon crescent of his vest; quick speaking, forthright, a dynamo of energy, given to gestures and grimaces, letting his voice run its full gamut from bass to falsetto." Like so many of the journalists whom Roosevelt befriended, White succumbed to his charm: "Roosevelt bit me and I went mad."

After being elected by a landslide in 1904, Roosevelt produced a flurry of legislative initiatives that had an impact on the open-range cattle industry. He regulated railroad rates and passed the Federal Meat Inspection Act and the Pure Food and Drug Act, two landmark consumer protection laws, as well as the Antiquities Act, which gave the president the power to declare national monuments of natural, historical, or cultural significance on any federal land. Devil's Tower in Wyoming would be the first of eighteen so designated by Roosevelt. And yet in hindsight, these accomplishments, as significant as they were, are dwarfed by what he achieved through his conservation initiatives.

Once in the White House, Roosevelt formed an alliance with Gifford Pinchot (pronounced PIN-cho), who headed up the Division of Forestry, mirroring Roosevelt's relationship with the *Forest and Stream* editor George Bird Grinnell a few years earlier. A member of Roosevelt's Boone and Crockett Club and the creator of Yale's School of Forestry, Pinchot was a committed conservationist, perhaps even more so than Roosevelt himself. Owen Wister picked up on this zeal when he remarked of Pinchot, "The eyes do not look as if they read books but as if they gazed upon a Cause." Pinchot wanted the federal government to maintain control over its public lands — not for the sake of beautiful scenery or the romance of the wilderness, but because the private sector was likely to exploit and destroy such lands and could not be counted on to act as a proper steward. "Conservation means the greatest good to the greatest number for the longest time," Pinchot would write in his 1910 book *The Fight for Conservation.* "It demands the complete and orderly development of all our resources for the benefit of all the people, instead of the partial exploitation of them for the benefit of a few." Proper government administration of public lands would come to mean retaining control of the land and leasing it for fees, rather than simply selling it off to the private sector as fast as possible, which had been the intention of the Homestead Act.

Roosevelt organized two national conservation conferences during his presidency, one in 1905 and one in 1907, giving the new movement greater visibility. He also created the National Conservation Commission, with Pinchot as its chairman, to take an inventory of the country's natural resources: its water, land, forests, and minerals. Then in 1905, by means of the Transfer Act, Roosevelt and Pinchot sneakily moved the administration of national forests out of the General Land Office of the Interior Department and into the Agricultural Department, where the Division of Forestry, which simultaneously morphed into the new United States Forest Service, could oversee them. Under Pinchot's oversight, the department's forestry experts, who used scientific management methods, could administer the national forests for the common good.

These two men would convert 150 million acres of federal land into forest preserves. Eventually, the western lumber and railroad interests began to push back against what they perceived as an assault against free-market principles. They retaliated in February 1907, when Congress passed an agriculture appropriations bill carrying an amendment authored by Senator Charles W. Fulton of Oregon; it removed sixteen million acres of forest from the control of the executive branch, restoring them to the control of Congress, where Roosevelt feared they would be "exploited by land grabbers and by the representatives of the great special interests." The approved bill was sent to the White House for Roosevelt to sign. Aware that they had only ten days to act, Roosevelt and Pinchot spread out maps on the floor of the White House and, with the help of a cadre of administration clerks working forty-eight-hour shifts, laid out twenty-one new forest reserves (eight of them in Oregon) and enlarged eleven others. The paperwork was drawn up, and these protected areas were then created, by executive order, only moments before Roosevelt signed the agriculture appropriations bill into law — effectively neutering Fulton's amendment. The new national forests would come to be known as the Midnight Forests. Senator Fulton, of course, was irate. Lawsuits ensued and ultimately were argued before the U.S. Supreme Court, where the justices ruled in Roosevelt's favor.

Although the open-range era had compounded an environmental disaster that began with the extermination of the bison, its great saving grace was immersing Roosevelt in the landscape of the West. It educated him as to the importance of the conservation ethic. And once he understood the dangers facing the wildlife, the forests, and the grasslands of the open range, he worked tirelessly to make sure that others understood too. Perhaps key among his accomplishments was getting the American public on the side of preservation. He did this through a barrage of speeches, articles, and interviews, such as the speech that he made before the Colorado Livestock Association in Denver in 1910, in which he argued, "It is also vandalism wantonly to destroy or to permit the destruction of what is beautiful in nature, whether it be a cliff, a forest, or a species of mammal or bird. Here in the United States we turn our rivers and streams into sewers and dumping-grounds, we pollute the air, we destroy forests, and exterminate fishes, birds and mammals — not to speak of vulgarizing charming landscapes with hideous advertisements. But at last it looks as if our people were awakening."

The conservation movement would develop two branches as the new century progressed: the "wise and multiple use" conservation approach favored by Roosevelt and the more purist environmental approach favored by writers such as John Muir, Aldo Leopold, and Bob Marshall, who lobbied to protect wilderness areas for the aesthetic and recreational opportunities they presented and for the less tangible contributions they made to people's quality of life. If he had lived long enough, Roosevelt likely would have straddled these two branches. A member of the National Rifle Association and a lover of expensive guns, he almost certainly would never have given up his weapons or his love of hunting. On the other hand, he would have grasped the notion of wilderness for wilderness' sake and championed the reintroduction of a keystone species like the gray wolf into Yellowstone, once he, like the rest of us, came to understand its role in the ecosystem. As a lifelong birder and animal naturalist, he would have embraced the science of ecology too, as it began to emerge.

The extraordinary national parks, national forests, and wildlife and bird refuges that endure in the United States today, thanks to the work of Theodore Roosevelt and his followers, are the envy of the rest of the world. The historian Stephen Ambrose accurately summarized Roosevelt's contribution: "He was one of America's first conservationists, and he is still her greatest, because of what he was able to do through the Boone & Crockett Club and as president of the United States."

Following his departure from the White House, Roosevelt embarked on what would prove to be a yearlong African safari, sponsored by the Smithsonian Institution and the American Museum of Natural History, with the intent of gathering specimens for their collections and advancing scientific knowledge. It may well have done just that, but it also proved to be a first-class hunting expedition for Roosevelt and his entourage. The expedition required two hundred bearers to carry the gear, which included four tons of salt for preserving specimens, as it wended its way across British East Africa and through the Belgian Congo. In total, the hunting party killed or trapped 11,397 animals, including insects. They shot 512 big-game animals, including eleven elephants, seventeen lions, three leopards, seven cheetahs, twenty rhinoceros (including, regrettably, six rare white rhinos), eight hippopotamuses, and ten buffalo. Though Roosevelt insisted that he was "not in the least a game butcher," his rifle accounted for 296 of those big-game kills. The total cost of the expedition came to seventy-five thousand dollars, subsidized in part by the steel baron Andrew Carnegie as scientific philanthropy. Roosevelt covered the rest with his fifty-thousand-dollar advance from *Scribner's Magazine* for his exclusive account of the trip.

In 1912 Roosevelt attempted to retake the White House on the Progressive "Bull Moose" platform after splitting from the Republican Party, only to lose badly to Woodrow Wilson in a rare four-way race for the presidency. But, as the historian Doris Kearns Goodwin has observed, "Although the Progressive Party met early defeat, the progressive causes would continue to influence American politics for years to come." She cited three progressive amendments to the Constitution as legacies of the movement: the Sixteenth, which allowed for a national progressive income tax, which in turn helped pay for the New Deal's social programs; the Seventeenth, which established the election of U.S. senators by popular vote; and the Nineteenth, which gave women the right to vote.

Soon after the loss of the election, Roosevelt put himself in harm's way one final time. He set off with his son Kermit to the Amazon River, to explore a tributary known as the River of Doubt. During the expedition he gashed his thigh while wading through a set of rapids. The wound festered in the jungle heat. Prostrate, beset with malaria, and unable to care for himself, Roosevelt grew feverish and slid in and out of consciousness; he nearly died. When he finally emerged from the jungle, he had lost over fifty pounds and suffered permanent impairments to his health.

The final blow came on July 17, 1918, when a dispatch arrived at his Long Island home, Sagamore Hill, with the news that his adored youngest son, Quentin, had been shot down over enemy lines in France while serving as a fighter pilot in the First World War. As reporters watched, Roosevelt paced up and down the front porch, anguishing over how to break the news to Edith. He finally steeled himself for the task and entered the house, closing the door gently behind him. Half an hour later he emerged to make a statement to the press: "Quentin's mother and I are very glad that he got to the front and had a chance to render some service to his country, and show the stuff that was in him before his fate befell him." Roosevelt then retreated to his study. As he dictated the day's correspondence to his private secretary, Josephine Strycker, tears streamed down his face and his voice choked with emotion. Not long after, Roosevelt was seen standing alone in the stable at Sagamore Hill with his arm draped over the neck of his favorite horse, sobbing.

Although favored to win the Republican nomination in 1920, he would never get the chance. On January 6, 1919, he went upstairs to bed after complaining of trouble breathing. He died in his sleep of a pulmonary embolism, a blood clot in the lung. He was sixty years old.

Late in his life, in a conversation with Senator Albert Fall, Roosevelt remarked that if asked to choose his favorite chapter or experience in life, he knew which he would choose: his time spent in the Badlands. "I would take the memory of my life on the ranch with its experiences close to Nature and among the men who lived nearest to her."

Few American presidents would ever attain the enormous popularity that Roosevelt enjoyed during his years in the White House. Part of this can be explained by his exuberant and charismatic can-do personality. But just as important was the fact that Roosevelt had come to embrace the ideals of the American West — independence, unwavering courage, and moral righteousness. He might have been patrician born and Ivy League educated, but he had forged himself into something far more universal. By embracing what he had learned in the Badlands, he came to embody the ideal American cowboy.

20

The Closing of the Range

The Johnson County War divides the Old West's open-range era of the trail drive, the cowboy, and the giant cattle ranch from the New West's world of the farmer, the homesteader, and the small-time rancher. By now the business methodology — including the heavy-handed tactics — of the cattle barons had been thoroughly discredited. Open-range ranching was simply a broken economic model. Henceforth no competent rancher would gamble on the availability of boundless public land or the fickle western weather. Doomed by false assumptions, by barbed wire, and by poorly conceived land laws and widespread ranch mismanagement, the cattle industry retrenched and then slowly began to restructure and rebuild.

Grazing on public lands continues to this day, but small ranches have replaced the massive ones that once dominated the northern plains. These smaller outfits grow their own hay and alfalfa, a more cost-effective approach, and they fence and shelter cattle on their own land. Many struggling ranchers chose to convert their outfits into guest ranches, or so-called dude ranches, to cater to visitors from the East who were eager to sample the cowboy lifestyle and see the western landscape firsthand. The three Eaton brothers, friends and neighbors of Roosevelt in Medora, were the first to succeed at this new line of work. Their ranch remains in the Eaton family and continues as a dude ranch to this day, although the family pulled up stakes in 1905 and moved to Wolf, Wyoming, on the eastern slope of the Bighorn Mountains. The most successful dude ranches were situated in areas of exceptional natural beauty, such as Jackson Hole, Wyoming, at the foot of the Grand Tetons.

The war also marked the passing away of lynching-bee justice and the start of a more orderly, law-abiding society in the West. The pioneering culture of the frontier came to a close as the modern urban era began.

The first to articulate this theory was a thirty-two-year-old historian named Frederick Jackson Turner, who, shortly after hearing Theodore Roosevelt speak on similar ideas, wrote and delivered a speech in 1893 that was later published as "The Significance of the Frontier in American History." Turner argued that the frontier had now closed and, with it, the first chapter in American history. More important, the frontier, and not our country's European origins, best defined the United States — its national character and its commitment to democracy. Thus the country should look to the West, and not across the Atlantic, for its true origins and historical identity. In the decades that followed, other historians championed, critiqued, and disputed the theory, but no one denied that Jackson had picked the right moment to formulate it. As the historian Maurice Frink wrote in *When Grass Was King*, "Certain it is that a scene unlike any other in economic history faded from view when the curtain fell on the open range days. There would be other acts, dramatic and exciting; there would never be another just like this one." Walter Prescott Webb echoed this sentiment when he described the open-range era as "one of the outstanding phenomena in America history."

But from another perspective — this author's — the events leading up to 1893 tell us less about the closing of the frontier and more about the economic evolution of the nation and its market economy. By means of substantial financial investments and the establishment of numerous cattle towns, the great cattle boom encouraged and accelerated the settlement, development, and industrialization of a vast open terrain, while kick-starting its biggest industry — meatpacking. That process, though disruptive to the environment, contributed mightily to the shaping of present-day America. The events of the cattle era mark a key moment in the maturation of the nation: the domestication of the Wild West. The inroads that the trappers and the miners made into the untamed rangelands were dwarfed by the transformations created by the railroads and the livestock ranchers, which in turn attracted the homesteaders. The former Great American Desert, subdivided first by barbed wire, was further checkerboarded into small plots by an influx of farmers. Boomtowns like Cheyenne grew into cities, a trend affecting much of the nation, as it became more settled, industrialized, and urban.

From then on, smaller towns grew up in tandem with cities scattered across the country's far-flung territories. Some communities thrived; others failed; all played a role in the ongoing process of investment, construction, homebuilding, and economic expansion — and its attendant cycles of success, failure, bankruptcy, and renewal. Economic development, much of it driven by business practices introduced during the cattle boom, proceeded in fits and starts over the ensuing decades, with periodic booms and busts. But the final remarkable significance of the cattle kingdom is the way it shaped our country into the landscape that we recognize today — a crazy quilt of wilderness areas, ranches, farms, forest cutovers, subdivisions, suburbs, towns, and cities.

The historian William Cronon put his finger on it: "The integrated city-country system in which all of us now live is so widely diffused across the landscape that we no long identify it with any single place . . . The immense region between the Appalachians and the Pacific has in the twentieth century been partitioned into the subregional hinterlands of the many cities and physiographic provinces of the continent's interior." By the end of the cattle era, St. Louis and Chicago had lost their status as "gateway cities" because the boundary to the so-called frontier had dissolved. No one, Cronon noted, referred any longer to the Great West, or for that matter, to the Great American Desert.

The Johnson County War did more than place an exclamation point at the end of the open-range cattle era. It also foreshadowed the bitter disputes over land practices that would become a lasting feature of life in the American West.

The idea that the land existed purely for exploitation — an infinite resource that could be tapped forever, without significant repercussions — was a view that the cattle ranchers espoused but that the Big Die-Up and the ravaged environment discredited. Wild animals were disappearing, and the health of the grasslands was imperiled. Even when left alone, overgrazed lands never properly recovered; the diversity of plants diminished, opening the door to invasive species such as cheatgrass and Russian thistle, better known as tumbleweed.

Finally, after years of argument propounded by conservationists like Roosevelt, Americans became aware that the land, the animals, the forests, in fact all the natural resources on the American continent, were finite; the looting undertaken by various commercial interests could not continue. A deep awareness took hold: the wilderness — something uniquely American — could be lost forever.

The new conservation movement had scored its first victory with the passage of the Forest Reserve Act of 1891, placing new restrictions on the use of important parcels of land; miners, cattlemen, and farmers could no longer exploit them. Many battles followed in its wake: Democrats versus Republicans, conservationists versus sagebrush rebels, East versus West, a political tug of war over the efficacy and fairness of new approaches to land management and regulation. Businesses and western governors regularly challenged the unilateral actions of the federal government, citing states' rights and the rights of citizens. In the western states today, suspicion and distrust of the federal government and its land policies remain widespread.

The Boone and Crockett Club did much to support the nascent conservation effort. It fought for the preservation of wilderness areas and forest reserves. It promoted seasonal hunting, thus allowing the hunted animals to breed before they were taken and protecting the females and the young. It also advocated for state hunting licenses and bag limits. Still, it was far from perfect in its conservation ethic: by keeping a running record of the largest trophy kills, the club encouraged hunters to focus on chasing the biggest possible trophies, which, in Darwinian parlance, "naturally selects" against large animals in the wild. Sure enough, the size of the antler racks of deer, elk, and bighorn sheep, and the size of the specimens themselves, shrank over time. The biggest animals were taken as trophies, and with them, their genomes. By shooting all the big bull elks, the hunters were naturally selecting against big bull elks; over time, hunters found mostly smaller bull elks, with smaller antler racks. This process played out for aquatic species as well, in particular for big-game fish. Alas, this approach does not reflect natural predation as it occurs in the wild. It abrogates the rules of natural selection, which weed out the weak and the small; it replaces survival of the fittest with survival of the smallest.

Needless to say, many conservation (or environmental) initiatives could be controversial and unpopular at the local level. What right did the East Coast establishment and the federal government have to impose their will on the western states, especially when conservation initiatives could limit economic opportunity, potentially depriving citizens of the West of a livelihood?

It did not help that the conservation movement was born during an economically challenged period in the West. As Michael McCarthy has written, "At the turn of the century, with the frontier 'closing' and depression hemming them in from all sides, pioneer settlers equated shrinking land access with shrinking opportunity, and shrinking opportunity with economic destruction. Adopting, out of desperation, a 'last stand' mentality that permitted them no flexibility, they mourned more keenly than ever their lost rights." Western settlers came to believe that they had been economically damaged and disadvantaged by the conservation movement. Worse, the new policies seemed patently unfair: the eastern states had never been so handicapped in their own economic development! But these arguments overlooked the fact that the federal government's actions were entirely legal. Nothing in the Constitution gave westerners a sacred right to the land. On the contrary, Congress had always had the right to hold, manage, and dispose of public land as it saw fit.

The conservationists had a few convincing arguments on their side. They stated that a war much larger than the Johnson County War had been waged and lost: a war against the environment of the open range. "The invasion [of the West] by millions of head of exogenous horses, cattle, sheep, and goats in the span of a few decades must have come with the explosive, shattering effect of all-out war," according to the environmental historian Donald Worster. As early as the 1940s, the western historian Bernard DeVoto was writing scathingly of the arrogance of the cattle barons: "The cattlemen came from Elsewhere into the empty West. They were always arrogant and always deluded. They thought themselves free men, the freest men who ever lived, but even more than other Westerners they were peons of their Eastern Bankers and of the railroads . . . They thought of themselves as Westerners and they did live in the West, but they were enemies of everyone else who lived there . . . Nothing in history suggests that the cattlemen and sheepmen are capable of regulating themselves even for their own benefit, still less the public's . . . Cattlemen and sheepmen, I repeat, want to shovel most of the West into its rivers."

One of the worst casualties in this war against the environment was the gray wolf. The federal government sanctioned its extermination, and federal bounties largely paid for it. Even Theodore Roosevelt misunderstood the wolf's role in the ecosystem; he saw it as "the beast of waste and desolation" and called for its eradication. It wasn't until 1995 that the gray wolf was experimentally reintroduced to Yellowstone National Park in limited numbers (thirty-one animals) and to the Frank Church Wilderness of Idaho (twenty-three animals). The neighboring ranchers, not happy to see them return, remain to this day opposed to the reintroduction of the wolves, despite the fact that it has resulted in only modest predation of their herds, for which they are being compensated.

This reintroduction surfaced a remarkable discovery, with implications for cattle ranching. With Yellowstone as an ecological laboratory, scientists could watch the impact that the wolves had on the local food chain — one far more striking and widespread than anyone expected. The wolf, it turned out, was a keystone species that had a ripple effect on the rest of the environment.

The wolves were doing the ecosystem a favor: by forcing herds of elk to collect defensively in tight units, scaring them into avoiding open spaces, and encouraging them to keep on the move to avoid predation, the wolves had given the habitat around rivers and streams a chance to recover from overgrazing. Willows regrew there, shoring up the banks and protecting the soil from erosion. These willows in turn provided food for beavers — and only one beaver colony had remained in Yellowstone prior to the reintroduction of the wolves. The beaver dams created ponds for trout, which in turn helped the osprey and bald eagle populations to recover. The wolves helped reduce the coyote population, which, like the elk population, had been out of balance. Fewer coyotes meant that various small-rodent populations could recover, providing prey for raptors such as owls, whose numbers increased. Even the grizzly population benefited from the return of the gray wolf, because the grizzlies could once again steal the wolf kills to feed their young. Furthermore, the predation of elk weakened by disease resulted in stronger, healthier elk herds. These new herds, forced close together for their own safety, better aerated the soil with their hooves and better fertilized it with their manure, restoring the health of the grasslands. The appearance of the landscape began to improve, as the wolves reversed a process that was gradually turning Yellowstone into a desert. Suddenly the value of a complete and balanced ecosystem, replete with carnivores, was indisputable.

The gray wolf population across the United States has now recovered from three hundred animals in the wild to over four thousand. In the northern Rockies, the wolf has been removed from protection as stipulated in the Endangered Species Act, and in some parts of the country you can get a license to hunt it. The reintroduction can be judged a success despite the challenges that remain: balancing the conflicting interests of preservationists, hunters, and ranchers. Happily, the wolves have brought an unexpected economic windfall: recreational wolf watching is bringing revenues to certain rural areas.

The idea that the wolves were, in effect, herding the elk to the benefit of the environment soon had wider ramifications. Herding was precisely what the wolves had done with the great bison herds, forcing them into tighter units and keeping them on the move. This behavior possibly accounted for the richly fertilized grasslands of the Great Plains.

Support for this idea has come from as far away as Zimbabwe, in southern Africa. There, a former biologist and game ranger named Allan Savory, after years of experimenting with culling herds of African elephants to reverse deforestation and desertification, made a startling discovery. He realized that the answer was not smaller elephant herds but just the opposite: larger ones. He further deduced that the best approach to herding other animals, in order to reverse desertification, was to follow the methods of cattle herding used by the Masai tribes, who had grazed their cattle along the Great Rift Valley since the fourteenth or fifteenth century. According to Savory's controversial theory, we need more cattle herds, and bigger ones, kept in close quarters and moved frequently, which is exactly what happens when carnivores are present. Savory has persuasively demonstrated that his holistic and counterintuitive approach works on the Dimbangombe Ranch in Zimbabwe. Now others are adopting his methods.

One of those is Bryan Ulring, co-owner of the J Bar L Ranch in Centennial Valley, Montana, who sees himself as a cowboy acting like a wolf to keep his herd tightly packed and moving back and forth across his range. "See how they are moving around? They are like a bunch of mobile composting units that constantly recycle the grass into the ground," he explained to Dr. M. Sanjayan in the PBS series *Earth: The New Wild*. "I think they are the world's most perfect farming equipment — an all-in-one farming equipment. You have the harvester, the seeder, and the fertilizer all in one unit."

For environmentalists who have viewed cattle as an environmental menace, this new theory stands the prevailing wisdom on its head. As Dr. Sanjayan remarked on the PBS program, "As a conservationist I sort of hate cows. But Bryan has managed to get his cows to occupy the role once occupied by bison. Bryan plays the wolf. Together they are restoring this land back to health. And it's a hard truth that I almost don't want to accept because it feels like a betrayal, but Bryan has somehow figured out a way to make his cows fit, fit within the ecology of this place."

Savory's approach entails more than rotational grazing. He uses the cattle corral itself as an ecological tool, constantly relocating it before the grass in a given area becomes degraded. The trick is not to allow the hooves of the cattle to compact the soil so much that water cannot infiltrate, while making sure that they aerate the soil and stamp in grass seeds, along with their manure. To properly execute such holistic ranching requires a great deal of planning and monitoring. Whether this form of management will be broadly scalable across the West and other parts of the world remains to be seen. It likely will not work in more arid rangelands, where the ecosystem is simply too fragile to withstanding grazing of any kind. But a recent survey of ranches using this holistic approach reports strikingly positive results: "95% report an increase in biodiversity, 80% reported an increase in profits, 91% reporting improvements in quality of life. All report that biodiversity is now an important consideration in managing their land, where only 9% felt so prior to exposure with Holistic Management." The Circle Ranch, located in the high-desert mountains of Hudspeth County, Texas, has tripled the "animal days of grazing" that the 32,000-acre ranch can support.

The Savory approach has one final alleged benefit: by promoting grass growth and healthy biodiversity, it captures carbon, converting it into biomass — in short, the practice might help reverse global warming.

The notion that cattle might be used to improve soils, sequester carbon, and thus help save the planet has many conservationists dumbfounded. Not everyone is on board. "There is no such thing as a beef-eating environmentalist," remarked James E. McWilliams, an author and professor at the University of Texas who critiqued Allan Savory's approach in a TED Talk; for one thing, cattle do not behave like bison. Left to their own devices, they gather around water holes and trample the habitat in a manner that bison don't.

Others take issue with Savory's understanding of the biology of grasslands, questioning whether the trampling hooves actually do anything to plant grass seeds. And what about the large amounts of methane that cattle emit into the atmosphere? By some estimates, livestock produce carbon dioxide emissions approximately equal to the amount of exhaust produced by the entire transportation industry — cattle being the worst of the livestock offenders. Uniting cattlemen and conservationists simply sounds too good to be true. But peer-reviewed articles have disputed the disputers and discredited the discreditors. The latest evidence seems to suggest a Hollywood-like sequel to the open-range cattle era.

The Savory Institute is working aggressively to establish one hundred so-called Savory hubs, which will protect one billion hectares of grassland around the globe by 2025; plans are also going forward to create venues for training and supporting other practitioners of the holistic approach.

Despite progress, we humans remain woefully ignorant about the subtle workings of ecosystems and the biosphere, especially our grasslands. Nor have we been able to halt the destruction of these and other natural ecosystems and their native species. As Reed F.

Noss and Allen Y. Cooperrider wrote in their classic work, *Saving Nature's Legacy,* "Improvements in knowledge and technology have simply not kept pace with the forces of environmental destruction. These forces — fundamentally human population, resource consumption, anthropocentric arrogance, greed, selfishness, ignorance, and disrespect for living things — have encouraged higher rates of habitat destruction in spite of better science, stronger laws, and fancier technology."

21

Failed Second Acts

Many of the failing cattlemen in the years following the Johnson County War never understood that, as much as overgrazing and the weather and lax management had contributed to their demise, the meatpackers had been their greatest nemesis.

Moreton Frewen, who had predicted rising prices for beef because of an unmet and growing demand, failed to comprehend that high prices and profits would bring more and more entrants into the field, and eventually, even inevitably, an oversupply would sink those prices and profits. Frewen also did not grasp the pivotal role of the meatpackers in Chicago.

The Beef Trust had asserted itself at a critical juncture in the supply chain, where much added value was created in the business, which is to say, in the processing of the meat itself. Their modern management techniques, such as a vertically integrated business model, allowed them to achieve a stranglehold on the industry, controlling supply, distribution, and pricing. The meatpackers, especially the "Big Five," had done what all good monopolists do to shore up market share: they deliberately forced down prices. Much like Amazon, with its damn-the-current-profits strategy, the trust expected to recoup short-term losses through greater volume and market share and ultimately more autonomy concerning prices in the future. A side benefit was driving many competitors out of business. Everyone in the industry soon became beholden to the meatpackers. According to the historian Richard White, "The big packinghouses loaned money to commission agents, who loaned it to farmers seeking to buy feeders from the western range. The agents held a mortgage on both the corn and the steer. Long before the steer ever reached Chicago, Kansas City, or Fort Worth, the packers controlled it." The meatpackers' mammoth power — as the largest industry in the country until surpassed by the auto industry — had ultimately brought even the railroads, the other great industrial power of the era, to heel.

Across America, monopolies and trusts in industries from sugar to steel were behaving in this manner, which finally prompted President Theodore Roosevelt and the Justice Department to begin the hard work of breaking them up. Roosevelt would initially target J. P. Morgan's Northern Securities Corporation, a railroad holding company, and then, later, the greatest cartel of all, Standard Oil. Unfortunately, the trustbusters' assault on the meatpackers would come far too late to save the careers and fortunes of the great cattle barons.

Two of the most prominent of these men were especially notable for their inability to recover from setbacks in the American West: Moreton Frewen and the Marquis de Morès. In many respects, their failed efforts at cattle ranching would mark the high point of their business careers while tarnishing their future prospects. However, much as Roosevelt did after *he* left the West, both returned for extraordinary second acts.

It is hard not to admire Moreton Frewen's perseverance. No matter how consistent and colossal his business failures, he soldiered on. To the end of his life he sported an almost unparalleled self-confidence as well as a uniquely American brand of entrepreneurialism and hucksterism, which he had picked up in the American West. Forced off the board of the Powder River Cattle Company and desperate for money, he first tried promoting a new grease to lubricate locomotives and the wheels of railroad cars, taking a 10 percent commission on every sale. The grease was thicker in consistency and longer lasting than competing products, but selling it proved unprofitable. He moved on, in short order, to promote the prototype for an ice-making device. But that didn't sell either.

By now a number of his angry debt-holders, including the Earl of Wharncliffe, the former chairman of his cattle company, had expressed a determination to pursue Frewen in court. With a fresh plan to solve his financial problems, Frewen slipped off to Monte Carlo. He hoped to win big at the gambling tables, using a betting system that he apparently picked up from a friend. He lost two hundred pounds sterling on the first day. Dejected and complaining that the system was "unreliable and dangerous," he wrote his wife a letter that read, in part, "Sweet thing, I ought never to have come out here on such an errand. I blame myself for it, but it seemed the only chance, and that is now a very slight one. You can guess that not the worse part of the day was the loss; it was worse still to have to cable the news to you, sweet thing." And yet he stayed on in Monte Carlo for another four or five days, gambling every day, trying repeatedly, and ineffectually, to reverse his fortunes.

Back in London he regaled friends at his clubs with anecdotes of his western adventures until, at last, through the help of his brother-in-law Randolph Churchill, he managed to secure an assignment guiding Sir Salar Jung, the immensely rich twenty-four-year-old hereditary (but recently deposed) prime minister of Hyderabad, India, on a tour of Europe. The job also entailed serving as the former prime minister's private secretary and adviser. But Jung, who weighed over three hundred pounds and consumed three bottles of whiskey each day, drank himself to death over the next two years, leaving Moreton once again unemployed.

By 1887 Moreton and Clara had been married for six years and were raising three young children. But Moreton was so often away on business that in all those years the couple spent only a few weeks at a time together. To avoid being dunned by creditors, he took to avoiding London altogether. "What a curse poverty is," he wrote his wife from India. "It kills all the pleasure in life." He was terrified of going bankrupt because his precious social clubs would then request his resignation, and by now he was a member of the Carleton Club as well as White's.

He began to champion bimetallism, a controversial monetary standard by which the unit of a country's currency is determined by both gold and silver, with a fixed exchange rate between the two metals. Theoretically, bimetallism can help stabilize commodity prices and facilitate exchange rates. Moreton's interest in the topic was hardly an accident. In his mind, price declines and currency-exchange issues had taken a heavy toll on his cattle business and, more broadly, his family's fortune, as well as those of the British "squirearchy," the social class he identified with. Gold, he believed, empowered the bankers over the common man, while silver could expand the money supply and, inflation aside, make everyone richer — and he was all for that! He wrote widely on the subject, styling himself an expert and going so far as to advise his friend William Jennings Bryan on "Free Silver" during the celebrated orator's three unsuccessful campaigns for president of the United States.

Moreton's next effort, predictably, was an attempt to corner the silver market. But when he couldn't raise the huge sums of money the scheme required, he settled on forming a syndicate to drive up the stock of the diamond dealer De Beers. More friends went in on this venture, including his accountant and his brother Stephen, who ponied up £18,290, a chunk of it on margin. It was virtually every penny Stephen possessed. For a time the plan seemed to be working and the stock rose, from £15¾ to £23½, but then, unexpectedly and inexplicably, the price collapsed into the single digits. Stephen wrote Moreton to inform him that he had gone bust. "It is a great blow to me, I needn't tell you, and don't see what is before me now at all." He asked Moreton to keep an eye out for a job for him. Stephen's reduced financial circumstances ultimately forced him to abandon his career in the military in pursuit of better pay.

Thanks in large part to Moreton's luckless investments, by now all of the Frewen brothers were in deep financial trouble, including the eldest, Edward, heir to the family's two great Sussex estates. Both properties had been heavily mortgaged earlier in the century when making money in agriculture was still a sure thing and mortgage indebtedness something of a way of life for the landed gentry. But when the flood of imported grain and beef (live and frozen) arrived, the annual rental income earned on the Frewen lands — mostly from tenant farmers — was cut in half, from twelve thousand to six thousand pounds. Edward was forced to move into a farm cottage and rent out the stately homes for additional income. By the 1880s the mortgages were in arrears. The Law Life Insurance Company, which held the mortgages, as well as other liens on the property, proceeded to clear-cut the estates of their timber in lieu of foreclosing on the loans. Countless ancient specimen oaks and ornamental timber were destroyed and, equally tragic, a lovely heronry known as Great Sawdons, which once held the nests of hundreds of birds. Frewen wrote to a newspaper editor how heartbroken he was over the loss of "the most cherished association of my childhood — a wood which shelters the largest heronry in the British Isles, a beauty of sylvan scenery beyond all price, a great national possession — no more, no less."

Similar calamities afflicted many other great British landed estates in these years, as the great agricultural depression that began in 1870 continued to erase longstanding family fortunes. Britain's slow slide off its perch as the world's preeminent empire had begun. The aristocracy's and the landed gentry's financial problems would continue well into the twentieth century, when soaring death duties and rising labor costs compounded the pressures on these estates. Countless irreplaceable stately homes were demolished as the old families lost their wealth to the pressures of globalization, the costs of war, and their own financial negligence and ineptitude. A 1952 edition of *Burke's Landed Gentry* would report that fully half of the families listed had disposed of, or lost, all of their holdings in land.

To his credit, Moreton Frewen at least was determined to do something about his family's fading glory, and that of any other family willing to join him. One reason he succeeded so often in raising money from his friends in the squirearchy was because they desperately needed his help. Many viewed his endeavors to restore their family finances as one of their last and best hopes.

Frewen's next great venture was the Crawford Gold Crusher, a device used to extract gold from slag heaps in abandoned gold mines of the American West. The prototype, a miniature model that performed perfectly on his dining room table, persuaded more friends to risk more money. He even convinced his mother-in-law to invest in the gold crusher. To do so she sold a diamond rivière given to her by her husband, Leonard, to wear at the court of Napoleon III. "I have got the ball at my feet once more, and this time I'll keep it — you will see," Moreton wrote to Clara, full of hope and false confidence.

And for a time it looked as though the contraption would work. Dozens were sold. As Frewen wrote to his wife, "I never felt better, stronger or more confident. It is a blessing to have a mind. I don't feel as though all the ill-luck in the world could keep me down long now." But when the crushing machines were actually installed at the mines in the West, the technology, once scaled up from the model, would not operate effectively, or as a friend put it, "neither inventor nor invention could be made to working order." Moreton's hopes collapsed: "I am so utterly perplexed to know where to turn and what to do for the little money you need — for your diamonds [now pawned], darling, for the most pressing bills and for the Duke's rent. I have not a penny of my own now, nor have I any means here of raising any. I am at the last gasp."

On to the next project. How about shipping Siberian timber through the Northwest Passage? No takers. How about British Electrozones, a smelly disinfectant made from electrified seawater, which could be sold variously as a bath oil, a meat sauce, a cure for both boils and rinderpest, "a corrective" for stale fish, or a fluoride-like substance to protect teeth from decay? But chemists refused to stock it. The wife of a friend who invested in the product described how she tried unsuccessfully to dispose of hers: "I poured mine down the sink and it smelt for a fortnight. Other ladies who thought they had received eau de toilette were perfectly furious." The product went on — without Moreton Frewen — to become an improbable hit as a deodorant.

What about sulfides, which properly applied could separate tin from zinc? A fortune could be made selling them. Again, there would be, but Frewen's option on the product was "not entirely correct in legal form." His company went bust and took with it another four thousand pounds and two years of hard work. "He left babies on other people's doorsteps," remarked Dr. Jameson, a renowned physician and British colonial politician.

By now Moreton's indebtedness had soared. In letter after letter to his wife, he wrote entreaties like this one: "Do get hold of some money. I am as usual worried to death." At around this time his hair turned prematurely white. "He avoided bankruptcy by an agility that exceeds praise," noted his nephew Shane Leslie, in a portrait of Frewen published in his book *Studies in Sublime Failure.*

Although Moreton never neglected to pay his club dues, he did for a period fail to pay his servants, in particular, his loyal Irish manservant, Mack. He rationalized this oversight by arguing that the longer he failed to pay his help, the more necessary it would be for them to stick around — and the sooner they would come to think of themselves as members of the family! Mack, ever loyal, chose to stay on. At one point, Frewen borrowed heavily from trusts that his father had set up for Moreton's children, a decision that left his kids encumbered with his debts at the time of his death.

In one sense, the cattle fever Moreton Frewen contracted in his youth never left him. Each of his schemes was a new chance to vindicate himself for that first great costly, unforgettable folly in the American West. Did any man ever pay such a penance for the vanity and overconfidence of his youth?

Oddly, it was in the literary arena where Moreton likely did the most good. Here he did the English-reading public a service by discovering the work of an aspiring young author whom he met in Calcutta. The young Brit was writing sketches for the local newspaper in Allahabad. "I will do my best to get some of his stuff published in England," Moreton wrote Clara. "He really has a talent. His name is Rudyard Kipling." Frewen dutifully submitted a few of Kipling's stories and ballads to a pair of London newspaper editors; he knew both through the articles he had written on bimetallism.

The editor of the *Daily Telegraph* replied dismissively: "Dear Moreton, I think your friend's work has merit, but hardly reaches the standard of a position on the staff of *The Daily Telegraph*." The second editor, however, was William Earnest Henley, the editor of the *National Observer* and himself the author of the inspirational poem "Invictus." The red-bearded Henley walked with a peg leg and a crutch, having lost one leg below the knee to a tubercular infection of the bone; he thereby provided the inspiration for the pirate character Long John Silver in *Treasure Island*, written by Henley's close friend Robert Louis Stevenson. Furthermore, Henley's sickly daughter (who died at five) was the inspiration for Wendy in J. M. Barrie's *Peter Pan*, adding further luster to the Henley family's literary fame. Legend has it that Henley danced in delight on his peg leg upon receipt of Kipling's great barrack ballad "Danny Deever." He published it on February 22, 1890, and launched Kipling's career in Great Britain. Kipling would be the first English-language author to win the Nobel Prize for Literature — and he may well have had Moreton Frewen to thank for it.

Another of Moreton's contributions to the literary world came when he offered to serve as Winston Churchill's literary agent, to shepherd his nephew's first book through the publishing process. It began when Winston, aware of his uncle's reputation as an editorial writer and pamphleteer on bimetallism, solicited his literary advice. In one remarkable exchange that occurred when Winston was just twenty-one, the future prime minister and famed orator wrote to "Dear Uncle Moreton" on the subject of prose style: "I am very grateful to you for your letter and for the encouraging criticisms therein. The only great prose writer I have so far read is Gibbon — who cannot certainly be accused of crispness. It has appeared to me — as far as I have gone — that composition is essentially an artificial science. To make a short sentence — or a succession of short sentences — tell — they should be sandwiched in between lengthy and sonorous periods. The contrast is effective." To encourage the aspiring writer, Moreton bought Winston his first typewriter.

But when it came to the proofreading of Winston's first book, Frewen bungled the job. The book, titled *The Story of the Malakand Field Force: An Episode of Frontier War,* offered a firsthand account of a punitive British military campaign against Pashtun tribes in what is now Pakistan, a campaign for which Churchill had volunteered. Frewen not only did a miserable job of the proofreading, but he proceeded to alter the punctuation, which a reviewer in the highbrow literary magazine *Athenaeum* decried: "sentence after sentence ruined by the punctuation of an idiot." Winston, crestfallen, wrote a letter to his aunt Leonie in which he moaned, "Moreton let me in most sadly by the careless way in which he revised the proofs and his terribly illiterate punctuation. I telegraphed to stop the sale but it was already too late."

Churchill recovered from this early literary setback and, like Kipling, went on to win the Nobel Prize for Literature. He was cited for "his mastery of historical and biographical description as well as for brilliant oratory in defending exalted human values." Moreton Frewen deserves full credit — for providing the typewriter.

The Marquis de Morès, the last of the cowboy aristocrats, fared little better than Moreton Frewen once he too reentered the real world. After a failed effort to finance and build a railroad through the jungle in Vietnam, stretching from the Chinese frontier in Yunnan Province to the Gulf of Tonkin, he returned to Paris, where he launched a political movement that bizarrely combined socialism and rabid anti-Semitism. The members of his party took to wearing cowboy attire and ten-gallon hats to call attention to themselves on the streets of Paris. In speeches and newspaper articles, de Morès attacked, among others, the Rothschilds, the leading bankers of the day, denouncing them as monopolists. He quickly made other powerful enemies among the French elite. Anti-Semitism, of course, had been rife in France for generations and was especially prevalent among the aristocracy, which was fervently Catholic. But in many respects, socialism proved to be far more unacceptable at the time. After declaring his socialist sympathies, de Morès was snubbed at the Jockey Club, where he heard loud whispers denouncing him as a traitor to his class. His father, *le duc*, went a step further and publicly disowned him.

As Moreton Frewen subsequently noted, "Wherever Morès went he was a lightning rod for any local ructions." Indeed, de Morès fought at least three well-publicized duels over the following five years against outraged Jewish adversaries in the French elite. The most widely publicized of these was fought against Captain Armand Mayer, a professor at the École Politechnique and an expert in the épée, a small three-sided dueling sword. This duel took place in a *salle d'armes* on Île de la Grand Jatte on the Seine, on the morning of June 23, 1892. It was not intended to be a duel to the death but rather to "first blood." In such a duel, strict provisions forbid close-quarter fighting, and the contest was to end the instant one or the other was wounded. Still, it proved deadly.

On command, the two men began the slow-tempo sword fighting that characterizes the épée, interrupted by the occasional burst of a thrust and counterthrust. Finally, Mayer lunged in on the attack. The Marquis, using the exceptional strength of his wrist, parried Mayer's épée with his own sword and, in the same movement, countered. As Mayer finished his sally, de Morès's weapon penetrated Mayer's armpit and went through his lung to his spinal cord. "I'm hit!" exclaimed Mayer, staggering backward. De Morès, perhaps not realizing the severity of the blow, promptly stepped forward and offered his hand. "Captain Mayer, will you permit me to shake your hand?" The two men shook, and Mayer stumbled off to seek the care of a doctor. Although the wound bled little, Mayer died later that evening.

De Morès's life came to a gory end in 1896, in an appropriately western-style shootout that occurred in an unlikely place: the desert of Tunisia. In June of that year, pursuing a far-fetched plan to drive the British (and the Jews) out of Egypt, he traveled to North Africa, hoping to rally Islamic groups to join him in his quixotic campaign. The British, with French help, had occupied Egypt in 1882, in part to gain control of the strategically important Suez Canal. But the French and the English were now at political loggerheads. De Morès was convinced that his campaign would prevent the British from advancing farther into Saharan Africa. And if he could help France further colonize and exploit the resources in the area in the aftermath of such a coup, he could restore his reputation and earn himself a fortune in the process. His self-assigned mission was a simple one: "Give the Arabs land, justice and the Koran and march with them, with Algeria as the base, in the peaceful conquest of Africa." He set about organizing an expedition to rally the various desert tribes to his cause. At the dock in Tunis, he said goodbye to his American wife, Medora. His last words to her were his motto: "Travaillez et priez!" Work and pray!

The French authorities warned him that they could not vouch for his safety, yet nonetheless he proceeded by caravan into the Tunisian desert. Some two dozen Tuareg men escorted him; he had hired them as his guides and protectors. A month into the journey, he grew suspicious when new tribesmen joined the caravan, and some of his possessions were stolen at night. When his head guide then attempted to take the caravan on a detour from the prescribed route, de Morès protested. At that instant the Tuareg men turned on him. One tried to wrest de Morès's rifle from the scabbard on the saddle of his horse. Others grabbed at his revolver holster, dragging him out of his saddle in the process. A third swung at him with a saber. De Morès ducked, but the blade sliced through his hatband and grazed his forehead, causing profuse bleeding. Revolver in hand, he shot the saber-wielding Tuareg dead on the spot. Then he exchanged gunfire with his other betrayers. Ever cool under pressure, he managed to kill a second man and wound two others.

At that point the Tuareg men retreated. De Morès, alone, with his back to a tree, bleeding from his forehead, reloaded his pistol. The Tuareg men sent one of their leaders forward to try to negotiate his surrender, but de Morès seized the man as a hostage. When the fellow attempted to escape, de Morès shot him dead too. The firing resumed. At this point de Morès was shot twice, once in his side and once in his neck. Mortally wounded, he knelt and attempted to reload one final time. At that moment the leader of the tribesmen raced up behind him and buried a knife in his back, killing him instantly.

To make certain he was dead, the men fired numerous shots into his corpse. They then stripped him of his money belt and his clothing. They castrated him and dragged his naked body by one ankle behind a horse, eventually abandoning it in some bushes near the well of El Ouatia. Two of his Tunisian servants were also killed in the skirmish, but one managed to escape. A day or so later this Tunisian made it back to a French army post, where he reported what had happened. Eighteen days later the French authorities recovered the body of de Morès and returned with it to the port city of Gabes. His *homme de confiance*, William van Driesche, was waiting there to identify the remains.

From comments her husband had written in his letters, de Morès's wife was convinced that the French government had conspired to have her husband killed. She offered a large reward for his assailants, and eventually three men were captured. One died in jail; the other two were tried and sentenced to "life at hard labor." But the marquise was never able to prove that the French government was complicit in her husband's assassination.

Can the disastrous subsequent careers of Moreton Frewen and the Marquis de Morès be blamed directly on what had happened to them during the cattle boom? There seems little question that their financial reverses as cattle ranchers dented their youthful confidence. One suspects that Moreton Frewen knew by the time he left the West that his brother Richard was right: Moreton couldn't manage his schemes, and each subsequent venture was almost tailor-made to prove that thesis. Perhaps he felt doomed to failure — that could perhaps explain why he never returned to investing in cattle, the one subject he arguably knew something about and an endeavor in which he might learn from his mistakes.

De Morès, for his part, retreated to his earliest career roots, and to his family roots, by becoming a soldier. Financial arbitrage wasn't for him, nor, it would seem, was cattle ranching and beef packing; so instead, ever vainglorious, he would aim even higher and try to become the next Napoleon, conquering new territories for the glory of France. In the process, he rode intellectually and politically off the deep end.

What can be said for Moreton Frewen and the Marquis de Morès in comparison to the other young, privileged ranchers of the cattle kingdom? In a sense they surpassed Hubert Teschemacher because they, at least, attempted new endeavors. But they did not rebound from their losses in the way that Theodore Roosevelt did. In the American West Roosevelt found himself, while in many ways his peers lost themselves. TR's experience there endowed him with a mission and a rational direction in life.

22

Myths of the Old West

———

Theodore Roosevelt's good friend Owen Wister, frustrated
at his inability to get an opera produced about the career
of Montezuma and disappointed by a dull legal career, first
turned his hand to writing fiction in 1891. Wister hailed from a
distinguished Pennsylvania glassmaking family, which included a
signer of the Declaration of Independence and, more dubiously, the
author of the fugitive slave clause of the Constitution. He was also
the grandson of Fanny Kemble, the leading British Shakespearean
actress of her day. As a boy he attended a Swiss boarding school
and then St. Paul's School in New Hampshire before enrolling at
Harvard, where he graduated summa cum laude. While majoring
in music, he wrote a Hasty Pudding theatrical show titled *Dido and
Aeneas*, which proved so successful on tour, it largely paid for the
club's new theater.

After his graduation, Wister's intellectually formidable mother
took him abroad, and in London introduced him to her lifelong
friend the writer Henry James. His grandmother, Fanny Kemble,
arranged for him to perform a piano recital of his own work in front

of *her* good friend, the great Hungarian virtuoso Franz Liszt, who declared Wister to possess *un talent prononcé*. But Wister's father refused to support his career in music, so he drifted into banking and then law, hating both. He grew depressed and eventually suffered a nervous breakdown.

At this point — in 1885 — he first came out to Wyoming for a rest cure, at Roosevelt's suggestion. On arriving in Cheyenne, he was taken for lunch and drinks at the Cheyenne Club. A day or so later, he headed out to the VR Ranch, in an exceptionally lovely setting on Deer Creek in Converse County. This financially imperiled ranch was the one owned by Major Frank Wolcott, who would subsequently lead the Johnson County invasion. Here Wister boarded for the summer. On this, the first of his fifteen trips to the American West, he joined Hubert Teschemacher and Richard Trimble, his fellow Porcellians, on the memorable moonlit roundup. Wister took copious notes during every subsequent trip, recognizing instinctively that the culture, the lore, and the landscape were uniquely American and still fresh and unfamiliar to an East Coast and European audience — perhaps material for a future opera.

Then one night in the fall of 1891, during a conversation with his friend Walter Furness over dinner at the Philadelphia Club in downtown Philadelphia, Wister wondered aloud why no one had yet featured the American West in the way that Rudyard Kipling was using India as a setting for a series of fictional tales. Roosevelt was writing the natural history and Frederick Remington was creating the illustrations, but where were the short stories and the novels? After all, the subject matter was inherently dramatic and would sell — in fact, a literary career might be built upon it. The moment Wister uttered these words, he knew that he should be that author. He remembered exclaiming to his friend, "Walter, I'm going to try it myself . . . I am going to start this minute." He left the dinner table, hurried upstairs to the club's library, and by midnight had composed a draft of "Hank's Woman," the first of two short stories that within a matter of months would appear in the pages of *Harper's Monthly Magazine* and garner immediate acclaim. An early story (written in June 1892) featured the nameless figure known only as "the Virginian." At some point Wister realized that this mysterious character could be the protagonist of a novel.

Roosevelt read and admired his friend Wister's early short stories and encouraged him to continue in this western vein. Roosevelt objected only to some of the violence in the stories, which he considered sadistic. He advised Wister to tone down the gore, citing a scene in which a vicious rancher abuses his horse. It was based on an episode Wister had witnessed firsthand on a pack trip taken with David Robert Tisdale — one of the two Tisdale brothers who participated as invaders in the Johnson County War. At one point Tisdale whipped and kicked his exhausted and unresponsive horse, then used his thumb to gouge out one of its eyes.

But more important, Roosevelt wanted the Virginian to be a model of manly virtue — "a natural aristocrat" whose superiority was a product of his exposure to the natural world and the cowboy's outdoor way of life. After all, why couldn't the western cowboy, freed from the corruption of urban industrial society in the East, be a reborn, archetypal male, a model of the Rooseveltian "vigorously led life," a more virile, noble, and heroic fellow than his eastern or southern counterparts? To his credit, Wister embraced this new, more positive conception of the protagonist. He took Roosevelt's suggestions and dedicated the book to him.

According to the historian Douglas Brinkley, "Roosevelt believed that Wister, far from selling out, did America a favor by making his masculine archetype a man of virtue, not vice." The public agreed. Published in 1902, *The Virginian: A Horseman of the Plains* was a sensational bestseller. The book sold 200,000 copies in its first year and went through fifteen printings. As already mentioned, the book would be made into a movie five times and inspire a television series by the same name, which ran for nine years on NBC. According to Keith Wheeler in *The Old West: The Chroniclers*, "*The Virginian* became more than a best-seller. It was the archetype that fixed the myth of the West."

Up until this point, the cowboy was typically depicted as a gunfighter, a wild, untamed man who frequented brothels and shot his way out of a jam. But this image had been changing as the cowboy evolved from the villain of dime-store novels (such as Deadwood Dick) to the hero of pulp fiction. Wister, with his prod from Roosevelt, gave that mythic image its last big push in a positive direction. The fact that the Virginian remained nameless was central to that myth. He became the quintessential American everyman, the figure that every boy, or every cowboy wannabe, could identify with. He was a gentleman, polite to women, kind to animals, law-abiding, and honest — the antithesis of the outlaw. When he wasn't engaged in cowboy activities, his job was to distinguish right from wrong. The character is virtually the same as Alan Ladd's Shane in the movie version of Jack Schaefer's 1949 novel of that name, or from Gary Cooper's role in *High Noon,* or from the many roles played by John Wayne in the John Ford westerns. In works of fiction, Wister's hero paved a similar path, making possible the work of writers from Zane Grey to Louis L'Amour.

And yet, oddly, *The Virginian* also defended vigilantism. When the book's heroine, Molly Wood, expresses skepticism regarding lynching and asks Judge Henry, who is clearly intended as the moral conscience of the novel, "Have you come to tell me that you think well of lynching?" The judge replies, "Of burning Southern negroes in public, no. Of hanging Wyoming cattle-thieves in private, yes. You perceive there's a difference, don't you?" When she says that she does not, he explains that since ordinary citizens created the Constitution, the laws were therefore their laws, and if a situation should arise whereby the laws of that Constitution were not being enforced, then it was okay for the citizens to enforce those laws themselves: "When they lynch they only take back what they once gave." The narrator argues that the problem with a democracy is that by deferring to others in the interests of "equality," democracy often serves the interests of the weak and the corrupt. Or, to put it more explicitly, *quality* was needed as well as *equality.* Wister's words justify the existence of a sort of self-appointed American elite, who can take matters into their own hands and act in the interests of a higher good, outside the law if necessary, to protect or restore civilization. This was not an uncommon notion in the nineteenth century. One historian of the era, N. P. Langford, published in 1890 an apologia for vigilantism titled *Vigilante Days and Ways,* in which he wrote, "Montana owes its present freedom from crime . . . to the early achievements of these self-denying men who . . . established law where no law existed."

Wister's novel promotes other questionable ideas. First is the presumed superiority of men and their dominion over women: the women in the book are either whores or saints whose salvation lies in submitting to the more powerful men. Second is the idea that the American West is a playground for young white Anglo-Saxon men. The book's sexism, a prejudice that was commonplace at the time, is somewhat surprising coming from Wister, given the accomplishments and the dominating personalities of the women in his family. Perhaps he was expressing some wish fulfillment. Although the Johnson County War does not feature in the book, it informs its politics, and the book implicitly defends the invaders' actions, which is hardly surprising: Wister was a close friend of a dozen of the Cheyenne cattlemen, including Wolcott and Teschemacher. He actually visited Wyoming at the time of the invasion. It wouldn't be until 1940, with the publication of Walter Van Tilburg Clark's *The Ox-Bow Incident,* that vigilantism received the literary treatment it deserved. Clark's book deftly overturns the western stereotypes and depicts lynching for what it was: morally reprehensible mob violence and a subversion of justice.

Wister had some other ideas that ranked high on the morally questionable scale, and these grew more apparent in his later life and work. For example, while serving as an overseer (trustee) of Harvard University, he urged support for President Lowell's proposal to institute a quota system that would reduce the number of Jewish students at the university. His reasoning: "Jews are perfectly free to found colleges of their own." His later novel *Lady Baltimore* (1906) outrageously defended a racist antebellum South. To his credit, Roosevelt loathed the book and immediately condemned it.

Of course, sexism, elitism, anti-Semitism, and arguments in defense of lynch law were not what readers cared about, or why they bought Wister's book. They loved its western setting, the romance, and the handsome, virile figure of the Virginian. They came to the book looking for a hero to root for, especially in the climactic shootout with the bad guy, Trampas. When the moment arrives, the two pistol-bearing foes face off on the main street of Medicine Bow at dusk. Wister delivered the Virginian's coup de grâce obliquely, with admirable economy and melodrama: "A wind seemed to blow his sleeve off his arm, and he replied to it, and saw Trampas pitch forward. He saw Trampas raise his arm from the ground and fall again, and lie there this time, still. A little smoke was rising from the pistol on the ground, and he looked at his own, and saw the smoke flowing upward out of it."

The myth of the noble, honorable cowboy that Wister helped to create would prove durable. Indeed, it only seemed to grow over time. As the historian Robert Athearn has written, Hollywood in particular has outdone itself trying to make westerns ever more western: "The unbelievable followed the incredible, and the improbable was set aside for the impossible." Regardless of the medium, something about the western connects with American identity. "Sure it was hokum, snake oil, but we are still slathering it on ourselves today," noted Michelle Latoilais, an English professor at the University of California at Irvine. "The Western is a major American genre, one that goes to the heart of our famous patriotism. 'Bring 'em on' is voiced from the Oval Office in reference to Iraqi militants. It is the cry of the cattle drive, the wagon train pulling out of St. Jo, the sharpshooters poised in rock crevices, the fierce Indians below — the desire for a foe, a challenge which will reaffirm our national character."

Perhaps it is the highly aspirational nature of that iconic image of the cowboy — galloping on horseback across a wide-open plain — that helps the myth endure. "Disregarding actuality, we see these knights of the range in our mind's eye wandering the open prairies, free from the confines of the city, of marriage, of capitalism, and of the many other fetters and fetishes that plague our lives," wrote Lawrence Clayton in *The Cowboy Way*. At a time when the young men of the country began abandoning the farms for the cities in pursuit of better-paying jobs in factories, it is hardly surprising that the outdoor life and the perceived freedom of the cowboy became quickly and fervently idealized. In today's even more urban world, the cowboy retains his anti-urban allure.

Because of the cowboy's immense popularity with the public, his myth has been exploited by politicians, actors, business leaders, and musicians, all wanting to assume the cowboy's mantle of individuality and incorruptibility. One can only hope that they do not take that myth too much to heart. As the Wyoming historian T. A. Larson has written, "The suggestion that a Secretary of State can confront the enormous ambiguities of international policy by perceiving himself as a lonesome cowboy falters with only slight analysis." And the same applies, he added, to the chief executive officer of a corporation who sees himself as the Marlboro Man. The myth may have reinforced a reckless, imperialistic streak in our foreign policy. The cultural critic and historian Richard Slotkin has argued that the myth of the cowboy has directly influenced U.S. foreign policy by imbuing it with a "frontier mentality" and ultimately dangerous notions of American exceptionalism. One example would be Theodore Roosevelt's applause for the U.S. conquest of the Philippines in 1899 — calling Americans "a fighting race" and dismissing the islanders as "Apaches." President Lyndon Johnson would quote a gunfighting Texas Ranger named L. H. McNelly in defense of his 1965 decision to expand the Vietnam War, remarking that "courage is a man who keeps on coming." Theodore Roosevelt went even further with his corollary to the Monroe Doctrine, in his 1904 State of the Union address; he argued that the United States would henceforth intervene to police Latin America, correcting wrongs or restoring justice as it saw fit. While initially intended to preempt European involvement in the area, the policy provided justification for a variety of interventions: in Cuba (1906–9), Nicaragua (1909–10), Haiti (1915–34), and the Dominican Republic (1916–24), to name a few. Much like a vigilance committee, the nation began to pursue its own imperialistic goals and what it perceived to be the higher good, while paying lip service to international law — "walking softly and carrying a big stick" on the international stage, in Roosevelt's phrasing — too often to its own detriment.

Thus, it can be argued that a direct link connects vigilante justice on the open range and U.S. involvement in Vietnam, or Iraq, or most recently our vigilante-like drone strikes in Pakistan and elsewhere. No wonder *The Economist* once described President George W. Bush's foreign policy as "cowboy unilateralism." In this respect, the influence of the American cowboy myth has not always been innocent or harmless. But neither has it been deterministic, as Slotkin himself has cautioned: "The history of the Frontier did not 'give' Roosevelt or Kennedy or Reagan the political scripts they followed. What they did — what any user of cultural mythology does — was to selectively read and rewrite the myth according to their own needs, desires, and political projects."

One other link should be highlighted, and that is the contribution of the European aristocrats and grandees — men like Moreton Frewen and the Marquis de Morès — to the formation of the cowboy myth. Lawrence M. Woods presents a startling hypothesis in his book *British Gentlemen in the Wild West: The Era of the Intensely English Cowboy:* Owen Wister may well owe some of the most striking attributes of his character the Virginian to the English and Scottish nobility who launched so many of the western cattle companies. He argues that a cattle company was really a domestic microcosm of the British Empire, and essential principles of the empire governed it: "The right to rule the range was underwritten by a compact of like-minded men, and their presence and agreement were enough to guarantee that it would function. But it deserves to be remembered that the reason they were able to agree on such a compact stemmed from their common attachment to the principles of gentlemanly conduct."

This casts Cheyenne and its Cheyenne Club in a whole new light — that of a late-Victorian outpost of the British Empire. Although most of the cattle barons were not European by birth, many (like Wister himself) who hailed from the Eastern Seaboard were often confirmed Anglophiles who aspired to emulate the English aristocracy in their manners and mores, to say nothing of their gentlemen's clubs, their hunting habits, and their other social activities. Roosevelt rode to hounds on Long Island; Frederick DeBillier played polo in Cheyenne. Wister played cricket at St. Paul's School. It is not much of a stretch to argue that the manners of the Virginian, the "natural aristocrat," in Roosevelt's words, are recognizably European: gentility toward women and adherence to principles of honor. As Woods observed, "The ground of that relation is a concept of nobility and honor; and these values have lived on in our society, although they are no longer expressed in terms of duty to sovereign and country, or even in the simpler formulations Wister chose for his Virginian."

Perhaps what we admire about the iconic and heroic cowboy of books, television, and film, whether we realize it or not, is this curious blend of American everyman and chivalrous Victorian nobleman — an amalgam of Teddy Blue's sense of fun and love of adventure (and his skill with a lariat), Roosevelt's self-possession and endurance, the Marquis de Morès's notions of honor and nobility (and his proficiency with weaponry), and Moreton Frewen's pride, daring, and boundless self-confidence. Combine them all, and you have a character in a Stetson hat who can be played by Alan Ladd or Gary Cooper, Paul Newman or Robert Redford. Perhaps this potent mixture explains why the now mythical cowboy remains popular across the developed world. In a surprising number of countries, children grow up playing cowboys and Indians. In countries located in different hemispheres, such as Germany and Japan, cowboy clothing and the cowboy lifestyle are revered. Drinking and line dancing in cowboy bars and saloons remain popular around the world.

Both Wister and Roosevelt knew that the cowboy era was over by the time *The Virginian* was published, in 1902. And both felt nostalgia for it. As Wister wrote in the introduction, the cowboy "rides in his historic yesterday. You will no more see him gallop out of the unchaining silence than you will see Columbus on the unchanging sea come sailing from Palos with his caravels." As Roosevelt put it in his autobiography, "That land of the West has gone now, 'gone, gone with lost Atlantis,' gone to the isle of ghosts and of strange dead memories. It was a land of vast silent spaces, of lonely rivers, and of plains where the wild game stared at the passing horseman. It was a land of scattered ranches, of herds of long-horned cattle, and of reckless riders who unmoved looked in the eyes of life or death."

Early historians of the cattle era stretched themselves rhetorically to make great claims for the importance of the cattle kingdom. But their claims did not withstand the test of time, and the period became characterized as a short, quirky moment in the nation's development, known best for knitting together North and South in commerce and thereby helping to heal the nation in the aftermath of the Civil War. The cowboy endured admirably in his folkloric and mythic incarnation, but not as an actual historical figure in the national narrative, where he began to fade. In retrospect it seems clear that the enterprising cattlemen, with their big ranches, made a far larger historical contribution to posterity than the lowly cowboys who worked for them. The cattle kings' efforts to conquer and industrialize the West converted its vast open spaces into productive agricultural land and helped build the beef business into an industry of grand proportions. And yet, like the cowboy, the individual names of the cattle barons have largely been forgotten, perhaps justifiably so, given how many of them failed financially. Other categories of American entrepreneurs, such as the Gilded Age robber barons or today's high-tech entrepreneurs, whose success is measured by their mammoth fortunes, are remembered far better than the big ranchers, whose strivings so often left them destitute.

Any study of the open-range cattle era offers up a host of lessons. It supports the idea that great men (and women — though not so many in this story) can play a disproportionate role in shaping his-

tory, a thesis first popularized by Thomas Carlyle in the 1840s. Look
to Roosevelt's shining legacy in conservation and Theobald Smith's
medical breakthroughs as proof. It also illustrates the sheer power
of economics to trump personality, character, and individual initiative — and let's not forget luck. To succeed in the cattle trade, as in
most businesses, you needed an inordinate competitive advantage
— monopoly control being the most obvious. Or you had to possess some unique proprietary skill or technology. Even with those
advantages, you needed to be well enough financed to ride out the
inevitable downturns, and canny enough to avoid con artists and
frauds. As with any form of investing, if you caught the boom just
right, and timed the market well, or exploited a first-mover advantage, you might well end up as rich as the cattlemen Iliff and
Wibaux, as the meatpacker Swift, or as the barbed-wire titans Glidden and "Bet-a-Million" Gates. But miss the opportunity, chase the
Wall Street herd, invest too late, lack the funding, or simply take
your eye off the ball, and you could end up on the slag heap of an
economic bust, as you would today, an experience shared by many
talented, hardworking people.

Mark Twain captured this sense of deflated expectations when
he reflected on his own adventures in the American West during
these years in his memoir *Roughing It.* He could be describing the
experience of nearly every twenty-five-year-old in the cattle kingdom when he wrote, "So vanished my dream. So melted my wealth
away. So toppled my airy castle to the earth and left me stricken and
forlorn." Like many of the cattlemen and cowboys, Twain had left
home at twenty-five to seek adventure, success, and wealth in the
West. Instead he found, in the historian Hamlin Hill's words, "cold-
blooded murderers, rigged juries, paper speculation in stocks, and
blighted hopes, including his own."

It was a Darwinian struggle across the open range, as it often
is in a capitalist society — a struggle to survive, to outcompete, to
adapt on the fly to changing circumstances brought on by new
technology, emerging monopolies, changing regulations, fluctuat-
ing markets, and fickle weather. From one angle, the story of the

great beef bonanza is a record of remarkable human ingenuity and technological advancement. From another, it is a case history of the calamities that befall those who ignore economic or ecological realities in a single-minded pursuit of the American Dream. The open-range cattle era and its role in shaping America deserve to be more broadly known, if only as an instructive cautionary tale.

Afterword:
"Unhorsed for Good"

In 1903, the year after *The Virginian* was published, Moreton Frewen took his children to see Buffalo Bill's Wild West Show at Earl's Court in London. The old scout and hunter Bill Cody, who had once helped the Russian archduke Alexis shoot his first bison, had gone on to worldwide fame as the proprietor of a traveling circus that gave foreign audiences a taste of the Old West, replete with live Indians, staged shootouts, galloping horses, and displays of sharpshooting by Annie Oakley. The show toured Europe eight times between 1887 and 1906 and helped popularize the myth of the cowboy worldwide. A few of Cody's crew from Wyoming spotted the tall Moreton Frewen in the crowd, recognizing him from his Powder River ranch days. They invited him to take the reins of the yellow Deadwood stagecoach that was now part of the show. With his brother-in-law, Sir John Leslie, riding shotgun beside him, Frewen steered the coach around the Earl's Court arena and through two Indian ambushes, to wild applause.

It was Moreton Frewen's final encore as a cowboy. And he

seemed quite happy to help caricature the myth that he had done his part to create.

His last great business venture was a deal that he undertook in 1906 on behalf of Canada's Grand Trunk Railway — to promote the port of Prince Rupert in British Columbia in return for an option on a thousand acres of land. But like Joseph McCoy thirty-nine years earlier in negotiations with a different railroad, Frewen neglected to secure the agreement in writing. The railroad, of course, reneged, and the ensuing lawsuits dragged on for years. Frewen never saw a penny for his efforts.

At a dinner party in Ireland during these years, Frewen encountered his old nemesis and cattle-ranching neighbor from Wyoming, Horace Plunkett, who had overseen the liquidation of Frewen's Powder River Cattle Company. The Irishman with the weak constitution had returned to his homeland and achieved considerable fame — and a knighthood — by promoting dairy cooperatives throughout Ireland in response to the long agricultural depression. The two men stared daggers at each other from their respective seats and refused to speak. They were reconciled only late in life, when Plunkett graciously forgave a longstanding Frewen debt.

Moreton's Irish valet, Mack, who had served him loyally ever since Moreton was a student at Cambridge, died of throat cancer and predeceased Frewen by two years. Mack had accompanied Frewen on over a hundred transatlantic crossings and had often worked without pay. At the end of his life, sporting a long white beard, he was said to bear a distinct resemblance to Leo Tolstoy. "I miss his morning call no end," Frewen wrote in his memoirs.

Frewen suffered a stroke in the spring of 1922. Believing perhaps for the first time that he was destined to die, he would sit in a chair in the shade of one of the great gnarled oaks on the grounds of his dilapidated home, Brede Place, and periodically bellow, "I AM DYING!" to anyone who would listen. He wrote letters to his friends, announcing that he was at the edge of the abyss, soliciting their sympathy now instead of their capital. He developed an obsession with his bowels, insisting during the winter months that, "to get a movement," he needed to be driven five miles down the road to the warmer water closets at Brickwall, the ancestral home where he had been born. His family lobbied to get him nominated for a K.B.E. (Knight Commander of the Most Excellent Order of the British Empire), but the honor could not be arranged, perhaps for the obvious reason that it was not deserved.

His memory and then his whole mind gave out at the end. He was moved to a nearby private nursing home, "his eyes flashing and his trouser flies undone." There, as one friend remarked, "he lay like a dying bull in the Sussex marshes." When he passed away at the age of seventy-one in September 1924, the clerk at the probate registry listed his effects as worth only fifty pounds.

His passing provided obituary writers with rich fodder. "Moreton Frewen, whose death is announced in another column, was a picturesque and in some respects a pathetic personality," wrote one. "He was always trying to get somewhere and never quite getting there." Another described him as having "a first class mind untroubled by second thoughts." But his friend Rudyard Kipling saw the dreamy, romantic side of Moreton's endeavors: "He lived in every sense except what is called common sense, very richly and widely, to his own extreme content. If he had ever reached the golden crock of his dreams he would have perished." Moreton Frewen was buried in the family cemetery at Northiam, where, "unhorsed for good," as his nephew put it, "he awaits the forgiveness of debts and the resurrection of Silver."

Moreton Frewen's autobiography, *Melton Mowbray and Other Memories*, which he had begun to write at a desk set up in the old chapel at Brede Place, remained only half complete at his death; it was, nevertheless, published posthumously in a limited edition.

In his memoir, Frewen wistfully recalled Hans Holbein's portrait of Lady Guildford, which had hung in the place of honor at the head of the grand staircase in the front hall of the family's Tudor mansion, Brickwall, when Moreton was a boy. His father had bought the portrait for sixteen pounds at a Christie's auction, when the trappings of the great country estate Stowe House went under the gavel, in 1848. He remembered how, despite his father's admonition never to sell the painting, his older brother Edward, desperate for cash in the 1880s, had parted with it for a modest sum. Moreton mused that if he had bought the painting from his brother, that single decision might have changed everything for him. Some years later he walked into William K. Vanderbilt's book-lined study in his chateau-like mansion on Fifth Avenue in Manhattan, and there, hanging over the fireplace, was the portrait of Lady Guildford, "well lighted, well hung, looking extremely prosperous." The only Holbein in North America at the time, it was worth a fortune.

Now it seems fitting that the painting, eventually gifted by William Vanderbilt to the Metropolitan Museum of Art, is no longer considered a Holbein, but rather a copy of a Holbein. Even posthumously, Moreton Frewen's dreams went sour.

Moreton Frewen, the man who had formed the first English joint-stock cattle company and orchestrated the formation of Johnson County when it was still virgin land in the Territory of Wyoming, would look back ruefully on that period: "The fortune which I ought to have made is lying about the creeks under the Big Horn Mountains in piles of whitening bones." In his memoirs he referred to his western adventures as the "Great Cattle Catastrophe" — which it was, for him and his many English compatriots. In all, the British lost some $20 million of the $45 million they had invested, or $478 million in today's money. That might not seem like so much, but it had the economic power in its day of something close to $33 billion. The English quickly wrote off some $10 million of their capital, and the Scottish around $8 million. Of course, much of it had earned dividends in good years, but the Scotsman John Clay thought it doubtful that a single cent had been earned, if you added up all the profits and losses of the open-range industry between 1870 and 1888.

Not all of this money simply evaporated in the Big Die-Up and the protracted recession that followed. Indeed, it can be argued that the investments made by men like Frewen and de Morès, although never recouped by the original investors, played an important role in funding the development of the American West. It helped to seed profitable new industries, such as the manufacture of barbed wire and Stetson hats, as well as many small mom-and-pop businesses in the cattle towns. And the British could take credit for improving the cattle breeds and introducing some of the best — and worst — ranch management practices.

A handful of the Scottish cattle companies stuck it out through the long downturn and managed to do well as the industry recovered. Unlike their English counterparts, who for the most part cut their losses and quit, the Scottish investors tended to take the long view, in many cases choosing to retrench and restructure. Experienced real estate investors, many of them had prudently bought portions of their ranch lands outright. A few of those ranches, the Matador, the Swan, the Prairie, and the Western, not only survived the post-bust depression years, but delivered modest dividends to their shareholders. Others made enough money off the eventual appreciation of the land to cash out early in the twentieth century with respectable profits. Today these same ranches sell in the tens of millions of dollars, more often than not as trophy assets for the ultra-wealthy.

One of the few cattlemen to survive the era with his net worth intact was John Clay. By 1913 he was in charge of a hugely successful Chicago cattle-commission agency — Clay, Robinson and Company — with $120 million in annual sales; it owned fifteen regional banks. In 1922 he took to the road to deliver a nostalgic speech titled "Coming Back to the Wagon." He argued for a return to the old ideals of the open-range system: "It is back to the wagon, back to the sheep wagon, back to work, back to the old bell mare, and the cook's unwelcome yell of 'Roll out boys.'" Only through hard work, focused management, and avoidance of government interference could the big cattlemen restore their fortunes, he argued. The open-range approach could still work and remained the best use for the otherwise unoccupied government lands that made up so much of the arid American West. With his reputation tarnished by his involvement in the Johnson County War, Clay was largely ignored. But if Allan Savory's ideas for using cattle herds to reverse desertification are borne out, the savvy Scotsman may have the last word. Perhaps he was a century ahead of his time.

The Montana cattle baron Granville Stuart always felt stirred by the sight and sounds of an approaching cattle drive, led by the remuda of trotting horses and the rattling mess wagon. To the rear marched the long, winding, jostling, lowing herd of cattle, that mass of bobbing heads and sharp, shiny horns — the rumble of their hooves rising as the herd drew closer. The sun always seemed to glint off the saddle conchos, the bridles, the spurs, and the mother-of-pearl handles of the cowpunchers' six-shooters. The red bandanas tied around the cowboys' necks added a bright dash of color to the scene.

When the great trail drives ended, blocked by the arrival of homesteaders, quarantines, and the installation of barbed wire, this memorable sight vanished, much like the giant bison herds, the sky-darkening flocks of passenger pigeons, and the swarms of Rocky Mountain locusts, all of which went extinct during the open-range era. Left behind in the drovers' dust was the myth of the noble, courageous, independent cowboy.

For Teddy Blue Abbott, it felt bittersweet to end up a farmer, much like his father before him. "I had always worked for big cow outfits and looked down on settlers, and now I was on the other side of the fence, and finding out how damn hard it was to start out poor and get anywhere." The work of farming, he discovered to his surprise, required considerably more effort — more physical labor and often more riding — than he had ever done during his years of earning forty dollars a month as a cowhand. To get started, he rented his first ranch house, a small, poorly insulated frame structure with no furniture or heating. The first night in their new residence, he and Mary slept on his cowboy bedroll, spread out on the bare floor. They never forgot how the pack rats scampered over them as they huddled together and tried to sleep.

He planted a small garden, chopped down trees to build a log cabin, and purchased his first few cattle. Every day he milked two cows, dug irrigation canals, and tended his garden. That first fall he spread out the newly cut oats on his bed tarp and beat them in order to remove the chaff. He sold wheat, potatoes, and butter to coal miners in the neighboring mountains. He made $680 in profit for the year and reinvested it all in the farm. He added ten more milk cows and began to sell milk daily to a boarding house in Maiden, Montana, seven miles away. By 1900 he had built up a modest herd of beef cattle and had secured grazing rights to two thousand acres of land. By 1919 he had fifty thousand dollars in the bank. Then along came the next cattle bust, and his luck turned: "I lost most everything. Such is life in the West."

He started over.

Teddy Blue and Mary raised eight children — five boys and three girls. At the time of his death he boasted of having fourteen grandchildren and one great-granddaughter. He watched the methods of raising cattle evolve to smaller ranches fenced with barbed wire, where the cattle were fed each winter with hay that was grown and baled on the ranches during the summer. He lived long enough to see most cowboys and cattlemen put their guns away, although he refused to give up his. "A six-shooter's an awful lot of company," he wrote in his memoir. "Suppose you break your leg, you can signal. If you're caught afoot, you can shoot a jackrabbit. If you're held up, you can defend yourself."

The open-range era was long gone now, and the wild cowboy had become, as Blue put it, "a prehistoric race." Although he admired the bronco riders in the local rodeos, he was disdainful of the current crop of cowpunchers: he didn't think riding fence lines, looking for slack or broken barbed wire, rounding up cattle in cow pastures, or bucking hay bales in the summer months could compare with the work that the old cowboys had performed on the open range. "A man has got to be at least seventy-five years old to be a real old cowhand. I started young and I am seventy-eight. Only a few of us are left now, and they are scattered from Texas to Canada. The rest have left the wagon. I hope they find good water and plenty of grass. But wherever they are is where I want to go."

On April 7, 1939, just a few days after his memoir *We Pointed Them North: Recollections of a Cowpuncher* was published, Edward Charles "Teddy Blue" Abbott, a cowboy, died peacefully in his sleep.

Acknowledgments

A family vacation spent at the 7D Ranch near Cody, Wyoming, and a pack trip into the Absaroka Mountains when I was nine years old gave me my first introduction to the American West. I went back the summer I was sixteen to work at Strang Hereford Ranch, then in Carbondale, Colorado, herding cattle, bucking bales, fixing fences, and riding a bronco in a rodeo. But the fact that my wife and I chose to move to Jackson, Wyoming, in 2006 was due to my mother, Betsy Wyman, who introduced us to the town. She had fallen in love with the area (and a cowboy) when she first visited with her father in 1946, staying as dudes at the renowned White Grass Ranch. No one was more appreciative of what the West had to offer than she was. I wish she had lived long enough to read this book.

My wife and I, with our Belgian Tervuren, Shadow, riding shotgun, toured the northern open ranges of the American West in the summer of 2014, visiting many of the sites mentioned in this book — Cheyenne, Wyoming; the Badlands of North Dakota; Theodore Roosevelt National Park; Miles City, Montana; and the TA Ranch outside Buffalo, Wyoming (site of the Johnson County War). We also visited numerous museums and roadside attractions devoted to the history of the West, all of them listed below. Those portions of the book concerning the role of English and Scottish investors in the emerging American cattle trade were researched at various libraries in London on trips in 2014 and 2015. A number of additional trips were made to the American Heritage Center at the University of Wyoming in Laramie, which boasts perhaps the best collection of records pertaining to the open-range cattle ranches.

For their help in the research and preparation of this manuscript, thanks are due to the following libraries (and librarians!), museums, and historical collections, both physical and digital.

Wyoming

John Waggener and Hailey Kaylenne Woodall and the American Heritage Center at the University of Wyoming, Laramie; G. B. Dobson's excellent website, *Wyoming Tales and Trails*; the Wyoming Stock Growers Association, Cheyenne; Wyoming State Historical Society and its fine website, WyoHistory.org; Suzi Taylor and the Wyoming State Archives, Cheyenne; the Buffalo Bill Center of the American West, Cody; Ray Hammond and Old Trail Town, Cody; Rainsford Historic District, Cheyenne; the National Museum of Wildlife Art, Jackson; the Teton County Library, Jackson; KeAnne Langford and Corrine Gordon and the Carbon County Museum, Rawlins; Jackson Hole Historical Society and Museum, Jackson; the TA Ranch, Buffalo; Sylvia Bruner and the Jim Gatchell Memorial Museum, Buffalo; Johnson County Library, Buffalo; Teton Raptor Center, Wilson; and Dubois Museum and Wind River Historical Center, Dubois.

Montana

The Range Riders Museum, Miles City; Little Bighorn Battlefield National Monument, Crow Agency; Lory Morrow and Montana Historical Society, Helena; C. M. Russell Museum, Great Falls; Montana Cowboy Hall of Fame and Western Heritage Center, Big Timber; and Legendary Virginia City and Nevada City.

North Dakota

Theodore Roosevelt National Park, Medora; Chateau de Morès State Historic Site, Medora; Medora Chimney Park, Medora; Theodore Roosevelt Center at Dickinson State University, Dickinson; North Dakota Heritage Center, Bismarck; and Sarah M. Waker and the State Archives, State Historical Society of North Dakota, Bismarck.

Other States and Countries

The Library of Congress, Washington, D.C.; National Park Service, U.S. Department of the Interior, Washington, D.C.; the Beinecke Rare Book and Manuscript Library, Yale University, New Haven, Connecticut; Sarah Yarrito and Chicago History Museum, Chicago, Illinois; the Theodore Roosevelt Collection at the Houghton Library, Harvard University, Cambridge, Massachusetts; Peter A. Trombetta and the Porcellian Club, Cambridge, Massachusetts; Tweed Roosevelt and the Theodore Roosevelt Association; Sagamore Hill National Historic Site, Oyster Bay, New York; Theodore Roosevelt Birthplace National Historic Site, New York, New York; the New York Public Library, New York, New York; the Morgan Library and Museum, New York, New York; Lauren Robinson and the Museum of the City of New York, New York, New York; National Cattlemen's Beef Association, Centennial, Colorado; Joyce Marsden and *The Cattleman* magazine, Fort Worth, Texas; Marva Felchin and the Autry National Center of the American West, Los Angeles, California; the National Cowboy and Western Heritage Museum, Oklahoma City, Oklahoma; Idaho Falls Public Library, Idaho Falls, Idaho; the Santa Ynez Valley Historical Musem and Parks — Janeway Carriage House, Santa Ynez, California; the Santa Barbara Museum of Natural History, Santa Barbara, California; the Santa Barbara Public Library, Santa Barbara, California; Luis Chavez and the University Club of Santa Barbara, Santa Barbara, California; Chastleton House and Garden, Moreton-in-Marsh, Oxfordshire, England; the London Library, London, England; and the Rare Books and Manuscript Collection of the British Library, London, England.

For their help with photo images, thanks are due to to Stacey

Byers of Captured Spirit Photography, Santa Barbara, California, and Chris Owen of Samy's Camera, also in Santa Barbara.

I would like to express my appreciation as well to the following friends and colleagues (in no particular order) for their support and kind words of encouragement: Dick Wien, Joe Downing, Barbara Doran, John Ferriter, Randy Stone, Luke Swetland, Prior Parker and Maria Canale, William and Susan Sheeline, Stephen and Joanna Colville-Reeves, Roger Tulcin, Ann Smith, Norman Pearlman, Dennis Baker, Ned Bacon, Duncan Coppack, Roger Smith, Amy McCarthy, Broughton Coburn, Maartje de Wolff, Scott Spector and Sandy Masur, Robert and Carolyn Pisano, and Steve and Terri Frenkel.

I am especially grateful to my family — first, to my father, Winthrop Knowlton, who thankfully brought up his children in a culture of books and ideas, but also to Win Knowlton, Oliver and Lisa Knowlton, Eliza and Mark Oursler, Samantha Knowlton, Stanley Knowlton, Tom Wyman Jr. and Lisa Wyman Stowell, Peter and Alice Wyman, and Michael and Janet Wyman. A warm thank-you as well to Maxine Groffsky for her advice over the years and for launching me in the writing trade. My in-laws, Peter and Angela Hames, have been especially encouraging. And I owe a huge debt of gratitude to my stepmother, Grace Knowlton, who among other things introduced me to the natural world by getting me hooked on ornithology when I was a boy.

I could not have asked for a smarter or more talented editor than Eamon Dolan at Houghton Mifflin Harcourt. His excellent reputation is richly deserved. In a similar vein, I am deeply grateful for the help of my agent, Jeff Ourvan of the Jennifer Lyons Literary Agency, whose wise counsel proved to be as invaluable as his impeccable literary judgment. Susanna Brougham performed deft editorial work on the manuscript. Laurence Cooper, Margaret Anne Miles, and Rosemary McGuinness at Houghton Mifflin Harcourt helped pull the book through production, while Kelly Dubeau Smydra gave the book its lovely design.

Last, not a word of this book would have been written without the love, support, and forbearance of my wife, Pippa, my English rose.

Notes

Introduction

and 1886 four states and territories—Colorado, Wyoming, Montana, and New Mexico—created 349 cattle companies capitalized at roughly $170 million (Gene Gressley, *Bankers and Cattlemen,* 109). Add in the cattle companies created in Texas, Kansas, Nebraska, Oklahoma, and the Dakotas and any preexisting herds, and again the figure is probably not far shy of $550 million.

highest median per capita income: Agnes Wright Spring, "Old Cheyenne Club," *American Cattle Producer,* July 1947.

xv   *"In our country, which is even now":* Theodore Roosevelt, *Ranch Life and the Hunting Trail,* 22.

xvii *"Think of riding all day":* E. C. "Teddy Blue" Abbott, *We Pointed Them North,* 176.

"and so we shot her": Ibid., 183.

a record kill: Lang, *Ranching with Roosevelt,* 247.

xviii *"One had only to stand":* Ibid., 251.

"This was the death knell": Stuart, *Forty Years on the Frontier,* 236–37.

"I am bluer than indigo": Theodore Roosevelt to Anna Roosevelt, April 16, 1887, *The Letters of Theodore Roosevelt,* vol. 1, edited by Elting E. Morison.

xix *over forty years since this story:* Most notably by Gardner Soule in *The Long Trail* (1976), Mari Sandoz in *The Cattlemen* (1958), Wayne Gard in *The Chisholm Trail* (1954), Edward Everett Dale in *Cow Country* (1942), Paul I. Wellman in *The Trampling Herd: The Story of the Cattle Range in American History* (1939), Walter Prescott Webb in *The Great Plains* (1931), and Ernest Staples Osgood in *The Day of the Cattleman* (1929).

xxii *50 to 80 percent of the various:* Some historians, such as W. Turrentine Jackson, dispute these numbers and argue that the actual losses were much lower. However, so many of the surviving cattle were so emaciated by spring that many cattlemen no doubt chalked them up as losses, and still others used the die-up as an excuse to rectify the inflated "book counts" of the cattle on their ranges.

the greatest loss of animal life: Donald Worster, *Under Western Skies,* 41.

1. The Demise of the Bison

3   *American hosts included luminaries:* Douglas D. Scott, Peter Bleed, and Stephen Damm, *Custer, Cody, and Grand Duke Alexis,* 38.

4   *seen as a geographical hinterland:* The explorer Major Stephen Long first described the area as the Great Desert in 1820 and deemed it "unfit for cultivation and of course uninhabitable by a people depending upon agriculture."

5   *one massive pasture:* Charles C. Mann, *1491: New Revelations of the Americas Before Columbus.*
    Dodge passed through a herd: William T. Hornaday, *The Extermination of the American Bison,* 390–91.

6   *They waited for hours:* Ibid., 393.

7   *"the transformation of the plains":* Richard White, in *Oxford History of the American West,* Milner et al., eds., 257.

8   *Bison could rub a pole out:* Nathaniel Burt, *Wyoming,* 44.
    "The buffalo hunters didn't wash": E. C. "Teddy Blue" Abbott, *We Pointed Them North,* 102.

9   *"The buffalo are strange animals":* Francis Parkman Jr., *The Oregon Trail,* 244.
    1,375 bison tongues: Hornaday, *The Extermination of the American Bison,* 474.

10   *If a horse was available:* Stanley Vestal, *Dodge City,* 47.

11   *"When I went into business":* Geoffrey C. Ward, *The West,* 263.
    "By the late 1870s, five thousand": Ibid., 263.
    "All this slaughter was": Abbott, *We Pointed Them North,* 101–2.

12   *"These soldiers cut down":* Dee Brown, *Bury My Heart at Wounded Knee,* 241.
    "So why do you ask us to": Ibid., 242.
    "let them kill, skin and sell": Roy Morris Jr., *Sheridan,* 342–43.

13   *"the phenomenal stupidity":* Hornaday, *The Extermination of the American Bison,* 465.
    breech-loading rifles: The progression from muzzle-loading muskets to breech-loading, or rear of the barrel loading, rifles was one of the great breakthroughs in the development of firearms,

allowing for much faster loading and firing, especially with the advent of needle-activated or pin-fired firing mechanisms first patented by Samuel Pauly in Paris in 1808.

"Such an accusation of weakness": Ibid., 520–21.

2. Cattle for Cash

15 *"It has been raining for three days":* George Duffield, "Driving Cattle from Texas to Iowa, 1866," *Annals of Iowa.*

17 *"The mounted men, always excellent":* Walt Whitman, *Specimen Days and Collect,* 48.

18 *his horns stretched more than:* J. Frank Dobie, *The Longhorns,* 206.

"sullen, morose, solitary": Wayne Gard, *The Chisholm Trail,* 17.

"Ask any old-time range man": Dobie, *The Longhorns,* 147.

20 *"had no tents, no tarps":* E. C. "Teddy Blue" Abbott, *We Pointed Them North,* 6.

"son-of-a-bitch stew": One full recipe: "Kill off a steer. Cut up beef, liver and heart into 1-inch cubes; slice the marrow gut into small rings. Place in a Dutch oven or deep casserole. Cover meat with water and simmer for 2 to 3 hours. Add salt, pepper and [Louisiana] hot sauce to taste. Take sweetbreads and brain and cut in small piece. Add to stew. Simmer another hour never boiling." See William H. Forbis, *The Old West: The Cowboys,* 87.

"About ten minutes to two": Abbott, *We Pointed Them North,* 199.

21 *"The horse's ribs was scraped":* Ibid., 37.

22 *he fainted and fell off:* Ibid., 200.

"When you add it all up": Ibid., 67.

23 *"They are Seminoles":* Duffield, "Driving Cattle from Texas to Iowa, 1866."

Fort Sumner: It was here, fifteen years later, in one of the ramshackle buildings of the deserted fort, that the outlaw Billy the Kid would be gunned down in a nighttime shootout with the local sheriff, Pat Garrett.

24 *perhaps the fiercest of the Plains:* For the best history of the Comanche, see S. C. Gwynne, *Empire of the Summer Moon: Quanah Parker and the Rise of the Comanches.*

25 *Loving died two weeks later:* W. J. Wilson, "W. J. Wilson's Narrative," in *The Trail Drivers of Texas,* edited by J. Marvin Hunter and George W. Saunders, 913.

26 *"The stricken cattle began":* Gard, *The Chisholm Trail,* 29.

27 *"Did they yield the steers":* Paul I. Wellman, *The Trampling Herd,* 98.

29 *"There was a freedom":* John Clay, *My Life on the Range,* vi.

30 *"It was here the romance of my life began":* Theodore Roosevelt, *Roosevelt Quotes,* http://www.nps.gov/thro/learn/historyculture /theodore-roosevelt-quotes.htm.

   "Doctors were scarcer": Forbis, *The Old West: The Cowboy,* 88.

31 *"I had severe shakes":* Duffield, "Driving Cattle from Texas to Iowa, 1866."

   some 35,000 head of cattle: Joseph Nimmo, *Report in Regard to the Range and Ranch Cattle Business of the United States,* 28.

32 *In all, some ten million:* R. D. Holt, "The Proposed National Cattle Trail," *The Cattleman,* vol. 29, 57.

   "From that time on": Abbott, *We Pointed Them North,* 6.

3. Birth of the Cattle Town

34 *"made an infidel of me":* E. C. "Teddy Blue" Abbott, *We Pointed Them North,* 23.

   "the Southern drover": Joseph G. McCoy, *Historic Sketches of the Cattle Trade of the West and Southwest,* 31.

35 *"one of the great single ideas":* Paul I. Wellman, *The Trampling Herd,* 131.

   Kansas Pacific would pay: McCoy, *Historic Sketches,* 32.

   "It occurs to me that": Ibid., 33.

36 *depriving St. Louis of:* Wellman, *The Trampling Herd,* 132.

37 *"I regard the opening":* McCoy, *Historic Sketches,* 75.

38 *"The agent seemed to relish":* Ibid., 40.

39 *"Medicine Bow was my first":* Owen Wister, *The Virginian,* 18. Wister made thirteen trips to the West specifically to research his book, meticulously recording everything he saw in tiny notebooks. They are among his papers at the American Heritage Center, University of Wyoming.

40 *"It is an ill-arranged set"*: Isabella Lucy Bird, *A Lady's Life in the Rocky Mountains*, 28–30.

4. Cattle-Town High Jinks

42 *"I bought some new clothes"*: E. C. "Teddy Blue" Abbott, *We Pointed Them North*, 40.

43 *But at eighteen years*: Frank M. Canton, *Frontier Trails*, 11.

44 *"Some of that frontier scamper juice"*: Ramon F. Adams, *The Old-Time Cowhand*, 325.

"Allegedly, medicinal and sometimes": Robert L. Brown, *Saloons of the American West*, 128.

45 *straight pool would not*: Victor Stein and Paul Rubino, *The Billiard Encyclopedia*, 183.

top of the pecking order: Michael Rutter, *Upstairs Girls*, 92.

46 *the saloon girls*: Keith Wheeler, *The Old West: The Townsmen*, 172.

"Some of those girls in Miles City": Abbott, *We Pointed Them North*, 107.

47 *"This line of work never"*: Rutter, *Upstairs Girls*, 1.

48 *Mag Burns's parlor house*: Mag Burns is Teddy Blue's fictitious name for the madam. Abbott, *We Pointed Them North*, 103.

49 *"a tall, graceful, pantherish man"*: Paul I. Wellman, *The Trampling Herd*, 166.

51 *"Sheets will be changed"*: Richard A. Van Orman, *A Room for the Night*, 50.

the term "red-light district": Wellman, *The Trampling Herd*, 195.

"By all accounts, she was": Ibid., 199.

52 *Ellsworth's lack of water*: Robert R. Dykstra, *The Cattle Towns*, 165.

"They didn't have any bull": Ibid., 175.

53 *so much as a scratch*: Lewis Atherton, *The Cattle Kings*, 51.

"highly unrealistic in their use": Ibid., 42.

54 *"The image of the ordinary"*: Leon Claire Metz, *The Encyclopedia of Lawmen, Outlaws, and Gunfighters*, 53.

A gunman adept at loading: Joseph G. Rosa, *The Taming of the West*, 138.

Surprisingly few ever saw: Atherton, *The Cattle Kings,* 42.

"two desperadoes, two low": Mark Twain, *Roughing It,* 349.

many were so illiterate: Paul Trachtman, *The Old West: The Gun-fighters,* 142.

Worse, the laws themselves: Metz, *The Encyclopedia,* xi.

55 *no one died in a cattle-town:* Wellman, *The Trampling Herd,* 159.

only forty-five homicides: Dykstra, *The Cattle Towns,* 144.

56 *in 1865 some 68,800 arrests:* Marc McCutcheon, *Everyday Life in the 1800s,* 266.

"Deadwood is just as lively": Edward L. Wheeler, *Deadwood Dick, the Prince of the Road; or, the Black Rider of the Black Hills,* 1877. Quoted in G. B. Dobson, *Wyoming Tales and Trails,* http://www.wyomingtalesandtrails.com/cheyenne4a.html.

57 *"He kept having hemorrhages":* Abbott, *We Pointed Them North,* 81.

"I went to a honky-tonk": Ibid., 82.

58 *a cowboy named Johnnie Blair:* Jeremy Agnew, *Medicine in the Old West,* 71.

59 *"The feeling today existing":* Joseph G. McCoy, *Historic Sketches of the Cattle Trade of the West and Southwest,* 43.

Ethnically diverse men: Atherton, *The Cattle Kings,* 2. See also Maurice Frink et al., *When Grass Was King,* 20.

"the fears thus engendered": Atherton, *The Cattle Kings,* 249.

60 *a creamery on the site:* Wayne Gard, *The Chisholm Trail,* 66, 11n.

5. Lighting the Fuse

61 *Macdonald was on assignment:* James Macdonald, *Food from the Far West,* xv.

62 *"Guess that's a Gunion":* Ibid., 3.

64 *It cost Eastman only:* Mary Yeager, *Competition and Regulation: The Development of Oligopoly in the Meat Industry,* 54.

The canal enabled steamships: The Suez Canal ruined the hopes of the Northern Pacific Railroad to become the primary conduit for goods traveling between the Orient and Europe. The railroad would need to look for other cargo — and cattle soon became a priority.

65   *"Keep few, keep good, keep well"*: Macdonald, *Food from the Far West*, 306.

      "the tide of emigration has": Ibid., 50.

66   *"The financial officers of that"*: John Clay, *My Life on the Range*, 128.

      £25 million of English capital: Claire E. Swan, *Scottish Cowboys and Dundee Investors*, 13.

      the western cattle trade: W. Turrentine Jackson, *The Enterprising Scot*, 73.

68   *the same social and sporting clubs*: Swan, *Scottish Cowboys and Dundee Investors*, 21.

69   *A later act, in 1862*: Harmon Ross Mothershead, *The Swan Land and Cattle Company, Ltd.*, 34, n34.

70   *"The acknowledged profits"*: John Clay, "Royal Agriculture Commission: Report of Mr. Clare Sewell Read and Mr. Albert Pell, MP, Clare Read," September 1, 1880, *The British Trade Journal and Export World*, 482.

      "It was said that the announcement": Edward Everett Dale, *Cow Country*, 96.

71   *The value of the land*: John Martin Robinson, *Felling the Ancient Oaks*, 26.

      at Chastleton House: It was at Chastleton House that the field rules of croquet were first codified and published — by Walter Jones Whitmore on April 7, 1866.

      the family's financial ruin: British farmland devoted to wheat would be cut in half between 1878 and 1902, from 3 million acres to 1.5 million acres, according to William Trimble, "The Historical Aspects of the Surplus Food Production of the United States, 1862–1902," *Annual Report of the American Historical Association*, 231.

72   *Other careers in the military*: Monica Rico, *Nature's Noblemen*, 51.

      "What Shall I Do with My Son?": A sequel, "Whither Shall I Send My Son?," appeared in the same periodical in July 1883.

      "They had too much time": Anita Leslie, *Mr. Frewen of England*, 35.

73   *"It is time for Wyoming"*: John K. Rollinson and E. A. Brininstool, *Wyoming Cattle Trails*, 318.

sixty-three articles extolling: Gene M. Gressley, *Bankers and Cattlemen,* 40.

74 *"Every Western state":* Ramon F. Adams, *The Rampaging Herd,* xvii.

"a complete lack of restraint": Gressley, *Bankers and Cattlemen,* 49.

75 *"It will be plain to any one":* A. A. Hayes Jr., "The Cattle Ranches of Colorado," *Harper's New Monthly Magazine,* 891.

a herd would double: William Thayer, *Marvels of the New West,* 553.

76 *Brisbin insisted that his numbers:* Charles I. Bray and James S. Brisbin, *Bankers and Beef: The Beef Bonanza,* 51.

77 *"Cattle is one of those":* Charles Wayland Towne and Edward Norris Wentworth, *Cattle and Men,* 262.

"I do not hesitate to say": David W. Sherwood, "Cattle-Raising in Colorado," in Charles I. Bray and James Brisbin, *Bankers and Beef: The Beef Bonanza,* appendix, 198.

"To this date, however": Thayer, *Marvels of the New West,* 554.

78 *thirty-six companies would sink:* Jackson, *The Enterprising Scot,* 100.

"Eastern and European aristocrats": Lewis Atherton, *The Cattle Kings,* 22.

6. Cowboy Aristocrats

79 *the Duke of Devonshire:* Moreton Frewen, *Melton Mowbray and Other Memories,* 253.

80 *best cures for hangovers:* Anita Leslie, *Mr. Frewen of England,* 23.

"a child could ride Shaughraun": Frewen, *Melton Mowbray,* 79.

"Am I wrong in saying": Captain "Brooksby" Pennell-Elmhirst, *The Cream of Leicestershire,* 192–94.

"So grand a fox": Ibid.

81 *"Without a single exception":* Allen Andrews, *The Splendid Pauper,* 250.

82 *"He could clean breeches":* Leslie, *Mr. Frewen of England,* 24.

"The great game in those days": Frewen, *Melton Mowbray,* 147.

"The dear, handsome little horse": Ibid., 148.

83   *"I never backed a horse after":* Ibid.

"Color, action, symmetry, manners": Ibid., 103.

Bertie, the Prince of Wales: One of Bertie's "conjectured" fifty-five liaisons, Langtry had a three-year affair with the prince before being unceremoniously dumped for the French stage actress Sarah Bernhardt.

"If I was the devil": Leslie, *Mr. Frewen of England,* 89.

84   nine *successive American presidents:* Frewen, *Melton Mowbray,* 21.

85   *"a rather stagy-looking Corsican":* Ibid., 195.

"As a one-man army": Donald Dresden, *The Marquis de Morès,* 19.

87   *"I shall become the richest":* Edmund Morris, *The Rise of Theodore Roosevelt,* 193.

88   *"a big, powerful man":* Theodore Roosevelt, *Theodore Roosevelt: An Autobiography,* 260.

"a sickly and timid child": Albert Britt, *Turn of the Century,* 57.

89   *"I do not think there is a fellow":* Theodore Roosevelt to Theodore Roosevelt Sr., October 22, 1878, in *The Letters of Theodore Roosevelt,* vol. 1, edited by Elting Morison, 18.

a popular book on game fish: Douglas Brinkley, *The Wilderness Warrior,* 84.

90   *"The light has gone":* Theodore Roosevelt, "Theodore Roosevelt's diary the day his wife and mother died, 1884," *Rare Historical Photographs,* rarehistoricalphotos.com.

aggravated his medical condition: Roger L. Di Silvestro, *Theodore Roosevelt in the Badlands,* 67.

92   *standard poodle, Mifouche:* This is not as strange as it might seem: standard poodles were popular hunting dogs into the late nineteenth century.

fourth member of the Porcellian: The disproportionate role played by members of Harvard's Porcellian Club in the open-range cattle era has never been reported before. Teschemacher, Wister, and Roosevelt remained loyal members of the club throughout their lives, returning for graduate dinners and reunions. Their contributions to the larger Harvard community were even greater. Hu-

bert Teschemacher would leave three-quarters of his fortune to
Harvard and the rest to Phillips Exeter to endow scholarships to
Harvard. Wister and Roosevelt would serve on Harvard's Board
of Overseers. Roosevelt also served as president of the Harvard
Alumni Association.

a feature film on five: Cecil B. DeMille directed the first film version, a silent one, starring Dustin Farnum, in 1914. Later versions
starred, in order, Kenneth Harlan (1923), Gary Cooper (1929), and
Joel McCrea (1946). A 2013 version, starring Trace Adkins, never
had a major theatrical release and went straight to DVD. There
were also successful stage versions, and the television series that
aired on NBC for nine years, from 1962 through 1971. As Darwin Payne wrote in his biography of Owen Wister, *Owen Wister:
Chronicler of the West, Gentleman of the East,* "It is impossible to
calculate the effect of these many presentations for the American
public."

"The more I have looked into": H. W. Brands, *American Colossus,*
221.

93   *the finest bowie knife:* R. L. Wilson, *Theodore Roosevelt: Hunter-
Conservationist,* xvi.

both guns were intricately adorned: Ibid., 46. The revolvers are on
display at the Autry National Center in Los Angeles.

95   *"To my mind there is no memorial":* Wilson, *Theodore Roosevelt,*
264.

97   *"Rich men's sons":* E. C. "Teddy Blue" Abbott, *We Pointed Them
North,* 191.

7. From Stockyard to Steakhouse

103   *"Tourists might hesitate":* William Cronon, *Nature's Metropolis,*
207.

A city of saloons, hotels, restaurants: Ibid., 210.

107   *more workers than any other industry:* Jimmy M. Skaggs, *Prime
Cut,* 90.

109   *The remaining 140 pounds:* Walter Bueher, *Meat from Ranch to
Table,* 74.

double in size by 1900: Skaggs, *Prime Cut,* 77.

110   *"However impressive individuals":* Cronon, *Nature's Metropolis,* 254–55.

      daring in his use of leverage: Louis F. Swift, *The Yankee of the Yards,* 28.

112   *"it doesn't take long":* Lately Thomas, *Delmonico's,* 148.

      "The historical fact is that": Joe O'Connell, "Delmonico Steak: A Mystery Solved," August 25, 2001, http://www.steakperfection .com/delmonico/Steak.html.

113   *"Severed from the form":* Cronon, *Nature's Metropolis,* 25.

8. The Rise of Cheyenne

114   *"the fascination of a horse":* Andy Adams, *The Log of a Cowboy,* 12.

117   *Herefords arrived by ship:* Alexander Swan, Conrad Kohrs, John Clay, and Moreton Frewen all took credit for being the first to introduce Herefords to improve the quality of their herds. W. S. Ikdard is credited with introducing the first Herefords to Texas, but they died of Texas fever. Edward Everett Dale, *Cow Country,* 81.

118   *a remarkable eight millionaires:* Samuel Western, "The Cattle Boom," WyoHistory.org.

121   *"If it can be made in leather":* G. B. Dobson, *Wyoming Tales and Trails,* http://www.wyomingtalesandtrails.com/cheyenne4a.html.

122   *thirty dollars for a later:* Susan Karina Dickey, "Work Clothes of American Cowboys: The Pictorial Record," in *The Cowboy Way,* edited by Paul H. Carlson, 103.

124   *"That night I shall never forget":* Richard Trimble to Merritt Trimble, August 27, 1882, Richard Trimble Collection, American Heritage Center, University of Wyoming.

125   *"I am going to think this all over":* Ibid.

      "I don't think I shall come East": Ibid.

127   *"I am sorry thee has so little":* Ibid., February 22, 1883.

      highest median per capita income: Agnes Wright Spring, "Old Cheyenne Club," *American Cattle Producer.*

      some $15 million by 1886: Ibid.

      "Millions are talked of": *Miles City Daily Press,* August 2, 1882.

128 *The contracts always stipulated:* Gene M. Gressley, *Bankers and Cattlemen*, 187.

130 *"We do not propose doing":* Spring, "Old Cheyenne Club."

131 *an excuse to expand: Cheyenne Daily Sun*, April 19, 1884.

"No wonder they like the club": Bill O'Neal, *Historic Ranches of the Old West*, 194.

"We wired you last week": William Sturgis to Park & Tilford, October 19, 1882, Cheyenne Club records, American Heritage Center, University of Wyoming.

"It lacked almost entirely": Ibid., August 10, 1882.

132 *"Converse was one of the few":* John Clay to Robert Hanesworth, April 4, 1930, Cheyenne Club Records, American Heritage Center, University of Wyoming.

133 *"dictatorial and disrespectful language":* Cheyenne Club Records, American Heritage Center, University of Wyoming.

"a motley group full of ginger": John Clay, *My Life on the Range*, 53.

a lengthy dinner at the club: John Clay, "The Cheyenne Club: Recollections of an Organization Once Famous in Connection with the Development of the Western Cattle Trade," *The Breeder's Gazette*, 1182.

"a sailor who had a girl": Clay, *My Life on the Range*, 77.

134 *"one centered on relaxation":* Howard R. Lamar, *The New Encyclopedia of the American West*, 117.

9. Barbed Wire: The Devil's Rope

136 *a surprisingly significant impact:* The Spanish in Cuba in 1896, as part of their *Reconcentración* policy, were the first to use barbed wire to incarcerate humans. The British were quick to pick up on the development and used barbed wire in the Boer Wars in South Africa, starting in 1899. Barbed wire would play an even deadlier role in World War I. Battlefields crisscrossed with barbed wire created areas that soldiers could not safely cross, so that neither side could make progress; they stayed hunkered down in trenches. Also, barbed-wire fences offered no barrier to machine-gun fire, making it more pervasive and deadly. Developing a response to the problems caused by barbed wire became a priority. The first military tank, created by the British in 1916, made it

possible to cross barbed-wire barricades (and trenches), allowing movement to resume on the battlefield.

all three men had filed: They were not actually the first. That feat is credited to Lucien B. Smith, of Kent, Ohio, whose patent was filed in 1867, but he never succeeded in commercializing his invention.

some thirteen of those: Earl W. Hayter, "Barbed-Wire Fencing: A Prairie Invention, Its Rise and Influence in the Western States," http://xroads.virginia.edu/~drbr/b_arb1.html.

138 *"This is the finest fencing":* Henry D. and Frances T. McCallum, *The Wire That Fenced the West,* 71.

139 *some 482 million pounds:* Ibid., 72–73.

Different styles of barbs: Hayter, "Barbed-Wire Fencing."

10. Frewen's Castle

142 *tiny two-man alpine tents:* Moreton Frewen, *Melton Mowbray and Other Memories,* 160.

143 *thirteen deep streams:* John W. Davis, *Wyoming Range War,* 287, n4.

144 *"Not a human habitation":* Frewen, *Melton Mowbray,* 167.

145 *"Twenty of us can dine":* Moreton Frewen to Clara Jerome, July 25, 1880, Frewen Records, American Heritage Center, University of Wyoming.

British polo was first formally: The game dates back to at least 600 BCE; nomads in Central Asia played it. Modern polo is thought to date from 1859, with the founding of the Sichar Polo Club in Manipur, India.

146 *"I feel a proprietary right":* Moreton Frewen to Clara Jerome, July 7, 1880, Frewen Collection, American Heritage Center, University of Wyoming. Quoted in Peter Pagnamenta, *Prairie Fever,* 255.

"stories without a vestige of truth": Frewen, *Melton Mowbray,* 185.

147 *"Never in my life was I":* Ibid., 174.

buying a coal mine: L. Milton Woods, *Moreton Frewen's Western Adventures,* 44.

148 *"New York is a much larger town":* Frewen, *Melton Mowbray,* 179.

150 *a $2.5 million dowry:* The young duke allegedly told his new American wife as they departed from their wedding ceremony

that he loved another woman and had no intention of ever returning to the United States, which he loathed.

"Now there was no understanding": Moreton Frewen to Clara Jerome, April 2, 1881, Frewen Collection, American Heritage Center, University of Wyoming. Quoted in Woods, *Moreton Frewen's Western Adventures,* 29.

151   *"This is our* real *honeymoon"*: Clara Frewen to Leonie Jerome, August 23, 1881, reprinted in Anita Leslie, *Mr. Frewen of England,* 66–67.

152   *"drunken, déclassé and half-witted"*: Linda Stratmann, "Oscar Wilde and the Marquess of Queensberry," June 18, 2013, http://www.huffingtonpost.com/linda-stratmann/oscar-wilde-and-the-marqu_b_3459456.html.

    "A big bear which measured": Frewen, *Melton Mowbray,* 205.

    "We had a fearful row": Woods, *Moreton Frewen's Western Adventures,* 25.

153   *"ornamental" or "guinea pig"*: David Cannadine, *The Decline and Fall of the British Aristocracy,* 407.

154   *"I tell you plainly, you can not"*: Richard Frewen to Moreton Frewen, May 18, 1882, Frewen Collection, American Heritage Center, University of Wyoming.

    "Do not stint yourself": Moreton Frewen to Clara Jerome Frewen, May 4, 1883, Frewen Collection, American Heritage Center, University of Wyoming.

155   *"Dear vulgar money"*: Moreton Frewen to Clara Jerome Frewen, March 7, 1881, Frewen Collection, American Heritage Center, University of Wyoming.

    "Nor is it reasonable": Moreton Frewen, *Free Grazing,* 8.

157   *Built out of white kiln-dried ash:* Howard R. Lamar, *The New Encyclopedia of the American West,* 1075.

    "Bathe your feet before starting": Marc McCutcheon, *Everyday Life in the 1800s,* 69.

158   *The reinsman held the three:* Ibid., 1075.

    "Ready?" asked the man: Hermann Hagedorn, *Roosevelt in the Badlands,* 213.

160   *"My plan is altogether feasible"*: Ibid., 61.

162   *"My God, de Morès has got":* Donald Dresden, *The Marquis de Morès,* 135.

163   *"His power of self hypnotism":* Hagedorn, *Roosevelt in the Badlands,* 333.

11. The Nature Crusader

165   *"I have been having a glorious":* H. W. Brands, *American Colossus,* 221.
      "So I have had good sport": Theodore Roosevelt to Anna Roosevelt, September 20, 1884, *Theodore Roosevelt: Letters and Speeches,* 15.
      "Nowhere, not even at sea": Theodore Roosevelt to Bamie Roosevelt, June 23, 1884, *Memorial Edition: Works of Theodore Roosevelt,* vol. 1, edited by Hermann Hagedorn.
      "I regard the outlook": R. L. Wilson, *Theodore Roosevelt: Hunter-Conservationist,* 43.

166   *he was in the saddle:* Ibid., 59–60.
      "He was foolish to stand so near": Theodore Roosevelt, *An Autobiography,* 377.

167   *"A great many men had falls":* Wilson, *Theodore Roosevelt,* 66.

168   *"I looked pretty gay":* Ibid.
      "It's a mere trifle": Ibid.
      "I waited until they were": Ibid., 64.

169   *"a fearless bugger":* Edmund Morris, *The Rise of Theodore Roosevelt,* 327.
      "If you are my enemy": Ibid., 301.
      "Most emphatically I am not": Ibid., 303.

170   *"restless raged wolf feeling":* Theodore Roosevelt to Anna Roosevelt, May 15, 1886, *The Letters of Theodore Roosevelt,* vol. 1, edited by Elting Morison.

171   *"By Godfrey, but this is fun!":* Hermann Hagedorn, *Roosevelt in the Badlands,* 43.
      "Cocking my rifle": Wilson, *Theodore Roosevelt,* 51.
      "I never saw any one so enthused": Ibid., 45.

173   *"I ran in and stabbed him":* Theodore Roosevelt to Theodore

Roosevelt Jr., January 14, 1901, *Theodore Roosevelt: Letters and Speeches*, 223.

174   *"There is no fundamental difference"*: Charles Darwin, *The Descent of Man*, 66.

176   *"No doubt it had some influence"*: Douglas Brinkley, *The Wilderness Warrior*, 189.
       eastern and western species: Ibid., 205.

177   *"the sheet anchor and the soul"*: Wilson, *Theodore Roosevelt*, 83.

12. Teddy Blue and the Necktie Socials

181   *some twelve million cattle:* Edward Everett Dale, *Cow Country*, 85.
       "The cattleman's empire of grass": Ibid., 85.
       "I'll bet you a dollar I can": E. C. "Teddy Blue" Abbott, *We Pointed Them North*, 158.

182   *"After I got some sense"*: Ibid., 150.
       He and Teddy Blue would remain: Ibid., 167. Teddy Blue was also a great friend of the artist Charles M. Russell.

183   *Remarkable for their documentary:* Mark H. Brown and W. R. Felton, *Before Barbed Wire*, 31.
       "Oh, boy, but life was good": Abbott, *We Pointed Them North*, 89.

184   *"You have too much snap"*: Ibid., 96.
       "If I say it myself, I was": Ibid.

185   *"The night never gets so dark"*: Ibid., 97.

187   *"In the first stage the victim"*: R. Michael Wilson, *Frontier Justice in the Wild West*, xvii.

188   *"Went to join the Angels"*: George Parrott display, Carbon County Museum, Rawlins, Wyoming.

189   *"the magpies' wings got broke"*: Abbott, *We Pointed Them North*, 119.

191   *he had lost at least 3 percent:* Granville Stuart, *Forty Years on the Frontier*, 195.

192   *"Yes, madam, and by God"*: Abbott, *We Pointed Them North*, 135.
       "There was ranches every few": Ibid., 91.

193   *"We were blamed for everything"*: Stuart, *Forty Years on the Frontier*, 196.

195   *"an overworked, underpaid hireling"*: Wallace Stegner, "Who Are Westerners?" *American Heritage*, 36.

"a hired hand on horseback": Lewis Atherton, *The Cattle Kings*, xi.

196 *Among their demands:* Cowboy wages were comparable to the average industrial worker in Texas at this time, who earned twenty-three dollars a month for a sixty- to seventy-two-hour workweek, according to Paul H. Carlson, *The Cowboy Way*, 80.
the offending cowboys were: Ibid., 77–87.

198 *"I always wanted a dark-eyed woman"*: Abbott, *We Pointed Them North*, 149.
"It was a wonderful outfit": Ibid., 129–36.
"The Stuart girls were [half Indian]": Ibid., 141.

199 *"The Stuart girls had prettier"*: Ibid., 142.
"I was so damn in love": Ibid., 187.
"She is sure enough a Daisy": Ibid., 202n.
he "reformed" and "got civilized": Ibid., 187.

200 *"The influence which he exerted"*: Hans Zinsser, *Biographical Memoir of Theobald Smith, 1859–1934*.

13. Mortal Ruin

202 *"a more satisfactory realization"*: Report of the Directors and Statement of Accounts to November 30th, 1884, Frewen Collection American Heritage Center, University of Wyoming.
"When the winter has been good": William H. Forbis, *The Old West: The Cowboy*, 65.

203 *Freight rates on the railroads:* Robert G. Athearn, *Westward the Briton*, 107.
near the bottom of the list: Maurice Frink et al., *When Grass Was King*, 241.

204 *"gaily libeled his opponents"*: Allen Andrews, *The Splendid Pauper*, 87.
"You might sometimes": T. P. O'Connor, "The Late Mr. Moreton Frewen: A Personal Memoir," *Daily Telegraph*, September 1924, Frewen Collection, American Heritage Center, University of Wyoming.

205 *Frewen promptly mortgaged it:* L. Milton Woods, *Moreton Frewen's Western Adventures*, 92.
"I shall have to plot and scheme": Moreton Frewen to Clara Je-

rome Frewen, about 1884, Frewen Collection, American Heritage
Center, University of Wyoming.

206 *"We have got to face this":* Helena Huntington Smith, *The War
on Powder River*, 96.

"I have now to inform you": Moreton Frewen to Mr. Tomkins,
Frewen Collection, American Heritage Center, University of
Wyoming.

"As to this hound": Smith, *The War on Powder River*, 96.

"Boss, can we clean get out": Moreton Frewen, *Melton Mowbray
and Other Memories*, 222.

207 *Eton-educated, but frail-looking:* Woods, *British Gentlemen in the
Wild West*, 77.

"the monument of Frewen's folly": Diaries of Sir Horace Plunkett,
1881–1932, November 6, 1887, National Library of Ireland.

208 *a stodgy if well-intentioned bore:* At that time, Manchester's wife,
Louise Montagu, was having a torrid affair with Lord Harrington,
nicknamed "Harty-Tarty," the future Duke of Devonshire. When
Harrington eventually married her after Manchester's death in
1890, she became the famous "Double Duchess."

"a nice old gentleman": Woods, *Moreton Frewen's Western
Adventures*, 90.

"I hope things may now go": Frewen, *Melton Mowbray*, 234.

"ways of dealing with elderly men": By 1950, following a steady
succession of ill-conceived investments that included a move into
Kenyan farmland, the Manchester family estates, including the
stunning Kimbolton Castle (final home of Catherine of Aragon),
47,000 acres of land, a 13,000-volume library, and a priceless collection of Holbeins, Rubenses, Titians, and Van Dykes, had all
been sold off — a not uncommon fate among British aristocrats
in the twentieth century.

209 *"The board have been very much":* Woods, *Moreton Frewen's
Western Adventures*, 121.

"I have wished a thousand times": Ibid., 148.

"For myself I wish": Ibid., 128.

"My relations with a lot of good": Frewen, *Melton Mowbray*, 233.

"Mud was thrown freely": Woods, *Moreton Frewen's Western
Adventures*, 139.

"Your brother's action absolutely": William Mackenzie to Richard Frewen, December 23, 1886, Frewen Collection, American Heritage Center, University of Wyoming.

210 *"I think you will admit"*: F. R. Lingham to C. W. M. Kemp, Secretary of the Powder River Company, November 24, 1886, Frewen Collection, American Heritage Center, University of Wyoming.

"I had a very great interest": Frewen, *Melton Mowbray*, 235.

211 *"If we are forced to repay"*: Woods, *Moreton Frewen's Western Adventures*, 179.

Frewen's personal financial condition: Ibid., 134.

212 *"Get the house sold if possible"*: Moreton Frewen to Clara Jerome Frewen, September 26, 1886, Frewen Collection, American Heritage Center, University of Wyoming.

"Poor Archer": Moreton Frewen to Clara Jerome Frewen, November 15, 1886, Frewen Collection, American Heritage Center, University of Wyoming.

"I am shortly to resign": Horace C. Plunkett, "Report to the Shareholders of the Powder River Cattle Company, Limited, by the Manager, December 18, 1886, Frewen Collection, American Heritage Center, University of Wyoming.

213 *"Raise all you can"*: Horace C. Plunkett to Moreton Frewen, November 15, 1886, Frewen Collection, American Heritage Center, University of Wyoming.

"Well whatever happens": Woods, *Moreton Frewen's Western Adventures*, 158.

"Had we but known it": Frewen, *Melton Mowbray*, 234.

14. Poker on Joint-Stock Principles

214 *"I now learn for the first time"*: Gene M. Gressley, *Bankers and Cattlemen*, 251.

216 *"He don't stop at one"*: Charles Wayland Towne and Edward Norris Wentworth, *Cattle and Men*, 264.

sold posthumously: Jim Fenton, "English Cowboy: The Earl of Aylesford in the American West," in *The Cowboy Way*, edited by Paul H. Carlson, 67.

217 *was nearing bankruptcy*: Gressley, *Bankers and Cattlemen*, 255.

"In our business we are often": William H. Forbis, *The Cowboys,* 64.

twenty million cattle grazed: Richard White, "Animals and Enterprise," in *The Oxford History of the American West,* edited by Clyde A. Milner et al., 265.

218   *1.8 million acres:* J. W. Williams, *The Big Ranch Country,* 255.

219   *no fewer than fifteen hundred:* Monica Rico, *Nature's Noblemen,* 51.

the British formed thirty-three: W. Turrentine Jackson, "British Interests in the Range Cattle Industry," in Maurice Frink et al., *When Grass Was King,* 222.

some $45 million: Ibid., 223.

220   *"The Scotchmen arrived":* Cheyenne Sun, August 31, 1889.

221   *at a dollar per acre:* The Union Pacific Railroad allowed payment over ten years at 6 percent interest, reducing the cost to the cattlemen to 5 cents per acre per year. See Ernest Staples Osgood, *The Day of the Cattleman,* 212.

enclosing twice the acreage: Ibid.

"Among the new questions": Thomas Sturgis, "Minutes of the Wyoming Stock Growers Association Annual Meeting at the Opera House in Cheyenne, April 6–8, 1885," WSGA records, American Heritage Center, University of Wyoming.

222   *"If I laugh at Americans":* Moreton Frewen, *Melton Mowbray and Other Memories,* 196.

"these western men": Bill O'Neal, *Historic Ranches of the Old West,* 191.

"I did not like the cowboys": Lady Rose Pender, *A Lady's Experience in the Wild West in 1883,* 46.

223   *"Of all the English snobs":* Cheyenne Daily Sun, November 3, 1887.

"We want no caste, no upper classes": Peter Pagnamenta, *Prairie Fever,* 285.

"Together, big corporations": Ibid., 268.

224   *the exclusive private use:* Donald J. MacLeod to *The Independent,* republished in *The Week,* January 24, 2015, 27.

"Through the ornamental windows": San Francisco Chronicle, June 8, 1881. Quoted in Pagnamenta, *Prairie Fever,* 267.

225 *"It is impossible to exaggerate"*: Chicago Daily Tribune, March 23,
1885. Quoted in Pagnamenta, *Prairie Fever*, 271.
valued at roughly $340 million: Joseph Nimmo, *Report in Regard
to the Range and Ranch Cattle Business of the United States*, 55.
21 million acres: Pagnamenta, *Prairie Fever*, 278.
The foreign owners of the largest: Ibid., 278.

226 *"We are at present permitting"*: Congressman Lewis Payson, *Congressional Record*, 49th Congress, July 31, 1886, 7830–31.
limited new foreign investment: In 1897 the law was revised to
exempt mining lands. When the territories became states, they
were no longer covered under this statute.
"only poker on joint-stock principles": Edinburgh Courant, January 28, 1884. Quoted in Maurice Frink et al., *When Grass Was
King*, 157.
the book counts inflated: Harmon Ross Mothershead, *The Swan
Land and Cattle Company*, 30.
never again pose a serious threat: The British would go from investing in cattle ranches to investing in the U.S. beer business.
They would buy up more than eighty American breweries, which
led to the franchising of saloons. By 1900 four out of five saloons
were tied to a brewery, a model that persists in the UK to this
day. See Richard Erdoes, *Saloons of the Old West*, 239.

15. The Big Die-Up

228 *Weeks might go by*: William H. Forbis, *The Old West: The Cowboys*, 92.
"They tell a story about": E. C. "Teddy Blue" Abbott, *We Pointed
Them North*, 125.
"There wasn't anything to do": Ibid., 125.
cowboys who took to memorizing: Forbis: *The Old West: The Cowboys*, 82.

229 *"So after that it was nothing"*: Abbott, *We Pointed Them North*,
125.
"some young lady": Reuben B. Mullins, *Pulling Leather*, 111.
"All the noise to be heard": Ibid., 112.

230 *"hung on the floor"*: Ibid., 81.

"Many writers of fiction": Ibid., xii.

231 *the temperature sank*: L. Milton Woods, *Moreton Frewen's Western Adventures*, 176.

"Something dreadful always": H. Norman Hyatt, *An Uncommon Journey*, 285.

"As the South Sea bubble burst": John Clay, *My Life on the Range*, 174.

232 *"It is told of one untruthful manager"*: The Yellowstone Journal, Illustrated and Historical Edition, September 27, 1900, 4.

higher in the Montana and Dakota: Dr. Randy McFerrin and Dr. Douglas Wills, of New Mexico State University and University of Washington at Tacoma, have written ("Searching for the Big Die-Off: An Event Study of the 19th Century Cattle Markets," *Essays in Economic and Business History*, vol. 31, 2013) that a statistical analysis of the receipts of the Union Stock Yards shows no disruption of the supply of western range cattle arriving in Chicago for the period following the Big Die-Up, calling into question the entire narrative of such an event. They argue that the notion that the land was overgrazed and overstocked was wildly exaggerated by the press of the day and likely an excuse for cattle barons to readjust their book counts downward from inflated numbers. While theirs is a clever piece of statistical analysis, there seems little doubt there was an oversupply of cattle before the die-up and that the glut of steers in Chicago might well have continued after, as ranchers liquidated their herds. Also, the local newspapers had every incentive to minimize, not exaggerate, the reports of the damage, as the truth would only further depress the value of cattlecompany shares.

But even if the lower estimates: W. Turrentine Jackson, "The Wyoming Stock Growers Association: Its Years of Temporary Decline, 1886–1890," *Agricultural History*.

"Times hard. Money short": Ibid.

"He was vain and loved": Clay, *My Life on the Range*, 50.

233 *His net loss: $23,556.68*: Douglas Brinkley, *The Wilderness Warrior*, 198.

He reportedly salvaged only: Lawrence M. Woods, *British Gentlemen in the Wild West*, 170.

234 *The calf crop came in at:* Woods, *Moreton Frewen's Western Adventures*, 172, 187.

235 *The French cattle baron Pierre Wibaux:* Ibid., 196.

sold off the refrigeration plant: Ibid., 97.

retire on his own terms: Edward Everett Dale, *Cow Country*, 104.

"My own unissued shares": Moreton Frewen, *Melton Mowbray and Other Memories*, 235.

237 *"Your telegram from Denver":* Merritt Trimble to Richard Trimble, May 21, 1887, Richard Trimble Collection, American Heritage Center, University of Wyoming.

238 *"The Marquis de Morès has gone":* Donald Dresden, *The Marquis de Morès*, 184.

The financier had reportedly: Ibid.

239 *the two had become involved:* Ibid., 211.

cost his father some $250,000: Virginia Heidenreich-Barber, *Aristocracy on the Western Frontier*, 11.

"It is necessary for me": Dresden, *The Marquis de Morès*, 189.

16. The Fall of Cheyenne

240 *"I do not think I ever saw":* Walter Prescott Webb, *The Great Plains*, 236, n1.

"Range husbandry is over": *Rocky Mountain Husbandman*, March 17, 1887.

"The big guns toppled over": John Clay, *My Life on the Range*, 173.

241 *Membership in the once:* Bill O'Neal, *Cattlemen vs. Sheepherders*, 90.

"I find that my cattle": E. P. Breckinridge to Thomas Sturgis, August 23, 1887, in W. Turrentine Jackson, "Wyoming Stock Growers' Association: Its Years of Temporary Decline, 1886–1890, *Agricultural History*.

"Ambitious cowboys, and others": John Rolfe Burroughs, *Guardians of the Grasslands*, 144.

Small parcels of 80 to 640 acres: Webb, *The Great Plains*, 393.

242 *"I said, 'Any young man'":* Reuben B. Mullins, *Pulling Leather*, 191.

243 *"I reviewed my past life":* F. M. Polk, "My Experiences on the Cow

Trail," in *The Trail Drivers of Texas,* edited by J. Marvin Hunter
and George W. Saunders, 146.

"I had never saved a dime": E. C. "Teddy Blue" Abbott, *We
Pointed Them North,* 205.

"from now on I wasn't a cowpuncher": Ibid., 207.

246 *"Probably discovery of Texas Fever":* Claude E. Dolman and Richard J. Wolfe, *Theobald Smith, Microbiologist,* 113.

"He was in the first exciting": Ibid.

247 *the last of the jaguars:* C. F. Eckhardt, "Texas Fever, the Winchester Quarantine," July 5, 2009, TexasEscapes.com, http://
www.texasescapes.com/CFEckhardt/Charley-Eckhardt-Texas
.htm.

"To those who have the urge": Hans Zinsser, *Biographical Memoir
of Theobald Smith,* 265.

248 *"It is useless to look":* John Willingham, "The Cowboy Strike of
1883 and the Demise of Old Tascosa," *The Edge of Freedom,* April
15, 2013, http://edgeoffreedom.net/the-cowboy-strike-of
-1883-and-the-demise-of-old-tascosa/.

four-fifths of the stores: Joseph G. McCoy, *Historic Sketches of the
Cattle Trade of the West and Southwest,* 168.

250 *"Cheyenne dull and doleful":* Diaries of Sir Horace Plunkett,
1881–1932, December 3, 1889, National Library of Ireland.

"a town of many shattered hopes": Philip Stewart Robinson, *Sinners and Saints,* 61.

Keely Institute for the treatment of drunks: Charles B. Penrose,
The Rustler Business, 7.

251 *bullet through his head:* Clay, *My Life on the Range,* 78.

17. The Rustler Problem

256 *left to struggle wildly:* John Clay, *My Life on the Range,* 14.

a threat to his water supply: Jim Averell had written a letter to
a local newspaper — the *Casper Weekly Mail* — published on
April 7, 1889. In it, he criticized the cattle barons, and implicitly
Bothwell: "They are land-grabbers, who are only camped here as
speculators in land under the desert land act. They are opposed
to anything that would settle and improve the country or make
it anything but a cow pasture for eastern speculators. It is won-

derful how much land some of these land sharks own—in their minds—and how firmly they are organized to keep Wyoming from being settled up. They advance the idea that a poor man has nothing to say in the affairs of this country, in which they are wrong, as the future land owner in Wyoming will be the people to come, as most of these large tracts are so fraudulently entered now that it must ultimately change hands and give the public domain to the honest settler."

258 *"Much of their work is":* Bill O'Neal, *The Johnson County War,* 25.

260 *"Special to the* Wyoming Derrick*":* Wyoming Stock Growers Association Records: Johnson County War 1892, American Heritage Center, University of Wyoming.

261 *"The attack on Nate and Ross":* John W. Davis, *Wyoming Range War,* 105.

262 *drenched in blood:* "Shot in the Back," *Cheyenne Leader,* December 4, 1891.

265 *"He was a fire-eater":* Clay, *My Life on the Range,* 138.
sure to end in disaster: Robert K. DeArment, *Alias Frank Canton,* 122.

266 *"strongly advised against such action":* Clay, *My Life on the Range,* 268–69.

269 *blacks, but also Catholics and Jews:* The first lynchings were public whippings carried out by a vigilance committee led by one Colonel Lynch in Virginia, in the late eighteenth century.
Among the delegates: John Rolfe Burroughs, *Guardian of the Grasslands,* 75.

270 *"There were some good men":* O'Neal, *The Johnson County War,* 105.

271 *a founder of the WSGA:* Ibid., 35.
$150,000 in debt: Burroughs, *Guardians of the Grasslands,* 37.

18. Nate Champion and the Johnson County War

272 *"Their education and wealth":* John W. Davis, *Wyoming Range War,* 139.

273 *"an unwavering sense of responsibility":* John Rolfe Burroughs, *Guardian of the Grasslands,* 130.
"angry and excitable": Davis, *Wyoming Range War,* 138.

275   *"Me and Nick"*: Charles B. Penrose, *The Rustler Business*, 33.

276   *"It is now about two hours"*: Ibid.
      "Nick is dead": Ibid.

277   *"It's about 3 o'clock now"*: Ibid., 34.
      loaded *"wide and high"*: Ibid., 18.

278   *"Well they have just got through"*: Ibid., 34.
      "By God, if I had fifty men": Davis, *Wyoming Range War*, 154.
      the version of the diary: It appeared in the *Chicago Herald* on
      April 16, 1892.

279   *"a fresh [rude] young man"*: Penrose, *The Rustler Business*, 24.
      "fell back on the pillow dead": *Cheyenne Leader*, April 16, 1892.

282   *That night the skies were clear:* The moon was full on April 12,
      1892.
      "I don't care how good a fighter": Bill O'Neal, *The Johnson County
      War*, 42.
      "When I took off my overshoes": Penrose, *The Rustler Business*,
      21.
      the bullet had not penetrated: Davis, *Wyoming Range War*, 170.

283   *"five beans in the wheel"*: O'Neal, *The Johnson County War*, 143.
      "Each man gave up hope": Davis, *Wyoming Range War*, 173.

284   *"Mr. Blaine got a message through"*: Allen Andrews, *The Splendid
      Pauper*, 169.

286   *"The Long Suffering Ranchmen"*: "Wiping Out Rustlers," *Chicago
      Herald*, April 13, 1892.

287   *"This article, though profoundly"*: Davis, *Wyoming Range War*,
      241.

288   *"They drank it as they drank"*: Penrose, *The Rustler Business*, 36.

289   *"I started out taking"*: O'Neal, *The Johnson County War*, 214.
      "They soon, or at least many": Penrose, *The Rustler Business*, 36.
      "Mr. Baxter was called": Maurice Frink, in Maurice Frink et al.,
      When Grass Was King, 114.

290   he *"snapped over"*: Maria Sandoz, *The Cattlemen*, 399.

291   *"Come at once, bring"*: O'Neal, *The Johnson County War*, 209.
      receive proper medical attention: High altitudes, according to a
      common medical misconception of the era, were believed to be
      a contributing cause of nervous breakdowns.

292 *"died alone and single":* John Clay, *My Life on the Range,* 78.
293 *Van Devanter destroyed many of his papers:* Lori Van Pelt, "Willis Van Devanter, Cheyenne Lawyer and U.S. Supreme Court Justice," WyoHistory.org.
294 *Entire books have been written:* In 1914, the surgeon on the expedition, Dr. Charles Penrose, wrote his account of what happened, with the biased assistance of fellow invader Billy Irvine. Penrose's pamphlet makes clear Governor Amos Barber's complicity in the affair from the outset. Much is accurate in the Penrose/Irvine account, but it repeats the myth of a rustler problem in Johnson County, arguing that it justified the invasion. Billy Walker, one of the two fur trappers who witnessed the killing of Nick Ray and Nate Champion, wrote a memoir titled *The Longest Rope,* nearly fifty years after the event, with the help of a ghostwriter, as did the son of the invader Malcom Campbell. Frank Canton, John Clay, and others touched on the events in their own memoirs, skewing the details to fit their personal agendas.
  "a century of obfuscation": George W. Hufsmith, *The Wyoming Lynching of Cattle Kate, 1889,* vi.
  "We were in Wyoming as paid": O'Neal, *The Johnson County War,* 220.
295 *"People of the same trade":* Adam Smith, *An Inquiry into the Causes of the Wealth of Nations,* 54.
296 *"Human experience long ago":* Ida M. Tarbell, "The Price of Oil," *McClure's* (September 1904), in Ida M. Tarbell and David Mark Chalmers, *History of Standard Oil Company: Briefer Version,* 194. Quoted in Doris Kearns Goodwin, *The Bully Pulpit,* 338.
  the gray wolf had become nocturnal: Theodore Roosevelt, *Hunting Trips of a Ranchman,* 28–29.
297 *"In the present winter of 1892–93":* Theodore Roosevelt, *The Wilderness Hunter,* 701.
  In 1886 in northern Montana: Theodore Roosevelt, "Wolves and Wolf-Hounds," *The Wilderness Hunter.* See *Hunting Trips of a Ranchman & The Wilderness Hunter,* 721.
298 *wolves were such a pestilence:* Bill O'Neal, *Historic Ranches of the Old West,* 55.

19. The Cowboy President

301   *"I had studied a lot about men"*: Ogden Tanner, *The Old West: The Ranchers*, 177. This echoes Herman Melville's claim of fifty years earlier: "A whaleship was my Yale College and my Harvard."

302   *"No one who saw Roosevelt"*: Arthur Lubow, *The Reporter Who Would Be King*, 195.
     "Every man behaved well": Theodore Roosevelt to Corrine Roosevelt Robinson, June 25, 1898, *Theodore Roosevelt: Letters and Speeches*, 150.

303   *soon came to despise him*: Doris Kearns Goodwin, *The Bully Pulpit*, 527.
     "a tallish, yet stockily built": William Allen White, "Remarks at the Theodore Roosevelt Memorial Association, New York, N.Y.," October 27, 1934.

304   *"The eyes do not look as if"*: Edmund Morris, *Theodore Rex*, 486.
     "It demands the complete": Gifford Pinchot, *The Fight for Conservation*, 48.

305   *"exploited by land grabbers"*: Theodore Roosevelt, *An Autobiography*, 404.
     a cadre of administration clerks: Morris, *Theodore Rex*, 487.

306   *"It is also vandalism wantonly to destroy"*: Theodore Roosevelt, "Roosevelt Quotes," Theodore Roosevelt National Park, U.S. National Park Service, http://www.nps.gov/thro/historyculture/theodore-roosevelt-quotes.htm.

307   *"He was one of America's first"*: Stephen Ambrose, introduction to Theodore Roosevelt, *Hunting Trips of a Ranchman* & *The Wilderness Hunter*, xix.
     "not in the least a game butcher": R. L. Wilson, *Theodore Roosevelt: Hunter-Conservationist*, 173.
     "Although the Progressive Party": Goodwin, *The Bully Pulpit*, 741.

308   *finally emerged from the jungle*: The best account of this expedition is unquestionably Candice Millard's *The River of Doubt: Theodore Roosevelt's Darkest Journey*.
     "Quentin's mother and I": Michele May, "Aviators: Quentin Roosevelt — He Died Fighting," *Aviation History*.
     tears streamed down his face: Edward J. Renehan Jr., "Theodore

Roosevelt's Family in the Great War," http://www.worldwar1
.com/dbc/roosev.htm.

with his arm draped over: Millard, *The River of Doubt,* 343.

309 *"I would take the memory":* Frederick S. Wood, *Roosevelt as
We Knew Him,* 12.

20. The Closing of the Range

311 *"Certain it is that a scene":* Maurice Frink, in Maurice Frink et al.,
When Grass Was King, 122.

"one of the outstanding phenomena": Walter Prescott Webb, *The
Great Plains,* 225.

312 *"The integrated city-country system":* William Cronon, *Nature's
Metropolis,* 379.

313 *opening the door to invasive species:* Richard White, "Animals and
Enterprise, *The Oxford History of the American West,* edited by
Clyde A. Milner et al., 269.

314 *advocated for state hunting licenses:* Ibid., 705.

naturally selecting against: Douglas Brinkley, *The Wilderness
Warrior,* 704.

survival of the smallest: See Chris T. Darimont, Caroline H. Fox,
Heather M. Bryan, and Thomas E. Reimchen, "The Unique Ecology of Human Predators," *Science,* August 21, 2015.

"At the turn of the century": Michael McCarthy, "The First
Sagebrush Rebellion: Forest Reserves and States Rights in Colo-
rado and the West, 1891–1907," http://www.foresthistory.org
/Publications/Books/Origins_National_Forests/sec13.htm.

315 *"The invasion [of the West]":* Debra Donahue, *The Western Range
Revisited,* 114.

"cattlemen came from Elsewhere": C. L. Sonnichsen, *Cowboys and
Cattle Kings,* xv.

"the beast of waste and desolation": Theodore Roosevelt, *The
Wilderness Hunter,* 699.

317 *The gray wolf population:* Mission: Wolf, http://www.mission
wolf.org/menu/wild-wolves/.

318 *"See how they are moving":* Episode 2: "Plains," in *Earth: A New
Wild,* www.pbs.org/earth-a-new-wild/home/.

rotational grazing: Allotment management plans devised by

the Bureau of Land Management came to the fore in the 1960s. Today they ensure that more attention is given to range management and rest-rotation grazing on public lands.

"95% report an increase": "Talking Points Regarding Savory," Savory Institute, http://savory.global/institute and Planet Tech Associates, http://planet-tech.com/blog/talking-points-regarding -savory.

319 *"There is no such thing as"*: James E. McWilliams, "All Sizzle and No Steak: Why Allan Savory's TED Talk About How Cattle Can Reverse Global Warming Is Dead Wrong," http://www.slate.com /articles/life/food/2013/04/allan_savory_s_ted_talk_is_wrong _and_the_benefits_of_holistic_grazing_have.html.

livestock produce carbon dioxide: In all, 14.5 percent of emissions come from animal agriculture. See "Racing Extinction," *Discovery Channel,* 2015 Oceanic Preservation Society, Vulcan Productions Inc.

320 *"Improvements in knowledge and technology"*: Reed F. Noss and Allen Y. Cooperrider, *Saving Nature's Legacy,* 326.

21. Failed Second Acts

322 *"The big packinghouses"*: Richard White, "Animals and Enterprise," in *The Oxford History of the American West,* edited by Clyde A. Milner et al., 269.

323 *"Sweet thing, I ought never"*: Moreton Frewen to Clara Jerome Frewen, March 3, 1887, American Heritage Center, University of Wyoming.

326 *fully half of the families:* Giles Worsley, *England's Lost Houses,* 18.
"I have got the ball at my feet": Allen Andrews, *The Splendid Pauper,* 158.
"I never felt better, stronger": Anita Leslie, *Mr. Frewen of England,* 126.
"I am so utterly perplexed": Andrews, *The Splendid Pauper,* 171.

327 *"I poured mine down the sink"*: Leslie, *Mr. Frewen of England,* 129.
"He left babies on other": Shane Leslie, *Studies in Sublime Failure,* 279.
"Do get hold of some money": Moreton Frewen to Clara Jerome

Frewen, 1883, Frewen Collection, American Heritage Center, University of Wyoming.

"He avoided bankruptcy": Leslie, *Studies in Sublime Failure,* 279.

329 *"The contrast is effective":* Andrews, *The Splendid Pauper,* 191.

"Moreton let me in most sadly": Ibid., 192.

Moreton Frewen deserves: Frewen did further service to literature when he rented his dilapidated country estate, known as Brede Place, to a tubercular American writer named Stephen Crane, the author of the great Civil War novel *The Red Badge of Courage,* and his common-law wife, Cora Taylor. She was the ex-wife of the son of the commander-in-chief of India; a former Florida hotel/brothel madam (Hotel de Dream), she was also one of the first female war correspondents. At Brede Place, Crane wrote two of the earliest and best literary western short stories — "The Bride Comes to Yellow Sky" (1898) and "The Blue Hotel" (1898). Increasingly ill and unable to pay the rent, Crane lived at Brede Place until shortly before his death, when Cora moved him to a sanitarium in the Black Forest, where he died at age twenty-nine of a pulmonary hemorrhage. Moreton and Clara Frewen created a posthumous fund to help repay Stephen Crane's debts.

took to wearing cowboy attire: Donald Dresden, *The Marquis de Morès,* 230.

330 *"Wherever Morès went":* Moreton Frewen, *Melton Mowbray and Other Memories,* 193.

331 *"Give the Arabs land, justice":* Dresden, *The Marquis de Morès,* 234.

332 *One died in jail:* Ibid., 256.

22. Myths of the Old West

336 *dedicated the book to him:* The dedication read as follows: "To Theodore Roosevelt. Some of these pages you have seen, some you have praised, one stands new-written because you blamed it; and all, my dear critic, beg leave to remind you of their author's changeless admiration."

"Roosevelt believed that Wister": Douglas Brinkley, *The Wilderness Warrior,* 467.

"The Virginian *became more":* Keith Wheeler, *The Old West: The Chroniclers,* 206.

337 *But this image had been changing:* Richard W. Etulain, "The Rise of Western Historiography," *Writing Western History,* 6.

"When they lynch they only": Owen Wister, *The Virginian,* 282–84.

338 *"Montana owes its present":* N. P. Langford, *Vigilante Days and Ways,* vol. 2, 448.

"Jews are perfectly free": Robert Shulman, introduction, in Wister, *The Virginian,* xiv, n13.

Roosevelt loathed the book: Theodore Roosevelt to Owen Wister, April 27, 1906, *Theodore Roosevelt: Letters and Speeches,* 459.

339 *"A wind seemed to blow":* Wister, *The Virginian,* 313.

"The unbelievable followed": Robert G. Athearn, *Westward the Briton,* 3.

"Sure it was hokum, snake oil": Michelle Latoilais, introduction to John Williams, *Butcher's Crossing,* xiv.

"Disregarding actuality, we see": Lawrence Clayton, "Today's Cowboy: Coping with a Myth," in *The Cowboy Way,* edited by Paul H. Carlson, 206.

340 *"The suggestion that a Secretary of State":* T. A. Larson, *Wyoming: A History,* 142.

Roosevelt applause: Frederick Allen, *A Decent Orderly Lynching,* 358.

"courage is a man who keeps on": Richard Maxwell Brown, "Violence," in *The Oxford History of the American West,* edited by Clyde A. Milner et al., 422.

341 *"cowboy unilateralism":* The Economist, November 1, 2014, 53.

"The history of the Frontier": Richard Slotkin, *Gunfighter Nation,* 658.

"The right to rule the range": Lawrence M. Woods, *British Gentlemen in the Wild West,* 192.

343 *"rides in his historic yesterday":* Wister, *The Virginian,* 6.

"That land of the West": Theodore Roosevelt, *The Rough Riders* and *An Autobiography,* 346.

a disproportionate role: Thomas Carlyle argued that "the history of the world is but the biography of great men."

344 *"So vanished my dream":* Mark Twain, *Roughing It,* 224.
"cold-blooded murderers": Hamlin Hill, introduction to Mark Twain's *Roughing It,* 20.

Afterword

346 *the yellow Deadwood stagecoach:* The coach is on display today at the Buffalo Bill Center of the West in Cody, Wyoming.

347 *"I AM DYING":* Allen Andrews, *The Splendid Pauper,* 248.
soliciting their sympathy: Many of them responded, including former senator Henry Cabot Lodge, who wrote back, "I cannot bear the thought that your affection and sympathy are to be taken from me." J. L. Garvin, the editor of *The Observer,* wrote, "Nobody used to equal you in the wonderful power of hope. You gave it to us all. You must not let it sink now." Quoted in Andrews, *The Splendid Pauper,* 247.
an obsession with his bowels: Ibid., 248.

348 *"his eyes flashing":* Ibid.
"He lay like a dying bull": Shane Leslie, *Studies in Sublime Failure,* 294.
"Moreton Frewen, whose death": T. P. O'Connor, MP, "Moreton Frewen Obituary," date illegible, Frewen Collection, American Heritage Center, University of Wyoming.
"a first class mind untroubled": Anita Leslie, *Mr. Frewen of England,* 88.
"He lived in every sense except": Leslie, *Studies in Sublime Failure,* 295.
"unhorsed for good": Ibid.
portrait of Lady Guildford: She was the wife of Henry Guildford, comptroller of the currency under Henry VIII.

349 *went under the gavel:* This was the first of two great estate sales. The second occurred in 1921 and included the house.
"The fortune which I ought": Leslie, *Mr. Frewen of England,* 86.
something close to $33 billion: For an excellent discussion of how to measure historical worth in terms of various measures of relative value, see Samuel H. Williamson, "Seven Ways to Compute the Relative Value of a U.S. Dollar Amount, 1774 to present,"

Measuring Worth, April 2016. Numbers used in the text for today's money equivalent reflect the increase in the Consumer Price Index (CPI) from 1880 to 2015.

The English quickly wrote off: W. Turrentine Jackson, "British Interests in the Range Cattle Industry," in Maurice Frink et al., *When Grass Was King,* 315.

if you added up all the profits: John Clay, *My Life on the Range,* 174.

350   *Others made enough money off:* W. Turrentine Jackson, *The Enterprising Scot,* 308.

"It is back to the Wagon": John Clay, "Coming Back to the Wagon," Cheyenne, 1922. Quoted in Gene M. Gressley, *Bankers and Cattlemen,* 277.

352   *"A six-shooter's an awful lot":* E. C. "Teddy Blue" Abbott, *We Pointed Them North,* 210.

"a prehistoric race": Ibid.

"A man has got to be at least": Ibid., 230.

Bibliography

Abbott, E. C. "Teddy Blue," and Helena Huntington Smith, *We Pointed Them North: Recollections of a Cowpuncher*, rev. ed., University of Oklahoma Press, 1955. First published 1939 by Farrar & Rinehart.

Adams, Andy, *The Log of a Cowboy*, Houghton Mifflin, 1903.

Adams, Ramon F., *The Old-Time Cowhand*, Bison Books, 1989. First published 1961 by the Macmillan Company.

——, *The Rampaging Herd: A Bibliography of Books and Pamphlets on Men and Events in the Cattle Industry*, University of Oklahoma Press, 1959.

Agnew, Jeremy, *Medicine in the Old West: A History, 1850–1900*, McFarland & Company, 2010.

Allen, Frederick, *A Decent Orderly Lynching: The Montana Vigilantes*, University of Oklahoma Press, 2004.

Allen, Richard M., "Harvard Men in the Range Cattle Industry," *Harvard Graduates Magazine*, vol. 2, 1894, 183–92.

Anderson, Terry L., and Peter J. Hill, *The Not So Wild, Wild West: Property Rights on the Frontier*, Stanford Economics and Finance, 2004.

Andrews, Allen, *The Splendid Pauper*, George G. Harrap & Company, 1968.

Aron, Stephen, *The American West: A Very Short Introduction*, Oxford University Press, 2014.

———, "A History of the American West in the Twilight Zone," *YouTube*, August 21, 2013.

Athearn, Robert G., *High Country Empire: The High Plains and Rockies*, McGraw-Hill Book Company, 1960.

———, *Westward the Briton*, Bison Books, 1962. First published 1953 by Charles Scribner's Sons.

Atherton, Lewis, *The Cattle Kings*, Bison Books, 1972. First published 1961 by Indiana University Press.

Baber, D. F., *The Longest Rope: The Truth About the Johnson County Cattle War*, Caxton Printers, 1940.

Barbour, Michael G., and William Dwight Billings, *North American Terrestrial Vegetation*, 2nd ed., Cambridge University Press, 1999.

Bird, Isabella Lucy, *A Lady's Life in the Rocky Mountains*, G. P. Putnam's Sons, 1886. First published in 1879 in London.

Bollinger, Gil, and the Jim Gatchell Memorial Museum, *Buffalo: Images of America*, Arcadia Publishing, 2009.

Brands, H. W., *American Colossus: The Triumph of Capitalism, 1865–1900*, Doubleday, 2010.

Bratt, John, *Trails of Yesterday*, Bison Books, 1980. First published 1921 by University Publishing Company.

Bray, Charles I., and James Brisbin, *Bankers and Beef: American Farmers and the Rise of Agribusiness*, Arno Press, 1975 (reprints of the 1928 and 1881 editions of *Financing the Western Cattleman* and *The Beef Bonanza*, respectively).

Brinkley, Douglas, *The Wilderness Warrior: Theodore Roosevelt and the Crusade for America*, HarperCollins, 2009.

Britt, Albert, *Turn of the Century*, Barre Publishers, 1966.

Brooks, Chester L., and Ray H. Mattison, *Theodore Roosevelt and the Dakota Badlands*, National Park Service, 1958.

Brooks, John, *Business Adventures: Twelve Classic Tales from the World of Wall Street*, Open Road Integrated Media, 2014.

Brown, Dee, *The American West*, Charles Scribner's Sons, 1994.

———, *Bury My Heart at Wounded Knee: An Indian History of the American West*, Open Road Integrated Media, 2000.

Brown, Mark H., and W. R. Felton, *Before Barbed Wire: L. A. Huffman, Photographer on Horseback*, Bramhall House, 1961.

Brown, Robert L., *Saloons of the American West*, Sundance Publications, 1978.

Bueher, Walter, *Meat from Ranch to Table*, Morrow, 1956.

Burns, Ken, *New Perspectives on the West: Episode Seven, The Geography of Hope*, PBS.org., 2001.

Burroughs, John Rolfe, *Guardian of the Grasslands: The First Hundred Years of the Wyoming Stock Growers Association*, Wyoming Stock Growers Association, 1971.

Burt, Nathaniel, *Wyoming*, Fodor's Travel Publications, 1995.

Cannadine, David, *The Decline and Fall of the British Aristocracy*, Random House, 1990.

Canton, Frank M., *Frontier Trails: The Autobiography of Frank M. Canton*, University of Oklahoma Press, 1966. First published 1930 by Houghton Mifflin.

Carlson, Laurie Winn, *Cattle: An Informal Social History*, Ivan R. Dee, 2001.

Carlson, Paul H., *The Cowboy Way: An Exploration of History and Culture*, Texas Tech University Press, 2000.

Carson, Rachel, *The Sea Around Us*, Oxford University Press, 1951.

———, *Silent Spring*, Houghton Mifflin, 1962.

Clark, Walter Van Tilburg, *The Ox-Bow Incident*, Modern Library, 2001. First published 1940 by Random House.

Clay, John, "The Cheyenne Club: Recollections of an Organization Once Famous in Connection with the Development of the Western Cattle Trade," *The Breeder's Gazette*, 1916, vol. 70.

———, *My Life on the Range*, University of Oklahoma Press, 1962 (reprint of the 1924 self-published edition).

———, "Royal Agriculture Commission: Report of Mr. Clare Sewell Read and Mr. Albert Pell, MP," September 1, 1880, *The British Trade Journal and Export World*, vol. 18.

Coburn, Walt, *Pioneer Cattlemen in Montana: The Story of the Circle C Ranch*, University of Oklahoma Press, 1968.

Cook, James, *Longhorn Cowboy*, Putnam, 1942.

Craighead, Frank C., *For Everything There Is a Season: The Sequence of*

Natural Events in the Grand Teton–Yellowstone Area, Falcon Press Publishing Company, 1994.

Cronon, William, *Nature's Metropolis: Chicago and the Great West*, W. W. Norton & Company, 1991.

Current, Karen, *Photography and the Old West*, Harry N. Abrams, 1986.

Dale, Edward Everett, *Cow Country*, 2nd ed., University of Oklahoma Press, 1965. First published 1942.

———, *The Range Cattle Industry*, University of Oklahoma Press, 1930.

Danz, Harold P., *Of Bison and Man*, University Press of Colorado, 1997.

Darimont, Chris T., Caroline H. Fox, Heather M. Bryan, and Thomas E. Reimchen, "The Unique Ecology of Human Predators," *Science*, August 21, 2015.

Darwin, Charles, *The Descent of Man, and Selection in Relation to Sex*, 2nd ed., D. Appleton & Company, 1927. First published 1871 by John Murray.

Davis, John W., *Wyoming Range War: The Infamous Invasion of Johnson County*, University of Oklahoma Press, 2010.

Davis, Richard Harding, *The West from a Car-Window*, Harper & Brothers, 1892.

DeArment, Robert K., *Alias Frank Canton*, University of Oklahoma Press, 1996.

Di Silvestro, Roger L., *Theodore Roosevelt in the Badlands: A Young Politician's Quest for Recovery in the American West*, Walker & Company, 2011.

Dobie, J. Frank, *The Longhorns*, University of Texas Press, 1982. First published 1941 by Little, Brown and Company.

Dobson, G. B., *Wyoming Tales and Trails*, http://www.wyomingtalesand trails.com/cheyenne4a.html.

Dodge, Richard Irving, *The Hunting Grounds of the Great West: A Description of the Plains, Game, and Indians of the Great North American Desert*, 2nd ed., Chatto & Windus, 1878.

Dolman, Claude E., and Richard J. Wolfe, *Theobald Smith, Microbiologist: Suppressing the Diseases of Animals and Man*, Boston Medical Library, 2003.

Donahue, Debra L., *The Western Range Revisited: Removing Livestock from Public Lands to Conserve Native Biodiversity*, University of Oklahoma Press, 1999.

Dresden, Donald, *The Marquis de Morès: Emperor of the Bad Lands,* University of Oklahoma Press, 1970.

Duffield, George, "Driving Cattle from Texas to Iowa, 1866," *Annals of Iowa,* vol. 14, no. 4, April 1924.

Dunlop, Thomas R., *Saving America's Wildlife: Ecology and the American Mind, 1850–1990,* Princeton University Press, 1988.

Dykstra, Robert R., *The Cattle Towns,* Alfred A. Knopf, 1968.

Eckhardt, C. F., "Texas Fever: The Winchester Quarantine," July 5, 2009, TexasEscapes.com, http://www.texasescapes.com/CFEckhardt /Charley-Eckhardt-Texas.htm.

Erdoes, Richard, *Saloons of the Old West,* Alfred A. Knopf, 1979.

Etulain, Richard W., *Writing Western History: Essays on Major Western Historians,* University of New Mexico Press, 1991.

EyeWitness to History, "The Hanging of Tom Horn, 1903," www.eye witnesstohistory.com, 2012.

Flag, O. H., *A Big Horn Tale: Volume 8, A Review of the Cattle Business in Johnson County Wyoming Since 1882 and the Causes That Led to the Recent Invasion,* the Jim Gatchell Memorial Museum Press, 2008 (reprint from the 1892 series of *Buffalo Bulletin* articles).

Forbis, William H., *The Old West: The Cowboys,* Time-Life Books, 1973.

Frantz, Joe B., and Julian Ernest Choate Jr., *The American Cowboy,* Thames and Hudson, 1956.

Frewen, Moreton, *Free Grazing: A Report to the Shareholders of the Powder River Cattle Co. Limited,* Steel & Jones, 1883.

——, *Frewen Papers 1823–1934,* Library of Congress.

——, *Melton Mowbray and Other Memories,* Herbert Jenkins, 1924.

Frink, Maurice, *Cow Country Cavalcade,* Wyoming Stock Growers Association, 1954.

Frink, Maurice, W. Turrentine Jackson, and Agnes Wright Spring, *When Grass Was King: Contributions to the Western Cattle Industry Study,* University of Colorado Press, 1956.

Gage, Jack R., *The Johnson County War Is/Ain't a Pack of Lies,* Flintlock Publishing, 1967.

Galbraith, John Kenneth, *A Short History of Financial Euphoria,* Penguin Books, 1990.

Gallogly, Elmore E., "Letter to Mary A. Gallogly," February 10, 1887, Gallogly Family History, Montana Historical Society.

Gard, Wayne, *The Chisholm Trail,* University of Oklahoma Press, 1954.

Goodspeed, Thomas W., "Gustavus Franklin Swift, 1839–1903," *The University Record,* vol. 7, no. 2, April 1921.

Goodwin, Doris Kearns, *The Bully Pulpit: Theodore Roosevelt and the Golden Age of Journalism,* Simon & Schuster, 2013.

Goplen, Arnold O., "The Career of the Marquis de Morès in the Bad Lands of North Dakota," *North Dakota History,* vol. 13, nos. 1 and 2, January–April 1946.

Gressley, Gene M., *Bankers and Cattlemen,* University of Nebraska Press, 1971. First published 1966 by Alfred A. Knopf.

———, "Teschemacher and DeBillier Cattle Company," *The Business History Review,* vol. 33, no. 2, Summer 1959, 121–37.

Gutherie, A. B., Jr., *The Big Sky,* Houghton Mifflin, 1952.

Gwynne, S. C., *Empire of the Summer Moon: Quanah Parker and the Rise of the Comanches,* Scribner, 2010.

Hagedorn, Hermann, *Roosevelt in the Bad Lands,* Houghton Mifflin, 1921.

———, *Works of Theodore Roosevelt,* memorial ed., 24 volumes, Charles Scribner's Sons, 1923–26.

Haight, Gordon S., *The Portable Victorian Reader,* Viking Press, 1972.

Hayes, A. A., Jr., "The Cattle Ranches of Colorado." *Harper's New Monthly Magazine,* vol. 59, November 1879, 891.

Hayter, Earl W., "Barbed Wire Fencing: A Prairie Invention, Its Rise and Influence in the Western States," http://xroads.virginia.edu/~drbr/b_arb1.html.

Haywood, C. Robert, *Cowtown Lawyers: Dodge City and Its Attorneys, 1876–1886,* University of Oklahoma Press, 1988.

Heidenreich-Barber, Virginia, *Aristocracy on the Western Frontier: The Legacy of the Marquis de Morès,* State Historical Society of North Dakota, 1994.

Holt, R. D., "The Proposed National Cattle Trail," *The Cattleman,* vol. 29, 1943.

Horn, Tom, *Life of Tom Horn: Government Scout & Interpreter,* University of Oklahoma Press, 1964. First published 1904 by John C. Coble.

Hornaday, William T., *The Extermination of the American Bison,* U.S. Government Printing Office, 1889.

Hufsmith, George W., *The Wyoming Lynching of Cattle Kate, 1889,* High Plains Press, 1993.

Hunter, J. Marvin, and George W. Saunders, editors, *The Trail Drivers of Texas*, University of Texas Press, 1985 (reprint of the 1924 edition).

Hyatt, Norman H., *An Uncommon Journey: Book One of the History of Old Dawson County, Montana Territory, the Biography of Stephen Norton Van Blaricom*, Sweetgrass Books, 2010.

Igler, David, *Industrial Cowboys: Miller and Lux and the Transformation of the Far West, 1850–1920*, University of California Press, 2001.

Jackson, W. Turrentine, *The Enterprising Scot: Investors in the American West After 1873*, Edinburgh University Press, 1968.

——, "The Wyoming Stock Growers' Association: Its Years of Temporary Decline, 1886–1890." *Agricultural History*, vol. 22, no. 4, October 1948, 260–70.

Jamieson, Dale, *Reason in a Dark Time: Why the Struggle Against Climate Change Failed—and What It Means for Our Future*, Oxford University Press, 2014.

Jones, Stephen R., and Ruth Carol Cushman, *A Field Guide to the North American Prairie*, Houghton Mifflin, 2004.

Kehoe, Elisabeth, *The Titled Americans: Three American Sisters and the British Aristocratic World into Which They Married*, Grove Press, 2004.

Kennon, Bob, *From the Pecos to the Powder: A Cowboy's Autobiography*, University of Oklahoma Press, 1965.

Kludt, Amanda, "Remembering Delmonico's, New York's Original Restaurant," June 29, 2011. http://ny.eater.com/2011/6/29/6673317/remembering-delmonicos-new-yorks-original-restaurant#4289408.

Knight, Dennis H., *Mountains and Plains: The Ecology of Wyoming Landscapes*, Yale University Press, 1994.

Kramer, Jane, *The Last Cowboy*, Harper & Row, 1978.

Krell, Alan, *The Devil's Rope: A Cultural History of Barbed Wire*, Reaktion Books Ltd., 2002.

Lamar, Howard R., *The New Encyclopedia of the American West*, Yale University Press, 1998.

Lang, Lincoln A., *Ranching with Roosevelt*, J. B. Lippincott Company, 1926.

Langford, Nathaniel Pitt, *Vigilante Days and Ways, Volumes 2 and 3*, D. D. Merrill Company, 1893. First published 1890 by J. G. Cupples Company.

Larson, T. A., *History of Wyoming,* University of Nebraska Press, 1965.

——, *Wyoming: A History,* W. W. Norton & Company, 1977.

Leppart, Gary, *Medora and Theodore Roosevelt National Park,* Arcadia Publishing, 2007.

Leslie, Anita, *Mr. Frewen of England: A Victorian Adventurer,* Hutchinson & Company, 1966.

Leslie, Shane, *Studies in Sublime Failure,* Ernest Benn, 1932.

Lewis, Theodore B., "The National Cattle Trail, 1883–1886," *Nebraska History,* vol. 52, 1971, 204–20.

Limerick, Patricia Nelson, *The Legacy of Conquest: The Unbroken Past of the American West,* W. W. Norton & Company, 1987.

Lubow, Arthur, *The Reporter Who Would Be King: A Biography of Richard Harding Davis,* Scribner, 1992.

Macdonald, James, *Food from the Far West; or, American Agriculture,* William P. Nimmo, 1878.

Mann, Charles C., *1491: New Revelations of the Americas Before Columbus,* Alfred A. Knopf, 2005.

Martin, Cy, *Whiskey and Wild Women,* Hart Publishing Company, 1974.

May, Michele, "Aviators: Quentin Roosevelt — He Died Fighting," *Aviation History,* January 2008.

McCallum, Henry D., and Frances T. McCallum, *The Wire That Fenced the West,* University of Oklahoma Press, 1965.

McCarthy, Michael, "The First Sagebrush Rebellion: Forest Reserves and States Rights in Colorado and the West, 1891–1907," http://www.foresthistory.org/Publications/Books/Origins_National_Forests/sec13.htm.

McCoy, Joseph G., *Historic Sketches of the Cattle Trade of the West and Southwest,* Ramsey, Millett & Hudson, 1874.

McCullough, David, *Mornings on Horseback: The Story of an Extraordinary Family, a Vanished Way of Life, and the Unique Child Who Became Theodore Roosevelt,* Simon & Schuster, 1981.

McCutcheon, Marc, *Everyday Life in the 1800s: A Guide for Writers, Students, and Historians,* Writer's Digest Books, 2001.

McPhee, John, *Rising from the Plains,* Farrar, Straus and Giroux, 1986.

McWilliams, James E., "All Sizzle and No Steak: Why Allan Savory's TED Talk About How Cattle Can Reverse Global Warming Is Dead Wrong," http://www.slate.com/articles/life/food/2013/04

/allan_savory_s_ted_talk_is_wrong_and_the_benefits_of_holistic
_grazing_have.html.

Mechau, Vaughn, "John Bull in the Cattle Country," *Rocky Mountain
Empire Magazine*, March 28, 1948.

Mercer, A. S., *The Banditti of the Plains*, University of Oklahoma Press,
1975 (reprint of the 1894 edition).

Metz, Leon Claire, *The Encyclopedia of Lawmen, Outlaws, and Gunfighters*, Facts on File, 2003.

Millard, Candice, *The River of Doubt: Theodore Roosevelt's Darkest Journey*, Doubleday, 2005.

Milner, Clyde A., II, Anne M. Butler, and David Rich Lewis, *Major Problems in the History of the American West*, 2nd ed., Houghton Mifflin,
1997.

Milner, Clyde A., II, Carol A. O'Connor, and Martha A. Sandweiss, *The
Oxford History of the American West*, Oxford University Press, 1994.

Morris, Edmund, *The Rise of Theodore Roosevelt*, Modern Library, 2001.
First published 1979 by Coward, McCann & Geoghegan.

——, *Theodore Rex*, Random House, 2001.

Morris, Roy Jr., *Sheridan: The Life and Wars of General Phil Sheridan*.
Crown Publishing, 1992.

Mothershead, Harmon Ross, *The Swan Land and Cattle Company, Ltd.*,
University of Oklahoma Press, 1971.

Mullins, Reuben B., *Pulling Leather: Being the Early Recollections of a
Cowboy on the Wyoming Range, 1884–1889*, High Plains Press, 1988.

Muttulingam, Sanjayan, *Earth: A New Wild*, Episode 2: "Plains," National
Geographic Studios in association with Passion Planet, www.pbs.org
/earth-a-new-wild/home/.

Nash, Roderick Frazier, *The Rights of Nature: A History of Environmental
Ethics*, University of Wisconsin Press, 1989.

——, *Wilderness and the American Mind*, 4th ed., Yale University
Press, 1982. First published 1967 by Yale University Press.

Niemi, Steven M., "Theobald Smith: Brief Life of a Pioneering Compara-
tive Pathologist, 1859–1934," *Harvard Magazine*, July–August 2009.

Nimmo, Joseph, *Report in Regard to the Range and Ranch Cattle Business
of the United States*, Government Printing Office, 1885.

Noel, Thomas J., *The City and the Saloon: Denver, 1858–1916*, University
of Nebraska Press, 1992.

Noss, Reed F., and Allen Y. Cooperrider, *Saving Nature's Legacy: Protecting and Restoring Biodiversity,* Island Press, 1994.

O'Connor, T. P., "The Late Mr. Moreton Frewen: A Personal Memoir," *Daily Telegraph,* September 1924. Frewen Papers, American Heritage Center, University of Wyoming.

Officer, Lawrence H., and Samuel H. Williamson, "Measures of Worth," *MeasuringWorth,* 2012. www.measuringworth.com/worthmeasures .php.

O'Neal, Bill, *Cattlemen vs. Sheepherders: Five Decades of Violence in the West, 1880–1920,* Eakin Press, 1989.

——, *Historic Ranches of the Old West,* Eakin Press, 1997.

——, *The Johnson County War,* Eakin Press, 2004.

Osgood, Ernest Staples, *The Day of the Cattlemen,* University of Chicago Press, 1957. First published 1929 by the University of Minnesota.

Pagnamenta, Peter, *Prairie Fever: British Aristocrats in the American West, 1830–1890,* W. W. Norton & Company, 2012.

Parkman, Francis, Jr., *The Oregon Trail,* Caxton House, 1944.

Parsons, Cynthia, *George Bird Grinnell: A Biographical Sketch,* Grinnell and Lawton Publishing, 1993.

Payne, Darwin, *Owen Wister: Chronicler of the West, Gentleman of the East,* University of Nebraska Press, 1985.

Pelzer, Louis, *The Cattlemen's Frontier,* Arthur H. Clark Company, 1936.

Pender, Rose, *A Lady's Experience in the Wild West in 1883,* University of Nebraska Press, 1985. First published 1888 in London.

Pennell-Elmhirst, Captain "Brooksby," *The Cream of Leicestershire: Eleven Seasons' Skimmings, Notable Runs and Incidents of the Chase (Selected and Republished from "The Field"),* George Routledge, 1883.

Penrose, Charles B., *A Big Horn Tale: Volume 4, The Rustler Business,* Jim Gatchell Memorial Museum Press, 2008 (reprint of a 1914 firsthand account).

Pinchot, Gifford, *The Fight for Conservation,* Doubleday, Page & Company, 1910.

Punke, Michael, *Last Stand: George Bird Grinnell, the Battle to Save the Buffalo, and the Birth of the New West,* University of Nebraska Press, 2009. First published 2007 by Smithsonian Books.

Rabkin, Richard, and Jacob Rabkin, *Nature in the West: A Handbook of Habitats,* Holt, Rinehart and Winston, 1982.

Raine, William MacLeod, and Will C. Barnes, *Cattle, Cowboys, and Rangers,* Grosset & Dunlap, 1930.

Reiger, John F., *The Passing of the Great West: Selected Papers of George Bird Grinnell,* University of Oklahoma Press, 1972.

Renehan, Edward J., Jr., "Theodore Roosevelt's Family in the Great War," http://www.worldwar1.com/dbc/roosev.htm.

Richter, Robert W., *Crucible for Conservation: The Struggle for Grand Teton National Park,* Grand Teton Natural History Association, 1982.

Rico, Monica, *Nature's Noblemen: Transatlantic Masculinities and the Nineteenth-Century American West,* Yale University Press, 2013.

Roberts, Phil, David L. Roberts, and Stephen L. Roberts, *Wyoming Almanac,* 7th ed., Wyoming Almanac/Skyline West Press, 2013.

———, *Wyoming Almanac and History: History and Opinion,* http://www.wyomingalmanac.com.

Robinson, John Martin, *Felling the Ancient Oaks: How England Lost Its Great Country Estates,* Aurum, 2012.

Robinson, Philip Steward, *Sinners and Saints: A Tour across the States and around them; with three months among the Mormons,* Roberts Brothers, 1883.

Rollinson, John K., *Wyoming Cattle Trails,* Caxton Printers, 1948.

Roosevelt, Theodore, *An Autobiography, Volume 20* of *Works,* Charles Scribner's Sons, 1921.

———, *Hunting Trips of a Ranchman* & *The Wilderness Hunter,* Modern Library, 2004. *Hunting Trips of a Ranchman* first published 1885 by G. P. Putnam's Sons; *The Wilderness Hunter* first published 1893 by G. P. Putnam's Sons.

———, *Letters and Speeches,* Library of America, 2004.

———, *The Letters of Theodore Roosevelt,* Elting E. Morison and John Blum, eds., Harvard University Press, 1951–54.

———, *Ranch Life and the Hunting Trail,* Bonanza Books, 1978. First published 1888 by the Century Company.

———, "Roosevelt Quotes," Theodore Roosevelt National Park, U.S. National Park Service, http://www.nps.gov/thro/historyculture/theodore-roosevelt-quotes.htm.

———, *The Rough Riders* and *An Autobiography,* Library of America, 2004. *The Rough Riders,* first published 1899 by Charles Scribner's Sons; *An Autobiography,* first published 1913 Macmillan.

Rosa, Joseph G., *The Taming of the West: Age of the Gunfighter; Men and Weapons on the Frontier, 1840–1900*, Salamander Books, 1993.

——, *The West of Wild Bill Hickok,* University of Oklahoma Press, 1982.

Rutter, Michael, *Upstairs Girls: Prostitution in the American West,* Far-country Press, 2005.

Sandoz, Mari, *The Cattlemen: From the Rio Grande Across the Far Marias,* 2nd ed., University of Nebraska Press, 1978. First published 1958 by Hastings House.

Savage, William W., *Cowboy Life: Reconstructing an American Myth,* University Press of Colorado, 1993.

Schultz, Myron, "Theobald Smith," *Emerging Infectious Diseases,* December 2008, http://www.cdc.gov/EID/content/14/12/1939.htm.

Scott, Douglas D., Peter Bleed, and Stephen Damm, *Custer, Cody, and Grand Duke Alexis: Historical Archaeology of the Royal Buffalo Hunt,* University of Oklahoma Press, 2013.

Shillingberg, William B., *Dodge City: The Early Years, 1872–1886,* Arthur H. Clark Company, 2009.

Shirk, David L., and George T. Miller, *The Cattle Drives of David Shirk: From Texas and the Idaho Mines, 1871–1873,* Champoeg Press, 1956.

Silvestro, Roger, "Teddy Roosevelt's Ride to Recovery" *Wild West,* October 2009.

Simpson, Peter K., *The Community of Cattlemen: A Social History of the Cattle Industry in Southeastern Oregon, 1869–1912,* University of Idaho Press, 1987.

Skaggs, Jimmy M., *Gunfighter Nation: The Myth of the Frontier in Twentieth-Century America,* University of Oklahoma Press, 1998. First published in 1992 by Atheneum.

——, "National Trail," *Handbook of Texas Online,* Texas State Historical Association, June 15, 2010, http://www.tshaonline.org/handbook/online/articles/ayn01.

——, *Prime Cut: Livestock Raising and Meatpacking in the United States, 1607–1983,* Texas A&M University Press, 1986.

Slotkin, Richard, *The Fatal Environment: The Myth of the Frontier in the Age of Industrialization, 1800–1890,* University of Oklahoma Press, 1998. First published 1985 by Atheneum.

Smith, Adam, *An Inquiry into the Nature and Causes of the Wealth of Nations,* T. Nelson and Sons, 1852.

Smith, Douglas W., and Gary Ferguson, *Decade of the Wolf: Returning the Wild to Yellowstone,* Lyons Press, 2005.

Smith, Helena Huntington, *The War on Powder River: The History of an Insurrection,* University of Nebraska Press, 1966.

Smith, Henry Nash, *Virgin Land: The American West as Symbol and Myth,* Harvard University Press, 1950.

Sonnichsen, C. L., *Cowboys and Cattle Kings: Life on the Range Today,* University of Oklahoma Press, 1950.

Soule, Gardner, *The Long Trail: How Cowboys and Longhorns Opened Up the West,* McGraw-Hill Book Company, 1976.

Southworth, Dave, *Gunfighters of the Old West,* Wild Horse Publishing, 1997.

Spring, Agnes Wright, "Old Cheyenne Club," *American Cattle Producer,* July 1947.

———, *Seventy Years: A Panoramic History of the Wyoming Stock Growers Association,* Wyoming Stock Growers Association, 1942.

Stegner, Wallace, *Marking the Sparrow's Fall: The Making of the American West,* Henry Holt and Company, 1998.

———, "Who Are Westerners?" *American Heritage,* vol. 38, December 1987.

Stein, Victor, and Paul Rubino, *The Billiard Encyclopedia: An Illustrated History of the Sport,* 2nd ed., Blue Book Publications, 1996.

Streeter, Floyd Benjamin, *Prairie Towns and Cow Towns,* Chapman & Grimes, 1936.

Stuart, Granville, *Forty Years on the Frontier,* Bison Books, 2004. First published 1925 by Arthur H. Clark Company.

Swan, Claire E., *Scottish Cowboys and Dundee Investors,* Abertay Historical Society, 2004.

Swift, Louis F., *The Yankee of the Yards: The Biography of Gustavus Franklin Swift,* A. W. Shaw Company, 1927.

Tanner, Ogden, *The Old West: The Ranchers,* Time-Life Books, 1977.

Taylor, J. Golden, and Thomas J. Lyon, *A Literary History of the American West,* Texas Christian University Press, 1987.

Thayer, William M., *Marvels of the New West: A Vivid Portrayal of the Stupendous Marvels in the Vast Wonderland West of the Missouri River,* University Press of the Pacific, 2004. First published 1880 by Henry Hill.

Thomas, Lately, *Delmonico's: A Century of Splendor,* Houghton Mifflin, 1967.

Tirrell, Norma, *Montana,* Fodor's Travel Publications, 1995.

Towne, Charles Wayland, and Edward Norris Wentworth, *Cattle and Men,* University of Oklahoma Press, 1955.

Trachtman, Paul, *The Old West: The Gunfighters,* Time-Life Books, 1974.

Train, John, *Famous Financial Fiascos,* Fraser Publishing Company, 1995.

Trimble, William, "The Historical Aspects of the Surplus Food Production of the United States, 1862–1902," *Annual Report of the American Historical Association,* vol. 1, 1918.

Truettner, William H., *The West as America: Reinterpreting Images of the Frontier, 1820–1920,* Smithsonian Institution Press, 1991.

Twain, Mark, *Roughing It,* Penguin American Library, 1982.

Van Camp, Renee, "The Eradication of the Wolf," *Alliance for the Wild Rockies,* Wildrockiesalliance.org.

Van Orman, Richard A., *A Room for the Night: Hotels of the Old West,* Indiana University Press, 1966.

Van Pelt, Lori, "Willis Van Devanter, Cheyenne Lawyer and U.S. Supreme Court Justice," WyoHistory.org.

Vestal, Stanley, *Dodge City: Queen of the Cowtowns,* Harper & Brothers, 1952.

Von Richthofen, Walter, *Cattle-raising on the Plains of America,* D. Appleton and Company, 1885.

Wallace, Robert, *The Old West: The Miners,* Time-Life Books, 1976.

Ward, Geoffrey C., *The West: An Illustrated History,* Little, Brown and Company, 1996.

Washburn, Charles G., *Industrial Worcester,* Davis Press, 1917.

Webb, Walter Prescott, *The Great Plains,* Bison Books, 1981. First published 1931 by Ginn and Company.

Wellman, Paul I., *The Trampling Herd: The Story of the Cattle Range in America,* University of Nebraska Press, 1988 (reprint of the 1961 edition). First published 1939 by J. B. Lippincott.

Western, Samuel, "The Wyoming Cattle Boom, 1868–1886," WyoHistory.org.

Wheeler, Keith, *The Old West: The Chroniclers,* Time-Life Books, 1976.

———, *The Old West: The Railroaders,* Time-Life Books, 1973.

———, *The Old West: The Townsmen,* Time-Life Books, 1975.

White, G. Edward, *The Eastern Establishment and the Western Experience,* Yale University Press, 1968.

Whitman, Walt, *Specimen Days and Collect,* David McKay, 1883.

Whitmore, Eugene, *John Jacob Meyers and the Early Cattle Drives,* Western Brand, 1947.

Williams, J. W., *The Big Ranch Country,* Texas Tech University Press, 1954.

Williams, John, *Butcher's Crossing,* New York Review of Books, 2007. First published 1960 by Macmillan Press.

Willingham, John, "The Cowboy Strike of 1883 and the Demise of Old Tascosa," *The Edge of Freedom,* April 15, 2013, http://edgeoffreedom .net/the-cowboy-strike-of-1883-and-the-demise-of-old-tascosa/.

Wilson, R. L., *Theodore Roosevelt: Hunter-Conservationist,* Boone and Crockett Club, 2009.

Wilson, R. Michael, *Frontier Justice in the Wild West: Bungled, Bizarre, and Fascinating Executions,* Twodot, 2007.

Wister, Owen, "The Evolution of a Cowpuncher," *Harper's Monthly,* September 1895.

———, *The Virginian: A Horseman of the Plains,* Oxford University Press, 1998. First published 1902 by Macmillan Press.

Wood, Frederick S., *Roosevelt as We Knew Him: The Personal Recollections of One Hundred and Fifty of His Friends and Associates,* John C. Winston, 1927.

Woods, Lawrence Milton, *British Gentlemen in the Wild West: The Era of the Intensely English Cowboy,* Free Press, 1989.

———, *Moreton Frewen's Western Adventures,* Roberts Rinehart, 1986.

Worsley, Giles, *England's Lost Houses: From the Archives of Country Life,* Arum Press, 2002.

Worster, Donald, *Under Western Skies: Nature and History in the American West,* Oxford University Press, 1992.

Yeager, Mary, *Competition and Regulation: The Development of Oligopoly in the Meat Industry,* Elsevier, 1981.

Zinsser, Hans, *Biographical Memoir of Theobald Smith, 1859–1934,* National Academy of Sciences, 1936.

Index

Illustration Credits

Cattle Trails (map): Mapping Specialists, Ltd., Fitchburg, WI. *Bison skulls, 1870:* Courtesy of the Burton Historical Collection, Detroit Public Library. *Taking the Monster's Robe* (bison skinners): Photo by L. A. Huffman. Montana Historical Society (MHS) Research Center Photograph Archives, Helena, MT (catalog no. 981-013). *Cattle roundup:* Photo by Charles D. Kirkland. Chuck Wagon Scenes Photo File, American Heritage Center, University of Wyoming. *Joseph G. McCoy:* Courtesy of the Dickinson County Historical Society. *Drovers Cottage at McCoy's Stock Yard, 1867:* Photo by Alexander Gardner. Library of Congress, Prints and Photographs Division, Washington, D.C., (LC-USZ62-56808). *Teddy Blue Abbott at age nineteen, 1879:* Shobe Auction and Realty. Published in *We Pointed Them North: Recollections of a Cowpuncher*, by E. C. (Teddy Blue) Abbott and Helena Huntington Smith, copyright 1954 by University of Oklahoma Press. *Bar at the Wolf Hotel, Saratoga, Wyoming, ca. 1900:* Courtesy of Wyoming Stock Growers Association Records, American Heritage Center, University of Wyoming. *William Barclay 'Bat' Masterson, Dodge City, Kansas:* Kansasmemory.org, Kansas State Historical Society (DaRT ID: 188). *James Butler "Wild Bill" Hickok, 1873*: Photo by George Gardner Rockwood. Courtesy of Heritage Auctions. *Gustavus Franklin Swift, ca. 1903:* Library of Congress, Prints and Photographs Division, Washington, D.C. (LC-USZ62-72952). *Bird's-eye view of Union Stock Yards:* Photo by Gates. Courtesy of the Chicago History Museum (ICHi-24543). **In the Slaughterhouse, 1892:** From *Views in the Chicago Stock Yards* (The Albertype Co., New York). Courtesy of the Chicago History Museum (ICHi-29764). *Delmonico's restaurant:* Photographer unknown. Museum of the City of

New York (X2010.11.4294). *From* **Cheyenne, the Magic City,** *by Charles D.* **Kirkland, 1890** (p. 10): Wyoming State Archives, Department of State Parks and Cultural Resources. *Cheyenne Club:* Courtesy of Wyoming Stock Growers Association Records, American Heritage Center, University of Wyoming. *Laramie men in white tie:* Courtesy of Wyoming Stock Growers Association Records, American Heritage Center, University of Wyoming. *John Clay:* Courtesy of Wyoming Stock Growers Association Records, American Heritage Center, University of Wyoming. *Owen Wister:* Photographed in Yellowstone by Frank J. Haynes. Courtesy of Owen Wister Papers, Wyoming Stock Growers Association Records, American Heritage Center, University of Wyoming. *Joseph Glidden's original patent for barbed wire:* National Archives and Records Administration, Records of the Patent and Trademark Office, Record Group 241. *Roosevelt in buckskins:* Houghton Library, Harvard University, Theodore Roosevelt Collection (520.14-002). *Roosevelt on a roundup:* Houghton Library, Harvard University, Theodore Roosevelt Collection (520.14-006). *Theobald Smith:* Published by Bain News Service. Library of Congress, Prints and Photographs Division, George Grantham Bain Collection (LC-B2-188-6). *Moreton Frewen in buckskins:* Courtesy of Moreton Frewen Papers, Wyoming Stock Growers Association Records, American Heritage Center, University of Wyoming. *Frewen's Castle:* Courtesy of Moreton Frewen Papers, Wyoming Stock Growers Association Records, American Heritage Center, University of Wyoming. *Clara Jerome:* Courtesy of Moreton Frewen Papers, Wyoming Stock Growers Association Records, American Heritage Center, University of Wyoming. *Marquis de Morès:* State Historical Society of North Dakota (00042-090). *Medora von Hoffman:* State Historical Society of North Dakota (00042-060). *Chateau de Morès:* State Historical Society of North Dakota (00025-B-37). *Granville Stuart, 1883:* Photo by L. A. Huffman. Montana Historical Society (MHS) Research Center Photograph Archives, Helena, MT (catalog no. 981-260). *Big Nose George Parrott:* Carbon County Musuem (1948.021.0144). *Vigilante hanging, Billings, Montana, 1891:* Western Heritage Center. *Ella "Cattle Kate" Watson:* American Heritage Center, University of Wyoming. *Frank Canton:* Courtesy of Wyoming Stock Growers Association Records, American Heritage Center, University of Wyoming. *Nate Champion:* Courtesy of Johnson County Jim Gatchell Memorial Museum. *Johnson County invaders at Fort D. A. Russell:* Photo by Charles D. Kirkland. Courtesy of Wyoming Stock Growers Association Records, American Heritage Center, University of Wyoming. *Teddy Blue Abbott, 1928:* Courtesy of Billings Public Library Historic Collection. *Wolfer's Cabin:* Photo by L. A. Huffman. Archives and Special Collections, Mansfield Library, University of Montana (79-0032). *Hubert Teschemacher:* Courtesy of Wyoming Stock Growers Association Records, American Heritage Center, University of Wyoming. *Colonel Roosevelt and Skip during Colorado bear hunt:* Houghton Library, Harvard University, Theodore Roosevelt Collection (560.52 1905).